A PLACE
FOR US

BOOKS BY NICHOLAS GAGE

Bones of Contention

The Bourlotas Fortune

Hellas

Eleni

A Place for Us

A PLACE FOR US

NICHOLAS GAGE

A MARC JAFFE BOOK

Houghton Mifflin Company

BOSTON

1989

Library of Congress Cataloging-in-Publication Data

Gage, Nicholas.
A place for us / Nicholas Gage.
p.   cm.
"A Marc Jaffe book."
ISBN 0-395-45517-0
1. Gage, Nicholas — Childhood and youth.   2. Gatzoyiannis, Eleni —
Family.   3. Gatzoyiannis family.   4. Greece — History — Civil War,
1944–1949 — Personal narratives.   5. Massachusetts — Biography.
6. Greek Americans — Massachusetts — Biography.   7. Journalists —
United States — Biography.   I. Title.
CT275.G225A3   1989
949.507′4′.092 — dc20   89-35429
[B]   CIP

Printed in the United States of America

Q 10 9 8 7 6 5 4 3 2 1

To Joan,

Christos, Eleni, and Marina

Thou art the master neither of thy property nor of thyself; thou and thy estate, all these things belong to family; that is to say, to thy ancestry and to thy posterity.

— Plato, *Laws* XI

Voices ideal and beloved
Of those who have died, or of those
Who are lost for us like the dead.

Sometimes in dreams they speak to us;
Sometimes within thinking the brain hears them.

And with the sound of them for a moment return
Sounds from the first poetry of our life —
Like music, at night, in the distance, that dies away.

— C. P. Cavafy, *Voices*

Contents

A PLACE
FOR US

At the harborside in Piraeus, before boarding ship for America on March 3, 1949

GOING
TO AMERICA

Exiles feed on dreams of hope.

— Aeschylus, *Agamemnon*

THE BLACK-AND-WHITE photograph, like many others taken during the late 1940s, shows a group of refugees leaving their devastated homeland to make a new beginning in America. There are four travelers: two nearly grown young women in Greek peasant dress and two small children, a boy and a girl, who appear about eight years old. Behind them hover two men in stylish city clothes — relatives charged with seeing the orphans safely onto the ship that will carry them to their new country. In the background looms a huge naval vessel, and all around is the bustle of the Piraeus harborside.

But the four pilgrims stand still and solemn in the midst of the blur of activity, grimly facing the box camera of the street photographer who has been paid to record their last moments on Greek soil. The older girls, with long braids down their backs, are all in black, from their crude village shoes and stockings to their bulky wool skirts and cardigans. They are in mourning for their mother, who died so that they could make this journey.

Her name was Eleni Gatzoyiannis. Eight months earlier, in June of 1948, she arranged her family's escape from their mountain village because the Communist guerrillas occupying it had begun gathering children to send to indoctrination camps behind the Iron Curtain. But at the last minute Eleni was forced to stay behind, and she told her children to flee without her. In a refugee camp later, they learned that she had been imprisoned, tortured, and finally executed by the guerrillas in retribution for their escape. They dyed their clothing black in boiling pots over the fire and prepared for the journey to America, for their mother had told them that whatever happened to her, that was where they must go.

The little girl in the photograph proudly clutches a tiny plastic purse and wears new clothes purchased in an Athens department store. The little boy fled the village barefoot, and for the voyage to America he has acquired heavy brogans made in the refugee camp. In the photograph one of his shoes is untied, but no one notices and ties it. He wears an ill-fitting suit of gray wool with short pants and a bulky jacket with bulging pockets. His new haircut is so short that the scalp shows on the sides. He eyes the camera warily, as if he doesn't trust the photographer.

The boy is actually watching two cardboard suitcases just behind the photographer, for they contain all his family's belongings, including his mother's wedding scarf and the only photographs they have of her. Nearly as important to him is the canvas school satchel filled with notebooks from his lessons in the refugee camp. He hopes these will impress his American teachers with his academic skills.

I know what the boy was watching and thinking and what treasures filled his pockets because I was that child, nine years old, who set sail for America on March 3, 1949. My three sisters and I had passage on the *Marine Carp,* a converted American troop carrier pressed into service as a passenger liner after World War II. I was traveling with my oldest sister, Olga, twenty, my second sister, Kanta, sixteen, and my fourth sister, Fotini, ten. Our third sister, Glykeria, fifteen, was missing behind the Iron Curtain, perhaps dead. She had been left behind with our mother. After *Mana*'s execution, our sister was driven at gunpoint into Albania with the rest of the villagers by the retreating Communist guerrillas. Now we had no idea where she was.

Although I had lost my mother, the only parent I had ever known, we weren't really orphans, because we had a father in America. That's how we had managed to get from the corrugated tin Quonset huts in Igoumenitsa, where a hanging sheet separated us from other families, to the docks of Piraeus. Now we would set sail for a country that had always seemed as remote and mythological to us as Atlantis.

Mana used to read us letters from this father who sold fruit and vegetables in Worcester, Massachusetts, and was considered an American millionaire by all the village. He had left Greece for America in 1910, a boy of seventeen with $20 in his pocket, and returned to take a bride in 1926. My absentee father's American citizenship and rumored fortune created envy among the villagers, who referred to my mother as the *Amerikana,* although she herself had never traveled more than fifty miles from her birthplace.

There were times during my first nine years when I was secretly proud of my unknown father's wealth and status, but more frequently I resented him because of his absence and the embarrassment his nationality caused me. Being the son of an American "capitalist" often made me the scapegoat of village boys who had absorbed the propaganda of the Communist guerrillas. When blockades and the shortages of World War II brought famine and we were weak from malnutrition and rickets, searching the ground for weeds to eat and surviving on the scant ration of flour that my grandfather, a miller, grudgingly gave us, I blamed my father for not bringing us to America to join him.

In the brief period of peace between the end of the European war and the outbreak of the Greek civil war in late 1946, *Mana* wrote, begging her husband to finish filing our papers so that we could emigrate at once, but he hesitated, worried about the risks of bringing adolescent daughters to a worldly place like America. "You have no idea how free the girls are here, running with strangers from an early age . . . ," he wrote. He ordered my mother to arrange a match for Olga, my oldest sister, with a man of good name, and then he would bring us.

But then it was too late. In the fall of 1947 Greek Communist guerrillas occupied the northern Greek villages where we lived. All the men, including my grandfather, Kitso Haidis, fled the mountains to avoid being conscripted, leaving the women and children behind. *Mana* wrote to her husband for advice, and he counseled her to stay and guard the house and property. She had survived the invasions of the Italians and the Germans, he wrote; certainly she had much less to fear from fellow Greeks, who were only fighting for their rights.

My mother was an obedient peasant woman who never spoke to a man outside her family until she was betrothed at the age of eighteen to a visiting American fourteen years her senior. She had been brought up to follow men's orders. When the guerrillas came, she gave them our food without complaint and went on daily work details to help build fortifications and carry the wounded. She didn't object when they demanded our house for their headquarters and prison, but simply moved us into her parents' hut. Although the guerrillas and her neighbors made her the object of special indignities because she was the rich *Amerikana*, she remained obedient and uncomplaining.

It was when the guerrillas demanded that she hand over her children that Eleni Gatzoyiannis finally chose to defy them.

In the spring of 1948 the guerrillas held a compulsory meeting in our village to announce that all children from three to fourteen would be taken to camps in Eastern Europe, where they would be reared and educated as Communists. They set out a table of food before the starving villagers, saying that any children whose parents volunteered them would immediately be fed. But despite the cries of their famished children, most of the mothers refused.

Then one day, hiding in my grandmother's bean field, I overheard two guerrilla officers say that all the children, volunteered or not, would be taken by force. When I ran to tell my mother, she chose defiance for the first time in her life and began to plan the escape that ended with her imprisonment, torture, and execution.

As I stood on the dock in Piraeus, I blamed my father for contributing to her death; if only he had moved faster, he could have brought us out during the brief peacetime in 1946 and we would be whole, living in America as a family. Now we were torn apart. My mother's bullet-riddled body had been tossed into a shallow mass grave with other victims and found months later by my grandfather, who interred her remains in the churchyard near the ruins of our house. My fifteen-year-old sister Glykeria was lost to us behind the Iron Curtain. My other three sisters and I were still together, thanks to my mother's courage and love, but we were penniless, owning no more than a change of clothes, and we were about to leave our homeland, cross an ocean to a strange country where no one spoke our language, and live with a father whom I had never seen but had always thought of with a mixture of love, longing, and anger.

If he really loved us, I thought, he would have taken us with him to America at the beginning, instead of leaving his young bride in Greece and returning every few years to visit. When he left Greece for the last time in late 1938, as the clouds of war gathered over Europe, neither Christos Gatzoyiannis nor his wife, Eleni, knew that she was carrying the son they both had prayed for while suffering the births of four daughters.

Now I imagined my father's face and tried to suppress my anger at the man who failed to save us in time. Like any child who has only one parent left, I longed to admire my father. Love and hate for this unknown American warred in my breast as we watched the launch that would ferry us to the *Marine Carp* approach. I held my school satchel filled with my notebooks like a talisman, hoping that when he saw how good I was at arithmetic he would be impressed.

Even when he learned that his wife had been murdered and his children were living in a refugee camp, Father still had vacillated about sending for us. He wrote asking whether we would prefer to make our home in the village with our grandparents, go to Athens to live with our cousins, or join him in America. But our answer was quick and unanimous, because we remembered so clearly what our mother said on the day she told us goodbye, as the Communist guerrillas took her away to thresh wheat. She promised she would try to escape on her own with Glykeria and find us, but, she told Olga fiercely, "If we don't, I want you to telegraph your father and tell him to get you out to America as soon as possible. Your grandfather will try to talk you into staying behind. My parents only want someone to stay in Greece and care for them in their old age. But whether I'm living or dead, I won't rest until you're all in America and safe."

Then came the moment when she said goodbye to me and was led away down the mountain by the guerrillas until she disappeared into the distance, turning once to raise her hand in farewell. Nearly the last thing she told me and my sister Kanta was, "Remember this: anyone who stays in Greece, who doesn't go to America, will have my curse. When you leave the house tonight, I want you to throw a black stone behind you so you'll never come back."

With our mother's parting words vivid in our memory and the threat of her everlasting curse hanging over us, there was no way we would succumb to the pleas and threats of our grandfather to stay behind. "In America the smoke from the factories is so thick it blocks out the sky. You'll never feel the sun on your faces again," he warned. "You'll never eat olive oil, feta cheese, or lamb again. It's a country filled with foreigners. You'll wind up marrying Italians, or worse."

But we refused to listen to him as he escorted us from the refugee camp in northern Greece to Athens, leading us through the formalities at the American Embassy, where we got our passport — issued in the name of Olga, who was the only one over eighteen. And on that day, as the ship's launch drew near, the old man sulked, refusing to join us in our last portrait as Greeks.

When our cousins heaved the two suitcases onto the launch and I firmly refused help with my school satchel, I noticed my grandfather's lip begin to tremble beneath his white mustache. "Take a good look at that sky," he growled for the last time. "You'll never see it again!"

I looked, seeing the unclouded blue sky that had hung over me all my life, and wondered what it would be like never to see it again. But I didn't hesitate as I followed my sisters onto the launch. When we reached the ship we climbed up the shaky ladder onto the deck, which was crowded with passengers in strange, foreign-looking clothes.

As the ship began to pull away, I watched the figure of my grandfather shrinking. Suddenly he began to wave the walking stick he always carried, carved from the branch of a cornel tree and polished to a dark sheen by his hands. Finally it was only the frantic waving of his stick that distinguished him from the other dots on the harborside.

I put my hands in my pockets to take stock of the treasures I had with me — amulets to protect me against the uncertain future. There was the cross-shaped box on a chain that my mother had hung around my neck in the last moment we were together. It was her most magical possession, because it held a splinter of a bone from a saint, and it was the only thing she could give to protect me from being shot or stepping on a land mine during our escape. I had promised her I would be brave, and the cold hardness of the cross made me feel braver now.

I inventoried my other treasures. First, a white handkerchief my god-mother had given me on the day between the wars when she left the village with her son to join her husband, Nassio, in America. Nassio hadn't procrastinated like my father. While we were being starved and bombed in the village, his son was in America, no doubt playing with wonderful toys like the wind-up airplane his father had once sent him. I had always hoped my godmother would give me that airplane when she left, but the handkerchief was what I got, and now I touched it to ease my transition from one culture to another.

I fingered the reed whistle that my Uncle Andreas had whittled for me when he taught me to make birdcalls. Andreas had always been the kindest man in my life, not like my stern, irascible grandfather. Uncle Andreas was the one who cried when we left the refugee camp, as my ten-year-old sister Fotini ran to comfort him, giving him a tiny, nearly worthless coin that she had been hoarding.

Then my fingers touched something cold and smooth, and I pulled it out of my pocket. It was the small black stone that I had picked up outside my house on the night of our escape, because my mother had ordered me to throw one behind me so that I would never return to the place that gave us so much suffering. I had kept that stone in my pocket for eight months, and now it was time to toss it into the sea.

My mother had often told us the story of how my father, an itinerant tinker of seventeen, when he boarded the ship for America, trium-phantly tossed over the rail the fez that the Turkish occupiers of north-ern Greece forced men to wear in those days as a symbol of their subjugation. When the fez disappeared into the waves, she said, my fa-ther felt like a free man for the first time in his life.

Now it was my turn to throw this stone from my village into the same sea, to insure that I would never be pulled back to this land of war and famine, bombs, torture and executions. My mother had said that any one of her children who came back would receive her curse. Throwing the stone was the way to turn my back irrevocably on Greece and my face toward America, where my father waited.

But my mother's body was still in Greece, in the church only a few yards below our ruined house. They had called her the *Amerikana* and all her life she had dreamed of America, but she would never leave our mountains. My sister was still somewhere behind those mountains too, unless she was dead.

It was the only country I knew, and I loved the cruel beauty of the mountain peaks, the sound of the goats' bells in the thin air, the smell of wood smoke, and the annual transfiguration of the gray hillsides when the Judas trees and wildflowers burst into paschal colors in the spring. I wasn't sorry to be leaving Greece, but despite my mother's orders, I couldn't make myself throw that stone overboard and cut myself off from my native land forever. It was the only place I had ever felt I belonged, until the war killed my mother and washed my sisters and me away like the swells of the sea that frightened me so when I first saw its vastness.

I slipped the stone back into my pocket and turned to follow my sisters, who were descending the steel stairs into the bowels of the ship, crying out in dismay at the dizzying sway beneath their feet.

Until we walked down the mountain out of our village eight months before, my sisters and I had never seen a body of water larger than the millpond where our mother washed our clothes. Crossing over the Kalamas River, which separated the isolated villages of the Mourgana mountains from the rest of the world, riding in a large wicker basket suspended from a cable and pulley, seemed to us a daredevil adventure. And until the day of our escape, we had never seen a motor-driven vehicle. To descend into the belly of this great iron fish and abandon ourselves to an eighteen-day journey on a sea that disappeared into the horizon seemed to us as precarious as the descent of Orpheus into Hades.

Before the harbor was out of sight my oldest sister, Olga, moaning, threw herself onto one of the narrow metal bunks in our cabin and announced that she would never live to see America. While we hunted for a bucket, she vomited on the floor.

Our third-class accommodations were in a windowless cabin deep in the hold of the ship, where the throbbing of the engines felt like the beating of an enormous heart. There were double-decker berths lining the walls of the cabin to sleep twelve passengers. I climbed into a top bunk and stared at the ceiling. The metal thwarts overhead and the throbbing of the engines made me feel like I was listening to the heartbeat of the huge beast. I closed my eyes and wondered if Olga's grim prediction would come true and we would die at sea and have our bodies thrown overboard to be consumed by the fish.

As a babble of Greek voices filled the cabin, I leaned over and discovered that every berth was occupied by a woman — some, like my sisters, in coarse village woolens, but most in bright print city dresses.

"Kanta," I hissed at my second sister, who was opening one of our suitcases. "It's all women in this cabin!"

"Of course," she replied. "Do you want your sisters sharing a cabin with men?"

"But *I'm* a man," I protested.

"You're small enough, so they let us," she said, as if I should be grateful. "It's better than being in a men's cabin by yourself."

That was *her* opinion. Indignantly I jumped down from my berth and left the chattering women behind, Olga moaning and little Fotini also looking a bit sick, while I set out to explore the rest of the ship like a man.

On the main deck I found a half-dozen muscular boys playing a ball game while expertly balancing themselves against the sway of the ship. They shouted at me in a foreign language.

"They're inviting you to play," said a female voice behind me in Greek. I turned and saw a chestnut-haired woman in a smart wool coat sitting in a deck chair and smiling at me.

"Who are they?" I asked her.

"American boys," she replied. "But they're going to Israel with their families. They're Jews. Why don't you play with them?"

I looked at them harder — the first American children I had ever seen. One of them came over and spoke to the dark-haired woman while looking at me appraisingly. All the foreign boys were wearing long pants, and I was painfully aware of my protruding knees and crude peasant shoes. I buttoned my coat to hide the cloth suspenders holding up the baggy pants.

"He wants to know how old you are," she said.

"Almost ten," I answered, looking defiantly up at the American boy. "How old is he?"

I understood the answer before she translated it, because it resembled the Greek equivalent: "Nine."

I stared. Clearly, boys grew bigger in America. Perhaps that's why they were allowed to wear long pants like men. This did not bode well for my future.

"Go ahead, why don't you play with them?" the woman said encouragingly. I stood my ground.

"What's that they're playing?" I asked.

She spoke to the boy and replied, "Football."

I had seen enough to know this was not what I called football. In the refugee camp we played football only with our feet, never with our hands, and the ball was round. In America, it appeared, even the games were different from what I knew. "Tell him I'd rather just watch," I said, and the tall American boy shrugged and turned his back, walking away with the casual confidence of one whose long pants were held up with a real belt.

Naturally American boys were bigger, I reasoned. While we were digging roots to stay alive, they had more food than they could eat. My mother had told me that everyone in America was rich. But something was nagging at my mind.

"If those boys are from America," I asked the friendly woman in the deck chair, "and if America is such a wonderful place, then why are they leaving it?"

"It's because they're Jews," she explained patiently, "and for two thousand years the Jews have had no country of their own. Everywhere they went, they were strangers and often persecuted. Last year the United Nations gave them a country, and these children and their families are going there to help settle it. It's not that they don't like America — everyone says America is a wonderful place. But they want a place of their own."

I thought about the Jews. I knew that in the spring of 1944 the Germans had collected all of the Jews in our province's capital, Yannina, and transported them to death camps. I learned this because the Greeks of Yannina had divided up the businesses and possessions of the Jews, and a merchant from our village who had a store there brought clothing plundered from Jewish homes up the mountain and passed it out to the villagers. My mother refused to let Olga keep a length of fabric that he handed her, because, she said, these things wrongfully taken from the murdered Jews would bring a curse on the owner. I could sympathize with people who had no real home and were always pushed from place to place, but these children looked too healthy and well dressed to be refugees like me and my sisters.

"Aren't you an American?" I asked the pretty brown-haired woman. "How do you know their language?"

She explained that she was a Greek who had learned English in school and then met and married an American soldier stationed in Greece. He had been sent back and now she was going to the States to join him. Her name was Christina.

Seeing my disappointment that she couldn't tell me anything about America, Christina offered to give me lessons in English if I would meet her on the deck every morning after breakfast. I had time to learn at least some of the language, because we would be on the ship for two and a half weeks: the *Marine Carp* was going first to Haifa, Israel, then to Italy before heading back to the United States.

I accepted Christina's offer eagerly and asked if I could bring Fotini as well. When she agreed I rushed down to our cabin to share all my news with my sisters.

I found our cabin in an uproar. Olga, even paler than she had been before, was sitting on her berth yelping weakly, clearly in shock. Kanta, the more level-headed of my older sisters, explained that Olga had just gone to the bathroom to be sick and had a terrible fright.

When we had first arrived in Athens from the refugee camp, indoor plumbing had been one of the most fascinating discoveries we made. We had never seen a flush toilet before, and in the hotel Fotini and I kept sneaking down the hall to pull the chain in the W.C. so we could watch that thrilling waterfall over and over again, until the concierge finally made us stop. I wondered what startling new thing Olga had encountered in the ship's bathroom.

"It was a naked woman!" she finally managed to cry. "I threw up in the toilet and then I heard a hissing sound and I turned around and there was a stall with a tin disk on top and water was coming out. A totally naked woman was standing under it with her head up toward the ceiling like a chicken who has drunk from a pool and raises her face to heaven in gratitude!"

In our village, women washed in wooden tubs in the dark cellar of their hut and never saw their own body naked, much less that of another woman. No wonder Olga was upset, I thought. I assumed that some terrified passenger, overwhelmed like us with fear of the dangerous voyage, had gone mad and ripped off her clothes and was running amok in the bathroom.

"I'm never going in there again!" said Olga with a shudder.

A woman seated on the next bunk started to laugh. "She was only washing herself," she explained. "She was taking a shower." (She used the French word, douche, employed by sophisticated Greeks who had seen such things.) "It's cleaner than a tub."

"But anyone can walk by and see her body!" protested Kanta.

"Only women can go in there," explained the city woman.

Olga caught Kanta's eye. "If this is the kind of thing women do in America," she said, "I'm not surprised that Father didn't want us growing up there."

From then on, even though racked with seasickness, Olga never entered the bathroom without first listening at the door to make sure no shower was running. Throughout the voyage, all of us continued to wash only our faces, hands, and feet.

One of the young Greek women in our cabin took a protective interest in Olga after her traumatic experience and nursed her through her spells of seasickness, coaxing her to walk on deck when she felt strong enough. When she didn't, the woman entertained her and the rest of us with romantic and bloodthirsty tales of elopements, betrayals, family feuds, and ancient vendettas in her native region of Mani. Her care of Olga freed the rest of us to leave our sister that first evening and go up to the main deck to sample American food.

In the dining room we encountered a familiar face amid the sea of strangers: Prokopi Koulisis, a young man of nineteen originally from the village next to ours. Like us, he was traveling to join his father in Worcester, Massachusetts. He was a good-natured, gregarious fellow with a round face, wavy brown hair, and a muscular build, and I envied him his ease with strangers. Just before the guerrillas had come he had escaped our mountains with the rest of the men, and we hadn't seen him again until we accidentally met in the American Embassy in Athens when we took our physical exams to qualify for immigration. Prokopi's mother, like our sister, had been forcibly marched into Albania and had disappeared. I was glad Prokopi would be sailing with us on the *Marine Carp*, since I hoped that his presence would be some sort of protection on the hazardous voyage.

Now Prokopi invited us to sit with him as we awaited our first American food. After all the tales we had heard of American abundance we expected a banquet, but the plates the waiter set down left us staring in puzzlement. The meat was still pink, almost bloody. "Perhaps they ran out of coal for the oven," muttered Kanta. There were some soggy cylinders that we identified as carrots and a mysterious pile of white stuff like thick yogurt.

"What a terrible thing to do to potatoes!" exclaimed Prokopi when he tasted it. "They've beaten them to death, when it would be so much easier to roast them nice and brown, with a little oregano, some rosemary . . ." Our mouths began to water at the thought.

Fotini pushed her plate away, whining, "I can't eat this! The meat is *raw*, and everything else tastes like boiled weeds."

"Have some bread," advised Kanta. "They can't spoil bread." We all reached for the breadbasket, then exchanged shocked looks as we discovered, with the first bite, that American bread tasted like cotton.

Garlic, basil, rosemary, oregano, succulent lamb, spicy artichokes, eggplant, and okra . . . none of these delicacies seemed to have crossed the ocean to America. We knew we should be grateful for this food after nearly starving to death for ten years, but we couldn't help remembering what our mother could do with a bit of cornmeal and some onions, or even the entrails of a lamb, which she transformed into a spicy *kokoretsi*. America was the land of plenty, but why did it all taste so bland?

My first English lesson with Christina the next day provided more unpleasant surprises. She graciously accepted my sisters Kanta and Fotini in her impromptu class, but our enthusiasm waned when we found out that the English alphabet had two more letters than our Greek alphabet, and many of them were completely unfamiliar — they looked to me like chicken tracks.

"Don't give up," Christina encouraged us, adding a Greek proverb: "Bean by bean the sack is filled." I vowed to surprise her by memorizing the entire English alphabet for the next lesson.

That afternoon, in the middle of the siesta hour, people began to appear on deck and run toward the bow. I had been pacing the ship, reciting the American alphabet aloud, and I eagerly followed to discover the source of the excitement.

We were approaching the port of Haifa, but because it was the Jewish

Sabbath we had to wait until the following day to unload. The next afternoon, passengers were allowed to disembark and wander along the harborside, and even Olga roused herself, eager to feel firm ground beneath her feet again. We bought several blood-veined oranges from a fruit stand and marveled at their size and sweetness. Except for the oranges, Haifa seemed not very different from any Greek port city, and a poor one at that. I saw a bus full of passengers from the ship, including the well-dressed American boys who had played football on the deck, waving and singing, excited at arriving in their new home. Again I wondered: if this poor place seemed so wonderful to them, what could America be like?

As the *Marine Carp* sailed from Haifa westward toward Palermo, in Sicily, I became increasingly lost in the morass of the English language. Different sounds, Christina said, might be spelled with the same set of letters: "enough," "though," "through." In Greek the spelling of a word was logical and sensible: in English, nothing made sense. My head was spinning as I watched her copying a list of vocabulary words for us to learn out of her *Divry's Greek-English Dictionary*. At the rate of ten words a day, I figured, it would take me several lifetimes to learn this infernal language.

Fotini, still somewhat seasick, gave up after the first few lessons. "This is never going to help," she cried. "I'll never learn American. It's too hard!" Kanta had to tend Olga, and soon I was the only student left. I was so frightened of what lay beyond our landfall that I ran around the deck like a wind-up toy, repeating the strange-sounding words that would protect me in my new school and win my father's praise: "The sea is blue. The boat is big. Onetwothreefourfivesixseveneightnineten."

By the time the ship approached Palermo, Olga was convinced she was very close to death. She hadn't been able to keep anything in her stomach, especially the unpalatable American food. Drawing on village medical lore, she decided that the only thing that might save her life was wine. She summoned me to her bedside, and whispering with painful effort, she ordered me to find Prokopi Koulisis and to send him ashore to buy a bottle of wine from the Italians. She handed me some of the precious American dollars our father had sent, and looking as ghastly as the vampires and ghosts of our village tales, she said that if I failed in this task she would certainly die and be thrown overboard.

Clutching the crumpled bills, I raced up to the deck, where Prokopi and the rest were watching the docking procedure. I pleaded with him to buy some wine to save my sister's life. As the only man in the family, I felt personally responsible for Olga's safety, and if she died, I knew my father would blame me.

Prokopi was willing, but we discovered that no continuing passengers were to be allowed ashore. As we hung over the rail, Prokopi noticed Italians loading provisions into the hold of the ship. He told me to stay put while he went below deck and tried to bribe one of the sailors for a bottle of wine.

I stared at the commotion on the docks below. There were bands of ragged boys, even more undernourished and poorly dressed than any in the Greek refugee camps. They were shouting at the passengers on the ship in their musical language and gesturing toward their mouths, clearly begging. No one on deck had any food to throw, but many passengers tossed packages of gum and cigarettes at the skeletal children. I stared in amazement as boys smaller and younger than myself plunged into the filthy water to retrieve them. On the docks small boys expertly lit up cigarettes and inhaled with the aplomb of adults, all the while begging for more.

Suddenly I realized, looking down on this pack of street children, that if it weren't for my mother's sacrifice and my father's American citizenship, I would be just like them, begging for any scraps people would throw me, living like a stray cat, with no place of my own. In that instant I knew that the traumas awaiting me could never be as bad as what I was leaving behind. I remembered the scenes that often haunted my dreams: the Germans marching through our village, so close to the ravine where we hid that I thought they would step on us; the smoking ruins of the houses they burned, including the charred skeleton of an old woman they tossed into the fire. I remembered my sisters searching the ground for flower bulbs to eat and finding the half-buried corpse of a young woman who was still warm. I hid and watched captured soldiers being forced to dig their own graves before they were lined up and shot. And I remembered the day in the refugee camp when we learned our mother was dead, and the keening cries of my sisters that had driven me out of the tin shack to hide in the woods. All these images rushed in on me, overwhelming me with the memory of my terror and hunger, as I stared down from the ship at the starving Italian boys below.

My mother knew such things didn't happen in America. That was why she made us promise to leave Greece, even without her. Suddenly the nervous anxiety that had plagued me ever since we boarded ship vanished. I looked at the orphan boys on the docks of Palermo and realized that my mother had sacrificed her life so I wouldn't be like them. Now it was up to me to cope with whatever America held in store. All over the world in the last years of the 1940s homeless people, blown like leaves by the winds of war, were searching for a place that would take them in. Greece was the only home I knew, but my mother had died to send us to a better place, and I had to trust her judgment.

When Prokopi returned to the deck, clutching a wicker-covered jug of chianti, I felt certain it would save Olga's life and we would all survive this journey. My mother's blood had paid for our passage, so we couldn't fail to reach the Golden Land she had told us about so often.

Seated on the floor of our stone house, near the fireplace, she had read and reread to us the letters our father sent from America, including one memorable postcard from New York picturing the Empire State Building. "I am writing this from the top of the tallest building in the world," he had scrawled on the back. "It has 102 floors. On one side I can see the Atlantic Ocean and the statue of the woman called Saint Freedom, which is so big you can climb up and stand in one of her fingers. This is how America looks."

Our mother would embroider his words, spinning fantastic tales of a country where the streets were like canyons and buildings as tall as mountains were heated by burning black rocks — coal — instead of logs. She spoke of swimming-pool rooms right inside the houses of rich people. I strained my mind trying to imagine such things. Soon I would see them with my own eyes.

Throughout the remaining twelve-day voyage across the ocean, as Olga grew stronger and my English vocabulary increased, I summoned my mother's tales of America whenever the panicky fear threatened to engulf me.

On the eighteenth day of our journey, I got up before dawn to put on my scratchy woolen suit, then went up to the deck, much too excited to eat breakfast. As soon as the darkness lifted and the haze burned off I saw it — two strips of land reaching out to us, the arms of America pulling us to her bosom.

The deck quickly filled as the ship approached New York harbor. My sisters gathered around me, silent at the rail, and I could feel Prokopi Koulisis' hands on my shoulders.

When I could make out details of the land, I felt an ache of disappointment. There were pockets of dingy gray snow in the hollows and a grim, metallic sky overhead. I couldn't help thinking that now, in Greece, oranges and lemons were ripening on the trees under a warm blue sky.

"The Statue!" someone cried, and there was a stampede to the other side of the ship toward the immense figure of the woman my father called Saint Freedom. She faced us, holding the torch that had welcomed millions of refugees from famine, war, poverty, and persecution, each one no doubt as frightened as I was now. Everyone started shouting and pointing, but when we drew close, the throng fell silent, as if in the presence of a miracle.

When we neared the dock, I turned toward the crowd of people waiting on land, trying to recognize the father I had never seen. I expected him to tower over the rest like a colossus, so I paid no attention to a short, portly man in a stylish felt hat and gray chesterfield, standing in the very front of the crowd. But Prokopi Koulisis remembered my father from his visits to our village, and I felt strong arms lift me up off the deck, holding me high above the heads of the crowd like a trophy as Olga shouted, *"Patera!"* The stocky man on the dock snatched his hat from his bald head and began waving it.

Twenty-five years later, when he was eighty-one years old, my father described the scene in his broken English into a tape recorder.

"I was on the dock watching the boat," he began slowly. "Olga recognize me. And I wave to them. Prokopi Koulisis, he pick Nikola up and show him to me from the deck. First time I see my son. Oh, my tears! My heart broke that minute."

He paused, trying to collect himself while two small grandchildren played at his feet. "They start to come out," he went on doggedly. "I hugged him, his little arms. They was so cold. My own childrens!"

He turned toward the machine that was recording his words. "I think I have to stop now," he said apologetically, "because I'm going to cry."

His tearful words of remembrance, our cries of greeting across the water, the murmurs of wonder at the sight of the statue who lifts her lamp beside the golden door — all these sounds are part of the chorus of the millions who entered this harbor seeking a place where they would be safe and free. First they came from northern Europe to settle a raw new nation, then from southern Europe, at the end of the nineteenth century and the beginning of the twentieth, seeking sanctuary from pogroms and famines, dictatorships, death camps and genocide. Entering this place, each uttered the same hymn of thanksgiving in his own tongue.

Today that chorus has grown faint in our ears, for the old European immigrants have passed away, taking their memories with them. Their children have forgotten what it means not to be American. The new arrivals, fleeing from Asia, Latin America, and the Middle East, are still trying to find homes and jobs, to learn the language and send their children to school. They have not yet found a voice to tell their tale.

This story of the children of Eleni Gatzoyiannis in America is the recollection of an immigrant who arrived at midcentury, old enough to be molded by the traditions left behind but young enough to belong in this new world. The particular calamities, heartaches, and triumphs in these pages are unique to my sisters and me, but our odyssey is as old as the nation: the arduous journey across the bridge that separates an old familiar world from a new and frightening one, to find a place for ourselves on the other side.

Christos (right), his partner (in the cab), and an employee posed with the REO Speedwagon

THE FIRST DAY
OF SPRING

Behold, I stand at the door, and knock.

— Revelation 3:20

INSIDE THE CAVERNOUS customs building on Pier 44, it seemed that we would never be summoned to cross the barriers and officially enter the United States. Silent knots of people with dark levantine features who had boarded our ship in Haifa were called forward, and exuberant groups of Italians, grandmothers in black with babies in their arms, were summoned and passed through the doors, behind which we could hear the excited cries of reunions in many languages. But we sat forlornly beside our cardboard suitcases, waiting.

Christina was called; she embraced us all and, to my embarrassment, kissed me on top of my head. "You're my prize pupil," she said, touching my cheek. "Don't look so worried. By Christmas you'll be speaking English like a native."

Finally we heard an immigration officer struggling with our unpronounceable name: "Ga-ga-yan-is."

Trembling in the presence of authority, we went forward as a group, and Olga thrust out passport number 247, issued by the American consul in Athens, Robert B. Memminger, on February 19, 1949, in the name of Olga C. Ngagoyeanes and her minor sisters and brother: Alexandra, Fotini, and Nicholas. Olga was described therein as four feet eleven inches tall, with brown hair and eyes, occupied with household duties. Our passport was valid only for travel to the United States and expired on June 19, 1949. Olga had printed her name in Greek along the edge of the black-and-white photo that showed the four of us standing in front of a huge marble pillar of the U.S. Embassy, frowning at the camera in the bright sunlight.

The immigration official glanced from our health certificates and our passport to us, still in the same clothes we had worn for the photo. Without comment he stamped the documents and pointed toward the customs officer at a desk behind him, who rifled through our suitcases in a perfunctory manner and waved us on.

When we walked around the barriers and into the next room, our father was waiting for us, the very image of well-fed American prosperity in his gleaming black oxfords, gray overcoat, and broad fedora — an island of style in a sea of weeping and embracing refugees. As soon as he saw us, he took off his hat, uncovering a bald head with only a fringe of gray at the back. He knelt down to embrace me first, and I submitted, keeping my body stiff and unbending. He kissed both my eyes, then released me and embraced Fotini. I noticed that all my sisters seemed a bit restrained as he kissed them on both cheeks in the old-country fashion. After an absence of nearly ten years, he seemed like a stranger even to the older ones. But despite our restraint, all of us secretly considered him a fine figure of a man, even more prosperous-looking and richly dressed than we had hoped.

Father introduced us to a thin, rumpled older man standing beside him. He was Prokopi Koulisis' father, Spiro, who had shared the drive from Worcester. Spiro Koulisis had prepared a little speech of welcome for us. "This is the first day of spring," he said. "A good time to begin a new life. May it be well rooted, and may you live many years for your father."

We all thought immediately of our mother, who did not live many years, but we said nothing. As Prokopi Koulisis emerged from the barriers and embraced his father, both of them bursting into tears, I felt threatened by the emotions welling up inside me. To hide how frightened and close to tears I was myself, I wandered over to the edge of the pier to examine the great bow of the *Marine Carp,* which seemed a hundred times larger now that I was standing outside of it. I was balanced on the very edge, gazing into the murky water, trying to see how deep the ship's hull reached, when I heard a gruff shout: "Hey! Get away from there! Come back here right now!"

I turned to see my father gesturing in a peremptory manner. Two minutes after we meet and he's yelling at me already, I thought. Ordering me around like a schoolmaster. I walked back, very slowly and deliberately, to demonstrate that he couldn't push me around; I would come at my own pace.

My face must have revealed my thoughts, for when I reached him he knelt down, putting an arm around me. "First time I see you and I yell at you," he apologized. "But now that I've finally got you, I don't want anything to hurt you." He took my hand and led us all off the pier.

As we walked out the door, the sounds and sights of New York stopped us dead. In the far distance rose the spires of the city like a forest of cypress trees, just visible beneath the arch of the West Side Highway over our heads. But the most astonishing sight to us was the parking lot in the shadow of the elevated highway, filled with row after row of automobiles.

"All of Athens doesn't have this many automobiles," I exclaimed.

My father stopped beside a long blue DeSoto. "Here we are," he announced. He opened the trunk and told us to put our luggage inside.

"Is this *your* car, Father?" wondered Fotini.

"It is this week," he replied, smiling enigmatically. "Now, would you like me to take you to a restaurant and show you New York City?"

"No, let's go straight to our home," said Olga, expressing the opinion of all of us. "We don't like American food anyway."

"Home is far away," our father replied (how far, we had no idea). "But whatever you wish."

As we started to crowd into the car, Father put a hand on Prokopi's shoulder. "It's not suitable to have a young man sitting in the back with my daughters," he said. "Let the old man sit there. You and Nikola can sit up front and watch me drive."

Kanta heard this remark, which confirmed her father's strict and puritanical attitude toward his daughters, and exchanged an apprehensive glance with Olga.

Father started the car and, shifting gears smartly, pulled out onto the highway with a speed and skill that thrilled me. I had never been inside a private car before, and I thought he drove with the boldness of a racing driver.

"Slow down, Gatzoyiannis!" shouted Spiro Koulisis from the back seat. "I didn't complain on the way up here. You and I have eaten our bread. But now our children are in your hands."

Father laughed, and to my delight speeded up. "Ever since I traded in my horse for a truck, I haven't scratched a bumper, let alone hurt anybody," he retorted. "And I don't need advice from a dog eater from Babouri who's never sat behind the wheel of a car."

"If we Babouriotes eat dogs, at least we're as clever as dogs," muttered Spiro. "But you Liotes are famous as donkey eaters, and we all know what *that* does for the intelligence."

I was heartened to hear the two men trading the usual insults. It proved that my father had a sense of humor and remembered the chauvinistic banter of our villages as well. I was also fascinated by the way he would ease up beside a car ahead, pick up speed and pass it, then pull in neatly, smiling with satisfaction.

"If you have no care for our skins, Gatzoyiannis, think of the car rental agency," persisted Spiro. "They want their DeSoto back in one piece."

As I turned to look at my father inquiringly, he changed the subject. "The children must be starving," he said, clearly feeling some pangs of hunger himself. "Prokopi, you open that bag of fruit."

We all stared in wonder as the young man pulled from the bag at his feet a cornucopia of plenty: apples, oranges, pears, tangerines, and green grapes. Fotini said what we all were thinking: "Is that real, *Patera?*"

"Of course it is," he replied. "What do you think?"

"But this is March!" protested Kanta. "In Greece we don't get pears or grapes before August."

"In America, there's fresh fruit all the time," Father bragged. "From places where it's always summer — Florida, California. You want oranges in December, you go to the store and buy them. Great country, America!"

We shook our heads and began devouring the fruit with good appetite after eighteen days of tasteless food. Father bit into a pear. "Not bad," he said judiciously, "but it can't compare with the Bartletts I sold from my truck. That's why we could charge twice as much as the pushcart Greeks and our customers were glad to pay it. All the big shots and their cooks wouldn't buy from anybody but Christy & Christy."

We all knew the story of Christy & Christy and their famous truck, the REO Speedwagon. "REO," as my father called it, was as famous in our village as the winged horse Pegasus. A framed picture on the carved mantelpiece in Lia showed our father, Christos Gatzoyiannis, and a youthful employee standing beside this splendid vehicle while Father's partner, Christos Stathis, grinned from the driver's seat. The truck seemed as long as our schoolhouse, dark and gleaming, embellished with a gold stripe and glass windows. FRUIT AND VEGETABLES FRESH DAILY was emblazoned on the side in large, seemingly three-dimensional letters, and on the door of the cab: CHRISTY & CHRISTY, 1 Ledge St.

The photograph was taken in the midst of the Great Depression; an NRA poster is displayed in the window, but both Christys appear well fed, and proud of their wonderful steed. And no wonder. Even in the worst of the Depression, when born Americans were standing on street corners selling apples, Christy and Christy, two immigrant boys from Greece, were pulling in $90 to $95 a week each. Their early success with the truck had enabled each of the partners to return to his native village in the late 1920s and marry in magnificent style, after choosing a suitable bride.

The produce truck continued to support Christos' family after his children were born, and made him one of the most prosperous and respected Greek immigrants in Worcester until his partner, Stathis, became ill and convinced him to let Stathis' brother-in-law, Nassio Economou, take his place. A great ladies' man, Nassio resented the long hours and the need to get up at five-thirty A.M., and when my father left the business in his partner's hands to visit Greece in 1937, Nassio secretly sold the truck and the business for $1200 and bought himself a diner near the railroad terminal from a bankrupt fellow immigrant. When he casually handed my father $600 — all that was left of the business he had spent his life creating — Father went after him with a knife, but was finally placated by the promise that Nassio would eventually make him a partner in the Terminal Lunch Diner.

But as we drove along the Merritt Parkway toward our new home in Worcester, we could see that our father still mourned the loss of his beloved REO and the produce business that had been his glory. We knew that the partnership with Nassio had never materialized and that there was some bitterness between the former colleagues, but we were bound to Nassio's family by stronger ties than money: Nassio had baptized my sister Glykeria, his mother had baptized Fotini, and his wife, Eugenia, had become my own godmother before Nassio brought her and their son to America in the brief peacetime between the wars. This tie of the baptismal font was as sacred as ties of blood and had to be respected despite any disagreements over matters like money. "You do not fight with people who have poured oil on your children," my mother often said when the subject of Nassio's perfidious business dealings came up.

In fact, before my godmother Eugenia departed for America with her son, she and my mother were the closest of friends, whatever their "bachelor" husbands were doing in Worcester. They wept bitterly when it was time to part. "When you see Christos in America," my mother begged Eugenia on the day she left, "tell him that coming to join him is all we want in the world."

Remembering that day, I reached in my pocket to touch the white handkerchief Eugenia had given me as a parting gift. "Will we live near my godmother, *Patera*?" I asked now, hoping to distract him from the loss of his truck.

"They live at the other end of town," he replied. "But your *nouna* is in our house right now, cooking dinner for us, waiting to welcome you."

Soon he pulled into a roadside gas station, and once again I was impressed by his confident manner as he chatted with the attendant in the guttural English language. He conveyed an air of good-natured authority, and the attendant bustled about, checking the oil, cleaning the windshield, as if pleasing my father was his greatest desire. I could see our father commanded respect in this new world.

As we drove through the lush Connecticut countryside, Father proceeded to inquire about all our relatives, with the conspicuous exception of our mother, while my sisters answered his questions tersely, wondering when he would ask about her. He asked about our grandparents, our cousins, our maternal aunt and uncle, and his own older brother Foto, the black sheep of the family. Foto had once been jailed for killing a Turk who had insulted his first wife, and Father had sent him enough money to open a coffeehouse within the prison. Later Foto produced nine children by his second wife (who was executed at our mother's side). Despite the fact that our father had supported him and his family for all the years before the war, Foto had refused to give us a bite of food during the famine or to share the gamebirds he trapped. He fled the village ahead of the guerrillas without a word to us, and when we were living in the refugee camp, our father naively sent the money for our support to Uncle Foto, who pocketed most of it, claiming it never got through.

"And how's my worthless brother?" Father asked. "Do you know, when that idiot filled out the immigration papers for you in Igoumenitsa, he put Nikola's birth date as 1935 instead of 1939, so I had to pay full fare for him on the ship — $450 instead of $225. Yes," he mused, "it cost me a fortune to bring you over here. But it's worth it."

"*Barba* Foto was drunk when he made out our papers, *Patera*," Olga said.

"Well, drunk or sober, he *is* my brother," Father said in a tone of forgiveness, as he drove over a bridge so long and so high that my sisters clutched each other in fear. "Look, we're just coming up on Hartford, Connecticut. See that onion dome with gold stars? That's not a church, it's a warehouse. Strange country, America!"

We stared at the skyscrapers of Hartford in silence, but once the city was behind us, Kanta suddenly burst out with the question the rest of us had been too afraid to ask. "Well, *Patera*," she said coldly from the back seat. "You've asked us about our grandparents and our uncles and aunts and every cousin we have. Aren't you going to ask us about your wife — how she suffered and how she died? Aren't you going to ask us about the famine and the beatings? Don't you want to know how she suffered to save us?"

My father seemed to deflate before my eyes, as if he had been struck a blow. He lowered his head momentarily in silence, then he pulled the car over to the side of the road and stopped. He turned off the ignition, and the car was silent except for the sound of Olga's sobbing. Then he turned around to look at Kanta, and I could see tears glistening in his eyes.

"We've got plenty of time for that, my child," he said. "We have years together. Nothing is going to separate us but God. I want to hear all those stories later, but this is the time for joy because we're together."

Kanta looked at him, mollified. "I thought you didn't care," she said softly.

"I care," he replied. "But now is the time for us to rejoice and to get to know each other."

Olga was still sobbing. "We have to tell it!" she cried. "It's our duty to tell the torments of our mother! We have to bear witness to her sacrifice!"

"You're my children and I want you to be happy today," said my father with finality, turning the key in the ignition. "We'll have plenty of time later for tears."

We drove on and there was a new lightness in the car, a sense of relief because we had spoken of our mother. We realized that she would have agreed with our father — this was a day for rejoicing, because for four of her children, her dream had finally come true.

It was nearly twilight as we entered the outskirts of Worcester, where we would make our new home. We expected something like Athens, the only large city we had ever seen. But although Worcester was the second largest city in New England, with a population of 200,000 in 1949, it did not impress us.

The city seemed to consist entirely of long, low mills, factories, and wooden tenement houses, just as my grandfather had predicted. When we stopped outside one of the tenements to let Prokopi and Spiro Koulisis off, I climbed out of the car and searched the heavens to see if my grandfather was right that I would never see the sky again — but to my relief it was clearly visible through clusters of clouds, darkening to sapphire with the dwindling light.

Father drove through a brightly lit commercial area, with crowded stores. "At least it's cleaner than New York," remarked Kanta. "And the people are better dressed than those on the docks."

We drove onto a wide street that ran beside a railroad track. Beyond the track was a factory that seemed to go on forever — grimy brick buildings, towering smokestacks, and gray wooden barracks that reminded me of the army camps I had seen in Greece. On the opposite side of the street from the factory buildings, wooden three-decker tenements, built as housing for the factory workers, ranged up hills in rows as far as the eye could see.

Suddenly my father turned up one of the side streets and stopped in front of a wooden three-decker, a mammoth beige-and-brown structure planted solidly on the sloping, tree-shaded street, with no ornamentation except a rounded bulge to the left of the front door that contained three layers of bay windows, and a small, square-columned front porch, also in three layers, for each floor of a three-decker is exactly like the other two.

We had no eye for architectural details as we tumbled out of the car, for my godmother was rushing out of the side door and down the driveway toward us, drying her hands on her apron and crying, "My poor children, my souls!" The sight of us children, whom Eugenia had last seen in our mother's company on the day she left Greece, sent her into a fit of weeping, which set Olga sobbing too.

Father came up and said sternly, "That's enough, *Koumbara*. I don't want my children upset. Let's get the suitcases inside and show them the house."

While Olga was weeping on Eugenia's ample bosom, Kanta was studying my godmother, amazed at how the woman had changed from a black-dressed peasant with a black kerchief hiding her hair. Now the headscarf was gone and Eugenia had short hair that brushed her shoulders. She wore a smart brown American dress, and on her wrist was a gold wristwatch. That last elegant detail sent a stab of pain through Kanta as she thought, "My mother didn't have bread to eat while my *koumbara* was in America wearing a gold wristwatch."

As the rest grappled with the suitcases, I climbed back in the front seat, drawn by an irresistible urge that had been growing in me ever since New York. I pressed down the center of the steering wheel, and a highly satisfying blast of the horn made everyone jump.

"Stop that!" Olga shouted as my godmother pulled me out of the car and enveloped me in her embrace, still weeping. "My precious child," she cried. "Come into the house so I can look at you."

She led us up the driveway and through a side door which revealed a small hall and a staircase leading up to higher floors where others lived. A private door opened into a tiny entry hall and our own kitchen, which made us all stop and stare. Olga couldn't take her eyes off the yellow-patterned linoleum floor, like a carpet of golden leaves. Our kitchen in the village had a floor of dirt.

As we gaped, we saw a pretty, round-faced young woman standing there watching us. Eugenia introduced her as Chrysoula Tatsis, and we realized that this was the first Greek woman to immigrate to America from our village. Chrysoula, "the golden one," had been only sixteen in 1936 when Leo Tatsis, owner of a wholesale grocery business in Worcester, came to Lia, married her, and spirited her away.

As the wife of a prosperous man twenty years her senior, Chrysoula had proved quick and clever in her mastery of the American language and customs. All the other Greek immigrants who came later, especially the women, turned to her as a role model and arbiter of taste in this new land. She knew about things like beauty parlors and silk stockings. Most important, as our father would often point out, Chrysoula had adjusted to life in America without damaging her moral reputation. You would not see Chrysoula Tatsis walking around in trousers like some of the tramps in America, he often said, directing my sisters to take her as a model of how a woman could live in this country without compromising her virtue.

We all stared at Chrysoula in awe, taking in her kind, wholesome face, her smartly waved hair in a demure bun, her silky green dress, her lips touched with just a hint of pink. She greeted us quietly and a bit shyly, not wanting to intrude on the emotional reunion with our godmother.

When we tore our eyes away from Chrysoula to look around the kitchen, Eugenia acted as our guide, showing Kanta and Olga the wonders of modern American technology. "Look, my treasures," she said. "This is a refrigerator. You put food in it instead of on the windowsill and it won't turn bad and start to smell. And look here," she said, opening the stove. "Now you won't cook over a fire and you won't need to go to the bakery and pay to have a pan full of beans or *pastitsio* cooked, because you can cook your own food right here in your own oven."

"That means we can make bread every day!" exclaimed Kanta, who had been terribly homesick for the taste of crusty Greek bread. More than the rest of us, Kanta cared about good food, although she never got fat. The aroma of the things cooking in the oven and on top of the stove reminded us how hungry we were. For the first time in eighteen days we inhaled the delectable aromas of giant white lima beans in garlic and tomato sauce, spicy green beans cooked with chunks of lamb, tangy goat cheese and mellow olive oil, rich flaky cheese and spinach pies. Suddenly we were all famished.

But the wonders of our kitchen continued. Eugenia pointed to a barrel-shaped white enameled machine on legs with a set of double rollers above it. "Washing clothes is nothing in America," she explained. "Instead of beating the laundry with branches on rocks beside the pond, you throw the clothes in here, where one machine beats them clean and this one on top squeezes them nearly dry in these rollers. Just watch you don't catch your fingers," she warned, glaring at me and Fotini.

We shook our heads, unable to absorb such a variety of new technological marvels, but Father was pointing at a door to another room.

"Olga, put your suitcase in there," he ordered.

"You mean this is ours too!" she exclaimed, opening the door to reveal a corner bedroom with two double beds.

"Yes, and put the other suitcase in that room," he continued, and we rushed to a second door and discovered another bedroom, smaller, with one double bed.

"But this is huge!" exclaimed Kanta. "In Greece, a family needs only one room."

Father smiled modestly. "This is *all* ours," he said. "Open every door and whatever you see is ours!"

This created pandemonium. There were four doors off the kitchen in addition to the one we had entered, and we rushed about, exploring our new home. The biggest surprise was the bathroom, which was sandwiched between the two bedrooms. We had discovered indoor plumbing in the hotel in Athens, but even our sophisticated cousins who lived in attached townhouses in that city had to use a privy in the courtyard. We had never expected to find a toilet in a private home.

"You see, my darlings," Eugenia crooned, "here in America you don't have to go outside to the bathroom, you don't have to go out to the spring for water, you don't have to go into the woods to cut firewood."

We ricocheted from one room to another, each one bigger than the last. The grandest were a dining room with a built-in, glass-fronted china closet and beyond that, through arched mahogany doors, a huge, echoing parlor. It echoed because it was empty except for a few folding chairs. The dining room too was empty of furniture. "I decided to wait until you came to buy furniture," my father explained, when we asked why the rooms were empty.

We didn't mind. This house in America seemed a virtual palace to us, good enough for a king. The only homes we had ever had before were our mud-floored stone hut in the village, with the animals living in the basement, and the corrugated tin barracks in the refugee camp, which we shared with other families, with only a hanging sheet to protect our privacy.

By the time we had explored every corner and returned to the kitchen, both Olga and Kanta were crying because our mother, after dreaming all her life of America, had not lived to see this magnificent home. To distract us, our father directed Eugenia and Chrysoula to put the meal on the oilcloth-covered kitchen table. Soon our grief was forgotten as we stuffed ourselves with the first palatable food we'd had since leaving Greece.

Afterward, Father looked at our grimy clothing, trying not to show his distaste, and said it was time for each of us to take a bath and put on the new pajamas and underwear he had bought for us. Proudly he opened the bureau drawers in the bedroom to reveal brand new underwear and pajamas in neat piles. Chrysoula had been sent to buy the girls' things, and their pajamas were in a soft, silky fabric printed with little pastel flowers.

"But I can't wear these, *Patera!*" exclaimed Olga. "I'm in mourning for *Mana*. I'm going to wear black for five years."

"Me too!" echoed Kanta, somewhat less decisively, as she ran her hand over the soft, silky fabric. "I can't wear these colors."

Our father sighed. "Just put them on tonight for me, children," he said. "Then tomorrow we'll talk about wearing black."

Chrysoula demonstrated to a fascinated audience how to fill the tub with water and described how each of us would sit in the water and wash our bodies all over. Olga blushed at the thought, but Father insisted. The American virtue he cherished above all others was cleanliness. Even when he had gone back to Greece on his long visits, he had prided himself on bathing every week in a tin tub before the fireplace. The villagers, who rarely bathed, considered this an eccentric and possibly life-threatening idiosyncrasy.

By default I was chosen to be the first to risk the dangers of the bathtub. When I emerged, feeling grown-up and manly in my striped pajamas with long trousers, I saw that my father's two former partners, Nassio Economou and Christos Stathis, were just coming in the door.

I stared at Nassio with curiosity. Even in the village I had heard rumors of his wild ways. Now, in his pin-striped suit and bow tie, he looked to me like one of the dandies I had seen in the fashionable Kolonaki section of Athens. In contrast, Christos Stathis had a square, stern face and body like my godmother. Clearly brother and sister, they were both as solid and steady as our mountains.

But Nassio was looking us over like a buyer at a horse auction. I became increasingly nervous, waiting for his judgment. We all returned his stare balefully.

Gesturing at Olga and Kanta, Nassio said to my father, "Cut off the braids, get rid of the black. Don't let anybody see them looking like this!"

"Don't you worry," replied Father, trying not to show his annoyance. "I'm taking care of all that."

"What's that one got on her neck?" continued Nassio, pointing at Olga, who blushed.

"It's just a goiter," she replied defensively. "Lots of people in the village have them. This is just a small one."

"How're you going to marry her like that?" Nassio asked Father. "This is America, Dr. Gage. You've got daughters now. You can't keep them locked in the house, wearing black. Face it, you've got to let them go out, go to school, go to work."

"I don't need you to tell me what I'm going to do with my daughters," snapped our father. "You're no authority on how to raise virtuous women, in my opinion."

I saw a flicker of annoyance pass over Nassio's face as he turned to examine Fotini, who looked frightened. "No color in her cheeks," he observed. "Pale as flour. You got to fatten her up. Where's the boy?"

My turn next, I thought. I threw out my chest and pulled myself up to my full height, trying not to falter under his scrutiny as he looked me over from top to bottom.

He clicked his tongue and turned to my father to deliver his verdict. "Pineapple juice!" he announced. "Make him drink pineapple juice four times a day, Dr. Gage, and he just might grow to normal size. Otherwise you got a midget on your hands."

"He'll grow! My son has years to grow," shot back my father. "But for you, little man, there's no hope at all."

Nassio didn't flinch. "I'm big enough where it counts," he bragged.

"Nassio, for God's sake, not in front of the girls," begged his wife.

"You think they don't know about these things, even in the village?" he retorted.

I saw my father's face flush with anger, and Christos Stathis saw it too. He laid a hand on Nassio's shoulder. "Plug it up," he said. "We came here to welcome the children and learn the news from over across, didn't we? Not to listen to your foolishness."

Father struggled to control himself, and Nassio momentarily backed down. I was secretly pleased that my father had come so quickly to my defense.

"What about the other girl?" said Christos Stathis, trying to change the subject. "What news of Glykeria?"

"Glykeria's still in Albania in one of those camps where the guerrillas drove them like cattle," Father replied. "I sent her some money but haven't had any word. She's in God's hands."

"You might as well throw your money in the sea," remarked Nassio. "You think the Albanians are going to give it to her?"

"I sent it through the Red Cross," Father said with mounting irritation.

"They're thieves just like the Communists," taunted Nassio. "They take people's blood for free and then turn around and sell it to sick people. You know, my friend, in that camp, with no father, brother, or mother to protect her, she won't come back as spotless as she went in."

Father leaped out of his chair, his face the color of a tomato. "She's fifteen years old, you bastard!" he cried, while Christos Stathis and Eugenia ran between them. "I don't want you in my house, talking like that."

"She's *my* godchild, isn't she?" Nassio replied coolly. "I'm only saying that nothing matters except her life."

It took all the energy of the women to calm the two antagonists, but after a round of ouzo and some *mezedakia,* Christos Stathis tried again to elicit news of the village.

Just before our departure for America, Olga had insisted on returning to Lia in the company of our grandfather. She was determined to remove my mother's body from the distant ravine where she and other victims of the firing squad had been thrown and to transfer it to the sanctified ground of our church, where *Mana* had prayed every day of her life. In the nearly deserted village, Olga and our grandfather slept in the house of our Uncle Foto.

As we sat around in our new kitchen, Olga told the story to the hushed group: "*Papou* and Uncle Foto rose before I was awake and went early up to the ravine," she said. "They didn't want me to see her body and be upset. But I guessed where they had gone and ran up the mountain. They were coming down, carrying a box with both *Mana's* body and Aunt Alexo's in it. It was only about this long," she said, stretching her hands a yard apart. "And I screamed, 'I want to see my *mana!*' but *Papou* wouldn't let me. He said, 'Your mother's hair is just the same, gold and shining like silk, but her skull's broken in pieces — perhaps when they piled the boulders on top.'"

As Olga talked and wept, I couldn't bear to listen any longer. I got up quietly and slipped into the corner bedroom where our suitcases were. I curled up on the bed and covered my ears, but I still could hear her crying. In an effort to distract myself, I got very busy picking out my belongings from the suitcases and setting them around the room, trying to make it seem more familiar, more like my home. I hummed loudly, trying to drown out the sound of Olga's words, trying not to listen, but it was useless. It seemed her voice was inside my skull.

"I got this idea in my head that the Communists had stoned her to death," Olga went on in the other room, "the way they executed some people in other villages, and I cried all night thinking of her dying that way. And then when I finally fell asleep, *Mana* appeared to me in a dream. 'No, my child,' she said to me. 'Don't cry so. They didn't kill me with rocks, they shot me here,' and she put her hand on her heart. And then I woke up and I felt better because my mother's remains were finally in the church beside the bones of our ancestors."

I slipped back in the kitchen and saw everyone in tears, even Nassio. Pretending I didn't notice, I walked over to my godmother. "Look, *Nouna,*" I said. "I still have it, your present." I held up the white handkerchief she had given me on the day she left.

It only made her cry harder, and she took me in her arms. Although I usually didn't let people treat me like a baby, I stayed on her lap until the drone of the conversation started to put me to sleep. Eventually my father carried me into the bed I would share with him. When he came to bed I saw him pause for a moment, facing the iconostasis in the eastern corner, and cross himself three times. Even in his striped pajamas he looked imposing.

The next morning I woke alone in the huge bed, dazzled by the sunlight streaming in the windows. I waited to feel the rocking of the ship, then remembered where I was. Soon I became aware of a delicious aroma and followed it to find my father in the kitchen, expertly flipping omelets filled with feta cheese, gilding them to perfection on both sides. He set one before me with a flourish, and I could imagine nothing more tempting than that golden puff oozing cheese. By the time I had devoured the last crumb, I was convinced that my father must be the best chef in all of Worcester.

When we had all finished breakfast he announced, "Now we're going to go into town and buy you some clothes to make you look like Americans."

At this news Kanta flushed with excitement. All her life she had hoarded American fashion illustrations from the magazines her father sometimes sent, dreaming over them for hours in the solitude of the outhouse. In her fantasies she was dressed in the latest American styles — soft, silky fabrics in bright colors — and always in her dreams her hair was cut short and wavy. In the village she had liked to stand with the sun at her back and look at her shadow on the ground, arranging her braids so she could pretend her silhouette had short hair and wore an American dress with a short skirt and short sleeves. Kanta knew that none of this was suitable apparel for a village girl of good character, but she didn't care; she longed to be stylish and up-to-date, and now her father was going to let her.

Olga, however, immediately protested. Since she was the oldest, she felt responsible for upholding the standards her mother had taught her and making sure her younger siblings did too. "I'm not going to put on anything but black, *Patera*!" Olga exclaimed. "We're in mourning for *Mana* and I'm going to wear black for five years."

"We'll try to get you the closest thing to black," replied Father. "You can't wear these clothes every day. You have to have at least one good outfit for church."

"Church!" cried Olga, outraged. "No self-respecting girl beyond the age of eleven lets herself be seen in church until her wedding day. You know that!"

"It's like that in the village, I know, my child," said our father gently. "But things are very different here in America. All the Greek girls go to church, just like the men and women. Of course their parents escort them and they don't speak to men, but showing your face in church doesn't mean you're immodest. Nassio was right — you'll have to learn some new customs in America."

"Well, *I'm* not going to church," retorted Olga. "*Mana* taught me the proper behavior, and I'm going to honor her by doing what she taught."

Nevertheless, even Olga crowded into the DeSoto with the rest for our excursion to the stores, eager to see our new country by daylight. Father drove up our sloping street, Greendale Avenue, to the corner and turned left. "There's where you and Fotini will go to school," he said to me, pointing across the street at a huge red brick building. "You see, it's only a stone's throw from the house, so you can come home for lunch in two minutes."

I was taken aback by the size of this immense building, bigger than our village's church, school, and coffeehouse all put together. "Aren't we going to wait until the new school year starts in the fall?" I asked hopefully.

"The longest part of a journey is the passing of the gates," recited my father, who had a proverb for every occasion. "No point in putting it off."

My mouth went dry as I surveyed this forbidding structure, surrounded by a diamond-patterned wire fence. It looked more and more like a prison.

"What about Olga and me, *Patera?*" inquired Kanta from the back seat. "Will we go to school?"

"You're lucky," he said. "They have a place here called Lamartine Street School where foreigners learn the English language — immigrants from every country, even old people. But you have to be thirteen years or older to go there. The little ones have to go right into the public schools, sink or swim."

I sat in silence, trying to fight down my fear of next Monday. Would I sink or swim? My father didn't know that on my first and only plunge into the ocean, near the refugee camp in Igoumenitsa, I would certainly have drowned in the unfamiliar surf if some older boys hadn't pulled me out, laughing the whole time at my panic and the hand-knit underpants that I wore instead of bathing trunks.

My father continued to drive around our block and then onto the wide main street, West Boylston, past the endless factory buildings and railroad tracks that had reminded me the night before of an army barracks.

"Norton Company," Father, said pointing. "Founded sixty years ago by a couple of Swedes. Now it employs thousands of people and makes most of the grinding wheels in the world. That's something like sandpaper. Most of the people who live around here are Swedes, descended from workers brought over by Norton. Very nice, quiet people."

"But where are the Greeks?" asked Kanta.

"They live closer to the center," he answered. "Not as nice as this neighborhood. You have to take a bus to get there."

"But won't there be any Greek children at school?" I quavered. "How are they going to understand me?"

"You're a smart boy, you'll do fine," he said, with more optimism than I felt was warranted. "It's best to grab the new language with both hands," he added. "Sink or swim."

Mentally I reviewed the English lessons Christina had given me on board the ship. "Onetwothreefourfivesixseveneightnineten," I recited proudly.

"Very good!" my father answered, first in English, then in Greek. "You say that for the principal, he'll be very impressed. Smart boy!"

In the cold light of day, the city of Worcester did not strike me as a friendly place. Nothing looked familiar — no black-kerchiefed old ladies leaning out of windows to gossip, no painted olive-oil tins of sweet basil and geraniums outside each door, no round tin tables where men sat over cups of coffee, watching the world go by. Worcester, built on seven hills, seemed an endless barricaded city of ugly wooden tenement buildings and even uglier brick factories.

When we reached the municipal buildings in the center of town, things looked more familiar. The huge gleaming granite building with a Doric portico supported by white columns, which father said was the civic auditorium, seemed to me a replica of the Parthenon. Main Street was lined with imposing white marble structures: the courthouse, churches, and office buildings, all demonstrating the influence of classical Greece on Worcester's settlers.

As we continued on Main Street, a parade of stores, banks, and commercial buildings, my father pulled over and pointed proudly to City Hall, a sprawling four-story granite structure with a soaring belltower. Behind City Hall extended a rectangle of green — the city common, my father explained, where America's Declaration of Independence had been read for the first time in public, in 1776. Here many of Worcester's early patriots were buried. "In this country, they have so much land, they leave the dead buried in the ground," expounded our father, "instead of digging them up after three years and putting the bones in the church."

We refrained from saying that in our eyes, this seemed sacrilegious.

Beyond the common, Father told us, behind the stores and banks that surrounded the green square, was Union Station, the heart of the bustling city, where all the train tracks converged. And opposite Union Station, we knew, was the Terminal Lunch, the diner that Nassio Economou had bought for a song from a ruined gambler, where he and

Christos Stathis now made a prosperous living managing a business that by rights should have been partly owned by our father. But none of us spoke of the Terminal Lunch, for we had eyes only for Sherer's Department Store, the palatial emporium on one side of the city common where, our father assured us, only the most high-class American clothing was sold.

Whispering as if in a church, we tiptoed behind him into its gleaming, luxurious interior, where everything seemed to have been polished that very morning and the light of crystal-prismed chandeliers reflected off silks and jewels and the finest leathers. We drew together, suddenly aware of the coarse cloth and ugly colors of our garments and the heavy clunk of our village shoes treading the soft, jewel-toned carpets.

Our father seemed unperturbed at being trailed by this gaggle of ugly ducklings. He nodded and tipped his fedora in a gracious and familiar way to the attendants who waited behind the counters; clearly he was a man of taste and distinction who was a welcomed customer here.

He led us first to the shoe department on the ground floor and issued orders to the young men in three-piece suits who hurried up to attend us. I tried to hide my homemade brogans from their sight by winding my feet around the struts of the chair, but by the time my father was done, we all had new shoes as well as a pair of slippers to wear inside the house, for it was our custom to remove our shoes at the door. My shoes were brown wing-tipped oxfords like my father's. The older girls took off their black crepe-soled lace-up shoes to try on high heels. Kanta received a pair of blue sling-back shoes and was so thrilled that she refused to let them be wrapped or boxed but carried them clutched to her bosom. Olga, staunchly choosing the most severe style, got a black pair.

Dresses and suits were upstairs, announced our father, gesturing, and we followed him to a cubicle lined with mirrors where a young man in uniform was waiting. This was our first sight of an elevator. In Greece we had been impressed and confused by the large mirrors and plaster mannequins of Diamantopoulos' department store, but compared to Sherer's American bounty, Athens' finest retail store now seemed pathetic. Our father was waving us into an elevator where a young man dressed like an army officer was about to spin a wheel and send us shooting heavenward. We all took a deep breath and followed him in, except for Olga, who stood helplessly frozen outside.

"Get in, get in," our father hissed to Olga. "Do you want all the world to take you for a country bumpkin? It's not going to eat you." Trembling, she followed, and as the door closed and the elevator jerked upward, we all swallowed the cries that rose in our throats.

Father chuckled and made some jovial comment to the young elevator operator, clearly identifying us as his children, newly arrived from Greece. The young man turned around with a smile and gazed at us curiously. Again we were aware of the contrast between our village clothes and our fine surroundings.

In the women's dress department Olga glowered at the profusion of brightly colored dresses spread before her, while Kanta nearly swooned at the abundance of American fashions. There wasn't a black dress in the lot. Finally Olga grudgingly accepted a dark navy blue dress with some discreet pindots of white on the bosom. Kanta's selection was a light blue dress to match her new shoes. It had a brown velvet collar and a pleated skirt, and when she put it on Kanta discovered that her thin body was acquiring a little potbelly from all the food she had consumed in the past day or so. Our father also bought all the girls wool coats; Olga chose one in dark brown, the others opted for pastels.

After buying Fotini a dress with puffed sleeves and lace that made her look like a dark-haired angel, Father led us all to the boys' department, where he issued some commands in the mysterious English tongue. The hovering salesladies produced a tan trenchcoat that was an exact miniature of a man's coat, and a rakish brown suit that featured leather insets on the shoulders and sleeves. Best of all, the suit had full-length trousers! There was a white oxford shirt and a narrow knitted tie with two-inch-wide stripes, and some striped polo shirts for everyday wear, but those were only frosting on the cake. The main point was that I had suddenly been promoted to manhood and long trousers.

Flushed with excitement, balancing stacks of boxes and bags filled with our new finery, we endured the elevator ride to the ground floor with the aplomb of experienced shoppers. As we were heading for the exit, a woman's voice cried out in Greek: "Christos Gatzoyiannis! Don't tell me these are your children!"

A rosy-cheeked, well-dressed woman of middle age hurried up, fussing over us as our father made the introductions. He said that this was Mrs. Sigalos. She admired our purchases and complimented our taste, and then said in a conspiratorial voice to our father, "Christos, may I have a word with you in private?"

With suddenly aroused suspicions, we watched him walk out of earshot with the woman and listen attentively as she whispered in his ear. Then he replied. She smiled and reached out to pat his hand. We exchanged horrified glances, all stricken with the same thought: we had escaped war-torn Europe to join our widowed father, and here he was, perhaps already ensnared by the charms of this conniving interloper. No doubt she had designs on our father and his fortune and intended to become our stepmother. We turned to stare at her with looks of unanimous outrage.

We rode home in stony silence, and when we carried our purchases into the house and Father sank into a chair and asked Olga to make him a cup of coffee, no one moved. He turned to find us all glaring at him accusingly.

"What's the matter with you?" he asked, bewildered. "Why aren't you trying on your clothes? Aren't those the finest clothes you've ever seen?"

"What's that woman to you?" Olga snapped.

"What woman?"

"That Mrs. Sigalos," shot Kanta.

"The wife of a friend!" he said. "Why are you all looking at me like that?"

"Why did she take you away to whisper to you?" charged Olga.

"And why did she pat your hand?" added Kanta. "We saw that."

Father slumped in his chair. "If you think there's something between Mrs. Sigalos and me, forget it," he sighed. "How could I think about another woman after your mother? Now that she's gone, I'll never marry again, so you don't have to worry."

"So why was that woman patting your hand?" Kanta persisted.

He shrugged and decided to tell the truth. "She took me aside to ask me if I could pay for all those things I bought you. She offered to lend me money. I thanked her and told her I didn't need a loan. That's when she patted my hand."

"But why on earth would she offer you money?" Kanta asked him in astonishment. We all stared. Anyone could see our father was a rich man by his fine clothes and his easy authority with the salespeople.

"Well, she heard I was out of a job," he said, somewhat defensively.

"Out of a job!" we all echoed.

"But you told us you were a chef in a big restaurant!" piped up Fotini.

"I was," said Father defensively. "At the Alpha Lunch. Right by City Hall. But the Lerner Company bought the store to make it into a dress shop and it had to close, so I'm temporarily between jobs."

"Then how on earth can you buy us all these clothes?" demanded Kanta, like a lawyer.

"Don't you worry, I've got plenty of money," retorted our father. "My credit's good anywhere. And besides, I've got unemployment."

"What's unemployment?" asked Olga, suspicion in her voice.

"Here in America, if you're laid off and it's not your fault, the government gives you some money to tide you over until you get a new job," he explained. "I keep telling you, this is a great country. Not like Greece. But your father can get a job in any restaurant in Worcester, that's how good my name is. I could get a half-dozen job offers before noon, if I wanted to. The important thing, now that you're here, is to get just the right job — close to home, so I can check up on you; plenty of money, so we can live well. Every restaurant owner in the city has begged me to come cook for him, but I need to look over my options carefully, make the right choice."

"Is this why you didn't buy furniture for the living room?" Kanta demanded. "Because you ran out of money?"

"Of course not!" exclaimed Father, beginning to get angry. "I just thought maybe you'd like to help pick out the furniture and carpets. I could have bought everything on credit, like I did the clothes at Sherer's today. Every big store in Worcester knows I have excellent credit."

"How much do you owe now?" insisted Kanta. "What are your debts?"

"What are you, my banker?" he growled. "For your information, if you add up everything, including the cost of your passage, all the immigration papers, what I bought for this house, the clothes, some odds and ends, it comes to . . . say, in the neighborhood of three thousand dollars."

There was a heavy silence as we all considered this sum, trying to convert it to drachmas — an operation that involved such astronomical figures we couldn't possibly manage without a pencil and paper. Finally I walked over and touched my father's sleeve.

"Does this mean you're not rich?" I asked.

"Rich! What's rich?" he exploded. "I've got my children here and that makes me rich. What more do I need?"

He put one arm around me. "I'm a rich man because I've got my good name and my reputation. Ask any man in Worcester who's the number one chef around here, they'll tell you Christy Gage. That's what all the Americans call me, 'Christy Gage.' Tell you what, my son, tomorrow you go around with me, we drop in at the different restaurants, you help me decide where to work. You'll see that when a man has a good name and skilled hands, he doesn't need to be rich."

That night, as I lay in bed watching him surreptitiously from under my eyelashes, he seemed to pause longer than necessary before the icons on the family altar. I studied his face, trying to decipher whether he was really as confident of finding a job as he said. My mother had always promised that if we ever got to America, our father would give us a fine life, and I still hoped she was right, but I was shaken by the day's revelations. In my first decade of life, every time things seemed about to get better, they got abruptly worse, a pattern that climaxed with the arrest of my mother on the eve of our escape and then the news of her murder. I had convinced myself that in America this pattern would be broken. Now I reassured myself that my father would find a job as easily as he said and would be so good to us that it would make up for his failure to rescue us sooner. I watched him secretly, trying to find clues to his feelings in the ritual he followed as he prepared for bed.

He crossed himself, then walked over to the wall and studied a sepia photograph of us all taken in the village, gathered around our mother; the girls blond, barefoot urchins, my mother thin and serious under her black kerchief. For his entire life my father had been the prosperous and esteemed absent patriarch of a family that lived across the sea. Now those shadow children had become large and very present responsibilities. I knew from my mother's stories that when Christos Gatzoyiannis had first set foot on American soil, a rosy-cheeked teenager, his only goals had been to send money back to support his mother and brothers and to acquire for himself a fine American wardrobe. Something about the way he studied the old photograph made me realize what a blow it was to him to become suddenly the sole parent and provider of four big children.

3

Top: Christos (left) and two brothers, George and Andreas. The picture was taken in 1915, when Christos still had his hair.
Bottom: Wedding portrait of Christos Gatzoyiannis and Eleni Haidis, 1926

PASSAGE TO KASTRIGARI

As for life, it is a battle and a sojourning in a strange country.
— Marcus Aurelius, *Meditations*

CHRISTOS GATZOYIANNIS was one of thirteen children born before the turn of the century to a tinker in the tiny mountain village of Lia in a northwestern Greek province that was still under Turkish occupation. He believed his birth year was 1893, but in those days Greek mothers postponed registering the birth of sons so they would have extra time to grow before being conscripted into the Turkish army; therefore Christos may have been born as early as 1891.

None of the four girls of Fotini and Nikolaos Gatzoyiannis reached adulthood. The one who lived longest, Vasiliki, died of the evil eye at the age of seventeen, according to my father, when a passing priest remarked on her beauty. Priests were well known for being unwitting carriers of the evil eye, and when Vasiliki returned home that day feeling dizzy and told about the priest and his compliment, her relatives quickly retrieved dirt from his footprints, boiled it, and made her drink it, but she died all the same.

Father was closest to the brother born just before him, Constantinos, a deaf-mute who could communicate only in writing. According to my father, the boy lost his hearing and speech from taking a nap under the walnut tree in the yard.

Christos' mother, Fotini, suffered a shattering series of tragedies when he was about seven. Her husband, Nikolaos, died of pneumonia, leaving her pregnant, with enough gold to feed the children for only a year. When that last child, Marina, was born, she lived only three days. On the fortieth day after the father's death, as the family prepared the spiced boiled wheat, *kolyva*, to give to the church congregation in his memory, little Christos volunteered to climb the walnut tree to pick off the few remaining nuts. He fell, cracking his head open, and many years later, when he returned to the village for the first time from America, a man of thirty-one, he had to show that scar to his mother to convince her he really was her son.

When her dead husband's gold sovereigns ran out, Christos' mother was forced to take the eight-year-old boy out of school and apprentice him to a cooper in the distant village of Paramythia who would pay him twenty Turkish *grossia* a month: about $1. But the child wasn't strong enough to bend the metal rings for the barrels, and his master beat him. Finally Christos escaped back to his village. His mother then apprenticed him to a relative in Athens, an itinerant tinker who traveled throughout free Greece, especially to Syros, in the Cyclades islands, which Father remembered as a paradise for its warm climate, friendly people, lush fruit, and freedom from Turkish rule.

When Christos returned home for the first time in twenty months, now nearly ten years old, he discovered that his brother Constantinos had died, and he was inconsolable. On his next journey with the tinker, they traveled to the port of Patras, and the boy entered a dry goods store where he spied a fine gentleman wearing clothing such as he had never seen before — a foreign-cut suit and an elegant overcoat of the thickest, softest wool. As soon as the man left, Christos quizzed the shop owner, who told him this paragon had returned to Patras all the way from Chicago in America. "Where's America?" asked the boy, and was told that you had to sail through immense seas westward for twenty-five days to get there. "I was paying attention," Christos told his grandchildren some seventy-five years later. "He was so nice, well dressed up, I put everything in my mind for America. I was thinking, there's no future for me in Greece or Turkey."

Nevertheless, the boy followed his master all over Greece, to Cyprus, Crete, Thessaly, and as far as Constantinople, traveling from village to village, selling and repairing copper pots, breathing the fumes of the lye that they used to clean off the black soot, sleeping at night by the fires they built to melt the solder. And all the time the idea of America was growing in his mind. It was the fine foreign clothes that had seduced him.

The tinker paid him four times what the cooper had given him, and Christos returned to his village every year or so to give his mother his wages to help feed the family. In 1906, when he was thirteen, he headed back toward the mountains of Thesprotia after an absence of eighteen months. In a store in the last village before ascending the mountain he heard two women saying that Yianni, the eldest son of Fotini Gatzoyiannis, was very ill.

Without a word Christos checked out of his inn and began the two-day walk up the mountain. He found his eldest married brother, then in his thirties, close to death. Realizing that the family was likely to lose another wage-earner and there wouldn't be enough money to feed the rest, Christos said to his mother, "Sit down, *Mana*, I'm going to deliver you a message." He told her he was going to write to a relative in America, Constantinos Zikos, who lived in Worcester, Massachusetts, and ask him to send enough money to pay ship's passage for Christos and his youngest brother, Andreas, then about twelve. Christos recounted the story to his grandchildren: "When she hear that, my mother start to scream, crying, starts to talk stories. I said, 'I don't care, *Mana*, I'm going to do it. Either I go to America or I'm gonna be dead. Better cry life.' That made her worse, she didn't expect such high men's words from me, so she was crying three, four days. My brother who was sick, he didn't say a word."

Christos composed the letter to the relative and finally received a reply saying that Zikos would pay the fare for him but not for his brother, because the man couldn't recognize Andreas, and to bring him over he had to be able to pick him out of a crowd. Next he sent Christos' ticket, which cost $28.60. It had been booked on a Greek ship, *Themistocles,* by a Greek travel agent in Worcester.

In March 1910, Christos Gatzoyiannis, then seventeen years old, packed a suitcase with an extra suit that he had bought in Athens. "I was a model guy, a fussy kid," he recalled. "I was going to come to States and I don't want to embarrass my country." He traveled by muleback to the sea and eventually reached Patras, where he boarded the *Themistocles* for New York on March 24, with twenty British sovereigns sewn into a special pocket of his coat.

Of the nearly half-million European immigrants who thronged to the United States between 1820 and 1840, almost none were Greeks. Not until 1890 did the deluge of Greeks begin to arrive at Ellis Island, driven by the poverty and the disastrous Balkan wars back home and the glowing reports of wealth that the few Greek immigrants working in the mills of America were sending.

The first Greeks in Worcester were three brothers named Pappakostas who arrived in 1872 and opened a soda fountain, and a man named Constantinos Voultsos who came the same year and peddled fruit from his pushcart in downtown Worcester. Voultsos rose to own a tobacco importing company, and in 1910 he brought his wife to America, an unusual move because almost all the Greek immigrants in the first decades of the century were, like my father, *bekiarides*, bachelors, between the ages of seventeen and twenty-two. The records of exactly how many Greeks came to Worcester are vague, for the American government classified many of them as Turks or Albanians, because large areas of Greece were under foreign occupation. My father carried a Turkish passport for that reason.

The Greeks arriving at Ellis Island passed through an immigration depot called Castle Garden, which they pronounced "Kastrigari." To most of the early Worcester immigrants, the days in limbo at Kastrigari were like purgatory before the gates opened, allowing them to emerge into the glory of America. "I spent three terrible days at Kastrigari," one of Father's cronies told me. "We were all seasick and exhausted from the trip, and I spent most of the time staring at the city and the Statue of Liberty, until finally they pinned a ticket on me and I was on my way."

All the early immigrants remember the time they spent waiting to be processed and examined as a period of terrible fear, suspense, discomfort, and often disappointment, for many were rejected and sent back because they were ill or no one arrived to claim them. The ethnic memory of being processed through the maze at Castle Garden was so universally traumatic that the expression "We passed through Kastrigari" became a Greek-American proverb denoting a shared experience that is both joyful and agonizing.

My father, however, characteristically remembered his arrival on Ellis Island on April 18, 1910, as a triumph. Like me, he had spent the long voyage studying a Greek-English dictionary. "I was very smart," he told his grandchildren. "On the way over, I wasn't playing, I was reading every day from the dictionary. When we got out to Ellis Island, they took me as a greenhorn who couldn't speak the language. The judge from above started asking, 'How old is he?' and over here was the Greek man with the whiskers, interpreter. I said, 'Seventeen.'

" 'You speak English?' the judge ask me.

" 'I can answer the necessity words.'

" 'Where you go?'

" 'I'm going to Worcester.'

" 'Do you have any relative?'

" 'Yes, cousin, Constantinos Zikos.'

"He check . . . he had the papers right front of him. He says, 'Let him go, I wish everybody was like him. Very smart kid. He's going to be real American.' He got proud because I knew the English."

Despite my father's favorable impression on the official, some bureaucrat on Ellis Island mangled his name, Christos N. Gatzoyiannis, and stuck his middle initial onto the surname, so he emerged onto the streets of New York with a ticket to Worcester pinned on his coat and the legal name of Christos Ngagoyeanes.

Like most immigrants coming off Ellis Island, Christos was expected to find his way from the dock via the Third Avenue elevated train to Grand Central Station, where, after reading the sign on his chest, someone would put him on the right train for Worcester. Many immigrants went through this procedure, and many, ignorant of the language, got off at the wrong city and stayed there.

According to my father's account, as soon as he set foot on American soil he caused a sensation. There was an elegant woman in a long, sweeping skirt and flowered hat walking on Third Avenue with her husband and her little dog. She was so overwhelmed by the rosy cheeks, fair hair, and handsome features of the teenager with the ticket pinned to his chest that, as my father told it, "She grab my cheek — I was very red cheeks — and she kiss me, saying, 'Oh, nice-looking kid.' I understand the words. Oh, I blush right away, all red, boy, and I say, 'I'm going to have bad luck in this country with the womens chasing me.'"

Passed along from one conductor to the next, the red-cheeked boy arrived in Worcester's Union Station, where he was met by several countrymen, who took him to the unsavory Portland Street location where he would live with half a dozen fellow bachelors in a tenement flat. Without stopping to unpack, he made them take him to downtown Worcester to buy an American suit and necktie. "Boy, I was nice-looking then," he recalled with satisfaction. "Looked like real American kid."

The Worcester streets that greeted my father in 1910 were bustling with horse-drawn trolleys rattling over cobblestones and electric wires draped on wooden poles. The largest immigrant group among the 100,000 citizens of the city were the Irish, followed by the Swedes, Poles, and Lithuanians. To the approximately 325 Greek immigrants living in Worcester at the time, telephones and electricity were a novelty. They assimilated quickly into the crowded life of the tenements, eager to reap the gold of America, to send it home and bring over more male relatives to share the workload.

Worcester, built on seven hills like Rome, was bought from the Nipmuck Indians in 1674 for twelve pounds, two coats, and four yards of cloth. It burst into full bloom with the Industrial Revolution, inspired in part by the invention of the cotton gin by Worcester County resident Eli Whitney. The first corduroy, the first power loom, the first envelope-making machine, the first liquid fuel rocket — Worcester's achievements multiplied. The nation's supply of grinding wheels, dining cars, and barbed wire for settling the western frontier came from its factories.

The first train arrived in Worcester from Boston in 1835, and on it, no doubt, were the first of the immigrants who would provide the manpower for the city's looms and tanneries, mills and factories. Worcester became one of the nation's foremost industrial cities, with factories springing up, scattering working-class neighborhoods of wooden flats in all directions.

In the decades from 1880 to 1910, as the population exploded from 60,000 to 155,000, an army of immigrants arrived, moving through the white marble palace of Union Station and onto Worcester's streets, seeking hourly wages in the factories that belched gray smoke into the skies. Ranks of three-decker tenements — which would become Worcester's most characteristic form of architecture — marched up and down its hills, trampling the elegant neoclassical Revolutionary War homes in their path. These three-deckers, more than six thousand square, solid wooden structures, offered little aesthetic appeal, but they were eminently practical for housing the families of the factory workers, one family to each floor.

Each floor usually included two porches or balconies, front and back, called piazzas by Worcester natives. The back piazza, which offered a tranquil view of the tiny square of yard below, often had a revolving spider-web contraption for drying laundry. The front piazza (or, on the first floor, the front stoop) provided a cool spot to watch the traffic of the street and to keep an eye on the pranks and amorous adventures of the neighborhood's youth.

Worcester was a city of smoke and grime, twelve-hour workdays in sunless factories, yet it was a city full of life, and for the immigrant and his family there were compensations. Each neighborhood was a community centered on a church or synagogue. For a few pennies the trolley line was ready to transport citizens on their days off to the shores of Lake Quinsigamond, to savor nature's beauties from paddlewheels and rented canoes or to explore the worldlier attractions of the White City Amusement Park.

The average wage at the time my father arrived in Worcester was about $5 a week for seven days' work. Most of the Greeks began as fruit peddlers, factory workers, dishwashers, gravediggers, or shoeshine boys. The bachelors in the crowded flats would take turns preparing meals, and every Saturday evening they would wash their soiled laundry in the community washtub. They had no church until a small congregation began to meet in a rented room in 1915. The first Greek weddings, baptisms, and funerals were performed in Arabic in the Syrian Orthodox Church or by traveling Greek priests who occasionally visited the community.

On Sundays, the lucky ones who had a day off would celebrate by socializing at the Greek coffeehouses, attending the cinema or the vaudeville shows for a nickel, strolling through one of Worcester's two public parks, or boarding a trolley car to travel to a country spot they called

Krioneri ("cold water"), where they could picnic. They would also call on compatriots who were celebrating their name day, the feast day of the saint for whom they were named, which Greeks celebrate instead of birthdays. Some of the bachelors preferred to spend their Sundays at home in their crowded flats, playing Greek records on a gramophone, drinking, and dancing in shared masculine misery to songs lamenting the torment of *xenitia*, exile in a foreign land.

Within three days of his arrival in Worcester, my father, ablaze with the ambition to earn money, found a job in a factory making strainers. He was paid two and a half cents per thousand strainers, which brought him $6 to $7 a week. He took a second job at night, working from seven P.M. to one A.M., setting up pins in a bowling alley. This earned another $4.10 for six days, making a grand total of over $10 a week — about ten times his earnings as a traveling tinker in Greece. He had only five hours out of twenty-four when he wasn't on the job.

Within nine months the teenager had saved up enough money to buy a spa for $300, on Grafton Street in Worcester. ("Spa" is local terminology for an establishment that is a combination candy shop, soda fountain, and convenience store.) In 1912, Christos, who was not yet twenty years old, sent for two of his brothers to help him run his growing empire: George, about fifteen years his senior, a married man with a handlebar mustache, and Andreas, eighteen, who was too handsome for his own good. Christos bought a pushcart, from which George sold fruit in the summer while Christos ran the spa with Andreas' help. In winter, George put his pushcart in storage and took over the operation of the spa while Christos worked a press at Worcester Pressed Steel Corporation, and later Harrington and Richardson Arms Company. These factory jobs brought in much more money than the spa, because, as Christos remembered it, he was such an extraordinarily prolific worker.

A portrait was taken of the three well-dressed brothers seated in a Worcester photographer's studio in front of a painted sylvan background: George in the middle, tall, dark, and thin, with his waxed handlebar mustache; Andreas on the right, boyish and dark; my father, blond and earnest, on the left; all wearing three-piece suits, high celluloid collars, gold tie pins, and watch fobs. My father holds a pair of leather gloves in one hand. It is the only picture of him with a full head of hair; by the time the next picture was taken, when he was thirty-one, he was nearly bald and had acquired his trademark bow tie and the belly, extra chin, and dignified mien of a well-fed businessman.

Christos quickly realized that it had been a mistake to bring over Andreas, who was unable to save money in a seductive and permissive society like America, but spent it all on women and gambling. In 1914 my father sent Andreas back to Greece and wrote off his round-trip fare as a total loss. That was the year Christos sold the spa and bought a horse and wagon to deliver fruits and vegetables to private homes. In 1917, when America was about to enter the war, he sent George back to Greece too, to see the daughter that had been born to him after he sailed for America.

Neither of Christos' brothers returned to America. The torrent of immigrants from Greece slowed to a trickle by the second decade of the century. Between 1900 and 1915, nearly one out of every four males in Greece between the ages of fifteen and forty-five — some 400,000 men — said goodbye to his family and set sail for the U.S.A. Greeks generally became railroad workers and miners in the West, factory workers in New York, Chicago, and the New England mill towns, and busboys, dishwashers, bootblacks, and peddlers in the big cities. They were often recruited for American employers by exploitive Greek *padrones* and used to break strikes or to underbid the wages of earlier immigrant groups like the Irish. Greeks would work for almost nothing. An observer in the early years of this century wrote, "They are . . . ready to blacken our boots for ten cents, and they do it remarkably well, displacing negroes and Italians, until later they open stores and sell American candies to an undiscriminating public, hungry for cheap sweets."

The Greeks' eagerness to work for poor wages and their quick success created a ground swell of prejudice against them. During the era before and after World War I, Greeks were characterized in American newspapers as "the scum of Europe," "a vicious element unfit for citizenship," and "ignorant, depraved and brutal foreigners." In the West, Greeks were a special target of the Ku Klux Klan.

Regulations began to restrict their wholesale immigration, beginning as early as 1917. In 1921 Congress passed the first immigration legislation based on national quotas, and in 1924 the Reed-Johnson Act limited the number of entering immigrants by using a formula based on nationality distribution in the U.S. census of 1890. The Greek quota was set at only 100 per year (compared to the 28,000 Greeks who came in 1921). In 1929 this figure was raised to 307, where it remained for most of the next three decades. The only loophole by which Greeks might get in was to be members of the immediate family of an American citizen.

This legislation sent the Greeks already in America scurrying to acquire citizenship so that they could bring in their relatives. Until the 1920s, Greeks had been the least interested of all national groups in acquiring citizenship, because, like my father, they typically considered themselves only temporary sojourners in America. But with the tightening of immigration laws, they quickly changed their minds. My father was one of those who hurried to qualify for citizenship. He was naturalized in 1924, fourteen years after landing on American soil.

He always spoke in glowing terms about his early years in America, but occasionally he would recount incidents revealing that he hadn't escaped the growing hostility against Greeks. Once he was passing under a bridge in his horse-drawn fruit wagon when a group of boys above him dropped an old umbrella loaded with stones. Its tip missed his head by inches and hit the cart with such force that it went through the floorboards. "I was lucky that day," he always concluded.

Christos gave up his horse and wagon when the United States entered World War I in 1917 on the side of the Allies. He was declared unfit for the draft because of a back injury he had suffered while lifting heavy fruit crates, and he decided to interrupt his career as a fruit peddler, knowing that better money could be made working the presses in Worcester's munitions factories.

"The foreman said, 'This kid's a smart kid, very, very expert on machines,'" he recalled. "I was! Two Armenians used to put out seven, eight crankshafts a day, two of them, two machines. I took one machine, got twelve to fourteen a day. Didn't fool around. How much wages you think I get? Ninety, ninety-five dollars a week! I send money to my brother. He build up a new home in the village. I pay my mother's debts, send her money every month."

When the war was over, Christos used his new wealth to buy a truck, the famous REO Speedwagon, to sell produce in all the silk-stocking areas of Massachusetts — Holden, Shrewsbury, Sutton, as far as Woonsocket, Rhode Island. For twenty-four years he was the king of the fruit peddlers, commanding the highest prices and the finest trade.

As his business expanded, he took on a partner, Christos Stathis, a laconic man from the neighboring village of Babouri who later persuaded my father to add his brother-in-law, Nassio Economou, to the partnership. "I was working as a waiter in New London, making good money, but Stathis wanted me close to him because he was afraid I might drift off into the depths of America and abandon his sister," Nassio recalled forty years later. "We all lived together at 1 Ledge Street. Every morning Christy and Christy got up at five, went and bought the fruit, and picked me up at seven. We had some adventures. Once a woman owed us for some carrots, couldn't have been more than ten cents, so they sent me to collect. I didn't come back with the money, but I came back smiling." At this time, as Father often told us, he also could have had his pick of women; the cooks and the maids and even the aristocratic ladies themselves flirted with him. "Ladies so fine, skin so pale, that when they drink milk you can see it go down their throat," he used to say, before launching into yet another story of some woman who had set her cap for him. "But in all my life I only look at one woman — your mother," he always concluded.

It was in 1924 that Christos returned to his native Greek village for the first time in fourteen years and had to convince his mother of his identity by showing her the scar from the fall out of the walnut tree. Her fair-haired young boy had become bald and fat, or, as Christos put it, "She didn't recognize me because I build up myself here in America — eat good, sleep good, shower every Saturday."

It was on that first journey back to Greece, carrying forty pounds of salted codfish up the mountain as a gift for his mother, that Christos saw his village free of the Turkish flag for the first time. "It make me proud!" And it was on that trip that he chose a wife.

A young niece told him in confidence that she was best friends with a girl named Eleni Haidis, the second daughter of Lia's most prosperous miller, and that Eleni would make him a fine bride. She described Eleni to him as clever but modest and so beautiful that as she walked down to her father's mill, the villagers looking at her whispered, "God give me two more eyes."

Christos took the path to church that passed by the miller's property, and there he saw Eleni working in the garden. "Nice-looking girl," he recalled. "Something went off my body and went over to her body and I begin to like her. I was old enough. I was thirty-one."

Eleni Haidis was fourteen years younger than the foreign businessman in the elegant American suit. He was not particularly handsome when he came to call on her father, accompanied by his brother Foto, but he had a kind face, soft white hands, and fine manners. No doubt she concluded that he would treat her more kindly than her fiery, tyrannical, and parsimonious father.

No one asked Eleni her opinion of the suitor from across the seas, nor did the pair exchange a word, but she was not unhappy when her father directed her to bring the customary coffee and the stranger put an American $20 bill on the tray, clinching the engagement. Afterward the agreement was sealed with food, wine, and a fusillade of bullets fired at the heavens to notify the neighbors.

From that point on, Eleni was allowed to converse with her fiancé on the occasions when she walked with her parents to church. Christos strutted at her side in his straw boater, his starched white shirtfront radiant in the sun. He told her that when he returned to Lia in a year or two, he would pay for the finest wedding the village had ever seen. He would bring cloth from America and hire the best dressmaker in the region to make the wedding costumes.

True to his word, Christos returned in November of 1926, and on the last permissible day before the pre-Christmas fast, November 29, their wedding crowns were exchanged in the Church of St. Demetrios. Eleni was wearing her scarlet wedding kerchief and her gold-embroidered, blue velvet wedding jacket.

Eleni had told her groom in a tearful conversation before the wedding that she would not be able to go to America with him, because her mother, whom she always tried to protect from her father's violent temper, insisted she would kill herself on the day Eleni left the village. Christos was disappointed but not surprised. Few of his friends in America had brought over their wives; it was customary to leave wife, children, and property in Greece and to visit them now and then on long trips home, while living as one of the bachelors in America.

Christos installed his bride in his mother's two-room house and added on two more rooms, making it the largest dwelling in Lia. Before he left for America, the couple's first child was born, in January 1928. At the last moment, Eleni sent the midwife out of the room and called her husband in to catch the baby, because she was afraid the village women had dirty hands.

Eleni wept in shame at producing a girl instead of a son for her husband. They named her Olga. When Eleni produced three more girls on Christos' subsequent trips to Greece in 1932 and in 1937, the villagers began to whisper that the wealthy *Amerikana*, despite her fine home and possessions, was cursed. But Christos always reassured her that he was just as glad to have daughters as sons.

His long trips to Greece, when he reigned over the village *cafenion* like a lord, were always a pleasant interlude for Christos. His reliable partner in the fruit business, Christos Stathis, would send him $60 a month from the profits, allowing him to linger in luxury.

It was during the last trip to Greece, in 1937, that Christos left the truck with his irresponsible partner, Nassio Economou. But he was forced to put the business in Nassio's hands, because he had received a letter from his sister-in-law warning that Eleni was desperately ill. The sister-in-law, Nitsa, dictated the letter secretly to nine-year-old Olga because she was illiterate. "Come at once, you can always find America again," she dictated. "But if you lose your wife, you're not going to find her again. And what are you going to do with your daughters?"

Christos knew no one in the village would want his daughters if his wife should die. He left the REO Speedwagon in Nassio's control and set out for Greece. In June he arrived on the mountaintop, where the village women were trying to save Eleni by drawing evil spirits out of her with leeches and *vendeuses*: candles burning inside overturned cups on her chest.

Christos' youngest daughters, Kanta and Glykeria, didn't recognize their father. He took his ailing wife by mule and by ferryboat to the island of Corfu, where European-trained doctors saved her. By the time she had finished convalescing, she was pregnant with a fourth daughter, Fotini.

It was then that Nassio turned up in the village, dressed like a gangster, saying he had sold the produce business Christos had invested twenty-four years in for the sum of $1200 in order to buy the Terminal Lunch from a ruined card player. After Father lunged at Nassio, tried to kill him, and failed, he slowly forgave his partner, because it was so pleasant to have a crony from America to sit in the coffeehouse with him, telling tales of the golden land and buying drinks for the assembled peasants.

Nassio convinced Christos to extend his visit for another six months. "Matter of fact, I owe him plenty," recalled Father, "because he hold me back. Six months longer, then I got my son, miracle son. So I owe that to him; that's why I forgive him although he done a lot of dirty things to me."

When their money from the sale of the truck was nearly gone, Christos urged Nassio to leave for America. Nassio, always the big sport, convinced him to wire Christos Stathis to send them money to sail back in style from Paris on the *Queen Mary*. Christos protested that it was silly to travel all across Europe, but Nassio insisted, and Father quickly learned to adjust to a life of luxury.

When Christos told Eleni goodbye on November 8, 1938, neither of them knew she was pregnant again, this time with a son. Nor did they suspect that the impending war in Europe would prevent them from ever seeing each other again. Their life together was over. It had added up to fifty-four months, the total amount of time my father had spent in the village during his four visits since their marriage.

Christos and Nassio picked up the money order from Christos Stathis at the American Express office in Paris and sailed for America. Nassio entertained Father with his antics on board, addressing him as "Dr. Gage" and convincing the crew that Father was an important American doctor who deserved one of the best tables in the dining room, a story that was given credence by Father's fine wardrobe. In contrast to his first twenty-five-day journey on the *Themistocles*, packed in with other immigrants, sharing one toilet and washbasin, Christos traveled across the ocean in five days in his stateroom on the *Queen Mary*.

On the way, he began to worry about what he would do to support his growing family now that Nassio had sold the business out from under him and they had squandered most of the proceeds showing off in the village. Nassio had said that once he got the Terminal Lunch on its feet, he and Christos Stathis would take my father in as a partner, but that was in the future, and Father had to find a job right now.

As usual, Nassio worked out a plan. Spoiled by the glamorous, carefree, café society life on the *Queen Mary*, Nassio didn't relish returning to Worcester to cook in a diner beside his staid brother-in-law.

"Here's what we'll do, Dr. Gage," Nassio told Father. "I've got some presents for Nick Karabinas, friend of mine who owns a restaurant in Philadelphia; he'll put you up, you don't pay nothing. Nick's looking to open another restaurant — he'll teach you to cook, nobody's a better cook than Nick, then, when you know the business, you call me, I bring the money I've made from Terminal Lunch, I come to Philadelphia, we live together, open a restaurant there, have good times like now, lots of money, women, nobody to boss us around. I'll call Nick from the dock, set it all up. What d'ya say?"

As usual, Father was won over by Nassio's persuasive reasoning and did just as he suggested. After living in Philadelphia for several months, learning to be a chef from Nick Karabinas, Father called Nassio in Worcester and said everything was ready; Nassio should come to Philadelphia with his money and they would open their own restaurant. By then, however, Nassio had renewed his acquaintance with some young women in Worcester and wasn't so eager to leave.

Shortly after the phone call to Nassio, Father received a return call from Christos Stathis. "What's this nonsense Nassio's telling me?" thundered Stathis. "You taking his ideas, believing his pipe dreams? Remember, you're a family man, got responsibilities. Don't fool around. You associate with Nassio, you lose your reputation. You two crazy fools, you'll never succeed at anything without me to keep an eye on you. You come back here, work at Terminal Lunch for me if you want to keep your good name. Don't listen to Nassio."

As soon as he got this call, Father realized all the flaws in Nassio's plan and meekly returned to Worcester, where he made a paltry $50 a week cooking at the Terminal Lunch. When it eventually became clear that neither Nassio nor Stathis had any real intention of making him a partner, Father quit in a huff and traveled to Staten Island in New York, where a former Greek priest from Worcester had a son-in-law who owned a diner on Richmond Avenue.

The man hired Father at once: it was wartime and business was booming. For the duration Father made as much as $90 a week frying hamburgers and hot dogs in that Staten Island diner. It was good money, but as Father always said, "You don't get rich working for someone else." He had been his own boss for twenty-four years, and because his customers were wealthy, he did well even during the Depression, when other Greek immigrants in Worcester were giving up on America and going home by the hundreds. But throughout the booming war years, when everyone he knew with a business of his own was piling up profits, Christos remained someone else's employee. He blamed his fate on his two former partners, Nassio Economou and Christos Stathis. "When I was making big money with my truck and they had nothing, I made them partners. But when my luck changed and they had their restaurant, they shut me out," he often complained.

After V-E Day, Christos began to think of his family again. He was aware of the famine in Greece; so many were dying of starvation that the survivors couldn't bury them, and bodies lay piled in the streets of Athens. He had read of the atrocities committed on civilians by both foreign invaders and warring factions of Greeks. He had had no word from his own family, because the mail couldn't get out of northern Greece, but he prayed that Eleni had managed to keep their children alive throughout the war and the invasions of his village by the Italians and Germans. For the first time Christos began to consider bringing his family to America, once his wife found a proper husband for the oldest daughter.

New York was no place to raise daughters, Christos decided, even if he was making good money at the Staten Island diner. Worcester was a slower, more conservative city, where women could walk on the street without fear of being accosted. So in 1946 Father returned to Worcester, hired a room in a Front Street hotel for $8 a week, and went to work at the Alpha Lunch, a diner on Main Street owned by one of his old card-playing buddies.

It was in the solitary room on Front Street that Christos received a letter from a cousin in Athens that enclosed a tiny news clipping reporting that his wife had been executed by the Communist guerrillas. His children, the cousin wrote, had escaped and were in a refugee camp in Igoumenitsa. He would have to send money and arrange to bring them to America.

"I saw that letter, I was crazy," Christos recalled. "I had six bottles beer in closet. If I didn't have those bottles, I was going to go out, kill two Communists in Worcester. I drank that beer just like plain water. I got dizzy and went to bed. Kill my wife? For what? I know there was inside feelings from my own village people, jealous. I come back to conscious when they call me up from the restaurant to go to work. I said no, I ain't going to work for a week. I'm mourning my wife. So I did, I write letters here and there. Why they kill my wife? No answers, no details."

Christos mailed off all the money he could borrow: to his father-in-law in the refugee village to support the children, to Washington, D.C., to cover the papers and fares for their immigration. The children all had American citizenship, so the papers eventually came through, but in Greece most letters and money couldn't reach beyond the blockades that divided the country. The money that did get through was mostly pocketed by Father's brother Foto and by our grandfather, who doled it out a penny at a time.

While Father was waiting to hear whether we had received our papers, he learned that his employer at the Alpha Lunch had sold the restaurant, which would be torn down, and he found himself on unemployment just when he most needed a job. But Christos was a congenital optimist, and he told himself that everything would work out in the end, once his children arrived. After all, this was America, where he had made a fortune once, and he could do it again; anything was possible. "God bless America, God bless this soil," he said to his grandchildren in 1974, while recounting the story of his life. It was a sentiment he repeated every day, like a mantra. When he was in his eighties, Father bought a family plot in Hope Cemetery and erected a stone for himself on it, completely engraved except for the date of death. "This soil has been good to me," he told his grandchildren. "I left, seventeen years old, come to America, and I'm satisfied. I hope this soil take me when I die. I got my home ready."

But even Father's irrepressible optimism must have wavered on that day in March 1949 when his newly arrived children discovered that he was not the tycoon they believed but an out-of-work, fifty-six-year-old short-order cook. Since cunning — a trait on which every Greek prides himself — was not Christos' strong suit, he must have felt grave qualms as he studied the photograph of his family and wondered how he would ever support this houseful of children.

Christos and his new family on the porch of the three-decker on Greendale Avenue

ON FOREIGN GROUND

How shall we find our livelihood roaming in some far land?

— Sophocles,
Oedipus at Colonus

AT THE TIME that Worcester became my adopted city, in the spring of 1949, its prosperity had just peaked and a quarter-century of decline had begun as the postwar economy wound down and mills were moved to Southern states where cheaper non-union labor could be found. But Worcester's economic future was the furthest thing from my mind as I woke up on my second morning in America, donned my new long trousers, and prepared to accompany my father on his odyssey of restaurants requiring a fine chef.

He was dressed as smartly as always, from his fine fedora and his custom-tailored tan suit, cut to disguise his ample girth, to his polished shoes. He always walked with his chin held high, stepping lightly despite his weight as if leading a parade. When I headed for the parked DeSoto, he called me back. "We're going to walk today," he said. "I want you to learn the neighborhood, and all the restaurants are close by on West Boylston Street anyway."

I felt proud to be seen beside this imposing figure in my new clothes, and I tried to imitate his strut. He spoke to me in a confidential tone, man to man. "Of course, none of the local restaurants here in Greendale can pay me as much as I'm worth downtown by City Hall," he said. "I was making seventy-five dollars a week at the Alpha Lunch. But working on West Boylston would save my bus fare — that comes to sixty cents a day, or three dollars a week. And I'll be close enough so I could run right home in case you needed me in an emergency." Clearly he had been mulling over these points and was trying to convince himself of the wisdom of his decision.

As we marched down Greendale and then turned left and walked along West Boylston, across the street from the Norton factory complex and the train tracks, Father pointed out local landmarks. At the corner of Greendale and West Boylston, less than a block from our door, was Hamel's grocery store, where, he said, we children could go and charge things to his account, because he had already prepared the Scandinavian owner for our arrival. Further on West Boylston was the small classical façade of the Greendale Public Library, where, he claimed, I could take out books to read without paying anything. He pointed out the drugstore and the barbershop and the five-and-ten-cent store, but nothing intrigued me as much as Louis Ching's laundry, because I had never seen an Oriental person before. I stared at the owner through the plate glass window until Father dragged me away.

He told me that the whole area we would cover that day had the same name as the street on which we lived — Greendale. The Norton Company had begun as a pottery firm, he said, until two Swedish potters conceived the idea of mixing emery into clay to produce tough grinding wheels that would not explode like shrapnel in the faces of laborers trying to smooth the iron machine parts in Worcester's many ironworks. Soon the grinding wheels eclipsed the pottery business.

The Norton Company prospered to the point where it became the backbone of Worcester's economy. And when Norton expanded, so did the Scandinavian population of the neighborhood. "Most Norton workers can walk to work in minutes," my father continued. "All they have to do is cross West Boylston Street."

Although the Scandinavians dominated the neighborhood, he said, some Armenians had settled in the area as cobblers and tailors, and a few Greeks, mostly from our own province of Epiros, had brought their skills as confectioners and restaurateurs. These Greeks, being *patriotes*, knew him and respected his culinary skills, he added.

Our first destination, he informed me, was the Greendale Lunch, which proved to be a dark, smoky tavern just across the street from one of the gates to the Norton factory complex.

We pushed open the door and saw the owner, Yianni Keratsis, stocking shelves beside the bar's mirror, which displayed posters of Miss Rheingold candidates. When he saw my father, he came forward to embrace him. I noticed that like my father Keratsis wore a black tie, indicating that he was recently bereaved.

"So this is your son, eh, Christo?" he exclaimed, pulling out chairs for us at one of the tables. "May he live long for you. How about a little ice cream, boy?"

He went into the back and emerged carrying coffee and doughnuts for my father and a tin dish of vanilla ice cream. "We've both had our sorrows this year," Keratsis remarked to my father. "My brother Kosta's been dead three months now, and every morning when I walk in here I expect to see him behind the bar."

My father nodded. "I woke up hearing a woman's voice in the kitchen this morning," he said, "and for a moment I thought it was my angel Eleni, alive, but then I realized it was my daughter Olga's voice."

They contemplated their losses in silence, then turned to watch me eat the ice cream. I was astonished to discover how much tastier it was than the Greek variety. Americans might not know how to cook, I reflected, but they could surely make good ice cream.

After some gossip with Keratsis about mutual acquaintances, Father eventually got to the point. "As a good family man, Yianni," he began, "I know you appreciate the new responsibilities I have, with my children coming over. I need to work close enough to home to keep an eye on them. I've been offered plenty of jobs downtown, but I'd prefer to work here in the neighborhood . . . for you."

This caught Keratsis by surprise. "You're a damn good cook, Christo," he said. "Any restaurant would be lucky to have you."

Father sat up straighter and caught my eye to make sure I was listening.

"What a shame you didn't come by three months ago," Keratsis continued. "When Kosta died, I panicked and hired two new people to take his place. Now Norton's laying off a lot of workers and my business is down more than thirty percent. Every time Norton sneezes I catch a cold. I've had to put one cook on half-days already. . . . But as soon as Norton starts calling the workers back —"

"Don't give it a thought, Yianni," Father interrupted. "Of course I understand. No problem. As I said, I've got a lot of other offers."

"Look, Christo," said Keratsis. "Go further down, to Pallas' place. You know he draws all the Swedish families from the Heights as customers, the old people, the kids on dates. He's not dependent on Norton's and the after-work drinkers like I am."

"Right, Yianni. Thanks for the suggestion," said my father, sticking out his hand. "And again, condolences for your brother. Hurry up, Nikola, finish your ice cream."

We walked another five minutes along West Boylston and came to an intersection where a side road hit the main road at an angle. At the wide-angled corner was a one-story granite building divided into four parts: a dry goods store, a barbershop, a bakery, and, the largest section, a confectionery, which my father called the Boulevard Spa.

"This whole block of stores belongs to my friend George Pallas," Father informed me. "Smart man! He started selling hamburgers off a pushcart, but he realized this would be a prime intersection and put all his money into buying it. Now he owns the whole thing."

Once inside, I was transfixed by the trays of pastries and gilded boxes of chocolates in the glass cases. A jukebox was stacked with records. There were a number of round tables with curly wrought-iron chairs, and in the back a polished marble counter with a row of revolving stools.

"Yiorgo!" called my father.

"Christo!" exclaimed the small, gray-haired man in an immaculate uniform behind the counter. He spoke a Greek that struck me as over-refined. "What an unexpected pleasure to welcome you to my poor establishment, old friend," he said. "And this must be your boy. A fine-looking lad, but we have to fatten him up a bit. How about trying my specialty, son — milk and chocolate syrup and ice cream all shaken up in a machine. They call it a frappe. I could throw in an egg to give you strength."

"He likes ice cream," said my father.

"Then we'll just add a bit of hot fudge, for good measure," said Pallas, scooping a ball of vanilla ice cream into a fluted sundae dish. Even though I was already satiated from my previous dish of ice cream, when I took my first bite I decided this must be the ambrosia of the Olympian gods.

Next I discovered that the stool I was sitting on spun entirely around. I amused myself whirling until my father reached out and stopped me. "Behave," he snapped. He had been gossiping and now was getting to the part about wanting to find work near his children. The whole time my father talked, Pallas fussily filled the napkin holders, checked the salt and pepper shakers, wiped the counter.

"I need a good cook for my lunch business, Christo," Pallas said finally. "Of course, I can't pay like the restaurants downtown."

"I realize that, Yiorgo," my father replied. "But it's important for me to be near the children."

"Forty-five dollars a week," said Pallas, very busily straightening the edges of a pile of menus. "That's the most I can pay."

"Forty-five!" exclaimed my father. "I was getting seventy-five dollars a week at Alpha Lunch!"

"That was a different kind of place," Pallas replied smoothly. "The people who come in here order a little soup, an open-faced sandwich, maybe a piece of blueberry pie. Then they put a dollar on the counter and expect change. This isn't the kind of neighborhood where people tip a quarter for a shoeshine and think nothing of it."

"Don't tell me you built this building with nickels and dimes," my father said, trying to make a joke.

Pallas didn't smile. "Forty-five dollars is the most I can offer, Christo," he said. "That's final."

"Thank you for your time, Yiorgo," said my father, standing up. "With four children, there's no way I can cover expenses on forty-five dollars a week." He led me out the door without remarking on the fact that half my sundae remained uneaten.

"That Pallas is a real small-timer," he muttered as he pulled me farther down West Boylston and then across the street. "He has no vision, doesn't think big. Nick Skouras is another story. A big man with big ideas. You see that over there? Now that's what I call a *real* restaurant!"

He was pointing across a large parking lot at a steel-and-tile Art Deco establishment that had started life as a diner but had been extended in all directions.

"That's Stuart's," said my father, pointing to the red neon letters on the roof. "Nick Skouras bought it from some Yankee and he's been doing standing-room-only business ever since. Seats a hundred and fifty people at a time. Open from lunch until midnight. Pulls workers from all the factories in this area, not just Norton's. They come down the hill from Worcester Pressed Steel, Morgan Spring, Heald Machine. Family groups from the Heights come in for a big dinner. Nick's got a gold mine here."

When we went inside I noticed that the tables were already starting to fill up, although it wasn't yet lunchtime.

"Christo, you old pirate!" shouted a booming voice from the back that made the windows rattle. I followed my father to a table in the rear where a hugely fat man sat counting rolls of nickels, dimes, and quarters.

Nick Skouras gestured to us to sit down opposite him and summoned a waitress, whom he directed, in English, to bring us coffee, doughnuts, and ice cream. I started shaking my head.

"He's not hungry," said my father in Greek.

"He will be when he sees Stuart's famous banana split," bellowed the enormous man. He whispered something to the waitress, who smiled.

Nick Skouras formally welcomed me to America, addressing me as *synonomate*, meaning that we had the same first name. As my father was praising him on his obviously flourishing restaurant, he beamed.

"My customers love me and my employees love me because I treat them right," he boasted. "If you'd come to work for me, you'd know that by now, Christo. Look at that, *synonomate*," he said, pointing at the multicolored creation in a large soup bowl set in front of me. "Stuart's famous banana split. Ever had one of those?"

"No sir," I faltered, looking at the sundae with a sinking heart. I had never seen a banana before, and even if this hadn't been my third dish of ice cream, I had no intention of eating such a thing.

My father cleared his throat. "When you first asked, this place was too far away for me," he began.

"Too far away from the coffeehouse and the card games, you mean," said Skouras with a raucous laugh. "I hear they're going to put an engraved bronze plaque on your chair. You've sure paid for it by now!"

"That was just to pass my time," said my father with a touch of annoyance. "Now I've got my children here and I've moved them into a house on Greendale Avenue, and I need to find a job in the neighborhood so I can be close to home. So if you still want me, Niko, I'm available."

Nick Skouras shook his head with an ironic grin. "Christo, old friend, now that you need work, I don't need a cook!" he said. "I have Charlie in the kitchen, and I've promised to make him a partner soon. My son and my nephew handle the short orders behind the counter. And there's no job in the place I can't do myself if I have to."

"But you're open six A.M. to midnight and your business just keeps growing," my father insisted. "It's too much for just Charlie to handle. You need another cook."

Nick Skouras considered this for a while, stacking his rolls of coins in front of him thoughtfully. "All right," he said finally. "I'll give you two days a week for now, and if business keeps growing, I'll take you on full-time."

"Two days a week isn't enough," my father snapped. "I don't have just myself to think about anymore, I've got four children."

"I was just trying to help out," Skouras announced in tones that were audible throughout the restaurant. "I have to run my business according to *my* needs, not yours."

As faces turned toward us, Father flushed crimson, but he stood up with the demeanor of a potentate. He took two quarters from his pocket and threw them on the table next to the untouched, melting banana split. "Get someone else for your two days a week," he said. "This is for our food. Keep the change."

Nick Skouras rose to his full height, shouting, "Christo, you insult me!" His terrifying voice pursued us as I scampered behind my father out of the restaurant.

Once in the parking lot, Father came to a halt and seemed to pull himself together. He set his chin, and I saw a spark of determination in his eye. He appeared to be a person who has reached a decision.

"Pay no attention to that Nick Skouras," he advised. "He's just an overgrown windbag. No one respects him anyway — left a good Greek wife to take up with some American woman who was doing his bookkeeping. I wouldn't associate with a man like that! And he criticizes *me* for playing a little cards!"

He took me by the hand and led me directly across the street toward a red brick building topped with a tall white cupola. I took it for a church, but on closer inspection, I saw a marquee in front.

"Have you ever been to the cinema?" Father asked.

"No, but I heard about it in Athens," I replied. "Grandfather said films are a waste of money and they ruin children's morals as well."

"Your grandfather always was a cheapskate," replied my father. "Let's go see a movie."

He paid the price of my admission — fourteen cents for a double bill — and escorted me to a seat in the back of the dark, cavernous, nearly empty theater. He warned me never to sit too close to the front, and then, as I looked up and saw giant gray-and-white figures flickering across the screen above me, he disappeared.

Frightened at being alone in this strange place, I turned around and saw him coming down the aisle carrying a box of popcorn and two boxes of candy. "Take these and stay right here until I come back for you," he ordered. "Don't move from this spot. When the picture ends and the lights go on, stay in your seat, and they'll start another one. I may be a while, but don't worry. Before the end of the next picture I'll come back to get you."

Before I could protest he was gone, leaving me alone in the dark. The shadowy theater frightened me and increased my anxiety over what I had learned in the past twenty-four hours. Not only was my father not a tycoon, I now knew, he didn't even have a job. And despite his claims that every restaurant owner in Worcester wanted to hire him, I had seen him rejected three times over, and humiliated as well. By now, all my euphoria on the first day about our fine life in America, our palatial home, and my luxurious new clothes was gone. My resentment of my father for leaving us in Greece during the war was now heightened by anger at him for bringing us to a strange world where he obviously was unable to take care of us.

Even in the worst of the famine, my mother had managed to find us scraps of food and had begged enough flour to keep us alive. But another family in the village, with little land and no animals, gave up and boarded themselves inside their hut, parents and children, nailing the doors and windows shut to wait for death to end their suffering. Before long the other villagers realized what had happened, broke down the Hahos' door, and collected enough food from their own meager stores to keep the family alive, but the Hahos name became synonymous with poverty and desperation. Even when all of us were barefoot and starving, the Hahos family was worse. Now, as I sat in the dark theater, I imagined that my father, my sisters, and I might starve to death within our luxurious home, the furniture and our new clothes repossessed by creditors. We would become the Hahos family of Worcester.

As I sank deeper and deeper into my seat, the odor of the popcorn nauseated me and tears ached behind my eyes. I felt betrayed by my father and his land and longed for the familiar sights of my village. But then my attention was caught by a figure on the screen — a blustering fat man who so resembled Nick Skouras that I had to look closely to understand it was an actor, whom I would eventually learn to recognize as Sydney Greenstreet. Everyone in the film, including the fat man, seemed rich and well dressed. It was an unremarkable B movie, the story of an ambitious, amoral conniver who betrays everyone — colleagues, lovers, friends — in his ruthless climb to the top. The title, I would learn, was *Ruthless,* and the sinister protagonist was played by Zachary Scott.

Even though I couldn't understand a word, I was mesmerized by the visual images: impossibly chic apartments, glamorous nightclubs, elegant offices. All those people seemed to be pleading, weeping, imploring the rich businessman, who only smiled like a lizard and refused them. I began to suspect that in America, to acquire wealth, power, and luxuries like those I saw before me, it was necessary to destroy people. What chance, I wondered, would my innocent Greek father have to find a job in such a country, when I saw this man on the screen humiliating his own countrymen?

By the time *Ruthless* ended and the lights came up, I had forgotten my fears in my eagerness to see the second movie, which proved to be a western called *Angel in Exile,* starring John Carroll as an ex-convict who heads for an abandoned Arizona mine in search of stolen gold. This was a lot easier to follow than *Ruthless,* even without understanding the words, and soon I was holding my breath in suspense. I abandoned myself to this fascinating celluloid world and discovered a new passion that would become an addiction. As I grew, the movies would serve as my escape, my drug, and my teacher in America. Whenever life became too difficult, I would head straight for the nearest cinema to forget my own drab problems amid the towering passions and tragedies on the screen. It gave me hope to see that in the movies, evildoers always met their punishment and the good and the beautiful were always saved, succored, and rewarded before the fadeout.

At the climactic shootout of *Angel in Exile,* when my father slid into the seat next to me and said it was time to leave, I shushed him and sat transfixed until the hero won salvation, the treasure, and the girl, and the lights went up. Father looked at me in surprise, taking in my untouched candy and popcorn. "You must really like the moving pictures," he said. "They always put *me* to sleep."

As we headed home, I studied him out of the corner of my eye, trying to guess where he had been and what he had done since he left me, but he walked with the same confident, jaunty strut, and his expression gave no clues. We got to the house and he told Olga to make him a Greek coffee. When she set the foamy cup on the kitchen table, he summoned Kanta and Fotini to hear what he had to say.

"I've decided to accept a position as chef at Terminal Lunch downtown," he announced. "Nassio Economou and Christo Stathis have been begging me to work for them. I figured, why hold a grudge?"

"But I thought Nassio betrayed you by selling the produce truck and buying the restaurant and never making you a partner!" exclaimed Olga.

"Don't you always say that Nassio is the last man on earth you would work for?" added Kanta.

Father waved his hand wearily as if brushing away gnats. "Better the devil you know . . . " He sighed. "I've got to work, don't I?"

"What are they paying you?" demanded Kanta, the inquisitor.

"Fifty-five dollars a week," he muttered. "They said that was the best they could do."

"But that's twenty dollars less than you got in your last job!" exclaimed Kanta.

"And you'll have to pay three dollars a week for bus fare," I reminded him.

"And you'll be all the way downtown," complained Olga.

Father took a sip from his coffee. "At least we'll have money coming in," he said. "Anyway, I plan to keep my options open. If it's not enough to get by on, eventually one of you older girls may have to go work in a factory."

"No decent girl would work in a factory," Olga snapped.

"Leave me alone, Olga," he said with a sigh, looking every day of his fifty-six years. "I'm tired."

That evening, and every evening for the first month or so after our arrival, fellow immigrants came to call. All the Greeks in Worcester had relatives caught up in the civil war, and with the postal service disrupted, they were all desperate for news. Most of the northern villages, like ours, had been emptied as the retreating Communist guerrillas forced the civilians to flee with them into Albania. Everyone was trying to learn the fate of missing relatives.

The night after my disillusioning excursion with my father, we opened the door to find Jimmy Tzouras, an old friend of Father's, standing on our step holding a bag of fruit and puffing on his inevitable White Owl cigar. A beefy bulldog of a man about a decade younger than my father, Tzouras owned a thriving wholesale produce company in Worcester called Standard Fruit and lived in bachelor quarters, but he was lonely for the wife and daughter he had left behind in Greece. It was his habit to visit other Greek families every night, always bringing a gift of fruit and always falling asleep in their kitchen, because his business required him to rise at five A.M. Everyone liked Jimmy Tzouras, despite his foul-smelling cigars. As he snored quietly in a corner someone would always remark, "Wherever Tzouras goes, he brings melons and *morpheus*."

Tzouras came to call as soon as he heard of our arrival, for his daughter and wife had been taken by the guerrillas into Albania in the same group as our sister Glykeria. They had written to him describing the harrowing passage, first on foot, then by sea, as the kidnapped villagers were stuffed into the holds of coal barges and transported to northern Albania, to the city of Shkodra. There they were crowded into barracks that had formerly been used as stables.

Tzouras greeted us all, studying our faces, then settled himself into a comfortable chair. After he offered us the bag of fruit and lighted another cigar, he pulled a much-folded envelope from his pocket.

"I have news from Albania," he said, frowning. "A letter from my cousin in Shkodra."

"Does it mention Glykeria?" my father asked.

"It does, I'm afraid," Tzouras said.

"Is she dead?" we all screamed.

"No, no!" replied Tzouras. "Nothing like that! I'll read it to you."

His cousin had written a letter carefully phrased to pass through the Communist censors, knowing that few missives from Albania would ever reach America. "Dear Cousin," Tzouras read,

> I hope this letter finds you well. We are all as well as can be expected. Your wife and daughter are in good health as are our relatives. We hear that our gallant fighters are striking heavy blows against the monarcho-fascists in Macedonia and we look forward to returning to our homes when the Red Flag flies over our fatherland.
>
> A number of brave young women from our villages have been given the great honor of taking up the gun in the struggle. Among those recently sent from Shkodra to training camps in the south was the daughter of our cousin from Lia who is near you in Worcester. Unfortunately your own Spirdoula was deemed too young for such glory. We all send you . . .

"They've conscripted Glykeria!" cried Kanta, who had been briefly drafted by the guerrillas in our village but had fainted so often during training that she was sent back.

"Those scum! She's barely fifteen years old!" shouted my father. "Sending her to fight at the front!"

"They must be pretty desperate," agreed Tzouras with a nod. "Now that they've lost Grammos, they're collecting young girls, old men, anyone who can carry a gun, probably getting ready for a last stand in Macedonia this summer."

Olga, Kanta, and Fotini all were in tears at the thought of our sister's suffering.

"They didn't take your Spirdoula, who's nearly the same age," growled my father. "They picked on Glykeria, special, because they executed her mother . . . making an example of her."

"She'll have to put on pants and sleep in the trenches along with the filthy guerrillas, those animals!" wailed Olga. "If it was me, I'd shoot myself first."

"Shut up!" snapped Father. "Whatever happens to Glykeria, she's my daughter and your sister and we're all going to church on Sunday and pray for her deliverance. God brought you out and He can still bring Glykeria out." He crossed himself and then pulled out his handkerchief and blew his nose.

All that night my sisters wept over Glykeria and speculated on what terrible things were happening to her, until I nearly went crazy listening to them. None of us could eat any of the lentil soup my father had prepared. Finally he ordered us not to speak of Glykeria anymore until we went to church on Sunday and lighted candles for her.

"I'm not going to church and let men look at me," declared Olga. "The rest of you can go if you like."

"And *I'm* not going to church unless I get my hair cut first," announced Kanta. "I refuse to let all the Greeks in Worcester see me with braids down my back like a village bumpkin."

"All right, all right," sighed my father, rolling his eyes heavenward. "Olga, you stay home if you want, and Kanta, I'll get the Irish lady who lives upstairs to take you tomorrow to cut your hair. She's a good woman, Mrs. Butler, and she said if there was anything she could do to help my orphaned children, to let her know. A good, moral lady. We have to keep quiet down here so as not to bother her. No more screaming and wailing. Now go to bed."

The next day Mrs. Butler, a kindly old woman with an erect carriage, agreed to take seventeen-year-old Kanta for her first haircut. Kanta marched proudly down West Boylston Street, wearing her fine new shoes, dress, and coat. At the salon she was seated in the big chair, and the beautician, a plump woman with a mass of red curls, undid her braids and brushed out the silky cascade of Kanta's dark blond hair. The woman lifted it in both hands, shaking her head, then looked at Mrs. Butler, protesting that it was much too beautiful to cut. Both the women turned to gaze at Kanta in the mirror, but she understood perfectly well what they were asking and she was adamant. Making a scissors of her first two fingers, she pantomimed angry cutting motions just below her ears. "*Copse-to! Copse-to!*" she shouted, like a little tyrant, and with a sigh the beautician took her scissors and let the long silken sheaf fall to the floor.

When the hairdresser was done, Kanta surveyed her image with satisfaction. Now she really *did* look like an American. But she was a little disappointed to see her shorn hair so straight, almost like a Dutch boy's. She couldn't figure out why so many American girls had curls and she didn't.

On Sunday Father got all of us except Olga washed, brushed, combed, and dressed in our new American finery in plenty of time to make a grand arrival at church in the rented DeSoto. After the disconcerting surprises of our first few days in America, I was eagerly looking forward to church — a comfortable oasis of familiar sights and sounds in the midst of this confusing foreign world. While driving through the city, I would ask eagerly every time we passed a church, "Is this one ours, *Patera*?" but each time he would reply, "No, this is Catholic," or Lutheran, Episcopalian, Jewish ("for the unbaptized" is the way he put it). I finally lapsed into a puzzled silence, trying to figure out how Worcester could accommodate so many contradictory religions when in Greece every church I'd ever seen belonged to the Orthodox faith.

The Greek Orthodox church in Worcester was named St. Spyridon because the handful of immigrants who created it in 1924 came primarily from our province of Epiros, just next to the island of Corfu, where the body of Saint Spyridon is preserved and venerated. But more to the point, St. Spyridon's feast day in those years fell on December 25, the only day all the factories were closed, so the immigrants could celebrate their church's feast day without losing any wages.

When Father pulled up on Orange Street and pointed out our own church at last, I was disappointed to see a sprawling brown brick structure that was not in the form of a Greek cross. Once we pushed our way into the crowded narthex, the surprises multiplied.

In our village church and every church in Greece, the congregation walks directly into the nave, men moving to the front while women and small children stand in the back. There are no pews or chairs but a few niches against the wall where elderly men can lean their elbows on supports to help them make it through the long service. In Greek churches, a constant drone of gossip and chatter competes with the singing of the priest and the cantors. Worshippers tend to wander around, entering and leaving the church as the spirit moves them.

None of this prepared me for St. Spyridon's Church on Orange Street, where we entered the massive doors to find ourselves in a jammed narthex and the center of all eyes. There were at that time four hundred dues-paying families enrolled in St. Spyridon's and twice that number of worshippers who ignored the annual fee. I began to suspect that every one of them had turned out on that particular Sunday with the specific intent of examining the refugee children of Christos Gatzoyiannis.

On the way to church Father had interrogated me to find out if I could recite the Lord's Prayer, the Pater-i-mon, by heart. As modestly as possible, I replied that I not only knew it all the way through, I could recite the Creed, the Pistevo, as well. Now, after we pushed through the curious crowd toward the candlestand, my father purchased two long, thin candles for each of us to light — one for our mother and one for our missing sister. Then, after whispering to me, "Are you sure you know the *whole* Pater-i-mon?" he scribbled a note to the priest asking if I might be allowed to recite it during the service. This was familiar procedure to me, because in the village the schoolmaster chose a different pupil each week to declaim the Lord's Prayer at the proper moment in the liturgy.

"Those are the ones — the war orphans — poor things . . ." I could hear the whispers floating through the crowd, but Father paid no mind to the onlookers. After we lit our candles, placed them in the waiting brass candelabra, and paid reverence to the two icons for that Sunday, crossing ourselves, kissing them, and genuflecting, Father led us through the throng like Moses through the Red Sea, into the nave. We walked in a procession down the main aisle between the church pews while I gaped at the spectacle of people sitting down in church. All eyes watched our passage. Kanta and Fotini tried to hang back, but Father motioned them forward, hissing that women and men worshipped together in America.

He led us through the long nave all the way to the very first pew. When we were finally seated, trying to ignore the weight of all those eyes upon us, we looked toward the Beautiful Gate for the priest, but in vain. I was reassured to see the familiar faces of the saints, with their sorrowing Byzantine eyes, gaunt famished faces, and the dessicated arms clutching the symbols of their martyrdom, staring back at me from the altar screen. I inhaled the thick mist of incense and cast my eyes heavenward. Sure enough, above the shimmering chandelier that represents the Heavenly Light of God, there was the immense face of Christ Pantocrator — Christ the All-Powerful — glaring down on me with a sternness that always seemed more accusatory than protective. But today, instead of intimidating me and filling me with guilt for my sins, the Pantocrator seemed like an old friend, come all the way from my mountains to watch over me in my new home.

"That's him, that's the priest, Father Rizos," whispered my father as a robed figure appeared from behind the Beautiful Gate.

"That's no priest!" hissed Fotini indignantly. "He's got no beard, and his hair's as short as anyone else's."

"In America the priests don't have to have beards," whispered Father back.

"I don't care what you say," muttered Fotini stubbornly. "I'm not going to kiss the hand of any priest who doesn't have a beard."

It felt funny to be sitting down in church, and under my wool suit I was beginning to sweat and to itch uncomfortably. *"Irini pasi,* peace be unto all," sang out the priest. The familiar words calmed me a little, and I tried to lose myself in the majesty of the ritual. Suddenly a blast of supernaturally loud organ music nearly lifted me out of my seat. Then a peal of hosannas from a heavenly choir somewhere behind and above my head sent me spinning around, searching for the source. I had never heard any music in church except for the monotonous chant of the priest and the cantors, so I almost expected to see the heavens opened and a multitude of the heavenly host hovering somewhere just below the ceiling, but in fact it was a choir of black-robed singers standing in the balcony at the rear singing "Kyrie Eleison."

A jab from my father's elbow turned my attention back to the priest and the liturgy, sprinkled with a few unfamiliar words of English. Then Father Rizos neared the recitation of the Lord's Prayer and gave me a significant nod. My father's hand under my arm lifted me firmly to a standing position, and a shove propelled me forward toward the three steps to the *solea.* At the top I stopped, facing the grim saints of the iconostasis, the terrible mysteries of the great marble altar table with its gospel book of gold, candlesticks of silver, and the ark holding the sacraments of communion. I saw the dark-eyed priest glaring at me with a look of misgiving.

There was an excruciating pause as I tried to find my voice. For a split second I had a vision of the great chandelier, cut loose by the hand of the Pantocrator in the dome, crashing down to annihilate me before the entire congregation for the sin of forgetting the words to the Lord's Prayer. Then, from somewhere inside me, the familiar phrases rose to my lips and I piped up, in as strong a voice as I could muster, hoping that the Pantocrator would hear and stay His hand:

> *Pater imon O en tis ouranis*
> *Agiasthito to onoma sou . . .*

I shouted my way through the entire prayer and then turned, with the blood pounding in my temples, and found my way back to my father's side in the front pew. All around I could hear a rustle like the wind through a wheatfield and a murmuring of voices: "The poor little thing . . . lost his mother . . . tortured and murdered . . ."

When I was safely wedged between my sisters and my father, I looked up to see what he had thought of my performance. He was staring at the altar, his face expressionless, but I could see that his cheeks were wet with tears.

At the end of the service, since we were in the front pew, we were the first to file forward to receive the piece of bread called the *antidoron,* or "aftergift," and to kiss the hand of the priest as he gave it. Father Rizos' ominous visage relaxed into a grin as he said to me, "Well done, my child. Welcome!" When Fotini, right behind me, grimly refused to kiss his hand, he gave her a wink of forgiveness.

We walked out through a nave of beaming faces, and once into the narthex, we stopped and the congregation pressed around to congratulate us. I felt buffeted and accosted by the hands and eyes of hundreds of strangers, who ruffled my hair or pinched my cheek and then turned to give their opinion to my father: "Smart boy" . . . "Fine lad, Christo, he'll do you proud" . . . "Lots of responsibility, but they're a fine-looking lot" . . . "Where's the oldest girl? I hear she's ready for the wedding crown" . . . "You made your father proud today, son. . . ."

Worst of all were the black-kerchiefed *yiayias* straight from the villages, who attacked me with wet sloppy kisses and pulled my cheeks until they burned. Some of them even spit toward me to ward off the curse of the evil eye, which was sure to possess me because of all the compliments I was receiving. I tried to dodge the saliva as the old women croaked, "Garlic in your eyes, my child." (Later, on the way home, I discovered that one of them had slipped a real clove of garlic into the pocket of my new suit to protect me from the awful results of so much admiration.) Desperately I tugged on my father's arm, trying to get him in motion toward the car so I could escape these suffocating and repellent embraces.

As we were encircled by the crowd, I could see that my father was euphoric with pride. This was the presentation of his new family, especially his only son, to the Greek community, and I was glad for his sake that I had made a good impression. But I was heartily sick of being kissed, pinched, and spat upon and couldn't wait to leave the church and my new fame. I was glad I had remembered the Lord's Prayer, but that performance seemed a minor hurdle compared to what awaited me in the morning — my initiation into the American school system.

Fotini and I put on our best clothes for our first day at school, and each clutching one of our father's hands, we walked up the street and turned the corner. I had wanted to bring my satchel full of Greek lesson books from the refugee camp, but Father said, "They can't even read Greek, your teachers. The thing that will impress them is that you learned some English already. So when we register you with the principal, Nikola, and I give you a signal, you stand up and show him how you can count in English."

"What's so great about that, that he can count?" muttered Fotini, who had insisted on carrying her tiny blue plastic purse filled with a handkerchief, two pennies, and the key that would let us in the house at noon for lunch. "In the refugee camp I always got better grades than him, especially in arithmetic."

"You're both smart children," replied my father soothingly. "But it's more important for a boy to be smart, because he has to support a family. For a girl, the most important thing is to have a good name. You know what I always tell your sisters: 'Virtue is beyond price for those who have it and beyond reach for those who lose it.'"

I nodded and preened at his words, while Fotini kicked a stone angrily up the walk, scuffing her new shoes. I could tell she was as scared as I was, even though she was a year older.

Inside the school, Father led us to the corner office of the principal, a tall, craggy-faced Yankee who was a medley of grays: gray suit, gray tie, gray hair, gray complexion, even a sprinkling of gray dandruff on his shoulders. He sat in his swivel chair with his back to the window, tapping his nails on his roll-top desk and looking us over, then he motioned for our father to sit down in the chair next to him and for us to sit in smaller folding chairs near the door.

Father laboriously began filling out the necessary documents. He had already explained to me that our name, Gatzoyiannis, was almost unpronounceable to most Americans, and our legal written name was even worse because the customs official on Ellis Island had garbled it so badly, creating the jaw-breaker Ngagoyeanes. No wonder my father often used for convenience the last name Gage, which Nassio had jokingly given him during their days selling vegetables, borrowing the name of a distinguished customer, Dr. Gage, who like my father made a fetish of always having a fine wardrobe. I had noticed in church how many friends addressed Father as Gage. Now I devoutly wished I didn't have to enter school with a last name that neither Greeks nor Americans could spell or pronounce, but Father was adamant that I use our full legal name.

The principal was speaking to my father in a soft, firm voice, clearly telling him something he didn't want to hear. Father shook his head, protested, waved his hands to make a point; then he turned to me and gestured. Like a jack-in-the-box I popped up from my seat and spouted: "Onetwothreefourfivesixseveneightnineten."

"Not now, Nikola, not now!" exclaimed my father with irritation. Then he went back to arguing with the principal. Several times he pointed to me, and each time I jumped up and began to recite. Finally the man sat and listened to me patiently, all the way to "fifty," then nodded and stood. Hoping I had impressed him with my erudition, I followed him, my father, and Fotini down the hall. When he led us into our new classroom and I looked around, I decided that I must have really astounded him. All the children in this classroom were bigger than the two of us. Some seemed to be in their late teens, like my older sisters. I stood taller, trying to appear older, as they watched our entrance.

The principal handed us over to our teacher, Miss McGinley, a matronly woman with auburn hair and a dark burgundy suit, whose warm smile offset the severity of her appearance. She shook our hands, saying our first names carefully, then directed two towering students to give us their desks in the front of the room.

We sat down, somewhat abashed at being the smallest in the class, and watched our father and the principal leave. At the door Father stopped, turned around, looking angry and worried at the same time, and then, shaking his head, turned abruptly and left without a word.

When the door closed, Miss McGinley smiled at us again, clapped her hands, and then called a tall, muscular boy named Jerry to the board. He looked at least sixteen, so I watched in surprise as he picked up the chalk and, biting his tongue in concentration, drew two huge ungainly letters on the board. He turned toward the teacher, who said a few words of praise, and suddenly the tall teenager jumped up and down in glee, delighted as a two-year-old by her praise. Startled, I turned and looked around the room. All the students were grinning and nodding.

"Fotini," I hissed. "There's something wrong with these kids. They're not normal."

"Of course they're not," she replied in a superior tone. "They're Americans!"

After leaving us at Greendale School, my father returned home, collected Olga and Kanta, and drove them into town to register at the Day School for Immigrants on Lamartine Street, stopping to pick up our shipmate Prokopi Koulisis on the way. Just a week before, the *Worcester Telegram* had published a front-page article about the Lamartine School's success in absorbing the flood of war immigrants to Worcester. D.P.s QUICK TO LEARN ENGLISH was the headline of the piece, which reported that the class was attended by more than seventy displaced persons from at least thirteen countries, ranging from young teenagers to middle-aged men and women, none of whom knew any English when they enrolled.

The article listed the students as coming from Rumania, Poland, Lithuania, Latvia, Italy, Czechoslovakia, Canada, Turkey, France, Finland, Lebanon, and Armenia, with Greece being represented by seven displaced persons. The number of Greeks increased by three when my father led my sisters and Prokopi Koulisis into the school office. But because the Lamartine School would not take children younger than thirteen and there were no public school instructors trained to teach English as a foreign language, Fotini and I had fallen between the cracks and been placed in a class for the retarded.

Father registered the three, and then they were introduced to their teacher, Miss McCarthy, who impressed Kanta as tall, beautiful, and very sympathetic. After taking a look at their classmates, the new students left, to start regular lessons the next morning. They dropped Prokopi off and drove away along Water Street, a beehive of busy ethnic delicatessens, restaurants, small shops, and warehouses. As Father approached his old hangout on the street, Broadway Soda, he noticed in one of the windows above it a shiny new sign: DR. DANIEL M. SEIDENBERG, M.D.

"That's a doctor's office," he said to Olga, pointing. "Let's see if he can look at you, examine that thing on your neck."

"Why?" she exclaimed, alarmed. "It doesn't hurt. It's always been there. I don't want to go to a doctor!"

"Don't wait to sight the fox before mending the chicken coop," my father replied with resolution. "We'll just go up and ask if the doctor can see you. No point in letting the thing grow until it starts frightening away potential husbands."

Our first recess that morning in the Greendale schoolyard increased my suspicion that my classmates were not normal. When we erupted into the schoolyard, all the children from our room played together in the far corner, running about clumsily, reacting to every turn of the game with excessive excitement. When they collided with other students, I saw the others tease them by imitating their clumsy movements and bewildered expressions.

Fotini and I stood to one side of the playground, watching the interaction. When I accidentally bumped into a pudgy, crew-cut boy about my age, he unleashed a series of taunts at us. I couldn't make sense of most of them, but the refrain, picked up by his cronies, stuck in my mind. "D.P. dummies! D.P. dummies!" was the epithet they sang at us, laughing and nudging each other. I longed to attack the stocky leader, using the street-fighting skills I had learned in the refugee camp, but first I had to know what he was calling me, so I just glared back.

When the noon bell rang and Miss McGinley released us to go home for lunch, I led Fotini down the hill to our house at a trot. "You heard what they called us," I said. "I'm going to find out what it means."

"How are you going to do that?" she asked. "What *did* they call us, anyway?"

"D.P. dummies," I replied. This English phrase was already engraved in my memory. "I'm going to look it up in Father's dictionary."

While Fotini cut up the cold cheese pie that our father had left behind for our lunch, I paged through the thick *Divry's Greek-English Dictionary*, which he kept on the kitchen table, studying it every night in order to enlarge his vocabulary. I looked for "deepee" in the English section in vain, but I did manage to find the word "dummy," and saw that the third definition read in Greek "a person who is stupid or retarded."

This solidified my suspicions that we had been placed in a classroom of retarded children; we were doomed from the beginning to be classed as mentally deficient simply because we couldn't speak English. My virtuoso performance in counting clearly had failed to impress the principal. I realized why our father had looked so angry when he had left us there.

While Fotini ate and muttered about the rudeness of American children, I pored over the dictionary in the Greek-to-English section, trying to formulate some questions for Miss McGinley. There was something I wanted to know, and it couldn't wait.

As Fotini and I were walking back to school for the afternoon session, my father was trying to coax Olga up the steps to Dr. Seidenberg's office. The doctor, a short, ingratiating young man with curly brown hair, immediately won my father's confidence by treating him with flattering familiarity, as if they were equals. Ever since being conquered by the Turks, Greeks have been used to being browbeaten by anyone in a position of authority, such as doctors, lawyers, and petty civil servants. Father was overwhelmed by this American doctor's congeniality and was prepared to believe anything he said. Olga was much less captivated.

"Tell her to unbutton her dress so I can listen to her heart with my stethoscope," Dr. Seidenberg told Father. When the request was translated, Olga firmly crossed her arms across her chest and shook her head. Not one button would she open to reveal so much as her collarbone. Coming from a village where even her hair had to be covered to avoid igniting lustful feelings in passing men, Olga had no intention of letting some foreigner start unbuttoning her dress.

"It's not going to be easy to examine her neck if she won't open her collar," remarked Dr. Seidenberg to our father with a good-natured chuckle. "But if it makes her feel better, I'll try."

As soon as we got back to the classroom after the lunchtime break, I stalked up to Miss McGinley's desk with a look of defiance on my face that seemed to startle her. I consulted a scrap of paper in my hand, then made a sweeping gesture that encompassed the entire room, where the other, larger students were sitting, watching me curiously.

"What. Grade. This?" I demanded, pausing between each word.

She smiled uncertainly and made circles in the air with her hands. "Ungraded. All grades," she said.

I wasn't letting her off that easy. I jabbed my index finger against my chest and fixed her with an unwavering glare. "What grade *me?*" I insisted.

She stood up and smiled down at me in an encouraging way, patting me on the shoulder. "We'll see," she said, and gave me a gentle push back toward my desk.

I marched home from school at three-thirty with Fotini in my wake, determined to unleash on my father the anger and humiliation that had been building up in me all day. Instead of dazzling the American teachers with my academic skills, I had been tossed into a class for retarded children, embarrassed and ignored during lessons, and ridiculed on the playground. I intended to issue an ultimatum to my father: either have me put in a class consistent with my age and academic ability or I would never set foot in that school again.

But when I got in the door and saw him sitting at the table like a beaten man, his head in his hands, I sensed at once that something was very wrong. Kanta was puttering about the kitchen in an angry way, her eyes red from crying. From the bedroom I could hear the sound of Olga sobbing. Like anyone who has already experienced the worst thing he can imagine — in my case the murder of my mother — I instantly saw a succession of horrible possibilities flashing through my mind's eye, starting with Glykeria's death.

"What is it, what's happened?" I demanded, all my complaints about school forgotten. "Did somebody die?"

"Keep your voice down!" my father exclaimed, glancing toward the closed bedroom door. "Nobody's died. It's just that I took Olga to the doctor and he looked at her neck and he thinks she needs an operation. But don't say anything to her. We have to keep her spirits up. We'll pretend it's nothing but a goiter. But I'm afraid . . ." His voice trailed off, and he turned his head away so I couldn't see his expression.

"Afraid of what?" I demanded, thinking that it wasn't fair for fathers to be afraid. They were supposed to be fearless.

"I'm afraid that Olga's got the bad sickness," he said, referring to the disease so terrible that no Greek would utter its name for fear of inviting it in the door: cancer.

5

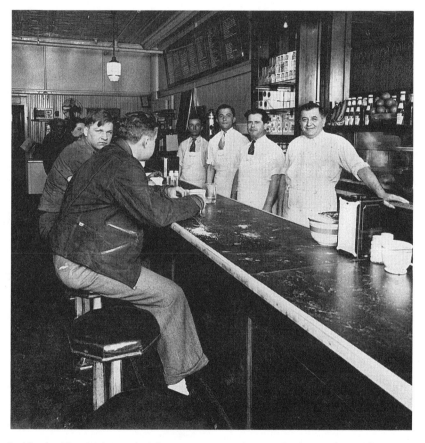

Inside the Terminal Lunch. The proprietors, Christos Stathis (right) and Nassio Economou (second right), are behind the counter.

DREAMS OF
DELIVERANCE

Lighten our darkness, we beseech thee.
— Book of Common Prayer

D R. SEIDENBERG sent Olga to two more doctors, but they all came to the same conclusion: the growth in her neck, a hard lump the size of an olive, would have to be cut out and sent to Boston for analysis. With no insurance and no savings, Father was hardly in a position to pay for an operation, but to him the doctors' word was absolute. He told Olga, during her second week at the Lamartine School, that she would have to go into the hospital.

Of all of us, Olga had the hardest time adjusting to our new country. In the village, as the first child, she had been the closest to our mother and the most pampered (except for me, the baby and the long-awaited son). Olga was the one who had gotten the best pieces of fabric for her dresses and the most appreciative glances from young men who passed her on the road. As the oldest girl she would have to be married before any of her sisters, and as the daughter of the American tycoon, she would surely make a brilliant match.

Our mother had never saddled Olga with the cooking, sewing, and cleaning but put her to work in the garden and fields and minding us little ones. Olga had whiled away her days dreaming of the groom she would choose and the wedding that would be the finest in all Thesprotia. As they had prepared her dowry, she had driven Mother to distraction, insisting that she would accept no village peasant who worked with his hands but only a professional man: a lawyer, doctor, or teacher — all species that were almost nonexistent in our isolated mountain region.

Now *Mana* was dead, the wonderful dowry had been destroyed in the war, and Olga felt responsible for the welfare of her younger siblings, for our mother had told her during their last farewell, "I hang the others around your neck." Of all of us, Olga was the most steadfast in obeying the strict rules our mother had taught. She refused to go to church, in fact to go anywhere; she would not cut her hair, wear anything but black, sing, or even smile. And as she sat in our new home alone, burdened with cooking and cleaning chores for which she had never been trained, Olga constantly mourned for our mother and the life she had left behind.

When she learned within weeks of our arrival that she had to go into the foreigners' hospital and have a strange doctor cut her neck open, Olga's depression became despair. She begged Father to make sure the operation would not disfigure her and make her unfit for marriage. On the Sunday afternoon when he helped her pack a few possessions in a paper bag, Olga wept pitifully, her tears soaking the front of her black dress. "Don't cry, *Foula*," I begged, using the affectionate term for "sister." "Everything will be all right."

Father led her up the imposing staircase into Doctors' Hospital on Lincoln Street — a large, turn-of-the-century mansion that had been converted into a small hospital. Olga recalls that she crossed herself as she entered and silently prayed that she would die under the ether, "so that I could be with my mother and not have to worry about anything anymore." She was put in a garret room with a middle-aged woman who smiled kindly, then my father left her alone.

The next morning Olga was given a hospital gown, which she modestly donned while hiding in the cramped bathroom. Then she was prepared for surgery and wheeled into the operating room, where all three of her doctors, Dr. Seidenberg, the specialist, and the surgeon, were washing up. Lying on the operating table, Olga tugged at the surgeon's sleeve, trying to communicate that he must put her soundly under the anesthesia before he cut her neck; she was afraid he would start too soon. "Please, Doctor, sleep," she kept repeating. "Please, Doctor, sleep."

The next thing she knew, she was lying in her hospital bed, the afternoon sun slanting through the window, and she could hear Father's voice. But when Olga opened her eyes, all she could see was the figure of our mother standing over her, her face full of compassion. Olga tried to speak and eventually managed a harsh whisper. "Please, *Mana*," she gasped, "bring me some water from Siouli's spring. Please, *Mana*, give me water!"

For a moment she passed out again, and when she came to she heard Father and then she saw him weeping. "Olga, my soul, it's me, your father, my poor child," he cried.

But Olga kept asking her mother over and over for water: *"Nero, Mana. Nero!"*

Fotini and I weren't allowed to go beyond the waiting room on the first floor. When Father came down that afternoon, we suspected from the pallor of his face and the redness of his eyes that things had not gone well. He hired a night nurse for Olga for the first couple of days, but while she begged all night for *nero,* the foreign woman would only rub ice on her lips, because she wasn't permitted to have liquids.

Olga spent nine days in the hospital, her neck swathed in gauze bandages. She discovered that her voice was completely gone except for a whisper, and she couldn't swallow a bite of the hospital food. Every day after work Father would bring her Greek soups he had prepared at the house, which the hospital nurses stored in the refrigerator and served to her at mealtime.

All day long Olga lay there feeling lonely, wondering how many hours remained until her father's visit. If a nurse came near she would reach out and seize her wrist to read her wristwatch, for none of us had such luxuries and Olga didn't know how to ask the time.

Olga passed her first Easter in America lying in the hospital bed, reflecting on the difference from the Easters she remembered in the village, for the resurrection of Christ is the greatest holiday in the Greek calendar. Even in the worst of the famine our mother had always managed to find an egg or two to dye red for the blood of Christ, and she would try to obtain a few bits of meat, even goat's entrails discarded by the guerrillas, to remind us of the roasted lambs, spicy sausages, honeyed pastries, and braided breads that marked Easter celebrations in better times.

In our house on Greendale Avenue, too, it was a bleak Easter, for Father had to work, and as soon as he returned home he rushed off to the hospital. The Americans' holiday fell on a different Sunday from the Orthodox Easter. I decided that a place where Easter is not celebrated with candles, church bells, red eggs, and fireworks must be a poor country indeed.

Several days after Olga's operation, when no nurses or doctors were around, she got up to go to the bathroom by herself. The cubicle was only big enough for her to stand in, but when she saw the mirror over the sink, she decided to unwrap her bandages and examine the scar. When the last bandage fell away, Olga couldn't even scream. The incision ran from behind her right ear all the way down to her right breast, with a crosscut clear around her jawbone. The tendon on the right side of her neck was gone, and where her neck had once been a smooth, rounded column, the entire right side was now a gaping cavity.

Her roommate pressed the call button in alarm as she heard the thump of Olga falling to the floor, unconscious.

After seeing how disfigured she was — unfit ever to be a bride —

Olga lost her will to live. She didn't seem to care that she couldn't speak. Father brought her home after nine days, but she lay in bed or sat in a chair with tears streaming silently down her face, and none of my attempts to distract or amuse her had any effect. "Every day," she remembers, "I prayed to die."

Father visited Olga's surgeon to learn the results of the biopsy. He asked if there was a malignancy, if she would live, and if so, would she ever be able to marry and have children?

"Don't you worry, Mr. Gage," the surgeon reassured him cheerfully. "We sent everything to Boston and your daughter is fine. She had nothing but a goiter. She can marry and have twenty children."

Relieved that his oldest child had escaped the dread disease, Father hurried home to tell Olga the good news.

About a decade later Olga, by then able to speak English, encountered the same surgeon when she was in Doctors' Hospital. He greeted her cordially. "What a coincidence!" he said. "I've just come from an operation on a woman that is identical to the one I did on you."

"I hope you do better job on her neck than you done on mine," replied Olga.

The surgeon flushed scarlet. "You shouldn't speak to me that way!" he shouted. "I saved your life! You had cancer, and if it wasn't for me you'd be dead now!"

"Bullshit!" replied Olga — one of the first English phrases she had learned. "If I have cancer, why you tell my father it was just goiter and I can have twenty children?" But the doctor stormed out of the room without answering her.

Thirteen years after that encounter, in 1971, Olga was trying on dresses in a shop when she noticed that the left side of her neck had started to swell like the right side had the first time. She burst into tears and rushed home, leaving the clothes on the dressing room floor. She decided to go back to Dr. Seidenberg, who had been the family doctor during her first operation, even though she now lived far from Worcester. He advised her to enter Doctors' Hospital for tests. After nearly ten days of testing, the same surgeon appeared in her room and announced that he had to operate on the remaining side of her neck.

Convinced she was dying, Olga became hysterical. She telephoned Fotini and Father, who came in a taxi and removed her from the hospital over the protests of the staff. They took her to specialists in Boston, who called the Worcester doctors to learn what tests had been done. Had they done this test or that test? Olga heard the Boston doctor ask. Again and again the answer was no. "Then what have you been doing with her for so long?" the doctor shouted into the phone.

It was just before Christmas when a Chinese doctor at Massachusetts

General Hospital inserted a needle into the swelling on Olga's neck and drew out blood. Then he said, "You're going to have a wonderful Christmas, my dear, at home with your family, because there's nothing wrong with you but a simple goiter. If you take a thyroid pill every morning for the rest of your life you'll never have a problem like this again."

Olga nearly wept with relief, but she couldn't help remembering a lifetime of dresses specially altered to hide her scarred neck. Back in 1949, when she was twenty-one and couldn't speak English, our father, like many immigrants, was so in awe of doctors that it never occurred to him to ask why it was necessary to remove half of Olga's neck if she had only a goiter — a common condition in our land-locked mountain villages.

After that first operation, as Olga convalesced, weeping in despair without even a voice to vent her grief, Fotini and I were still attending the ungraded class at Greendale School and being taunted every day on the playground as "D.P. dummies." I resented being forced to return to this daily humiliation, and my anger against my father for failing to save *Mana* was as strong as ever, but I didn't feel I could add my grievances to his heavy burden of financial difficulties and worry over Olga.

Every night Father emptied the change from his pockets into a pickle jar he kept on the table. He told me and Fotini that if we ever needed a few coins to buy candy or school supplies, we could dip into it. This seemed to me a bottomless cornucopia of wealth, and I quickly developed my own ways of forgetting my problems.

Whenever I had a quarter, I would head straight to Hamel's market at the bottom of our street and purchase five nickel Hershey bars. I had never seen chocolate until I left our village, and the first time I tasted it I was hooked. At Hamel's I went through a ritual with my Hershey bars that never failed to attract an audience. Standing right in front of Mr. Hamel's cash register, I would carefully unwrap all five candy bars, stack them into a solid chocolate sandwich, and then attack it like a shark, finishing it off in seconds.

My other method of forgetting my sorrows was to withdraw a quarter from the pickle jar every Tuesday, Friday, and Sunday and head for the new double bill at the Greendale Theater, where twenty-five cents would cover my fourteen-cent admission plus an ice cream sandwich and a box of popcorn and leave me a penny change.

The hours I spent in the darkness of the Greendale Theater, sitting on the scratchy velvet seats, inhaling the perfume of popcorn and Juju Fruits, temporarily obliterated the unpleasant realities of school, Olga's illness, and our financial problems. In fact, the hours I spent at the movies taught me more than anything I learned in Miss McGinley's class.

The very first double bill I saw after the one my father took me to was *Angels with Dirty Faces* and *They Drive by Night*. These two films introduced me to my two great heroes, Jimmy Cagney and Humphrey Bogart. They were both small, like me, but tough, cynical, and cunning, qualities that earned them great admiration. I chose them as my role models, and before long I was moving like Jimmy Cagney and talking like Humphrey Bogart with a heavy Greek accent. In fact, my Humphrey Bogart imitation, complete to the twitching curl of the upper lip, became so internalized that I couldn't stop it, even when ordered to by teachers and relatives.

I studied the movies for insights into American culture and real life, and they inspired dreams I never could have dreamed in my Greek village, where my wildest fantasy had been that the winter snow would turn to flour or sugar and we could all have enough to eat. In America, the movies taught, there is so much luxury and opportunity that anyone — a shoeshine boy, a farm girl, or an orphan — can become anything: president, tycoon, radio singing star. In the gloom of the Greendale Theater I realized that if I just played my cards right, I could be anything from a mafioso to a matinee idol — a revolutionary idea to a refugee from an impoverished and class-dominated country.

Revenge was a theme of many of the first movies I saw, igniting a thirst for vengeance in me. I watched Dick Powell track down the Nazi collaborator responsible for the death of his wife in *Cornered* and Gene Kelly mete out retribution to the Mafia killers of his father in *Black Hand*, and I decided that one day I would return to Greece to avenge myself on the murderers of my mother.

But first I would have to make a success in my new country, and the movies showed me how much I didn't know — about the refinements of life and the ways to seize power, and also about history. I was fascinated by historical and biographical dramas and frequently came home from the theater to quiz my father: Who was Madame Curie? Thomas Edison? Abraham Lincoln? Jerome Kern? Florence Nightingale? Richard the Lion-Hearted? Sometimes he would be able to answer me, but more often he would admit he didn't know. (One American celebrity he did know, however, was Jimmy Londos, the 175-pound "Golden Greek" who rose from bootblack to become the heavyweight wrestling champion of the world. Every Greek immigrant knew the names of Londos and our other countrymen who were American sports stars, such as major-league catcher Gus Triandos.)

My very favorite kind of film — even better than westerns — was the boxing movie, of which there were many at the Greendale Theater: *Body and Soul*, starring John Garfield; *Champion*, with Kirk Douglas; *Whiplash*, with Dane Clark; *City for Conquest*, with my hero Jimmy Cagney; and *Golden Boy*, starring William Holden. In these last two, reissues from a decade earlier, a young man, at great personal sacrifice, becomes a successful boxer in order to win financial security for his family. Slowly, as I sat there in the movies, my destiny became clear: I would become a boxer and make so much money that my father and sisters would never have to worry again. I was small, but I saw myself as wiry, clever, and tough, like Jimmy Cagney and Humphrey Bogart.

Fotini and I were slowly adjusting to being in the ungraded class with retarded and learning-disabled children. Shortly after our arrival, Miss McGinley found a Greek-American girl in the school to communicate with us. Through the girl's faltering Greek, we learned that we were to stay in the ungraded class for the rest of the year but in the fall we would be placed in classes with normal children, although no one said which grade. Meanwhile, we would be sent to study reading every afternoon with the regular second grade.

This was little comfort to me. I was still in the retarded class and taunted daily with shouts of "D.P. dummy." But there were some consolations in Miss McGinley's room. One was the kindness of our handicapped classmates, who adopted Fotini and me as mascots and put much energy into entertaining us. One of the girls in our class even taught us to play checkers.

The two who were nicest to me were Paul, who had an overlarge head, and Jerry, who looked like a normal teenager until he started to walk or speak. Miss McGinley made it a class project for the students to teach us the alphabet and the meaning of English words, which she had them act out. She might call Jerry to the front and say in a slow, clear voice, "I run to the window." Then, with enthusiasm as great as his clumsiness, Jerry would sprint to the window while the whole class shouted the sentence.

I was surprised by the kindness of the teachers at Greendale School, because in Greece teachers were often tyrants, and corporal punishment was standard procedure. When I was six, because my mother couldn't afford to buy me a separate notebook for each class, the village schoolteacher struck me so hard that my head glanced off the stone wall, which gashed my scalp. And in the refugee camp, when I muffed a recitation, the teacher bounced a hard blackboard eraser off my forehead.

But Miss McGinley never hit me and never shouted. In fact, when I went up to her desk to recite, she would put an arm around me. No one had done this since my mother's death, and Miss McGinley's gesture, her smile, and the perfume of her hair filled me with so much longing for a maternal touch that the new English words flew out of my head.

In the classroom I reveled in the attention of my teacher and my fellow students but on the playground I hated it when Paul and Jerry insisted on including me in their games and the other students stood around watching and shouting "D.P. dummy." My worst tormentor was Joey Doyle, a stocky, muscular boy who was a year younger than I but half a head taller. He lived on our block, and as we walked home for lunch, Joey would punch me on the shoulder, muttering "D.P. dummy." At the end of the day it was the same, with Joey and his sidekicks walking behind me, throwing things, laughing, and shouting the familiar insult.

One day in the spring as we walked down the hill something glanced off my head, sending a jolt of pain through me. I heard Joey's laughter, and suddenly I lost control. I spun around to confront him and he put up his fists, ready to box.

Although my goal was to be a professional boxer, as we parried, circling each other, I assessed the muscles on Joey's arms and decided this was no time for the Marquis of Queensberry's rules. Instead I opted for the street-fighting methods I had learned in Greece. As Joey jabbed at me, I grasped his collar, flipped him over onto the ground, grabbed his hair, and began pounding his head up and down, screaming every Greek curse I knew. Luckily, I was hammering his head on dirt, because if it had been cement I would have cracked his skull open like an egg. While his cronies watched, shouting, I pounded Joey Doyle's head until my fury began to abate. Then I let him stagger to his feet, covered with mud, snot, and blood, to run home sobbing.

From that day, the neighborhood boys cautiously avoided me like a vicious dog and no one on the playground yelled "D.P. dummy" anymore, but my only friends were still the handicapped children in my class.

While I was dealing with my problems in my own way, my father was facing overwhelming difficulties of his own. After a carefree existence as a *de facto* bachelor, his days divided between work and the pleasures of the Greek coffeehouse, his luck seemed to have turned bad overnight. He must have felt like Sisyphus, rolling the boulder up the hill only to have it roll back down on him. His wife's murder, his children's arrival, the loss of his job, his daughter's disfiguring operation — one catastrophe followed another. Most Greeks would have blamed the evil eye and called in the priest to perform an exorcism, but Father doggedly carried on, never admitting his frustration, while his days at the Terminal Lunch became more and more difficult.

The men he worked with, including Nassio Economou and Christos Stathis, who were now his employers, believed like most Greeks that a father's responsibility to his children, after begetting them, is only to feed them, police the daughters' virtue, and provide the girls with dowries. My father had never tended his children during his visits to Greece, but now that he was the sole parent, he became as solicitous as a mother hen. He took us to the dentist and the doctor and even escorted my sisters to the hairdresser; he chose our clothes, he cooked our food, and he called home several times a day to make sure Olga was all right and Fotini and I had come straight home from school.

Even though he made these calls on the diner's public telephone with his own nickel during slack periods, one of the other cooks at the restaurant, a man named Yianni, invariably complained about the calls: "For God's sake, Christo, you're on the phone again? You're always on the phone! We got work to do here!"

Sometimes Father would reply with dignity, "My children are new to this country. They don't know its ways. I have to look after them." Other days, provoked by the thought that his former partners might be putting Yianni up to the complaints, he would lose his temper and start to shout: "Who are you to tell me what to do? Who the hell is anybody here to question me? I had my own business in Worcester before anyone in this place. If it weren't for me, you'd all be working on some assembly line."

Father always considered himself one of nature's aristocrats, and his lofty manner annoyed his co-workers. Nassio's noisy, often vulgar practical joking was a torment to him, while Father's air of superiority only provoked the other, younger employees at the Terminal Lunch. One of them, a man in his early twenties, couldn't help needling our father whenever the opportunity presented itself by jabbing at his most sensitive spot: his daughters.

To every Greek, family honor is everything. A man might have millions, but if his family name is besmirched, even by some long-dead ancestor, he is treated like a leper. And a man's honor is based on the most fragile foundation: the behavior of the women in his family. A slovenly wife or a willful daughter can ruin a man and his descendants for all eternity. In Greece it was commonplace to hear of a man being acquitted of a crime of passion when his wife's or daughter's virtue was involved. A Greek like my father who had four daughters was vulnerable indeed.

The young man at the Terminal Lunch knew just how to infuriate my father. "I hear you have four daughters, Mr. Gage," he said one day, while chopping greens for the salads. "Four single daughters, all in need of husbands," he continued sympathetically. "What are you going to do with all those daughters, Mr. Gage, with no one at home to keep an eye on them?"

"Don't you worry about my daughters," bellowed Father, picking up the carving knife and advancing on him. "I don't need advice on raising my daughters! You can be sure they'd never look at an asshole like you!"

Another cook interjected himself between Father and his tormentor and managed to take away the knife, but every day Father's situation at the Terminal Lunch was becoming more intolerable. If he hadn't needed to feed his children, he would have told his perfidious ex-partners long ago what they could do with their $55-a-week job, but he had to hang on long enough to find some other way to pay our mounting expenses.

Olga's medical bills and our dentist bills, added to the debts he had already incurred in bringing us to America, drove Father to a desperate conclusion: he would have to put one of his older daughters to work. There was only one place in Worcester where a Greek immigrant girl with no skills and little English could get a job and not destroy her reputation. That was Angelo Cotsidas' Table Talk Pies.

My father and Angelo Cotsidas became fast friends almost from the first day the newcomer stepped off the train in Worcester (despite the fact that the sign pinned to his chest said "Boston"). Both men had the demeanor of gentlemen, although Cotsidas was so poor he bought his clothes in secondhand stores on Spring Street. Both frequented the pinochle games at Kritikos' coffeehouse.

Cotsidas soon knew all the Greek immigrants in Worcester, because he found a job delivering bread for the bakery of a relative named Zisis from his native village of Plesio. In the first two decades of this century, bread was truly the staff of life for the thousands of Greek men who lived in the tenements of Worcester and worked in its factories. They ate meat only on Sundays and survived the rest of the week on bean soup and at least one round loaf a day of the Greek bread produced by Zisis' bakery, because, as Cotsidas recalls, "It was filling and cheap."

When the first Greek immigrants began holding church services in a rented storefront in 1915, they devised an ingenious method of supporting their church by taxing the bread the immigrants ate. At the time of Cotsidas' arrival in the 1920s, there were 3500 Greeks in Worcester but only 50 Greek families; all the rest were "bachelors," or *bekiarides,* like my father, living crowded together in boarding houses, sending most of their salary back to their wives and children in the old country. Virtually all these men intended to return to their native village one day; they were only here to "steal America," as they put it, and in the meantime they formed societies for each village that sent back money for schools and churches in addition to the regular money orders that supported their families.

The Greek storefront church in those days charged each of the fifty Greek families twenty-five cents a month for dues, but the bachelors were charged one cent for every loaf of bread they ate. To make sure that no one cheated, the Greek baker was required to keep accounts of how many loaves were ordered by each colony of bachelors. In this way, the fledgling church collected as much as $300 a month from the frugal bachelors, whether they attended services or not.

Cotsidas worked at Zisis' bakery with another young immigrant, Theodore Tonna, and after two years the pair left the bakery to start their own business, renting a single upstairs room with a kitchen on Belmont Street. Their only collateral was an idea: they would make pastries and sell them wholesale to the 120 restaurants, stores, luncheonettes, and spas in Worcester that were owned by Greeks. The problem was, neither partner knew how to make pastries. Furthermore, there were already eighteen bakeries on Belmont Street, run by Swedes and Finns who had come over with the wave of Scandinavian immigrants headed for the Norton Company. But the two enterprising Greeks bought free drinks for a pair of talkative Finns until they elicited all their pastry-baking secrets.

Through the 1920s, Cotsidas and Tonna delivered doughnuts, coffee rolls, éclairs, jellyrolls, and turnovers to the diners and spas of Worcester. During the worst of the Depression, they charged only eleven cents for a dozen doughnuts. (At this time, recalls Cotsidas, a diner would offer a "special" lunch of soup, three lamb chops, coffee, and a piece of pie for thirty cents.) In 1933, Cotsidas and Tonna moved from their upstairs room, buying a bigger bakery and adding pies to their line. They dubbed their firm Table Talk Pies, inspired by a highly successful local business called Town Talk Bread. Although Town Talk sued, Table Talk's right to use the similar name was upheld.

Cotsidas and Tonna had forty young men working for them until the war broke out and almost all were drafted. They then hired women instead, struggling through the war despite rationed sugar and gasoline. Always an optimist, Cotsidas bought an old garage and converted it to a factory, and once the war was over he bought new machines that would mass-produce pies at a previously unimaginable rate. In 1945 the new factory opened, making only wholesale pies, and within four years the number of employees soared from forty to two hundred: Finns, Swedes, and Italians, and a few Greeks.

As with all immigrant groups, however, one Greek led to another, and by the time Table Talk's employees numbered four hundred — two hundred inside the factory, making a million pies a week, and two hundred outside, delivering the pies to all six New England states and eastern New York — 95 percent of the inside staff was Greek. That was why our father concluded that Table Talk was the only place that one of his daughters could get a job without seriously damaging her good name. Most of the staff, including the bosses, spoke Greek, and all would keep a sharp eye on the behavior of an unmarried Greek girl in their midst.

By the time Father decided he had to send Olga or Kanta to work, he and Cotsidas had known each other for nearly thirty years. Father knew he could rely on Cotsidas' friendship, even though Table Talk's owner was by then a multimillionaire and my father was an underpaid short-order cook who couldn't afford to feed his children. Cotsidas always welcomed Father, and aided him financially several times over the years, remembering that when their situations had been reversed, Father had been kind to him.

"When I came here, Christo Gatzoyiannis was the most prosperous Epirote in Worcester," he told me decades later. "Others were selling bananas at four cents a pound from pushcarts, he was selling them for twenty-five cents from a truck to the most aristocratic families in the county. He made big money and he was always a gentleman. That's why I helped him later. After Nassio Economou sold the truck, your father was never able to get his own business again. It's a pity you didn't know him in the old days."

Father decided to ask Cotsidas to employ his daughter, but he knew Olga was in no condition to work. After her operation she couldn't even speak, and besides, she was firmly opposed to women working in public. The only one who could take a job to help out financially was sixteen-year-old Kanta.

When Father was escorted into the office of the busy Table Talk factory, Cotsidas greeted him with his usual warmth. "Of course, *patrioti,*" he said, "I'll be glad to put your daughter on the line, as long as she's sixteen and has a Social Security card. Do you have her papers with you?"

To my father's dismay, when Cotsidas examined the immigration papers, he discovered that our Uncle Foto had written Kanta's birth date wrong, making it 1933 instead of 1932, so she was now officially listed as only fifteen, a year less than her real age.

"There's nothing I can do, Christo," said Cotsidas. "Bring her back on November sixteenth, when she's officially sixteen, and she can go to work at once."

With our income no better than before, Father continued working at the Terminal Lunch, becoming angrier every day. When school ended in June, I found myself stuck at home with no friends and nothing to do. Olga's depression was worse. Kanta tried to comfort her and handled most of the household chores, and Fotini had found a friend, a little girl who lived two houses away. Rather than stay in the house and watch Olga weep, I wandered around the neighborhood, haunting Hamel's grocery when I was hungry, and exploring new frontiers.

On one of the first hot days I wandered as far as Kendrick Park, across West Boylston and next to the Norton factory. In addition to a baseball diamond and playground equipment, there was a round pool or pond, not very deep, crowded with screaming children escaping the heat. I was wearing the short pants I had brought from Greece, so I plunged in too, being careful to stay away from the deep part in the middle.

Some days later I noticed red patches on my hands and an unbearable itching. Soon it spread all the way up my arms to my neck, down to my stomach, and to my feet as well. My sisters were not surprised that I got sick after my foolhardy plunge into that pool infested with the germs of foreign children.

When the rash turned into white pustules that began to ooze, creating crusts all over my body, my father called Dr. Seidenberg, although he could hardly afford more medical bills. By the time the doctor arrived at our house, the only parts of my body free of scabs were my face, my abdomen, and my upper legs. He looked me over grimly and then told my father that a dozen things could have set it off, from allergies to emotional problems like worry and grief. There was little that he could do, he said; it had to run its course, but he would leave me some ointment. The main thing was not to scratch, and to make sure I didn't, he wrapped my hands in rolls of gauze until I seemed to be wearing mittens. Then he departed, leaving me lying in bed in agony from the itching.

Life was reduced to the four walls of my father's bedroom, where I lay all day with the curtains drawn, staring at the ceiling and listening sporadically to the radio — "Our Gal Sunday" and "The Romance of Helen Trent" during the day and "The Lone Ranger" and "Inner Sanctum" at night — understanding a few more words every day. I often crouched at the window and watched the neighborhood boys playing ball in the back yard next door with a stick and a cork wrapped in yards of tape. Other times I would see them filling balloons with water and bombarding each other, screaming with laughter. Sometimes Greeks would come by to visit, and one old man, the last of the itinerant fruit peddlers, would occasionally take me and Fotini out in his ancient truck to buy ice cream. But on the whole, trapped inside with my gauze mittens and my flaking, itching skin, I thought the summer would never end.

By August new pink skin had begun to replace the weeping crusts. Olga had also begun to regain her voice, and then, near the end of the month, something so wonderful happened that it seemed our luck had finally changed.

The first two weeks of August, when Greeks fast in preparation for the Feast of the Virgin Mary, on August 15, were particularly painful for us because we were approaching the first anniversary of our mother's murder on August 28. As we limited our meals to fruit and boiled vegetables, we couldn't help imagining the torments she must have suffered a year before, during the two months between our escape from the village and her execution. And although none of us spoke of it, we were all wondering where our sister Glykeria was as the death-day approached: whether she was alive on a battlefield or dead and with our mother.

Then, on the morning of August 24, as Olga lay in bed between sleeping and waking, she saw our mother standing before her, wearing the blue dress she had on when she died, her kerchief around her hair. "Olga," she said in the vision, "Glykeria is free. If you want to continue mourning, that's up to you, but tell your sisters, your brother, and your father to put off black, for now it's time to dance and sing and be happy."

Olga sat straight up in bed as the image of our mother faded. She heard the sounds of Father shaving in the bathroom and went in to tell him what she had seen. He studied his reflection in the mirror, razor in his hand. Like most Greeks, Father had a dream book by his bed, and he knew that bad dreams — snakes, blood, death — meant impending windfalls, while good dreams — wealth, feasting, babies — meant something bad was in store. "It must mean that Glykeria's died and now they're together," he said. "Wherever she is, she's been killed."

This made Olga burst into tears. She was sobbing so hard that she couldn't answer the telephone when it rang. Throwing down his razor in exasperation, Father went to the phone. The next thing we heard was a shout: "Chrysoula, you bring that telegram over here and I'm going to kiss you, even if you are a married woman!"

As we crowded around, he told us the news: Glykeria had escaped from the front lines of the Communist guerrillas in the very last battle of the war, only fourteen days before, on the mountain of Vitsi in Macedonia. She had been held in a detention camp for prisoners near Kastoria, but somehow had convinced the Greek Army officers that she had been drafted against her will and wasn't a Communist. Now she was safe in Kastoria in the home of a merchant from Lia named Christos Tatsis. He didn't know our family, but he did have a cousin in Worcester — Leo Tatsis, the husband of Chrysoula, the pretty young woman who had been cooking in our kitchen on the day we arrived.

The very morning that Olga awoke with the voice of our mother in her ears, a telegram arrived at the office of Leo Tatsis' grocery supply business, asking if he could locate Christos Gatzoyiannis of Worcester to tell him that his fifteen-year-old daughter was alive and had escaped from the guerrillas.

We were overwhelmed with both joy and sorrow when we went to church that Sunday to hear Father Rizos read the memorial service for the anniversary of our mother's death and to pass out a tray of *kolyva* to the congregation afterward. That morning we cooked the *kolyva* at home — a concoction of boiled wheat, raisins, almonds, spices, and sugar. After spreading it on the tray and dusting it with powdered sugar, Olga decorated it, while tears ran down her cheeks. She formed a cross of candied almonds in the center, and used pomegranate seeds to make the alpha and omega on either side of the cross, symbolizing the beginning and the end. Finally she draped over the tray a blue ribbon, imprinted with gold letters spelling ELENI GATZOYIANNIS. Each worshipper would eat a bit of the boiled wheat as a symbol of the Resurrection, taken from St. John 12:24: "Verily, verily, I say unto you, Except a corn of wheat fall into the ground and die, it abideth alone: but if it die, it bringeth forth much fruit."

As I watched the congregation filing by, each taking a handful of *kolyva* and murmuring, "May her memory be eternal," it seemed to me that my mother had purposely lightened the pain we would feel on this day by causing the deliverance of her remaining child.

Despite our joy, Glykeria's escape meant new responsibilities and new expenses for our father. She wrote to us from Kastoria that she had walked out of the trenches wearing a baggy uniform and thoroughly infested with lice. She needed clothing, food, medical treatment. Father had to complete the papers for her immigration and pay for her passage. In the meantime he had to send money for her to travel to Igoumenitsa, where my grandparents were living, and pay for her keep until everything was ready for her to sail to America.

As his money evaporated, Father stopped putting change in the pickle jar on the kitchen table, because we emptied it too fast. Now there were no extra quarters to squander on movies and Hershey bars.

With my rash gone, I was eager to return to the cool darkness of the Greendale Theater and lose myself in the dramas on the screen. I asked Father for money, but that only got me a nickel or two a week, not enough for one double bill, let alone the three I had been seeing. Desperate to satisfy my craving for the movies, I decided to take the financing into my own hands. At night Father would come home, hang his jacket on a chair in the bedroom, and then go into the kitchen to eat dinner while Olga and Kanta kept him company. Fotini and I would lie on his bed in our pajamas, listening to his radio. I would wait until he was eating, then go over to his coat, remove his wallet, withdraw a dollar or a couple of quarters, and put it back. Fotini watched this larceny in awed silence but didn't tell on me.

After a few weeks Father noticed the deficit in his wallet and began asking questions, but we all claimed ignorance. Evidently it didn't take long for him to deduce the identity of the culprit, for one night, when I tiptoed over to the jacket, he and the older girls in the kitchen were listening and heard my steps. I rushed back under the covers as they burst in the door. Father checked his jacket and, finding the wallet missing, tore back the bedcovers to reveal the evidence lying next to my hand.

This proof of my guilt set off our customary family fracas, in which my father, bellowing with anger, whipped off his belt and charged at me while I leaped from the bed, out of the bedroom door, over tables and chairs, strewing furniture in my way, dodging obstacles in an effort to evade my rightful punishment, while my sisters screamed: "Don't do it, *Patera*! Don't hit him. You'll murder him! He's only a child!"

When he caught me, as he inevitably did, roaring in triumph, I cowered on the floor as the belt buckle whistled close to my quivering flesh, but Father could never bring himself actually to hit me with it. He contented himself instead with delivering horrifying threats of what would happen if I ever did such a thing again. Even though I always emerged from these encounters unscathed, the terror produced by my sisters' screams and the apparition of my father standing over me brandishing his belt always convinced me that I had narrowly escaped with my skin intact.

Although my father never actually beat me, these battles were further eroding my opinion of him. He had impressed me with his fine clothes and confident manner on the day we met, but within twenty-four hours I had learned he was out of work, in debt, and autocratic with us. My feelings for him had not improved when he had evaded hearing the details of my mother's suffering and let me be put in a class for the retarded. The confrontation over the stolen money only made me resent him more. Even though I knew it was wrong to steal, I felt he was forcing me to do it by taking away the jar of change. We were too poor even to afford a quarter to see the movies, and our poverty was his fault, I reasoned. After forty years in this land of plenty, he should have been the millionaire I had always thought he was.

In the village we suffered like the rest during the famine and the war, but we were always considered the richest family of Lia, because our house had five rooms instead of two and we owned such luxuries as a phonograph and a Singer sewing machine. Now, in Worcester, although we lived like kings by Lia's standards, we were among the poorest Greek families in the community. My mother had always portrayed my father as a great success, but I was coming to the conclusion he was a failure.

These feelings of resentment fueled my original suspicion that my father had purposely delayed bringing us from Greece, despite my mother's pleas, because he liked being free to live and spend his money as he pleased. If he had brought us during the period between the end of

World War II and the outbreak of the Greek civil war, as Nassio Econ-omou brought *his* family, then my mother would be alive now. I knew my sisters felt the same way and blamed Father too, but we were all still too insecure in our new life to risk showing him our anger and suspi-cions. Instead I badgered him with misbehavior, like the thefts from his wallet, while secretly resenting him and promising myself that one day, when I was ready, I would confront him with my accusations.

A detail from the third-grade class picture at Greendale School, 1949. Fotini is at the left in the second row, and Nick is in the center of the top row.

BETWEEN
TWO WORLDS

They change their skies above them,
But not their hearts that roam.
— Kipling, *The Nativeborn*

I PASSED THAT interminable first summer in America feeling like a prisoner, trapped in my itching, suppurating skin in a gloom-filled apartment, wishing I had never left Greece. Even when the eczema passed and my blisters healed, there was no reason to leave the house, because I had no money and no friends.

Then, during one of the worst dog days of August, I heard splashing, shouting, and laughter outside in the street and crept onto the front stoop to see Mr. Cummings, who lived across from us, spraying his children and others from the neighborhood, all wearing bathing suits, with a garden hose. He saw me watching and beckoned, shouting, "Come on over. There's plenty of water for everybody."

I was miserable from the heat and the water looked inviting, but I didn't own a bathing suit, so I just shed my trousers and ran across in my undershorts. This struck the others as screamingly funny, but they welcomed me into the melee anyway and we took turns running through the spray — even Joey Doyle and his sidekicks, who had been avoiding me since last spring.

That evening, as the sun was setting, Joey and his cronies — Brian Hackett, Steve Zilavy, and Marty Akerson — rang our back doorbell. "Wanna come out and play stickball?" Joey muttered when I opened the door. I recognized this brusque invitation as an overture of friendship, and beginning with the ballgame, I was part of the neighborhood gang.

In September, Fotini and I learned we were both to be placed in the third grade. This was a disappointment to me, because at ten I should rightfully have been in the fifth grade, and Fotini, at eleven, should have been in sixth. It was some consolation, however, that we weren't physically any larger than our classmates and that several of my new neighborhood friends would be with me in Miss Katherine Foley's third-grade class.

It was a relief to be included at last in the schoolyard games of the normal boys. I learned to play dodge ball, king of the hill, and war, and even mastered the American version of football so well that I was the second one selected, after Marty Akerson, when sides were chosen. But my old playmates from the ungraded class, especially Jerry and Paul, who considered me their protégé, watched in injured bewilderment.

One day, as I was pulling back for a touchdown pass against Steve Zilavy's team, Jerry lumbered over and clapped a large hand on my shoulder. "Hey, Nick," he said, "come on and play with us, okay?"

Feeling the eyes of my new friends on me, I shrugged his hand off and shouted in a voice that carried across the playground, "Leave me alone, dummy!"

The minute Jerry turned around to shuffle back to the retarded corner, I hated myself. All last year he had devoted himself to me with infinite patience and good intentions, and now I was treating him just like Joey Doyle had treated me. By the time Miss McGinley, my former teacher, came over, I was already hanging my head.

"That wasn't very nice, Nick," she said softly.

"I know. I'm sorry," I muttered.

But Jerry and Paul never again asked me to play with them, and I, finally promoted to the status of a normal kid, made no effort to join them.

Fotini and I both basked in the warmth of Miss Foley's attention. One day she asked, during recess, what had happened to our mother. This kind of question was so painful for me that I simply became mute and walked away, but Fotini readily explained that our mother had been shot by Communist soldiers. We saw tears in our teacher's eyes, and she didn't ask any more questions about our past.

It was Miss Foley who convinced my sister to call herself Tina, a name that would stick, because she could never master the pronunciation of Fotini, which in Miss Foley's mouth came out "Fortina." One day on the playground, noticing that Fotini, unlike the other third-grade girls, was beginning to develop breasts, Miss Foley asked, "Tina, how old are you?"

"Eleven," replied Fotini promptly. "But in Greek I'm twelve."

"But how can that be?" asked Miss Foley, mystified. She called over another teacher to hear this strange statement. Fotini could only repeat herself, for she didn't have enough English to explain that the Greeks, on a child's first birthday, say he is "stepping on" his second year, and so on. Thus we always seemed to be a year older in Greek than we were in English.

I had my own problems with the language. Despite my determination to outshine my classmates, the first time I was called to the front of the class to read out loud, I made a memorable gaffe. The unfamiliar word in the sentence was "weapon." Attempting to sound it out — a technique that always worked in Greek — I read it "wee-*pee*-on." Most of the class tactfully refrained from giggling, but Brian Hackett, a skinny, dark boy who was the worst student and biggest joker of our neighborhood gang, burst into guffaws. I could tell by the expressions on the children's faces that what I had said was somehow obscene. Since Brian happened to be sitting right in front of me, I closed the book and used it to strike him smartly on the side of the head. "Why you laugh?" I demanded, furious, as he wailed and rubbed his ear.

"Brian, you shouldn't make fun of Nicholas; he's just learning," Miss Foley reproved him, taking my side, but by this time everyone was roaring with laughter. From then on, I was reluctant to read aloud, for fear I would hit on another American phrase with embarrassing overtones.

Father had warned us that the English language was strewn with pitfalls. Early in his fruit-peddling career, he said, he had encountered one himself, as he delivered produce door to door. A dignified matron asked him to bring her some fruit or vegetable that wasn't available, and in an effort to say "I can't" he said simply, "Cunt." The outraged woman slapped my courtly, strait-laced father hard across the face, leaving him humiliated and bewildered. "A very risky language," our father warned us. "Ordinary words come out dirty, and there's no poetry in their curses, no imagination."

While Fotini and I were treading the minefield of the schoolyard, Olga and Kanta were also wrestling with strange new customs in the Day School for Immigrants on Lamartine Street. At least they had people who could translate for them.

By September, Olga had recovered her voice enough to attend Lamartine with Kanta, although she kept her neck swathed in scarves to hide her scars. It was progress to get her out of the house at all, but Olga never did feel comfortable in a classroom with young men. The teacher, Mrs. McCarthy, always began class by having the students stand up and sing "The Star-Spangled Banner." Olga, dressed in black from head to toe, including the black scarf around her neck, stubbornly refused to stand up, much less sing, although Kanta rose with the rest. "Olga, why don't you sing with the others?" asked Mrs. McCarthy each time.

After several days of this, Olga pleaded with a Greek female student who knew some English to explain to the teacher that she couldn't sing because she was in mourning for her mother, who had recently died.

"What happened to her?" asked Mrs. McCarthy sympathetically, and after some conversation in Greek, the woman who was translating said, "She was shot by Communist guerrillas."

"They wouldn't have shot her without a good reason!" piped up a young man whose brother was fighting with the guerrillas back in Greece. One of the older students told Kanta and Olga what he had said and they both rushed at him, screaming. Mrs. McCarthy finally restored a tense truce within the classroom and didn't ask Olga to sing again.

She did, however, prod Olga to repeat after her the simple sentence "Mary puts on her hat."

"Mary put on her hat," Olga mumbled.

"No, Olga!" said Mrs. McCarthy. "Mary puts on her hat. Say it. *Puts* on. *Puts* on."

Olga flushed scarlet, tears filled her eyes, and she muttered again, "Mary put on her hat." She was horrified because "puts on" sounded almost exactly like *putsa,* one word no well-bred Greek girl should ever say. All the Greek students in the class were choking with suppressed laughter.

"Come on, Olga, say it out loud. Call it by its rightful name," whispered a Greek woman sitting behind her, who rejoiced in the improbable name of Thelka Fourka. "Say it! *Puts on.*"

Finally Prokopi Koulisis, realizing that Olga was about to cry, said to the teacher, "Don't make her say it, Mrs. McCarthy. In Greek it's a bad word."

Good-natured Mrs. McCarthy was intrigued. "But what does it mean?" she asked Prokopi. By the time he had managed to explain that it was a slang word for the male member, Mrs. McCarthy was laughing so hard the tears were streaming down her cheeks.

Olga never did take to learning English the way Kanta did. After she had spent a month at Lamartine, our father decided to remove her altogether and have her stay home to clean and cook lunch for Fotini and me and make sure we came home straight after school.

That fall our upstairs neighbor, Mrs. Butler, was replaced by a young family: Hal and Rena Ball and their two small children. The Balls had bought the entire three-decker, so they were now our new landlords and collected our $25-a-month rent. Rena, a tall, striking woman of Italian extraction, became for us an interpreter of the strange customs of our new country, from peanut butter to Christmas trees.

The first time was in late October 1949. Olga was in the kitchen one evening cooking supper, and Fotini and I were in the parlor. The back doorbell rang and Olga opened it to find some bizarrely dressed children standing there, shouting something incomprehensible to her.

"Go away," said Olga, slamming the door in their faces. No sooner was she back at the stove than the doorbell rang again and more children, just as strangely dressed, were on the threshold shouting at her. "Go away," she said again, getting nervous, and she slammed the door. Olga suspected that some sort of vendetta was going on: the children of the neighborhood had decided to torment us because we were foreigners and didn't speak their language.

When the doorbell rang again, Olga called in desperation for me and Fotini to answer it. Bravely, we opened the door to find some of our schoolmates standing there, wearing bizarre faces that reminded us of the goblins that danced in the streets of Greece during Carnival; but that was spring and this was October, and besides, these children seemed to expect something from us.

"What you want?" asked Fotini.

"Trick-or-treat, money or eats," cried the children in unison.

Fotini and I looked at each other in bewilderment.

One of the boys, trying to make us understand, reached in his sack and pulled out a candy bar. It was a Mounds — Fotini's favorite, because she loved coconut — and she took it from him eagerly, saying, "Thank you."

At that, all the children burst into laughter, then they took more candy out of their bags and gave it to us, as we grabbed it greedily. When they finally left, shouting behind them "Happy Halloween," we had our hands full.

A few minutes later Rena came downstairs, drawn by all the commotion. Olga cried to her in dismay, "Miz Ball, all time, ring bell — talk! I cook — all time, ring bell — talk!"

"It's Halloween," Mrs. Ball explained. "It's the *custom*. They want you to give them candy. It's a holiday." But Fotini and I, stuffing our mouths with chocolates, had no intention of sharing, so the next time the doorbell rang we pretended there was no one home.

One American custom that immediately fascinated me was riding bicycles. Even the poorest boy in our neighborhood had his own bike, and our street, on a hill, was ideal for soaring downward at stunning speeds. A boy with a bike, I realized, had the whole world of Worcester to explore, while I, who had to go everywhere on foot, rarely got beyond Greendale. It seemed to me that I would truly become an American if I had a bicycle, and I nagged my father relentlessly to buy me one.

"Too dangerous!" he would snap. "You'd break your neck the first day. I didn't bring you all the way from Greece to have you kill yourself riding a bicycle." I suspected, however, that the real reason for his refusal had more to do with our financial situation than with my safety.

After school every day I sat at the top of our street, wistfully watching the other boys careen down the hill, especially Gary Setterlund, a year older than I, who was the paper boy and owned a dazzling red candy-striped Schwinn.

One day after school my pleas touched Gary's heart, and he agreed to let me take a turn on his bike. "You sure you know how to ride it?" he asked.

"It's easy," I declared. It certainly *looked* easy.

I mounted Gary's scarlet steed and, balancing carefully, headed down the street. Nothing blocked my descent, not a vehicle, not a person; the slope was clear all the way down to West Boylston Street. Like Icarus, forgetting his father's warnings in the euphoria of flight, I leaned into the wind as I whizzed past the watching children with incredible speed. As I reached the steepest part of the hill, it suddenly occurred to me that I didn't know how to stop.

Just like a tightrope walker who foolishly looks down, I lost my nerve and my balance together. The cuff of my corduroy pants became entangled in the chain, and the bicycle, pulled by gravity at a breakneck speed over pavement slick with fallen leaves, veered drunkenly into a tree. I became airborne, finally landing to the sound of the crack of my forehead against the curb.

Fotini and her friend Mary Anne Barrett, sitting on the Barretts' front stoop, had ringside seats. Convinced that I was dead, Fotini began to scream, which drew Mr. Barrett to the window. "Take him home!" he called out. "He has to go to the hospital!"

More worried about Gary Setterlund's bike and Olga's reaction than about dying, I put one hand to my forehead to stanch the flow of blood and staggered home, with Fotini at my side. Olga was standing in a closet on a chair, straightening Father's belongings. When she heard Fotini and saw me drenched with blood, she fell off the chair and began screaming twice as loud as Fotini, in the operatic, keening lament of the village, a sound that could be heard blocks away.

"*Foula*, don't be scared, I'm all right," I kept repeating, more frightened by Olga's cries than by my broken skull.

Finally Olga collected herself enough to dial the number at the Terminal Lunch. "Come home, Nick's killed himself!" she yelled when my father answered. "There's blood all over everything."

My father's nature was to be calm in a crisis and then to blow up afterward. He walked out of the Terminal Lunch despite his co-workers' threats, hailed a taxi, rode it to the house, wrapped my head in a bath towel, and took me straight to the nearest emergency room, at Hahnemann Hospital on Lincoln Street. There the gash in my forehead was stitched up by a blond female intern from Sweden who was so kind, her hands so gentle, that I felt no pain. I was so lonely for a maternal hand to coddle and console me that I was almost glad I had split my skull open.

The whole episode ended better than I anticipated. My father didn't hit or berate me for my carelessness but instead told me never to borrow another child's bike. "If it means so much to you," he said, "I'll get you a bicycle with training wheels for Christmas."

The next day I got to stay home from school and eat egg-lemon soup. In the afternoon all the neighborhood children came by to gaze in awe at my bandage and my stitches. "Didn't your father take a strap to you?" they asked.

"No, not *my* father," I announced proudly. "He not mad at all. He say, buy me my own bike for Christmas."

On November 16, Kanta turned seventeen. According to her immigration papers, she was now officially sixteen, old enough to be employed. That same day Father arrived at the Lamartine school to take her out of class and directly to Angelo Cotsidas' Table Talk bakeries. Mrs. McCarthy was reluctant to let her go, for Kanta was one of her best students. She explained that according to law, Kanta had to attend night classes at Commerce High School to learn English until she was eighteen. Before they left, my father had to sign papers promising that as her guardian, he would guarantee her attendance at those classes.

From the beginning, Kanta loved working at Table Talk, even though she worked six days a week, up to eleven hours a day, for ninety-five cents an hour. She loved the white uniforms and the hairnets, the camaraderie among the workers. Cotsidas began by putting her at the slowest machine in the shop, to set the empty pie tins on the wheel. Another woman added the bottom crust, another the filling, another the top crust, and so on. It was like the United Nations there, Kanta thought: Irish, Albanians, Poles, Lithuanians, but the majority were Greeks, and they all kept an eye on the youngest employee.

They were allowed ten-minute coffee breaks in the morning and afternoon and a half-hour for lunch (which Kanta brought from home). During those breaks the older Greek women looked Kanta over speculatively, saying, "You're so pretty, why don't you wear a little lipstick? . . . You're so pale, you need a little rouge on your cheeks."

These were daring suggestions. Kanta shuddered to think what her father would do if he caught her wearing makeup, but nevertheless, after several weeks, she agreed to try another girl's Tangee colorless lipstick, which slowly darkened on the skin. When it was time for her to go home, she scrubbed ruthlessly at her lips to get it off. Still, Father often asked, "Why are your lips so red?" and Kanta always answered, "It's just the cold." She couldn't go so far as to paint her fingernails scarlet like the other girls at work, but she put on colorless nail polish. When Father inquired suspiciously why her nails shone so, she would answer quickly, "It's all that oil in the pie dough!"

From the beginning, Kanta's weekly paycheck ranged between $60 and $70 a week, compared to our father's $55 — a fortune to us. She would turn her check over to Father every Thursday night and he would keep it all, except for her bus fare plus fifty cents to cover a nickel carton of milk every morning and afternoon. But Kanta always hoarded the milk money; she had better things to do with it.

One day, after Kanta had been working at Table Talk for some time, one of Father's Greek cronies brought his niece to work there. He caught sight of Kanta, the picture of a stylish factory girl in her uniform, hairnet, and cherry-red lips.

"You're painting your mouth with lipstick!" thundered the man, whose name was Vasili Stathis. "*Now* I'm going to tell your father!"

Kanta suffered an agony of guilt and dread throughout a day that seemed an eternity. She went home determined to confess before her accuser arrived. When Father got home, she faced him grimly and said in a quavering voice, "There's something I have to tell you, *Patera*."

He turned pale. "You've been fired!"

"No, no — nothing like that," she said quickly. "It's just that today, for the first time in my life, just as an experiment, I put on some lipstick, and Vasili Stathis came in and saw me."

Father sank into a chair, sighing, and pondered this new complication of parenthood. "Why would you paint your lips when you're already so pretty?" he asked finally.

"But *Baba*, all the other girls at work do it," she pleaded, "and I didn't want to look like a hick from the village. They make fun of me."

Father reflected a while longer. "All right," he finally said, to her astonishment. "If all the other Greek women at work do it, then you can too, but promise you'll never put anything on your cheeks, and never do it outside Table Talk."

Kanta's classical beauty was not lost on the male employees of Table Talk. One young man in particular, Greek but American-born, which made him unsuitable as a potential groom, always looked longingly at Kanta. When she passed he would say in Greek, using her proper name, "Good day, Alexandra."

"Don't you speak to me, or I'll tell my father and he'll come here and kill you," she always retorted, as a well-bred girl should. Nevertheless, in her heart of hearts she thought the young man attractive.

Three evenings a week Kanta attended English classes for immigrants at Commerce High School, as the law required. Cotsidas gave her permission to leave early on those days, and she would whip off her uniform and hairnet at seven o'clock and by seven-fifteen be at the nearby high school where she would attend classes until nine. Then she would catch the number 30 bus back from the center of town to Greendale Avenue and fall asleep by ten-thirty.

Kanta was young and strong and quick to adjust to work, but eleven-hour workdays plus three evenings of high school a week, with only one day off, left her exhausted. She would eat and fall into bed like a stone, too tired to gossip with Olga, who had been alone in the house all day and was longing for company.

Kanta was soon promoted to putting the top crust on the pies, before they were stamped down, neatly ridged around the edges, and propelled into the ovens. Pleased with her success as a working girl, she was horrified one day when she was called off the line by Theodore Tonna, Cotsidas' stern, bespectacled partner, because "the police are here for you." Tonna was furious. "Don't we let you off special to go to school, and now the police are here saying you never show up?" he demanded as they walked to his office. "What have you been doing with your evenings? We gave you this job as a favor to your father, you know. We don't need aggravation from the police."

Shaking, Kanta went in to face the two officers, and swore she had faithfully attended school. The police waved papers in her face and demanded proof. That evening she stormed in to the principal of Commerce High School and told him what had happened at work. "I want to learn English and I come here every night," she said. "Most of all, I don't want to lose my job. We poor people."

The principal pulled out the records and discovered that they had confused Kanta's last name, Gatzoyiannis, with that of another Greek immigrant, a girl named Karayiannis, who had been skipping classes. He agreed to write a note to Kanta's employers explaining the mistake. "Gatzoyiannis, Karayiannis — it all sounds the same," he muttered. (Later, when Kanta finished the classes for immigrants, that same principal wrote several letters to our father begging him to enroll her in regular high school night classes because she was so smart, but Father only tore up the letters in anger, saying, "You put him up to writing this. You only want to go there to run around with men!")

Glykeria's impending arrival in America and Kanta's profitable new job seemed portents that our luck was changing at last. A third stroke of good fortune occurred one morning as Father, waiting for his bus on the corner of West Boylston, heard someone call his name.

A sleek Oldsmobile pulled over, and inside he saw John Kotsilimbas-Davis, a fellow immigrant who had arrived in Worcester the same year as my father — 1910 — and found work in the factories. But John and his brother Charley had eventually pooled their money to purchase from some Yankees an establishment called Putnam and Thurston, which they had made into Worcester's finest restaurant. In the heart of the city on Mechanic Street, it was an elegant place with leather banquettes, crystal chandeliers, time-darkened oil paintings, and a wine list bound between gilded covers. It was to "Puts," as it was called by its regular customers, that Worcester's leading families, with names like Stoddard, Booth, and Jeppson, came to eat on Sunday after services at the Episcopal church on Park Avenue or during their sons' vacations from Groton or Exeter.

The Kotsilimbas-Davis brothers had risen far from their native village: they were each elected to a term as president of the Greek community, they wore diamond rings on their little fingers, and they sent their sons to Harvard. My father was flattered to have John Kotsilimbas pull over and call to him, "Where're you headed, Christo? Get in, I'll drive you there."

John, it turned out, was on his way back from a funeral, and he showed a warm interest in my father's welfare.

"I hear you're working for your old partners at the Terminal Lunch," he began. "They paying you well?"

"Fifty-five a week," replied my father, spitting out the words. "I'm worth twice that. But with my children here, I have to compromise."

"They treat you good over there?" inquired John solicitously. His prominent nose and deep-set, intelligent eyes gave him the look of a balding fox.

"They'd treat me like shit if I let them!" exploded my father, with his usual naive honesty, his injured ego making him completely forget any shred of cunning he might have. "Insults, griefs, every day! They don't know how lucky they are to have me!"

"You're right about that!" said John sympathetically. "I'll tell you what. Come work for me as a chef. You know we're the best in town. I'll match what they're paying you — I can't do any better right now, but we'll see how it goes. You'll get better treatment from me, I promise you that."

And that was how John Kotsilimbas-Davis managed to steal our father away from the Terminal Lunch without even having to increase his salary.

A satisfied grin spread over Father's face as he imagined the rage of Christos Stathis and Nassio Economou when he announced he was leaving them to cook for the best restaurant in town. It would be even more galling to his former partners that he was going to work for one of the Eleans — from the province of Elis in the Peloponnesus — for in the early decades of the century, among the Worcester Greeks, the Epirotes like my father and Nassio and the Eleans like Kotsilimbas-Davis had been bitter enemies.

The immigrant Greeks of Worcester split into two churches and two rival factions only two years after founding the first Greek church, St. Spyridon, in a dingy rented storefront on Grafton Street — a church so poor that, according to my father, there was only a single wooden chair for the bishop's throne, a wooden desk for an altar, and a washbasin for a baptismal font. In 1917 certain members of the congregation bolted to form their own church in another rented room, this one on Trumbull Street, under the name Saints Taxiarchae. The reason for the schism was the passionate hostility between the two political parties in Greece: the followers of the prime minister Eleutherios Venizelos and those loyal to the monarchy.

My father and all his fellow Epirotes had grown up in northern Greece under Turkish subjugation, and naturally they were attracted to Venizelos' "great idea" of winning back all the Greek-populated areas then held by the Ottoman Empire. The immigrants from Elis, in contrast, had grown up free Greeks and admired the monarchy, which they credited for the stability and prosperity of their province. The Eleans had had more opportunity for education and more access to the amenities of modern civilization, and perhaps that was why they assimilated into American culture a bit faster then my father's *patriotes*. Anglicizing their names, Costa Androtsopoulos became Charles Andreson, Panayiotis Belloyiannis became Peter Bell, and Yiannis and Konstantinos Kotsilimbas became John and Charley Kotsilimbas-Davis.

When World War I broke out in 1914, Prime Minister Venizelos wanted to commit Greece to the side of the Allies, whereas King Constantine I, educated in Germany and married to a sister of Kaiser Wilhelm, wanted Greece to support the Central Powers. The king resisted Venizelos so strongly that he forced him to resign as prime minister in 1915, and the country was politically divided for two years, until the Allies made Constantine abdicate in favor of his son Alexander and Venizelos was recalled as prime minister.

In Worcester the Greeks were no less passionately divided than their countrymen across the sea. Each faction had its own Greek-language newspaper, published in New York, to stay abreast of the news: the *Atlantis* for the royalists and the *Ethnikos Kyrix,* or *National Herald,* for the Venizelists.

In 1917 a political argument in one of Worcester's earliest Greek coffeehouses became so heated that it ended with one of the participants shot dead. The Venizelists and the monarchists discovered that they could no longer tolerate attending the same church, working in the same restaurant, or playing cards in the same coffeehouse as members of the opposing camp, and soon each faction created its own. Greek employers would go so far as to fire workers who were reportedly seen worshipping or gambling in the wrong place.

Over the years, these political schisms flared up periodically, despite the efforts of Greek prelates to unite the warring factions of their flock, for a Greek takes his politics just as seriously as he does the virtue of his wife or daughter. But Venizelos died in exile in 1936, and a charismatic bishop from Epiros — Athenagoras, who ultimately became patriarch of the Eastern Orthodox Church — was named head of the church in America and succeeded in uniting the Greeks once again. By the time John Kotsilimbas-Davis offered my father a job as chef at Putnam and Thurston, the old wounds had healed over. Father jumped at the chance to escape the Terminal Lunch, even if it meant working for an Elean. Not until much later did he realize that if he had answered John's questions a little more carefully, he could probably have negotiated a much better salary as well.

As the first Christmas in our new country drew near, I realized that this holiday was a much bigger festival to the Americans than it was to Greeks. In Greendale School we decorated the windows of our classroom and practiced special songs. The stores blossomed with decorations and a dazzling variety of temptations in every window. Even at our Greek church, where I had been inducted into the ranks of the altar boys, wearing blue satin robes and holding the incense burner every third Sunday when it was my turn, I saw children being coached to portray angels, shepherds, and the Holy Family for the Christmas Eve service.

Some of my third-grade classmates told me about a fat man named Santa Claus who came down the chimney on Christmas Eve to distribute gifts to good boys and girls, but I realized this was some kind of folktale and laughed derisively. In Greece there were the *kallikantzaroi*: evil goblins with red eyes, hairy as monkeys, who came out of the earth at Christmas to plague people with their pranks until the blessing of the water on Epiphany drove them back underground. They were blamed for souring milk, breaking mirrors, and frightening the livestock. Villagers used to keep a fire burning on the hearth for the entire twelve days between Christmas and Epiphany to prevent the little demons from coming down the chimney — the opposite of leaving milk and cookies to welcome Santa Claus. It was easier to believe in gremlins who caused tangles in girls' hair than in a fat philanthropist who left toys for all America's children in one night. I taunted my classmates mercilessly for their gullibility.

Father's only gesture to the holiday was to place some plastic electric candles in the windows of the room facing the street. "It's the American way," he said. "We don't want the neighborhood to think we're not Christians."

The excitement at school started to affect me. I could hardly go to sleep on Christmas Eve, so eager was I to see my new bike. The next morning Fotini and I got up early and ran into the kitchen where we found two wrapped boxes on the table. My heart sank when I saw that the one with my name on it was far too small to hold a bicycle. I tore it open and discovered in horror a wool suit in a dark shade of brown.

"Where's my bicycle!" I demanded, turning on my father. "You promised me a bicycle!"

"You need a suit, you don't need a bicycle!" he retorted. "Now that you're an altar boy and it's winter, that suit with the leather patches isn't good enough. You heard your godfather say it makes you look like a cowboy. Winter's no time for a bicycle anyway."

I could hardly believe that he had betrayed me this way, breaking his promise after I had told every boy in the neighborhood that I was getting a bike. I ran into the bedroom, slamming the door behind me, trying not to cry. Through the closed door I could hear Fotini's squeals of joy when she unwrapped a large doll with blond hair and a pink dress, which Kanta had bought for her at Woolworth's with the money she had saved from her milk allowance. At eleven, Fotini was already big for dolls, but she had never had one before, and she crooned over this one as though it were a real baby.

After a while I heard my father open the bedroom door. I was lying in bed, glaring at the ceiling, my Christmas gift in a pile on the floor. I refused to acknowledge his presence.

"Get up now and put on your new suit!" he barked. "People will be coming soon and I want you looking decent." A note of appeasement crept into his voice as he added, "There's *koulourakia* and *kourabiedes* in the kitchen. Your sisters have been cooking all week."

I knew that all his acquaintances would be coming around to wish my father "many years" for his name day, since Christmas is the feast day of everyone named Christos. I also knew there would be my favorite holiday pastries, for the scents of honey, cinnamon, and buttery shortbreads had filled the kitchen for days. But I was not in the mood to listen to people wishing my father good health and a long life. Because of him I was the only boy on Greendale Avenue without a bike, and now I had to figure out how to face my friends.

Eventually I was coaxed out of the bedroom by the promise of sweets. All afternoon and evening a stream of visitors arrived. They made a big fuss about my new Christmas suit, ruffling my hair (which I hated) and sometimes slipping a quarter into my hand as they said, "Many years for your father."

All the talk was of Glykeria's impending arrival — the papers were nearly ready, and she was expected to set sail from Greece in February. She had sent us a photograph taken by one of the nationalist soldiers when she was in the detention camp, after she convinced them she really was sympathetic to the government side and agreed to reveal details of the guerrilla locations. In the posed photograph, Glykeria, her round baby face contrasting oddly with the baggy man's uniform she was wearing, knelt on the ground, flanked by two other captured *andartinas* and surrounded by soldiers, while she pointed dramatically off to the side, presumably toward Communist emplacements. She had scribbled on the back of the photo, closing with the traditional sentimental farewell to absent loved ones: "Aug. 12, '49. Souvenir. These are soldiers with the lieutenant and me. You see a person without a soul, a body without blood."

The tiny photograph was passed from hand to hand and studied by all our visitors. "She's still a child," they murmured. "Imagine what she's been through, a young girl like that!" With a glance at us younger children, someone added cryptically, "We must pray that she has not been harmed."

This veiled suggestion that Glykeria might have been violated by the guerrillas clearly made my father nervous, for he retorted in a loud voice, "Her salvation is a miracle! We do not quibble with God's miracles. We will welcome her with open arms, whatever she has suffered."

As his temper rose, Kanta scurried out of the kitchen, bearing food. Although Olga was in charge of the cooking, she was too shy or too depressed to face the company, and Kanta did all the serving. The traditional ritual was to offer the visitor first a glass of cold water and a "spoon sweet," a candied fruit in syrup, on a silver tray. The guest would raise the glass, toast the honoree, and take a bite of the sweet, and then the dishes were whisked away to be replaced with alcoholic drinks like ouzo or brandy and bite-sized *mezedakia,* such as tiny triangular cheese or spinach pies, spicy meatballs, bits of lamb, tiny fried squid, and squares of rich *pastitsio.* Serving these courses kept Kanta on the run while Olga, in the kitchen, battled to replenish the supply of food. I, meanwhile, glowered on the edge of the room with a face like a storm cloud while strangers pinched my cheeks and wondered what could be wrong with the boy — so solemn on Christmas Day!

The next afternoon brought the visit I was dreading. The doorbell rang, and I opened the door to find Joey Doyle, Brian Hackett, Marty Akerson, and Steve Zilavy all standing there.

"Well, let's see your bike," said Marty. There was an expectant pause.

"I told my father, don't want a bike," I said. "I ask for new clothes instead." I was already wearing my new suit, in anticipation of their arrival, to prove I *did* get something.

They all started shouting at once. "You're crazy!" "You said what?" "You wanted clothes more than a bike?"

"I don't need a bike," I said, with a superior smile. "We get something better."

"What's that?" they all clamored.

"A car!" I lied. "My father buying a car."

"So what?" Marty said, the cagiest of the four. "You can't drive a car for years."

"He take me anywhere I want. I don't need a bike," I said, holding my ground.

"Gee, can I go with you sometimes?" asked Brian, the most gullible of the group, whose father owned no car.

Slowly they began to believe me. Before long I was believing it myself.

"Well, that's pretty neat," said Joey. "I guess a car *is* better than a bike. Feel like a game of football?"

I should have followed the wisdom of Greek sailors, who stay in port between Christmas and Epiphany so the *kallikantzaroi* can't do them any harm. Just as I was intercepting a pass from Steve Zilavy, I skidded on the pavement and tore a huge rip in the knee of my brand-new Christmas suit.

This time there was little chance that Father would overlook my crime. There was no way I could repair the damage, because he was the only one in my family who knew how to sew.

After quickly changing clothes, I decided I might be able to find a substitute pair of pants and pay for them on the installment plan, starting with the quarters I had been given for Christmas. A survey of all the stores within walking distance, however, revealed not a single pair of trousers resembling that strange shade of brown.

To hide the damage, I began to wear my raincoat indoors and out, whenever I had to get dressed up, always insisting, in answer to my father's queries, that I was cold. Every Sunday, as soon as I got to church I would dart into the altar boys' vestry and slip out of my raincoat and into the robes, which hung below the knees. By this ruse I managed to keep hidden from my family the damage I'd done to my new Christmas suit, but every Sunday and holiday I was terrified I would get caught.

Luckily, my father and Olga didn't notice anything, because they were so distracted by the approaching arrival of Glykeria, who set sail from Piraeus in early February 1950 on the steamship *LaGuardia*. Father borrowed $500 from Angelos Cotsidas to help pay for Glykeria's passage. When he arrived at Table Talk's head office to ask the favor, Cotsidas peeled five $100 bills off a roll and said, "Take it, old friend, and don't worry about paying it back. It's enough to know that your daughter has been spared."

Father, with characteristic dignity, shook his head. "You will have your money back within the year, Angelo," he said. "Christos Gatzoyiannis does not take charity."

That money plus Kanta's salary from Table Talk made it possible for us to buy some furniture to fill the empty parlor. Kanta and Olga went with Father to Glaser's Furniture Store, where they bought a massive, square living room set of blue and burgundy velvet, a couch and two overstuffed chairs. There was a blue glass coffee table to match, and they added doilies and antimacassars, gilded statuettes and plastic flower arrangements, prints of Greek saints and prelates; and my father's framed membership certificate in AHEPA, the American-Hellenic Educational Progressive Association, hung near the ceiling. They put up flowered draperies and lace curtains and then stood back to admire the luxurious effect of all those patterns and rich fabrics.

Just before Glykeria's arrival, Kanta, who had discovered from her co-workers how American women achieve an abundance of curls, went to a beauty parlor on Main Street to get a permanent. When her hair was rolled onto dozens of tiny electrodes connected by wires to a sinister-looking machine and she could smell it roasting, Kanta began to have qualms, but she told herself grimly, "I asked for this, now I've got to go through with it." After an hour of cooking and another half hour of work by the beautician, she emerged with a helmet of tightly marcelled waves. She held her head high, feeling like a real American at last.

We knew that Glykeria's arrival would bring even more visitors than Christmas Day had, all curious to learn about the girl's ordeal in the guerrilla army and if she had been changed by it. We children became more and more nervous as the day approached, for only Glykeria knew what had happened to our mother during the two months between our escape from the village and her execution. We wanted to know the details of *Mana*'s last days, but were afraid to hear them.

Father said we had better prepare a huge supply of spoon sweets for Glykeria's arrival. Olga, who had had no idea how to cook when we first arrived, had learned how to make these sweets, as well as cookies and pastries, from my godmother, Eugenia Economou, who coached her over the phone as Olga worked in the kitchen, cradling the receiver on her shoulder. From Eugenia, Olga had learned to make candied cherries and grapes and the braided cookies called *koulourakia*. Now she felt perfectly capable of candying the bags full of quinces that Father ordered from Jimmy Tzouras' Standard Fruit store. But Father insisted on overseeing the operation himself, to make sure the expensive *kedonia* came out just right. He told Olga to slice and clean the quinces and then to wait until he got home from work.

That night after dinner Father put the fruit in a huge vat of water and sugar on the stove and set it to boiling gently. It would take hours until the quince were done, and he and Olga were both exhausted, so he decided to set the alarm clock to wake him up at one A.M. and turn them off.

The pot of boiling quinces was so big that it suffocated the flame on the gas burner, and that night, as we slept, gas silently filled the house. The next thing Olga knew, she heard Father's voice shouting, "Children! Wake up! Are you alive?" She opened her eyes, but couldn't raise her head. There seemed to be a huge weight holding her down in bed. Olga noticed that Father's bald pate and forehead were all mottled with blue patches, as if he had spilled ink on himself.

Father had somehow awakened and managed to get the window open. He succeeded in rousing Olga and me, but neither Fotini nor Kanta could get up. "The child wants to wake up, but she can't," he cried, wringing his hands over Fotini. He dragged her to the back door and opened it, then went back for Kanta, who managed to stand up but immediately collapsed on the floor.

Finally he managed to drag all of us out to the square of green grass in the back, where a single apple tree grew. Leaning against the tree, we were all heartily sick, but, to my father's relief, alive. He didn't know what had awakened him in time, but he suspected that it was one of those miracles, like Glykeria's escape, that meant our mother was still watching over us.

The next day Father called John Kotsilimbas-Davis at Putnam and Thurston. "I'm not coming in today," he said. "We're all sick. We almost died last night. One more hour of sleep, and my daughter would have arrived from Greece to find her family all dead!"

Fotini and I didn't go to school that day either, but sat weakly on the front stoop, drawing deep breaths of clean air and occasionally leaning over the stairs to vomit again.

A few days later, on February 17, the steamship *LaGuardia* docked in New York harbor. Father was there to greet his last immigrant child. Because of our tight finances, he didn't rent a car this time but took a train to New York, and he didn't waste money on extra tickets. We children waited at home as the house filled up with relatives and friends.

On the dock Glykeria embraced Father happily, but on the train she started to cry, and she wept all the way to Worcester as she watched the grimy, unfriendly houses of America speeding by and compared the view to the whitewashed houses, flower-filled courtyards, and outdoor cafés of Greece. It was a dark February day, and filthy snow was everywhere. "How can I be happy in such a place, *Patera*?" she said weeping.

But when she climbed the steps on Greendale Avenue to embrace my sisters and me and hear the welcoming cries of a houseful of relatives, when she saw the maroon and blue velvet furniture, the green tablecloth, the blue coffee table, the lace curtains, and the cabbage-rose–printed wallpaper, she declared that it was the most beautiful house she had ever seen.

We all started to cry at the sight of our sister, whom we had feared was dead. Father called for silence and announced, "No tears! Now I have all my children here, alive and together. At last we can be happy, sing and dance and put away our black clothes."

When we pulled away to study Glykeria, we were a bit taken aback at her appearance. The little blond imp we remembered, after starving for so long, had gained forty pounds since she had escaped from the battlefront, greedily devouring all the candy she could buy with the money Father sent. In Igoumenitsa she had paid a dressmaker to make her a dress she felt was suitable for America: it was of dazzling green satin, with short sleeves and a full, flowing skirt. With it she was wearing white ankle socks and sturdy laced-up oxfords. Kanta looked at her in dismay, imagining what her girlfriends at Table Talk would say, and thought, "I've got to put her on a diet."

That night all the girls slept together in one bed, as they had slept together on the floor of our home in the village. They whispered and laughed for hours, but none of us asked Glykeria about our mother, for it was still too soon. The next day more visitors arrived, and the partying and laughing never seemed to stop. Along with the Greeks came a reporter and a photographer from the city's afternoon daily, the *Evening Gazette,* to do a story about the young refugee girl who had been forced to fight with the Communist guerrillas and had escaped to join her family in Massachusetts.

Father did all the talking to the reporter as Glykeria sat shyly by his side, her hands clasped in her lap. Then she was photographed wearing the same green satin dress she had arrived in, holding a Greek doll — a Klephtic warrior dressed in a white skirt, red fez, black embroidered vest, and shoes with pompons — a souvenir she had bought in Athens.

"She had a bad time," Father told the reporters. "Here, in her new home, she will learn to be young and happy again."

Like our father, we all smiled at the newspaper photographer and we smiled at Glykeria, but inwardly we were all worrying that when she revealed the details of the past twenty months, she would tell us things we couldn't bear to hear.

7

Glykeria, still dressed as an *andartina*, pointing to the mountain battleground where she escaped from the guerrillas

CHORDS OF
MEMORY

Oh, I will think of things gone long ago
And weave them to a song.

— Euripides, *Trojan Women*

GLYKERIA IS AN ancient name derived from the word meaning "sweet." From the beginning, it seemed a misnomer for my feisty, head-strong, fearless third sister.

In the village, Glykeria, a towheaded urchin, would always be at the very front of a funeral procession, eager to see the body being buried or the bones dug up three years later, while Kanta felt faint at the mere sound of funeral bells. Glykeria was always testing our mother's patience until it ran out; then, when *Mana* tried to punish her, the little girl would run through the village imploring all the saints to witness her death. She bossed us younger children like a tyrant and didn't hesitate to scold God himself when she felt He had made a mistake.

Now, as visitors filled our house to hear the latest news from Greece, Glykeria sat in the place of honor on the maroon velvet couch, resplendent in her green satin dress, and regaled her audience with tales of her adventures. No matter how often she told it, we all loved the story of how she had escaped from the Communist front lines in the last battle of the war.

After *Mana*'s execution, Glykeria was persecuted by the guerrillas in our village. They called her in for interrogations every day and made her a scapegoat, giving her extra work carrying supplies and wounded men over the mountains to make her pay for the escape of her sisters and brother. When the guerrillas finally retreated into Albania, taking the inhabitants of our village with them, one woman, who was a favorite of the Communists, made Glykeria carry all her belongings on her back.

After they finally reached Shkodra, in northern Albania, at the end of a terrifying journey by foot, army truck, and overladen coal barges on rough seas, the villagers were deposited in a two-story barracks that had been used as a stable and told to shovel the manure out of the cubicles where they would live. With not even a blanket for warmth, Glykeria shared a cubicle with fifteen other villagers. For six months they survived on daily rations of one scoop of beans and a piece of rock-hard bread. She washed her lice-infested dress in the lake and searched for wild greens to eat and firewood to burn.

Then, on an icy day in March 1949, Glykeria was dragged with other screaming girls onto an army truck to become an *andartina*, a female guerrilla, even though she was the only one under sixteen. The conscripted women were sent south by train toward the battlefront in northern Macedonia. There Glykeria had to walk from the train through the snow wearing only sandals of pigskin soles tied to her bare feet with string, while the Macedonian peasant women watched her in pity, murmuring "poor thing" in their musical tongue as she passed, the smallest of the conscripts.

Outfitted at the training camp with a baggy man's uniform and cleated boots, Glykeria proved to be hopeless as a fighter from the beginning. She fell asleep on guard duty, and when she learned that a girlfriend of hers from home, drafted along with her, had been cut in half by machine-gun fire, Glykeria threw down her rifle and refused to take it up again.

Finally the guerrillas decided to make the child a telephone operator so she could work at the switchboard in the relative safety of an underground bunker. With three other women soldiers she worked the phones by day, relaying calls from the field, and at night she laid telephone cables deep in the ground and fortified the lines with buried land mines.

As she told of the guerrilla life, Glykeria chuckled at the memory of her callousness. She became accustomed to seeing dismembered heads, arms, and legs on the battlefield, and once, she said, she was so thirsty during a battle that she drank from a stream even though it ran red with blood from the bodies clogging it higher up the mountain.

On the night of the last battle, August 10, 1949, as the nationalist artillery launched a surprise assault on the Communist guerrillas on Vitsi, attacking from five different points, Glykeria was working the telephones in the underground bunker with one other woman. Over the static of her earphones she heard the artillery shells and bombs, so she knew the soldiers were getting near. Suddenly the telephones in the guerrillas' front lines, which had been silent for an hour, crackled into life. A strange male voice asked, "Who is this?"

"What is the password?" Glykeria replied automatically, as she had been taught.

There was a pause. "I don't know," said the voice.

Glykeria realized she was talking to a soldier from the nationalist army. She could visualize exactly where he was standing, because she had placed the cables herself. With a glance at the other girl, who was busy at her own phones, Glykeria whispered into her mouthpiece, "Listen carefully." Then she described exactly where the guerrilla officers were based and where the underground pillboxes were concealed.

As the mortars of the attacking soldiers began to hit home, a guerrilla rushed into the bunker and told the operators to retreat, carrying the heavy suitcaselike telephones with them. Outside it was dark, the sky black except for the flash of mortars in the distance. All around they heard the shriek of bullets whizzing past their heads. When they reached a spot where they could look back, the two girls realized that the government troops were almost upon them. Glykeria seized the arm of the other girl, whose name was Marika, and cried, "Let's give ourselves up!"

Marika stared at her, then reached for the rifle slung over her shoulder. "Are you suggesting that we betray our comrades?" she asked. She leveled the gun at Glykeria's chest, and then, as an artillery shell barely missed them, Marika turned and disappeared into the shadows.

Glykeria dropped the telephones and hid in a ravine for hours. Eventually, when she heard the voices of the nationalist soldiers, she jumped into the path of an officer, screaming, "Mr. Lieutenant, I give up! The Communists killed my mother! My father's in America. I'm with you!"

Glykeria was one of many guerrillas, men and women, who surrendered that night and claimed loyalty to the nationalist side. They were herded into a prison camp, and many of the women were beaten because the soldiers didn't believe that they weren't Communists. Glykeria was saved by a Colonel Constantinides, a dazzling figure on a huge white horse who picked her out of the mass of prisoners, probably because she was younger and blonder than the others and her fair hair, ruddy skin, and wide forehead reminded him of the faces of his home province — Epiros.

When the colonel asked Glykeria the name of her native village, she discovered that he knew our grandfather, Kitso Haidis, and had even slept in his house in Lia. Colonel Constantinides said he would have her transferred to the detention center in the nearby town of Kastoria, where she would be treated more humanely than the Communist prisoners. Eventually he got her released into the custody of Christos Tatsis, a tall, graying shopkeeper in Kastoria who, like us, had originally come from Lia. After two weeks of pleading with the authorities to release the child, Tatsis came to collect Glykeria from the police station, carrying an umbrella to protect her from the rain. But our sister was so ashamed of her appearance in her filthy uniform and oversized boots, her hair matted and tangled, her body covered with lice, that she begged her benefactor, "Please, Mr. Tatsis, let me walk behind you so that nobody will guess you know me."

That was the day that Christos Tatsis sent a telegram to his cousin Leo Tatsis in Worcester, asking him to find Christos Gatzoyiannis and tell him that his daughter was alive and safe. The kindhearted shopkeeper kept Glykeria in his home, bought her new clothes, and fed her. With the help of his elderly mother and his sister he burned her uniform, cut off her long braids, which were too tangled to comb, and treated the sores that covered her. Every day the sister bathed the girl in a large wooden trough and applied a homemade ointment to the red welts.

After two weeks of living on the charity of the Tatsis family, Glykeria finally received a letter and a money order from our father. She was put on a small plane to Yannina, and screamed in fear the whole way. Our grandfather met her and took her to the refugee barracks in Igoumenitsa. There he and our grandmother launched a campaign to convince Glykeria to stay with them and care for them in their old age instead of joining the rest of her family in America.

Everyday *Papou* treated her to rich halvah and pastries stuffed with cream, walnuts, and honey, and Glykeria ate enough to make up for all the months of starvation she had suffered. But she remained unmoved by his pleas and threats. "I'm going to America, *Papou*," she insisted. "As soon as my papers come. Every day I pray I'll get my papers."

One day the old man came down the road from the post office holding something behind him and crying. "You prayed for the papers, and you see, they've come," he said. "Now there will be no more grandchildren for us, nobody left."

"Maybe I'll come back someday, Grandpa," Glykeria said, knowing that she never would. And when he put her on the *LaGuardia* in Piraeus and she watched him standing on the pier, she had a premonition that she would never see him again, but she didn't cry. She was going to America.

We all loved hearing about Glykeria's adventures as a girl guerrilla, despite the gory parts. The ending, of course, was a happy one. She would spin out her odyssey the way our grandmother, sitting by the hearth, used to entertain us with folktales and ghost stories. Glykeria never brought up the subject of whether or not the guerrillas had molested her, and none of us dared to ask. We suspected that she would tell us when she was ready.

Many of the callers who arrived at Greendale Avenue every night to question her were Greek "bachelors" like Jimmy Tzouras, whose wife and daughter had been taken by force from our village with Glykeria during the general evacuation and marched across the Albanian border. These civilians, mostly women and small children and the elderly, were by now dispersed among many Communist countries: East Germany, Czechoslovakia, Hungary, Bulgaria, Rumania, and Russia. Some of them would never return to Greece; others would trickle back after years of exile. Most of the inhabitants of our village, like Glykeria, were taken first to Shkodra, Albania, but the village children between the ages of three and fourteen had already been wrested from their mothers and sent to indoctrination camps in Rumania, where they were trained as Communist soldiers of the future — the fate our mother had died to spare us.

Glykeria answered our visitors' questions with horrifying tales of the diaspora: stragglers shot, executed priests buried with their heads protruding from the ground, heartbreaking glimpses of bands of kidnapped children, a terrifying voyage by sea to northern Albania on an overcrowded barge awash with vomit and urine. She told of the wretched living conditions in the refugee barracks in Albania. Finally she told of the day in March when the weeping teenaged girls were dragged from their parents' arms and thrown into trucks to be taken to the battlefields of northern Macedonia as fighters in the doomed Communist army.

These stories saddened us and left our visitors raging. "Why did you escape when my daughter is still suffering in that hell?" cried Jimmy Tzouras, who eventually made Glykeria his pet as a substitute for his lost daughter.

"I was conscripted into the army and she wasn't — that's why I escaped!" Glykeria replied defiantly. "Don't worry, I suffered plenty for my freedom."

She recounted even the most terrible details with animation and humor, and it was clear to us that whatever our sister had suffered, the privations of the battlefield and the refugee camp had not broken her spirit.

One evening, after many days of visitors, no one came to call. We all sat around the kitchen table as the clock moved toward ten. When it was clear that no one was coming, Olga said to Glykeria, "Tonight we have you all to ourselves. Now is the time for us to learn about *Mana's* ordeal."

I couldn't bear to sit there and listen as Glykeria revealed my mother's torment, so I escaped into the bedroom, just as I had done when Olga described the discovery of *Mana's* broken body. But I had to know the worst, because what I imagined was so terrible that the truth would probably be a relief, I reasoned, so I positioned myself close enough to the door to hear everything I could bear, and retreated to the opposite end of the room when Glykeria began to talk about how my mother was tortured. My father clearly wasn't any more eager than I was to hear the details of *Mana*'s suffering, but he no doubt concluded that he couldn't put it off any longer, so he poured himself a shot of ouzo and sat resolutely at the table to listen.

Glykeria didn't protest or flinch from describing our mother's last hours, although I could tell how much it cost her to relive those moments from the way the color drained from her face and she paused now and then as if marshaling the strength to continue. Glykeria hadn't been with us in the village when we first planned our escape, for she had been chosen in the spring as the one to fill the guerrillas' quota of a woman from each house to go harvest the grain on the other side of the mountains. *Mana* had sent Glykeria because she was stronger and healthier than either Olga or Kanta, yet so young at fourteen that it seemed unlikely she would arouse lustful feelings among the men guarding the women workers. Many weeks passed, and Glykeria did not return.

Then, on the day before our planned escape, the guerrillas came around demanding a second woman from our house to help with the threshing. *Mana* finally chose to go herself, hoping to join Glykeria on the other side of the mountains so they could run away from the wheat-fields together and eventually reach the nationalist lines in the distant foothills. She told the rest of us to carry out the original plan to leave the village with our aunt, grandmother, and others.

After telling us goodbye for the last time, *Mana* was marched with a group of village women to the distant fields where Glykeria and other girls were working. But they had only one night together, sleeping on the floor of an abandoned house, where my mother whispered to Glykeria the news of our plans to flee. Mother and daughter were separated the next day as the work details were split up and sent to different areas to cut the wheat.

Mother knew she couldn't go off on her own after that, because Glykeria might be killed in retaliation. And Glykeria, laboring in the sweltering heat on another mountain, had no way of knowing that our mother was arrested in the fields shortly after our escape, taken back to the village, and jailed, beaten, interrogated, and tortured to learn the details of our plot. Finally, while our sister still worked at threshing for the guerrillas in the heat of July, our mother was tried before the whole village in a kangaroo court, then sentenced to death and returned to the jail — the basement of our own house, which had been taken over as guerrilla headquarters. There she was tortured some more in a fruitless effort to make her confess to crimes she had never committed. Her death sentence had created such an outcry in the village that the guerrilla officers felt it necessary to make our mother appear an enemy of the people in her neighbors' eyes, to justify her execution.

It was on the morning of August 28 that Glykeria and the other women from Lia were released from the work detail and told to return to the village. Glykeria, who had been harvesting wheat and building fortifications for three months without so much as a change of clothes or a bed to sleep in, set out on the two-hour walk over the mountains in the company of a sixteen-year-old girl from Lia named Xanthi Nikou. As they passed over the peak above Lia, they crossed a green plateau where a troop of guerrillas were digging a large square hole, but the girls never suspected it was to be a mass grave for victims of an execution scheduled for that afternoon.

The girls reached a spot where they could see our village below, and an inexplicable fear seized Glykeria as she saw half a dozen guerrillas stationed outside our house. She and Xanthi ran down the steep path. At a spring, they encountered a neighbor woman who told them tearfully that Glykeria's mother and Xanthi's father were among the dozen villagers condemned to death and now held prisoner in the barred basement of our home.

The two teenagers ran to the gate of our former courtyard and screamed at the guards standing there, demanding to see their parents. Soon their cries attracted Xanthi's two older sisters. The four girls made such a commotion, drawing all the neighbors to their windows, that the leader of the guerrillas, a man called Katis, "the judge," told the guards to let them in — anything to shut them up.

The four frightened girls were led into the large upstairs chamber where Katis waited, frowning. He made a sign to the guards, and soon Vasili Nikou and our mother were led into the room, each supported by two guerrillas because they were unable to walk alone. The prisoners were dazed and confused, convinced they had been brought out of the dark, crowded basement to be killed. When the guards let them go, both slid down to the floor, their backs supported by the wall, their legs extended in front of them.

When Glykeria saw what had become of our mother, she started to scream. Still *Mana* didn't recognize her, but only blinked in the sunlight. Her lips were swollen and cracked, her eyes livid from blows; her hair, always neatly braided under a kerchief, was now loose and tangled, and her dress was torn. The worst thing, Glykeria said, was the condition of her legs: black and swollen to grotesque proportions from the torture called *falanga*. *Mana* seemed to recognize nothing until she caught sight of the familiar iconostasis in the corner of the room, where she had crossed herself every morning and night until the guerrillas threw us out. "My poor house!" she murmured. "What have you come to?"

Katis angrily ordered the guards to drown out the girls' screams by putting a record full blast on the gramophone — once our family's prized possession. Glykeria knelt on the floor in front of our mother and reached for her. "*Mana,* what have they done to you?" she cried.

At last our mother recognized the daughter she had been praying for every day. "My child," she said, speaking slowly to make herself understood. "Don't worry about me, my soul. Look at you! You're worn to a husk."

Glykeria pressed her face against her mother's breast and cried. "I missed you so!" she sobbed. "What have they done with the others?"

"The children left," *Mana* told her. "They're safe, and I don't care what happens to me now. You mustn't cry. I don't want to think of you crying like this."

Mother and daughter held on to each other, each trying not to frighten the other with her tears. Glykeria kept asking what she could do to help.

"Rest first," *Mana* told her, "then look to see if there are any tomatoes in the garden and bring me one. Go to Eugenia Petsis — she has our animals — and see if she can send any milk with you." She touched Glykeria's cheek. "If anything happens," she added, "I've left several *okas* of corn and wheat in the house for you."

Glykeria started to protest, but *Mana* silenced her. "You must save yourself," she insisted.

Finally the guerrillas told them the visit was over.

"Go now, child," our mother said unsteadily. "Go and rest and then come back. I want to see you again."

Bracing herself on Glykeria's shoulder, she struggled to her feet and studied her. "My daughter," she said. "May you live for me as long as the mountains."

Glykeria stared at our mother's haggard, bruised face, then seized her hand and pressed it to her cheek. They kissed, and then she turned and went out the door. When she turned around, she saw *Mana* standing in the doorway, holding tight to the doorjamb for support, staring after her as if to fix her image in her mind. As our mother raised her hand in farewell, Glykeria shouted, "Don't worry! I'll be back soon!"

She found the neighbor, who gave her tomatoes and milk and insisted that she eat something herself. "Before you go back to your mother, you must sleep a little," the old woman said. "You can't let her see you looking like this."

In the cool darkness of our grandparents' empty house, where we had lived until our escape, Glykeria lay down and fell asleep. It was two in the afternoon when she reappeared at the prison, carrying the food for our mother, but she saw at once that something was wrong: all the doors, including the one to the cellar, were wide open. The guards outside were lounging on the grass.

"Where's my mother?" Glykeria cried. "Where are the prisoners?" The guards reassured her, saying they had been taken up and over the mountain to another prison in Mikralexi, where they would be better off.

Not knowing what to do, Glykeria went a little higher up the path to the cool green place by the millpond where her mother and sisters used to wash clothes. She sat there in the shade all afternoon, holding the untouched food and crying. Late in the day another neighbor, Giorgina Venetis, descending the path from the heights, found her there. Giorgina was pale and trembling.

"What's the matter, child?" she asked.

"They've taken my mother and the others up to Mikralexi and I didn't get to say goodbye," Glykeria sobbed.

Giorgina Venetis looked away, mumbled a few comforting words, and hurried on. She did not tell our sister what had sent her running in terror down the path from the ravine. As she had passed near the execution site, Giorgina had heard a woman's voice utter a cry that seemed to contain all the sorrow of the universe: "My children!" It was followed by a volley of shots, then silence.

After encountering Giorgina, Glykeria went slowly back to the empty house of our grandparents and spent the night lying on a pallet, hugging our mother's brown dress in her arms for comfort.

The next morning she was awakened by a middle-aged guerrilla with a dirt-stained beard, his eyes narrow with apprehension. "You mustn't blame me for bringing you this news," he said. "Yesterday afternoon we executed your mother. I fired one of the shots myself. We had no choice. We were under orders. It was your own villagers who betrayed her."

Glykeria put her hands over her ears and fell to her knees, screaming, "*Mana! Mana!*"

The guerrilla moved a step closer. "Now you have to come up to the police station to answer questions," he said. "They sent me to bring you."

That was the beginning of days of isolation and grief for Glykeria. No one in the village would speak to her, and even our former friends and neighbors passed her with averted eyes. Every day she was taken to guerrilla headquarters and interrogated about rumors of a fortune buried somewhere by the *Amerikana,* and every day she was sent on grueling work details for the guerrillas, carrying wounded men and supplies on muleback over the mountain paths from one village to another. After each trip she would be sent out again with the words, "Now you've got to go for your sisters' turns, since they're not here." Sometimes she would be so tired by the return trip, she said, that she would fall asleep and tumble off the mule.

Three men who were Communist stalwarts in the village came to the door of our grandparents' empty house where she slept and took away the few pounds of flour and ears of corn that our mother had left behind. They even stripped the corn growing in the fields.

Glykeria went to our neighborhood church and cursed the saints for not preventing her mother's murder, then she went home and prepared to die of starvation. But the old woman who had promised *Mana* to look after our two goats secretly gave her enough food to stay alive until the day, a month after our mother's execution, when the Communists drove all the civilians out of our village toward Albania, leaving nothing behind but stray dogs, corpses, and carrion birds wheeling overhead.

By the time Glykeria finished her story, all my sisters were sobbing and my father's face was wet with tears. Olga and Kanta keened and called down fearsome curses on the guerrillas. I stood in the bedroom door and glared at my father in stony silence, convinced that he was the one to blame for the terrible things my mother had suffered. He had been trying to avoid hearing the agonizing details of her last days, but now he was face to face with the result of his selfishness and his failure to get us out of Greece in time.

"Those butchers, those Communist bastards," wailed Olga. "May their bones rot and may the vultures feast on their eyes and tear out their livers! May they die slowly, to feel what our mother felt!"

"Stop it!" shouted Father suddenly, and we all turned to look at him. "Don't waste your curses on the Communists. Curse me! It was *my* fault. *I'm* the one to blame!"

We all stared in astonishment as he launched into a violent self-condemnation.

"It was the biggest mistake of my life," he continued, "not to listen to my mother when I got married. 'Take your wife with you, she belongs beside you,' she said. But your mother's parents wouldn't let her go. Your grandmother said she'd kill herself the day Eleni left the village. And your mother, she was gentle and sweet, an angel! She listened to them and stayed. And I let her! I should have insisted. Now she's dead and I've lost the sweetest wife and my children have lost the best mother, all for nothing! I told her to stay and protect the house and the fields and she obeyed me. And it cost her her life. *I* killed her!"

He was weeping openly, his hands covering his face. My sisters rose to comfort him. "You didn't shoot her, *Patera*," Kanta murmured. "You couldn't know what would happen."

"Nobody knew, nobody could guess," added Olga. "It wasn't your fault. It was the damned Communists!"

While my sisters tried to console him, begging him not to blame himself, I shut the bedroom door so I wouldn't have to look at him. I was sick with grief for my mother and anger at my father. I still blamed him for *Mana's* death, now more than ever, but his impassioned *mea culpa* had pre-empted the perfect opportunity to vent my fury at him. Ever since our first disillusioning days in America, I had been waiting for the chance to speak my accusations, but by blaming himself, he had defused the hostility I knew my sisters also harbored and had even won their sympathy. I felt cheated and more frustrated than before. But I stored my anger away for the time being, knowing one day it would erupt when he couldn't hide behind tears and self-condemnation.

Glykeria's arrival and her constant place in the spotlight irritated Fotini, who, as the youngest girl, had always felt ignored. Fotini had been eclipsed as an infant by my birth — the longed-for son after four daughters. Ever since, she had felt she wasn't getting her fair share of attention. Now, with Glykeria soaking up all our father's affection and sympathy, she was seething with a bad case of sibling rivalry.

A few nights after Glykeria's revelations, Father, Olga, and Fotini were sitting on the couch in the living room waiting for visitors while Kanta and I took up the armchairs, when Glykeria came in.

"Move, Fotini," she ordered. "I want to sit next to *Baba.*"

"That's right, let your sister sit here," said Father. "We lost her for all this time and now I want to enjoy her company."

That was too much for Fotini, who had been her father's pet until this usurper arrived.

"Glykeria gets the best seat! Glykeria gets the best food!" she screamed. "She's a fat cow! Glykeria should go back to Greece and let the guerrillas mount her some more and leave us in peace!"

The sound of Fotini crying out our worst suspicions after we had avoided any reference to the state of Glykeria's virginity for so long sent us all into shock. Father stood up with a face like avenging doom and whipped off his belt to beat her. She glared at him defiantly. The rest of us held our breath, then Glykeria put a hand on his arm.

"Don't hit the child, *Patera*," said Glykeria. "She's just saying what everyone else is thinking. You can't blame her for being jealous, and besides, now that someone's had the courage to bring it up, I'll tell you . . . not a single guerrilla — no man in Greece or Albania, for that matter — even tried to lay a hand on me!"

Father sank back onto the couch as an explosive sigh of relief escaped him. We knew he had been agonizing over what he would do if Glykeria had been ruined by the Communist soldiers and was doomed to a life of spinsterhood.

"It's a strange thing," Glykeria went on. "The older girls used to talk about it. We might be sleeping side by side in the same foxhole, but no guerrilla even looked at a woman with lust. We decided they must be putting some sort of medicine in the food, to eliminate their sex drive."

Kanta laughed. "I heard the same rumors during the weeks I was an *andartina*, before they sent me home," she said. "I don't know if it's true or not, but don't forget that sleeping with a woman soldier was grounds for immediate execution without a trial. I remember one man was killed for screwing a woman, and they tied his body to a horse and rode it through all the villages as a warning to the other guerrillas. That's a better antidote to lust than medicine and cold showers!"

Father was beaming with delight, Fotini's outrageous behavior entirely forgotten. "My child!" he said, holding out his arms to Glykeria. "You've suffered terrible things, but you've come back to us as pure as a lamb! Now you're going to rest. I don't want you to work, I don't want you to go to school, I don't want you to worry about anything for a year. This is the time to be happy and to get rid of those terrible memories of what you've been through."

"And those forty pounds you put on in Igoumenitsa," muttered Kanta under her breath. "You're going on a diet."

Glykeria's arrival seemed to me to usher in a period of good luck. I was doing much better at school and winning the respect of the other students in both the classroom and the schoolyard. Fotini, however, despite the kindness of Miss Foley, was feeling more and more uncomfortable in the third grade, with children three years younger than herself. Because I was small for my age, I didn't seem as physically out of place as she did. As my English improved, I was becoming a leader of neighborhood boys like Marty Akerson and Steve Zilavy. But three afternoons a week I led a double life, when I took the bus downtown to attend Greek school.

Like nearly every immigrant group in America, the Greeks of Worcester had created after-school lessons in an attempt to keep their language, customs, and religion alive in the breasts of their offspring. This is inevitably an exercise in frustration. What American child, tired after a day at public school, wants to attend more lessons to learn a difficult language with squirming children who would much rather be outside playing stickball? But Greek immigrants saw it as a duty to their *patrida* to educate their children in their language and culture, so three afternoons a week several dozen Greek-American children sullenly gathered in some rented classrooms of the Oxford Street School in downtown Worcester, where underpaid and overworked teachers tried to cram some knowledge into their heads.

Unlike the other students, I felt more comfortable speaking and writing Greek than English, so Greek school was an opportunity for me to shine and to associate with boys my own age instead of those I knew at Greendale School. I was placed in the fifth grade at Greek school, and my friends there envied my proficiency in Greek. They didn't suspect, and I didn't tell them, my ignominious grade level in the American school. I easily kept them fooled because they attended public schools far from my own.

Our Greek-school teacher was Arthur (Athanasios) Kanaracus, a tall, sad-eyed, dark man with glasses, who limped as the result of losing a foot under a train in childhood while playing on the railroad tracks. Like many well-educated Greeks, Kanaracus originally came from Asia Minor, where he was born in 1909. But when he was only six, his mother had a dream in which the Virgin Mary warned her to take her children, flee Turkey, and join her husband in America, so Kanaracus immigrated to Peabody, Massachusetts, just in time to escape the Anatolian massacres that began in 1915. The Greek and Armenian minorities in Asia Minor were largely wiped out by the Turks — 2.5 million were slaughtered, and 1.3 million survivors arrived as homeless refugees in mainland Greece.

To his Greek-school students, Professor Kanaracus seemed sterner than our American teachers, a stickler for discipline and manners. We stood when he entered, chorusing "Good day, Mr. Kanaracus," and we learned to preface our statements by saying, "With your permission, Mr. Teacher." Perhaps more than my fellow students, I sensed Kanaracus' profound love of the Greek language as he patiently tried to drum it into our heads — classical poems, patriotic songs of the revolution, and philosophical essays — doggedly correcting the American twang that corrupted the words of Pindar and Palamas.

Until we read his obituary forty years later, we children didn't know or care that Mr. Kanaracus was struggling to support his wife and children with three part-time jobs while composing liturgical music for the Greek Orthodox churches in America, a children's operetta, and five major works for full orchestra. To us, his students, his main function was to spoil afternoons that would have been better spent on the baseball field and to coach us for the two big productions of the Greek-school year: the graduation ceremony and Greek Independence Day, March 25.

Probably because my Greek was better than my classmates', I was selected for the starring role in the Independence Day performance in 1950, shortly after Glykeria's arrival in America. I was to portray Germanos, the bishop of Patras, who launched the Greek uprising against the despised Turks after four hundred years of slavery. It was on the day of the Annunciation, March 25, 1821, that the venerable bishop blessed the Greek war flag — a blue cross on a white field — at the great monastery of Aghia Lavra in the Peloponnesus and then, raising it above his head, electrified the gathered Greek Klephtic warriors with the immortal cry "*Eleutheria y Thanatos!* Freedom or Death!"

Naturally, the role of Bishop Germanos was the plum of the Independence Day celebrations, which were faithfully attended by St. Spyridon's entire congregation. As Germanos, I got to wear the long ecclesiastical robes and stovepipe hat of a bishop, with a fleecy beard secured to my ears by loops of elastic. My Greek-school classmates chafed at having to appear in white tights and the white pleated skirts of the Greek warriors, although it was some consolation that they got to brandish their cardboard swords ferociously.

My father and sisters, as relatives of the star, sat in the first pew on the occasion of my theatrical debut. I dressed in my Christmas suit, swiftly covering it as always with my raincoat so that the ripped knee wouldn't show. As soon as I got to the church, I donned the robes of the bishop, which effectively hid the evidence of my carelessness.

In ringing tones only slightly muffled by the huge beard, I recited the bishop's stirring exhortation to the gathered freedom fighters. For the big finale, as the organist softly played the Greek national anthem, I held the heavy flag upright, shouted "Freedom or Death!" and sank to one knee, facing the congregation, staring dramatically upward at the spot where Christ is generally portrayed in Greek patriotic paintings looking down from heaven at the bishop, hand raised in benediction on this Christian crusade against the infidels.

Throwing myself into the part, I knelt on the *solea*, unaware that my naked knee protruded through the bishop's robes right in front of my father's nose. I lowered my gaze from the heavens to see Father rise out of his seat in horror, staring fixedly at my knee. With a sinking heart, I realized that, star of the show or not, I was in deep trouble.

To my surprise, the enthusiastic response of the congregation moved Father to overlook the damage to my Christmas suit, especially when I said it had happened only a few minutes before, because of a projecting nail in the dressing room.

"You made my heart soar with those great words, *Eleutheria y Thanatos*," he said, his eyes brimming with emotion. "I know what it is to live in slavery under the Turks, hiding when they come to the village to kidnap girls for their harems and boys for their armies. You make me proud today to be Greek and free. What's a pair of pants? I'll buy you a new pair of pants!"

As the snow melted in that spring of 1950 and warm weather returned, our good fortune seemed to be holding. Father and Kanta were both working, Glykeria was at home to keep Olga company and help with household duties, and I was doing well in both the Greek and the American schools. When the school year ended at last, we eagerly joined other Greek immigrants nearly every warm weekend on excursions into the countryside for day-long picnics at Davidian's farm.

These picnics were an opportunity for the Greeks in exile, especially the bachelors lonesome for home and family, to imagine themselves back in the old country. David Davidian was an Armenian farmer who sold produce to many of Worcester's Greek peddlers, and he generously allowed us to picnic on the rolling lawn that stretched from the front of his white farmhouse down to the fields of crops and the pastures dotted with his cows and sheep.

Arriving in a motley assortment of ramshackle trucks, borrowed cars, and even taxis, we carried our picnic food to Davidian's and set up spits for the roasting of lambs and goats and the spicy sausages made from their intestines. There was always an ample supply of resinated wine and *raki*, the fiery Greek moonshine, to fortify the men assigned to turn the spits slowly by hand. As the tantalizing aroma of roast meat filled the air, I staved off hunger with slices of chilled watermelon and explored the streambanks or watched my elders at play.

Eventually someone took out a clarinet and began to weave a mournful melody on the still air. Someone else brought out his accordion to take up the plaintive strain. As the music increased in volume and emotion, the farmer Davidian himself might come out on his front porch, set up his drums, and beat out the rhythm. (During breaks in the music I vied with other boys to examine these instruments.)

The folk music of our Greek villages, heavily influenced by the minor scales of Eastern melodies, was slow and mournful even on joyous occasions like weddings. Many of the songs were sung *a cappella* by two groups in question-and-answer fashion, as were the village wedding songs, with the groom's family demanding possession of the bride and the bride's family replying with laments for the loss of their finest flower. The Greek immigrants sang and were transported back to the land of their birth. As Nikos Kazantzakis wrote, "The modern Greek, when he begins to sing, breaks the crust of Greek logic. All at once the East, all darkness and mystery, rises up from the deep within him."

I used to watch the adults dancing, singing, laughing, and arguing, and wonder at the effect these picnics had on them. I enjoyed the outings too, for I knew my father and older sisters had a good time and I had rarely seen them happy; but I was young enough to wonder how they could really take pleasure in such maudlin songs.

All the lyrics bewailed the evils of poverty, disease, death, and faithless lovers. The saddest songs of all expressed the terrible pain of *xenitia*, exile in a foreign land. One popular *rebetiko,* entitled "Xenitia," lamented:

> This foreign life's making me old and eating me alive.
> I can't stand it, *Mana,* my body's wearing out.
> This foreign life holds sorrow and so much bitterness,
> It feeds on young men's souls and wastes poor bodies.

As the grieving of the clarinet and the fire of the wine and *raki* heated the blood of the Greek exiles, someone would get up to dance alone, lost in a trance, doing the hypnotic steps of the "eagle dance," his arms outstretched on either side, head bowed, cigarette dangling from his lips, eyes fixed on the ground. No observer violated the privacy of this solitary dancer with applause; there was only an occasional hiss to express empathy with the *kefi,* the strong mystical emotion, of the performer.

Sometimes men would dance in a line, arms on each other's shoulders signaling the precision steps of the *hasapiko,* the butcher's dance, or the *tsamiko* — dignified and warlike, with a leader, supported by a handkerchief held by the next in line, performing great leaps and somersaults and acrobatic feats.

My father's favorite trick, which never failed to delight the onlookers, was to dance at the front of the line with a glass of wine balanced on his bald head. Moving with great dignity, head high, balancing on one foot while the other foot described elegant circles in the air, he would lead the dancers in a winding path, proud as a king. I saw him perform this feat hundreds of times, at every picnic, dance, wedding, and baptism until he was in his late eighties, and I never saw him spill a drop of wine, no matter how much he had imbibed.

The young men performed feats of strength while dancing, leaping high in the air, lifting tables in their teeth, leaning forward to pick a wine glass off the ground and drain it without using their hands. The women would dance too, slow and dignified line dances identical to those portrayed on the marbles of the Acropolis. In a serpentine line, women and girls held hands, moving slowly sideways with a hesitating step, facing first right and then left. These steps showed off the grace and fine features, supple bodies and rich garments of the maidens, while never requiring fast steps that would compromise their modesty.

The young men, who could not speak to the young women, could at least watch from a distance and spy an inviting glance, a well-turned figure, a delicate ankle. My sisters, however, sat modestly on the sidelines, while our father glowered, alert for any male eyes that lingered on them.

As the sun sank behind Davidian's farmhouse, as the roasted lamb was gnawed to the bone and washed down by *retsina,* sun-warmed fruits, and honey-drenched pastries, the emotion of the music and the dance would sometimes escalate into quarrels: royalists versus republicans, leftists versus nationalists. Old family feuds and ancient disagreements over boundary lines and water rights would flare up. Many times I saw grown men nearly come to blows over the question of whose village had the sweetest water flowing from its springs. But most of these altercations, although filled with terrible curses and threats, were interrupted just short of bloodshed by bystanders, so the antagonists could depart satisfied that each had given his opponent a proper fright.

When it was too dark to tell red wine from white or first cousin from foe, we would gather our things to ride back to Greendale Avenue in whatever vehicle had brought us, singing all the way. The finest baritone of all belonged to Prokopi Pantos, a handsome young cook from Babouri who could make a stone weep when he sang his specialty, the lament of the Souliote women.

In 1803, the women of Souli, a village not far from our own, had chosen death before dishonor at the hands of the Turks. As the attackers climbed toward them, the peasant women threw their babies and children off the cliffs of Zalongo into a rocky ravine far below. Then, dressed in their crimson-and-gold-embroidered costumes, they began the circle dance of Zalongo, singing and moving hand in hand toward the precipice to plunge one by one to their death.

As we prepared to go home on those picnic Sundays, Prokopi Pantos would bring the festivities to an end with the song of the Souliote women, which always made me shiver with delicious horror at the tragedy and courage of those martyrs, so often cited by mothers as examples to their daughters.

When Prokopi began to sing, all activity, all conversation ceased as we gathered to listen. His manly voice began softly and rose toward the heavens like the prayers of the cantor in church toward the ear of God. Step by step the emotion increased with the volume of the song, until Prokopi seemed to reach the pinnacle of grief. The notes hung high above us like a hawk floating on a current of air, looking down on the prosaic scurrying of dull humanity, or like a kite bound to earth by a slender thread of economic need but borne heavenward by love for our homeland. When Prokopi sang, his listeners were no longer laborers, peddlers, and short-order cooks but poets, philosophers, and artists, united by the transfiguring grief of our shared *xenitia*, as we listened to the last words of the women of Souli:

> Farewell, unhappy world,
> Farewell, sweet life.
> And you, unlucky homeland
> Farewell forever.

Women of Souli haven't learned
Only how to live.
They also know how to die
And never be slaves.

Twenty-five years after our picnics at Davidian's farm, when he was forty-four years old, Prokopi Pantos was singing his famous lament at a Panepirotic Federation Christmas dance when he suddenly suffered a heart attack and died. On his marble tombstone in Hope Cemetery his brother engraved the words he was singing just before he fell: "Farewell, unhappy world."

Like all the other Greek immigrants, we returned from those Sunday picnics tired, satiated, emotionally drained, feeling as if we had been transported for a day back to the village of our birth. The smoke of the factories, the fatigue of twelve-hour workdays, the pain of *xenitia* had been alleviated for a while. When it became unbearable again, we would all go back to Davidian's for another picnic.

In the hottest part of that summer, I once again came down with an agonizing case of eczema, even though, as I swore to my sisters, I hadn't been anywhere near the Kendrick Park swimming pool. Again I was confined to bed with bandages wrapped around my hands to keep me from scratching, as my whole body erupted in boils. During that siege, a salesman appeared at our door one sultry evening selling encyclopedias. These volumes, bound in beige-and-maroon covers with gold lettering, contained all the knowledge of the world on every subject, he told my father, unfolding display cards from his black suitcase. With a set of encyclopedias, he said, my father's son would be sure to go on to college and become an educated man and a success in the world.

Father had always revered education, although his own schooling was rudimentary. To the end of his life he studied his Bible and his English-Greek dictionary every night, hoping to expand his vocabulary. Now he listened to the glib salesman and remembered how I often came home from the movies asking him questions he couldn't answer: Who is Captain Blood? When did Louis Pasteur die? What is the Green Hornet? The answers to these and every other question posed by the mind of man were to be found in the encyclopedia, the salesman assured him — all the accumulated wisdom of the world, in thirty-six volumes. The price of the set of books, which would come one by one in the mail, every month or so, didn't sound so steep: $5 a month. Of course, the salesman never mentioned that the whole set would cost a grand total of $180.

If my father had ever calculated that amount, he would have realized that a man who makes $55 a week and has five children can hardly afford such a luxury, but he was won over by the eloquence of the salesman, who treated him, an immigrant, like an equal and a friend. So Father signed on the dotted line and gave the man $5. That was how I eventually came to possess a complete set of the *New Funk and Wagnalls Encyclopedia*. I spent my long summer days of convalescence and the two years that followed reading through the entire set, from "aabenraa" to "zyzyn." My father's innocence and gullibility, coupled with his sincere reverence for education, bequeathed me the foundation of an education that was the cornerstone of everything that came later.

In the fall, even though Glykeria had been told by Father that she should take a year off to recover from her ordeal, she decided to join Kanta as an employee of Table Talk Pies. She would attend school at night to learn English. Fotini and I began fourth grade under a skinny, severe, old-maid Irish teacher. With all of us out of the house, Olga was left alone all day long.

Olga's depression, which had increased with her disfiguring operation and then been alleviated by Glykeria's arrival, now returned, worse than ever. Visitors no longer dropped by every night, hoping for news of Greece. There were no girlfriends for Olga to gossip with, as she had gossiped with the village women while beating the laundry on the rocks around the millpond. Her only confidante in America was her godmother, Nassio Economou's wife, Eugenia, who taught Olga how to cook over the phone and listened as she wept for her mother. "Your mother died to save you, child, so she's at peace," Eugenia would tell her when Olga railed against the evil destiny that had kept her mother from ever seeing the land of her dreams. "I came to America," Eugenia added grimly, "and believe me, it would have been better if I had stayed behind. My husband had learned too well to live without me."

Then suddenly one day, without warning, Eugenia's heart stopped while she was washing dishes in the back of her husband's restaurant. When Olga saw her godmother lying yellow and gaunt in her coffin, she wept as if her mother had died all over again. It was then that Olga surrendered to the despair that had been threatening to drown her.

She cried all day long, calling for our mother. The neighbors upstairs, Rena and Halbert Ball, and Mrs. Kadis from the third floor, heard her and tried to comfort her, but they spoke another language and she couldn't tell them why she was mourning. Sometimes Mother's presence seemed so real to Olga that she thought she was losing her mind. One day, as she stared out the front window of the parlor, a burst of wind set the branches of the trees outside swaying. Suddenly Olga seemed to be in our house in the village, watching the branches of the mulberry tree moving as Mother came up the path, carrying vegetables picked from the garden.

This was not the first time that Olga had feared for her sanity. Once, before we came to America, the despair was so bad that she temporarily went blind. It was when we children and our grandfather had left the refugee camp and were en route to Athens to board the ship, and we stopped at a hotel in Corfu. Olga, too depressed to eat dinner, remained behind in our room. She sat there, remembering how our mother had said on that last day, "I hang the other children around your neck." Now Olga was taking us to a strange country, without even her grandparents to help. "What am I doing going there?" she asked herself. "How can I protect them in America?" She was a girl suddenly thrust into the role of parent to her own siblings, and she couldn't bear the responsibility. Suddenly the hotel room went black. She saw nothing. She began screaming, groping for the walls, feeling her way to the door. She managed to open it and rush into the hall. Then, as suddenly as her sight had gone, the blindness lifted and she could see people hurrying to help her.

But now, left alone in the five rooms on Greendale Avenue, Olga's frightening symptoms began to return. She felt she had no reason to go on living. Her neck was mutilated, her beauty gone, her last confidante — her godmother — was dead. She sat at the front window, longing for someone to stop by. Every time a car turned down the quiet street she would pray for it to be some friend — old Jimmy Tzouras or another of her father's cronies, anyone to talk to. When the car drove on by, Olga would burst into tears.

One day a friend of our father's, Nicholas Bokas, did come to call. He climbed the front steps, and as he raised his hand to knock, he could hear Olga inside, weeping and keening, crying for her mother. When she opened the door her face was so haggard and swollen, her eyes so sunken, that the old man was frightened. He went immediately to Putnam and Thurston's kitchen, where Father was working, and said to him gravely, "Christos, if you don't do something about that oldest daughter of yours, you're going to lose her. The way she looked today, I don't see her living long enough to wear a wedding crown."

Father always believed the advice of the last person who had spoken to him, quoting that opinion as gospel until someone came along and told him something else. He was shaken by Nicholas Bokas' words and promised to speak to Olga that evening, to try to pull her out of this melancholy. He had never been a parent before, and he didn't know how to fathom what might be going on in the mind of a young woman of twenty-two, or how to see the warning signs of a real clinical depression.

Father knew from experience that some immigrants were unable ever to adjust to the terrors and temptations of their new country. One of his friends, a Rumanian, had brought over his wife and their four young children several years before, and while the children turned into Americans practically overnight, the wife slowly lost her grip on reality. At first she would walk to a nearby park, where she sat and breast-fed her baby, watching the world go by, but then she saw how the Americans stared at her strangely and she became embarrassed. Before long, she refused to leave the house at all. The children had to go out and shop for her. For the rest of her life, the unhappy woman never went out again, although she functioned normally inside the apartment.

It was the women, isolated by tradition and language, who had the hardest time adjusting, Father realized, and the older they were, the less easily they learned the ways of the new world. Olga, as the oldest and most conservative of his children, determined to uphold the moral standards of her mother, naturally resisted change. Kanta, the smartest and most progressive of the girls, had already learned English nearly as well as her father, much of it from listening to soap operas on the radio, weeping at the travails of the heroines and murmuring in Greek, "*Ach*! The poor thing!" To Olga, however, English was an impenetrable barrier.

A sermon wouldn't help Olga, Nicholas Bokas advised Father. The solution was to get the girl a job, even a few hours a week, no matter how she felt about the propriety of women working. She needed to get out and see people. Bokas added that he knew just the place for her: a small corset factory run by a friend of his, a Syrian, on Shrewsbury Street. It was light work and she would be surrounded by women. It would take her mind off her problems.

Working in the corset factory did distract Olga a bit. She was seated at a machine that sewed the little garter tabs for stockings onto the bottom of girdles. It was easy work, but none of the other women were Greek, so she couldn't confide in them. Nevertheless, it was better than sitting home weeping, and she made $47 for a five-day week.

One day, shortly after she had started at the corset factory, Olga saw her employer beckoning to her and pointing at the telephone. She picked it up and heard Father's voice. He was obviously calling because of an emergency.

"What is it, *Patera*?" Olga cried. "Has something happened to the little ones? Did Nikola break his head again?"

"No, no, my eyes," replied Father. "It's nothing like that. Don't worry. I just called to tell you I've betrothed you."

"You've what?"

"Betrothed you. I've found you a husband."

Holding the receiver, Olga sank into a chair, her thoughts spinning. In the whole two years since she had arrived in America, she had scarcely left the house and hadn't spoken to any man younger than her father.

"But who?" she finally managed to ask.

"Dino Bartzokis. He's a cousin of Tasso Bartzokis, our neighbor in Lia."

"Dino Bartzokis?" she repeated. "Doesn't he live somewhere in Greece?"

"Yes, my soul," Father answered. "He lives in Kastoria. He works in a bakery there. I had a letter today from Christos Tatsis [the man who took Glykeria into his home when she escaped from the *andartes*], and he said that Dino Bartzokis is a fine young man with roots in Epiros who wants to come to America and would make an excellent husband for any of my daughters. So I wrote him back that I accept this man as a husband for my eldest daughter — you."

"*Patera,* can't we talk about this?" replied Olga weakly. "Wait until I get home!"

"What's to talk about?" said Father airily. "I've taken the decision. I've sent the letter. The deal is done."

Dazed, Olga went back to her machine, too distracted to distinguish one end of a girdle from the other. Without warning, her fate had been decided. The entire rest of her life would be shared with a man she didn't know. In one morning her father had disposed of the problem that had obsessed Olga and her mother for years.

Olga and Dino dancing with Christos at their wedding

A STRANGER
FROM KASTORIA

And the day star arise in your hearts.
— Second Epistle General of Peter 1:19

OLGA'S LIFE, ever since she turned eleven, the age when village girls are taken out of school to separate them from the opposite sex, had revolved on the question of whom she would marry. At *Mana*'s side, Olga spent years sewing, embroidering, and preparing her "inside dowry" — enough dresses, embroidered shifts, and stockings to last her a year. These would be stored inside her carved dowry chest. Next she traveled by foot and by mule with Mother all the way to the provincial capital of Yannina, to barter for the "outside dowry" — the sleeping rugs, blankets, pillows, mattresses, and coverlets that were piled on top of the dowry chest.

For three days *Mana* and Olga shopped in Yannina, bargaining with the Vlachs, the Latin-speaking shepherds who wove the finest *velenzes*. These were shaggy, bright-colored sleeping rugs, and the prize of them all was the brilliantly patterned bridal *velenza* they bought to spread over the saddle of the mule when the dowry was paraded through the village behind the bride on her way to the groom's family home.

But who would that groom be? It was a question that drove our mother to distraction, because Father wrote her that he wouldn't complete the papers to bring us to America until Olga was betrothed to a man of good family in Greece. Mother was deluged with marriage proposals from relatives of eligible men. Olga, after all, was the most desirable maiden in the village, not only for her beauty and virtue, but mainly because she was an heiress, the daughter of an American tycoon. Every time *Mana* opened the door, there seemed to be a matchmaker standing on the step, singing the praises of some bachelor. One village swain left love notes for Olga hidden under stones near our gate, until Mother threatened to dump manure on his head if he didn't stop trying to communicate with her daughter.

There was no lack of suitors for her hand; Olga herself was the problem. She raised her chin defiantly, clicked her tongue, and folded her arms across her chest, insisting that she would consider only a doctor, a lawyer, or a teacher — in other words, a professional man — for a husband. *Mana* patiently pointed out that the only teacher in the village was already married and there wasn't a doctor or lawyer between Lia and Yannina. These arguments usually ended with Mother dramatically throwing open the front door and ordering Olga to depart for the convent of Yeromeri to become a nun. She would let Olga stay an old maid, she threatened, and find husbands for her other, more tractable daughters instead.

That was all before the civil war, when Olga could afford to be choosy. Mother had finally become so obsessed by the problem that she made a clandestine two-hour journey to the hut of an old hag known as Flijanou, who could read the future in a coffee cup, or *flijani*. A visitor who paid for her prophecy would drink a cup of Greek coffee brewed by Flijanou, draining it down to the muddy dregs. Then the old woman would invert the cup, make the sign of the cross over it, and wait for the residue to dry. The grounds would form patterns inside the cup like frost etchings on a window — patterns from which Flijanou could decipher the fortune of the coffee drinker.

Our mother was embarrassed at doing such a superstitious thing; she would never admit to her neighbors that she believed in the prophetic powers of the coffee cup (although Kanta eventually proved to have an uncanny gift for reading the grounds). But *Mana* desperately needed some clue to Olga's groom so she could make the match and we could all go to America.

When the old witch looked into Mother's cup, however, she shook her head and said that the omens were not good. "I see you have four daughters," she intoned, pointing with one bony finger at the swirling patterns traced by the dried grounds. "Here is the eldest. You want to know whom she'll marry, but the cup shows that the man is not someone she knows now. He'll swoop down and take her like an eagle takes a hen."

When Mother asked apprehensively why it was a bad cup, Flijanou replied, "I see here your house empty and everyone gone within a year's time. The head of the household is gone. The house is empty. I see death . . . within a year's time."

Mother left the hut of Flijanou in a fury. After all her trouble, she had learned nothing of Olga's future husband, and Flijanou had implied that her husband would be dead within a year.

Since then, the first part of the prediction had come true in a way *Mana* had never anticipated: our house in the village was empty and deserted, and the acting head of the household, our mother, had been murdered within a year of the reading. Now this young man from Kastoria . . . was he the eagle who would swoop down and carry Olga off?

My oldest sister knew she had to be more realistic than before. Her wonderful dowry was gone. We had buried it when the guerrillas seized our village. When Mother eventually was imprisoned and tortured in their jail, the guerrillas forced her to dig the dowry up before the eyes of the villagers. In the damp ground, all the beautiful rugs and blankets had rotted and were falling to pieces. Nevertheless, the guerrillas spread the remnants over the grass and shouted, "You see what treasures the *Amerikana* has hidden away!"

Even Olga's beauty had now been compromised by the surgeon's knife, although she hid the scars by wearing high collars. Furthermore, she could barely read and write, and in America there were many better-educated girls to win the affections of lawyers, doctors, and teachers. She could no longer afford to be so particular. All these thoughts ran through Olga's mind as she tried to sew garters onto the girdles that afternoon, which seemed to last an eternity.

As soon as the bus dropped her off at home, she hurried in to quiz Father about her prospective husband. He explained that he had accepted Dino Bartzokis' suit partly because he had once shared an apartment with Dino's father, Spiro, when the two men were newly arrived young immigrants working in the factories of Worcester. In 1917, Spiro Bartzokis had returned to the mountains of Epiros. Over the years, in addition to acquiring a wife and six children, he had established two tinker's shops that made copper pots and pans, one in a village near ours and the other in Macedonia, near Kastoria.

"If Dino Bartzokis is half as good a man as his father, you're a lucky girl," Father told Olga, smiling nostalgically at his memories of the old days, when the two of them were carefree young bachelors.

But these sentiments did not reassure Olga. As soon as Glykeria came home, she began an inquisition of her younger sister, who had met the future groom in Kastoria when she was recovering from her ordeal as an *andartina*. She had been invited to dinner at the home of Dino's parents, because they too had come from Epiros, and the Bartzokis family were eager to meet this young girl who had escaped from the Communist army.

Olga asked about the three vices she feared most in a man: was he addicted to drink, gambling at cards, or chasing women? Glykeria assured her that, judging from her meeting with him at his parents' dinner table, Dino seemed far too well bred to have any of those defects.

"That's all I care about," said Olga. "If he's lazy, I'll work hard enough for both of us. If he has a bad temper, I'll be very quiet and not provoke him. All those things I can tolerate. It's the cards, the drink, and the women that I can't accept."

Then Olga raised a question her parents would have considered completely frivolous but that preoccupies every bride. "What does he look like? Is he handsome?"

"Handsome as a movie star!" exclaimed Glykeria. She went on to describe him as tall (by Greek standards in any case, though he was only five foot nine), with dark wavy hair, deep-set brown eyes, high cheekbones, a wide forehead, a nice smile. "It's just that he's too thin," said Glykeria. "You'll have to fatten him up. I don't understand how a man who works in a bakery can be so thin!"

As Glykeria talked, Olga realized that she had in fact once seen this paragon: in the spring of 1943, when she was only fifteen years old, Dino Bartzokis, then nineteen, and another cousin had come to Lia to visit Tasso Bartzokis, whose family lived just up the path from our house. Rano Athanassiou, Tasso's young sister-in-law and Olga's best friend, ran down and whispered to Olga, "You have to get a look at the cousin who has come to visit! He's so handsome! I want your opinion of him."

Olga couldn't speak to a stranger, of course, or any other man, but when the visitors left the Bartzokis house, she followed them at a discreet distance down toward the village square. She saw Dino only from the back, but she remembered being impressed by the tall, erect figure of the dark young man with his trouser legs tucked into dashing army boots. "I hope when I grow up, my husband will look like that," she thought to herself, never suspecting that one day her father would choose that very man for her.

Thus, even though she probably wouldn't have recognized Dino Bartzokis if he had passed her on the street, Olga was pleased with her father's choice. Not until months later did she learn that Father hadn't really sent off the letter of acceptance to Christos Tatsis that same day, but kept it in his pocket until the next morning in case Olga violently refused to consider such a match. But Olga believed it was a *fait accompli* and threw no tantrums.

"Once Father told me he was from a good family, that was enough for me," she always said afterward. She would never admit that Glykeria's description of Dino's masculine beauty had had any influence on making up her mind.

Once the fateful letter reached Christos Tatsis, Dino himself wrote back to our father, and a correspondence started between the two men, who exchanged letters every ten days or so. Dino's first letter began,

"My dear future father-in-law, I greet you and my lovely future wife and the rest of your family." He then proceeded to outline the kinds of statements, official papers, visas, and forms that would have to be filled out before the postwar Greek government would allow him to emigrate.

He also included a wallet-sized black-and-white photograph of himself, which Olga snatched as it fluttered out of the envelope toward the floor. She studied it avidly. Dino was indeed as handsome as a movie star, with pomaded, wavy dark hair combed to one side, heavy eyebrows over deep-set, soulful eyes, chiseled cheekbones, and a self-confident but not excessive smile. He was wearing a gray pin-striped suit with the widest, most pointed lapels she had ever seen, a white shirt, and a wide, flowing tie in a dramatic graphic pattern. From his breast pocket protruded the tops of fountain pens and pencils. He might be only a worker in an army bakery in Kastoria, she thought, but he looked just like the lawyer or doctor she had always dreamed of marrying; perhaps a bit more glamorous.

Olga put the photo in her wallet. After much hesitation and discussion with her sisters, she finally chose a snapshot of herself to send back to him. It showed her in our tiny Greendale back yard under the apple tree, wearing her usual black dress, staring at the camera solemnly, with me on one side of her and Fotini on the other. She was a small figure, so shadowed it was hard to tell what she looked like. With apprehension she gave it to Father to send to Dino, hoping that this stylish young man with the wide lapels wouldn't think she looked too much like a peasant girl.

Father wouldn't let Olga write to Dino, for that would appear too forward, and if the two young people communicated with each other and then something went wrong — the papers were never completed and Dino never arrived in America — Olga's reputation would be ruined. What man would want secondhand goods, even if the only contact between the betrothed couple had been through the U.S. Post Office?

This correspondence between Dino and his future father-in-law began early in 1951. After about five months, Dino wrote that all the papers and visas seemed to be in readiness. At this point Father decided that it would be all right for Olga to add a line in her own hand as a postscript to his letter. Father stood over her and dictated the words as she wrote in her crude schoolgirl printing: "And from me, your promised spouse Olga, a kiss from across the sea."

This greeting in Olga's own hand elicited from Dino a letter addressed directly to her. "My lovely future wife," he wrote, "I should have taken the initiative to write to you first, but I know that your father follows a strict code on such matters and I didn't want to show him any disrespect . . ." There followed a love letter of such poetry and eloquence that Olga was suffused with an emotion she had never known before: she was hopelessly in love. Or, more precisely, she was infatuated with Dino's letters. His prose was intoxicating to a sheltered young woman like Olga. He wrote that he thought of her constantly, that he lived for the day when they would be together at last, that he kissed her picture every night.

For her part, Olga kissed the envelopes that Dino had addressed in his elegant flowing script. (She wondered what he thought of her short, awkward sentences and crude block letters.) She slept with his letters under her pillow, and she carried them with her everywhere, until they were falling to pieces from being reread so many times. One letter in particular touched her heart, and she would never forget the closing: "My lovely future wife, it's now twelve o'clock midnight and I am going to bed, but I won't sleep. I will lie awake in the darkness thinking of you." This image was so intimate, especially to a girl who had never been allowed to speak to a young man, that it seemed to Olga as if they were already married: Dino in Greece, lying awake at night sleepless with love for her; herself in Worcester, tossing feverishly, holding his letter to her breast. Dino's letters convinced Olga that he was the one man in all creation for her. Certainly no doctor, lawyer, or teacher could have written love letters of such eloquent beauty.

Then, just when Dino was about to purchase the ticket for his voyage to America, everything fell apart. It began when he wrote to Father: "The government won't give me an exit visa. They're suspicious that I won't return for my military duty. All I need is a temporary visa. Please write a letter saying that I must come to America to settle some financial matters left by my father. Write that your health is not good and these matters must be settled at once."

That night, at the coffeehouse, Father showed Dino's request to a gray-haired man called Peter Bell (born Panayiotis Belloyiannis), who had been the first Greek to graduate from a Worcester high school. He had anglicized his name and even obtained a law degree. Peter Bell was the man all the Greek immigrants turned to for legal advice.

"You must never write such a letter," Bell advised Father. "This is clearly a ruse to cheat you. Once he has a letter like that, your future son-in-law will come to America and claim that you owe his father money and show the letter as proof. He'll steal everything you own."

Father immediately believed Peter Bell, just as he believed any educated person who gave him advice, and he returned home white with fury at the deceit of this young man, after all the generosity he had extended to a penniless Greek bakery worker. "I regret that I cannot provide the letter you want," he wrote curtly to Dino that night. "Perhaps you should reconsider your plans to come to America." Then Father showed his letter to Olga, told her what her treacherous fiancé was trying to do, and announced, "The engagement is finished."

But Olga was a woman passionately in love. She took to her bed and refused to get up, ever. She cried ceaselessly, sobbing that she could never love another man. Father began to rue the day he had ever been so lenient as to let Dino and Olga correspond with each other.

Luckily for Olga's health and our family's peace of mind, Dino was cleverer than Father. He simply took the letter of rejection Father sent him, threw it away, forged a letter with Father's signature saying just what he wanted, put the counterfeit letter into Father's envelope, and took it to the local officials. Within days, Dino's papers came through, and he wrote to Father and Olga that he would be arriving within the month, sailing on the ship *Argentina,* which would reach New York harbor in September.

Olga rose from her sickbed like Lazarus from the dead, her heart bursting with joy. She had been laid off from the corset factory at the beginning of the summer owing to flagging business, but that was just as well, because now she had to prepare herself to meet her future husband.

With his own savings as well as the paychecks from Kanta, Olga, and Glykeria, Father had finally managed to buy a car — a 1946 light-blue Studebaker, which he loved as much as his late, lamented REO Speedwagon produce truck. Every evening he took us visiting in that car, paying calls on Greeks throughout Worcester, or sometimes just driving out to the countryside so we could enjoy the sunset over Lake Quinsigamond.

When Dino's arrival was imminent, Father decided to take both Kanta and Olga to New York a couple of days early so he could show his two oldest daughters the city. The three stayed in a hotel in the Times Square area, and Father took the girls everywhere: through the Lincoln Tunnel to New Jersey, on the ferry to Staten Island, where he had worked during the war as a cook in a restaurant, on a Circle Line cruise around Manhattan Island, past the Statue of Liberty. They strolled down Fifth Avenue, marveling at the luxuries in the shop windows. "It's just like Athens, only better!" exclaimed Kanta. "It's like something in a movie!"

In one of those shop windows, a mannequin wore a stylish dress of brown wool with a sophisticated black pattern. It had a high neck, and it seemed to Olga just the thing to impress Dino at their first meeting, a subtle change from her somber all-black dresses.

"Whatever it costs, I'll buy it for you," said Father. "You're my oldest daughter, and you have to look like a bride for your husband."

On September 21, 1951, the *Argentina* steamed into New York harbor with a thin, dark young man in a pin-striped suit at the rail. A young woman in a high-necked brown-and-black dress waited on the pier beside her father. On Broadway, Yul Brynner was acting in a new play, *The King and I*, not far from where three million New Yorkers had recently turned out to welcome home Douglas MacArthur, relieved of duty by President Truman. *I Love Lucy* was the popular new show on America's small television screens, *The Catcher in the Rye* was the bestseller among sensitive adolescents and *A Place in the Sun* was pulling in moviegoers with its steamy love scenes. Sweethearts danced to Nat King Cole's "Too Young" and Debbie Reynolds' "Aba Daba Honeymoon," and the U.S. Bureau of the Census had just purchased its first business computer to keep track of the country's growing population. Americans were discovering such newfangled conveniences as Dacron suits, push-button garage doors, and trading stamps.

But in New York harbor, Olga Gatzoyiannis and Dino Bartzokis knew nothing of such events and fads. As the great ship neared the dock, all Olga could think, while she strained to see across the distance, was that in a few moments she would meet the man whom her father had chosen for her, the husband who would share the rest of her life.

For Dino, it had not been an easy departure from Greece. He had had to pay the Greek authorities eighteen gold English sovereigns in lieu of eighteen months of military service. (He had started his army service years before, but after two months had come down with pleurisy and been sent home.) He had had to pay another ten gold sovereigns to be held in trust and given back to him when he returned to Greece, as promised, within three months. The gold sovereigns had depleted all his family's savings, and Dino knew he would never recoup any of it, just as he might never see his parents again. But he was an optimist and very ambitious.

Dino had always known he was cleverer than most of his contemporaries, and he considered it his rightful destiny to be a rich man. He was willing to work harder and longer than anyone else to get there, but he knew that in postwar Greece, no amount of work, ambition, or brains would make him a fortune. America was where opportunity waited, and getting through that golden door was worth any sacrifice. As soon as he had saved enough, Dino promised his siblings, he would send for them.

On the day Dino left his town of Kastoria for Athens, his father took him aside. "You have a quick temper," he advised his son. "Sometimes it flares up and you lose control. But you must be very gentle with your bride and treat her well, for she has no mother to protect her."

Dino finally emerged from customs, carrying one suitcase and wearing the same suit he had worn in his photograph. He recognized his fiancée at once. Father had coached Olga that she should kiss Dino on both cheeks, just as she would kiss anyone arriving after a long journey. She was too terrified even to speak a word to this apparition, who seemed even taller and handsomer than she had dreamed. But Dino had enough poise for both of them. He seized Olga's hand and raised it to his lips, a traditional gesture reserved only for one's future wife. Olga blushed scarlet at this display of affection in front of her father, and ducked her head. Then Dino kissed Olga on both cheeks and, turning to Father, embraced him and kissed him as well.

The moment his feet touched American soil, Dino started talking with the speed and energy of a machine gun — a dizzying fusillade of compliments, anecdotes, stories, questions, and jokes that left his listeners a bit dazed, especially Olga, who had not yet mustered the courage to say anything. When they reached the Studebaker in the parking lot, Dino fell silent for the first time. "Whose automobile is this?" he asked finally.

"Mine," replied Father, beaming proudly. "We'll go riding in it every day."

"You mean you own this car? It's all yours?" asked Dino, disbelieving.

"It's all mine," Father said with a nod.

Dino was, for once, at a loss for words. He had never before known a person who owned a car, and he concluded that his future father-in-law must be even richer than he expected.

Before driving to Worcester, Father stopped at a New York restaurant for lunch, but while Dino and Kanta devoured everything the waiter brought, Olga couldn't eat a bite.

"Why aren't you eating?" Dino asked gently.

"I'm not hungry," Olga mumbled.

She was painfully tongue-tied in the presence of her dashing groom. Dino seemed so sophisticated and at ease, able to speak on any subject without ever having to stop and think.

In agony, Olga wondered how to address him. She certainly couldn't call him Dino. In the village it was unthinkable for a woman to address her husband by his first name, even if they had been married for fifty years. No engaged girl would call her future husband anything, because they wouldn't have an opportunity to converse before the wedding. Olga wondered if she should call him "Effendi," the Turkish title of respect that village women sometimes used.

In the car her embarrassment grew. Father told Dino to sit in front with him, and he put Kanta and Olga in the back. There was a bag of fruit, and Olga wanted to offer some to Dino, but she couldn't work up the courage to speak. Every once in a while, Dino would pause in his conversation with Father long enough to turn around and look back at her with a wink of reassurance. Finally, when he did this, she managed to mutter, "Would you perhaps like a fruit?" Dino reached back and patted her cheek, saying, "Yes, my child, I'll have some grapes." A scarlet flush suffused Olga's cheeks, and she was so mortified she couldn't look him in the face.

Somewhere in Connecticut they stopped and Father took photographs of Olga, Dino, and Kanta standing beside the Studebaker — pictures for Dino to send back to Greece to astonish his family. For the rest of the journey, Dino chatted with his future father-in-law while Olga sat in the back, speechless with love and joy, and Kanta, to drown out Dino's chatter and express her high spirits on this momentous day, sang village wedding songs to Olga.

Until the wedding, Dino was given Father's place in our bedroom and shared the double bed with me, while Father moved to a cot in the other bedroom with Fotini, Glykeria, and Kanta. Olga slept on a cot set up in the kitchen. After the wedding, she would move into the bedroom with Dino, and I would be exiled to the living room couch.

I seemed to be the only one in the family who wasn't overjoyed at Dino's arrival. I resented this dark, glib, thin stranger who took my father's place in my bed and got up at night to pace and smoke cigarettes. He seemed too intense and talked so fast, punctuating his speech with choppy gestures, that I could hardly take in what he was saying.

Even though the future bride and groom were now living under the same roof, Dino and Olga scrupulously observed the proprieties. Sometimes at night, however, when Dino went out of the bedroom to go to the bathroom, he would find Olga awake on the cot and would sit next to her and talk. And sometimes he would give her a chaste kiss on the forehead before going back to bed.

Shortly after his arrival, Dino said to Olga during one of these private conversations, "Now that I see what kind of woman I'm getting for a wife, I realize that you're even finer than I had hoped. You're innocent and don't know about men and perhaps you fear me, but I'm going to tell you something. I'm a good person and will be a good husband and will treat you like a queen. You don't understand what I mean now, but someday you will."

The wedding was scheduled for October 21, exactly a month after Dino's arrival. The reception would be in the upstairs function room of Putnam and Thurston's restaurant, where Father worked. We had to cut corners; this wedding couldn't be an elaborate spectacle like the weddings in our village, which might go on for a week. There would be no preparation of the nuptial mattress, with the bride's attendants covering it with flower petals and coins and bouncing a small boy on it to insure male offspring. Since the bride and groom lived in the same house, there would be no procession of the groom's family to the house of the bride and no parade of the bride and her dowry through the village to the groom's house, stopping at the crossroads to distribute the braided wedding breads and Jordan almonds for fertility and luck. The dismal fact was, we had no relatives in Worcester to celebrate Olga's wedding with us and to uphold the traditions, and Dino was even more alone.

Olga knew a young married Greek woman, Katerina Bazoukas, who offered her own used wedding gown; all we had to do was have it dry-cleaned. Meanwhile, with Katerina's help, Kanta planned a bridal shower for her sister — an American tradition that the Greeks in Worcester eagerly adopted, because it gave the women a chance to celebrate together and to contribute to the dowry of the bride. Kanta and Katerina worked for days, cooking a feast of cheese and spinach pies, savory giant white beans in garlicky tomato sauce, *moussaka* and *pastitsio*, and rich honeyed desserts. Kanta rented a huge pink ruffled umbrella for the bride to sit under as she was showered with rose petals.

While our house was cleaned and decorated in readiness for the guests, Dino was sent upstairs in the care of Rena and Halbert Ball. Hal, our genial landlord, set about entertaining him until it was time for him to go downstairs for the opening of gifts. Hal had learned some phrases from his Italian-born wife, and Dino had picked up a few words of Italian during the years from 1941 to 1943, when Mussolini's troops had occupied his village, so the two men communicated in fractured Italian while Hal hospitably plied Dino with whiskey. "*Grazie!* "*Prego!*" "*Salute!*" they shouted as Dino drained his glass. He thought that the whiskey would be no stronger than the Greek ouzo he was used to, but when he tried to stand up, he discovered he had overestimated his capacity and was feeling the effects of the alcohol.

In our parlor Olga was seated under the huge pink umbrella, wearing a blue dress that made her look like a little girl at a birthday party. After the shower of rose petals was released by pulling a ribbon, Dino sat at her feet on the floor and ripped open the presents (which was really Olga's prerogative), laughing and exclaiming over each one. There were fine American sheets and towels, gleaming aluminum pots and pans, sets of tableware and a toaster, lacy lingerie and envelopes of money. Dino's eyes grew wide as the riches of America piled up around him. Finally, after the last guest had gone, Dino sat on the floor surrounded by gifts and crumpled paper and wept because his family wasn't there to see what wonderful things had been given to himself and his bride.

If Dino was surprised by the bounty of the bridal shower, he was thunderstruck when he learned the truth about Father's profession and his own future prospects. Sometime after Dino's arrival, while we were all sitting at the dinner table, Father explained to him with a touch of pride that he was the chef at Worcester's leading restaurant, the luxurious establishment where they would hold the wedding reception. That was why, he continued, he had been able to obtain for Dino a job as a salad chef, a beginning position that paid only (he cleared his throat) $28 a week. But Dino would be trained on the job, and he too could aspire to become a successful chef one day like his future father-in-law, who was bringing home (he cleared his throat again) $55 a week.

Dino stared at him in horror. "But don't you own the restaurant?" he stammered. "I thought — I mean, it was my understanding that you owned your own business and I would, as your son-in-law, come in as your assistant."

"We'll be working side by side," said my father reassuringly. "I'll teach you everything I know. After all, I'm considered the best chef in Worcester. Ask anyone about Christy Gage and you'll see . . ."

He trailed off, seeing that Dino wasn't listening but wore the stunned expression of a bull in a slaughterhouse who has received the fatal blow. That night, after Olga cleared the table, Dino sat scribbling figures on scrap paper, no doubt calculating what $28 was in drachmas. When Olga went to bed, he was still sitting there, the picture of dejection, his head in his hands.

Dino had believed the talk in Kastoria that Christos Gatzoyiannis was an American plutocrat, and when he saw that he owned a car his estimation of his future father-in-law's wealth increased. The truth came as a devastating disappointment, but he soon consoled himself that he was still better off in America than in Kastoria. He wrote his family that he had lots of ideas for making money, and once he was officially married, he would pursue them.

When it came time to pick up the wedding gown from the dry cleaners, I was the one entrusted with the $20 bill. As Father handed it over, he warned me to be very careful not to wrinkle the gown or to let it touch the ground on the way back from the Chinaman's. It was a bright fall day, and I scuffed through coppery piles of leaves on my circuitous journey to West Boylston Street. When I got there, Louis Ching stood patiently, his fingers resting on his abacus, while I turned out my pockets. Somehow I had lost the $20 bill. I knew it represented nearly all of my father's capital and I retraced my steps, combing every inch of my route, but without success. Desperate, I begged the Chinaman to let me have the dress on credit — I'd raise the money somehow — but he shook his head. On that miserable trek home, long after dark, I wondered if perhaps some devil deep inside me had whispered that without a gown, the wedding would have to be canceled and Dino would have to return to Greece and relinquish the other half of my bed.

After my father finished shouting at me, while Olga was still sobbing into her handkerchief, Kanta spoke up. "You know, *Patera,* this is all for the best," she declared. "Olga's your oldest child, and it's not fitting for her to get married wearing someone else's gown. We have to buy her a new dress, even if it's a cheap one. We'll pay for it on time. And eventually we'll save enough to get Katerina's dress back from the cleaners."

As usual, Father was swayed by the opinion of someone who seemed more assured than himself. Next came the challenge of shopping for the gown. Olga turned to Chrysoula Tatsis, the doyenne of the Greek immigrant community in Worcester. Just as she had advised us on every other aspect of American culture, Chrysoula was the ultimate arbiter of fashion style and taste.

Chrysoula escorted Olga to every shop in downtown Worcester, and at one of them they found the perfect dress, in a size five to fit her 109-pound frame. It cost $55 — a reasonable price. It had a turned-up satin mandarin collar to hide the scars on her neck, long sleeves, a modest bodice of satin with re-embroidered Alençon lace, little satin buttons down the front, and a long train. At the same store they chose the veil, which by Greek tradition was paid for by the *koumbaros,* or best man, who would exchange the crowns on the heads of the bride and groom.

Olga's *koumbaros* was Jimmy Tzouras, the cigar-smoking owner of Standard Fruit. Tzouras told Olga to buy the finest wedding veil she could find, whatever it cost, so she chose a lace-edged cloud of tulle held in place by a pearl tiara. The veil cost $30 — nearly as much as the dress — and Chrysoula convinced the saleslady to let Olga have the entire ensemble on credit, with only $10 down.

When Olga returned to the house in triumph, Jimmy Tzouras came by to learn what she had found. She told him about the dress bought on credit, and he whispered to her that he would pay for the whole thing, the dress and the veil, so that she could walk down the aisle on her wedding day wearing an ensemble that was entirely hers, free and clear.

On the day of the wedding, Olga and Dino dressed themselves with none of the panoply traditional in the village, where all the groom's cronies would shave and array him while getting drunk and singing until it was time to make the formal assault on the house of the bride, who had been carefully prepared by her own crowd of friends. Nevertheless, Olga had her sisters to help her dress, as well as some other women from the Greek immigrant community. She refused to let any of the girls put even a touch of makeup on her, but a clever matron took ice cubes and applied them so skillfully to Olga's cheeks and lips that her face glowed. Everyone remarked how appealingly the bride blushed throughout her entire wedding day.

A marriage is such a solemn, overwhelming event that a Greek bride rarely smiles, and many weep all the way down the aisle. Olga was so terrified by the arrival of this day that she had no trouble remaining properly solemn, and at the altar, after the exchange of the rings and before the crowning of the bride and groom, she burst into tears when the priest intoned, "Remember them, O Lord our God, and the parents who have nurtured them, for the prayers of parents make firm the foundations of houses." Olga was so overcome with grief that her mother could not be there, on this greatest day of her life — the wedding Eleni had dreamed of for so long — that she sobbed inconsolably, but she regained control of herself by the time the best man exchanged the wedding crowns three times.

To the ninety-six guests who attended Olga and Dino's ceremony in St. Spyridon's Church and the reception afterward in the American flag–draped banquet room of Putnam and Thurston, it might not have seemed like much of a wedding; we ate chicken instead of steak, and danced to records my father put on the Victrola instead of a live orchestra. But for Dino and each member of my family it was a turning point — the beginning of a new era, brilliant with promise.

For Olga, of course, it was the most important day of her life. From birth, a Greek girl is groomed for her wedding ("How can I marry you like that?" a Greek mother will invariably shout at a female toddler who has soiled her clothes). Everything that happens after a Greek woman's wedding day is an anticlimax, except the birth of her son. Although the black-and-white wedding pictures show Olga shy and solemn, Dino appears constantly beaming, stylish and at ease in his rented tuxedo. For Dino, this day was the end of twenty-seven years of hunger, poverty, and fruitless struggling, and now the future he had dreamed of, as a wealthy American, lay before him.

To Kanta, Olga's wedding day meant that she was free, at nineteen, to begin thinking of her own groom. To Glykeria and Fotini, it was a day to dress up and look beautiful in pastel satin gowns borrowed from other Greek bridesmaids in other weddings, and to sing and dance for the first time since our mother's death. For me, in a rented tuxedo, it was the first time I had seen my family so happy after a decade of war and famine and the murder of my mother. From this day forward, I was certain, we would have happiness and prosperity.

This wedding was a milestone for my father more than any of us. Until our arrival, he had always believed that one day he would return to Greece, to grow old and die in our village like a king. He had come, like the other Greeks, to "steal America," but instead Greece had stolen his wife and spit out his children, and now, with the wedding of his oldest child, he was irrevocably putting down roots in the new land. This daughter would have children, his other daughters would wed, his roots would grow deeper into the earth, and he would become the patriarch of a clan — an American clan. He might still feel the pain of *xenitia* when he heard a clarinet's lament or smelled the pungent aroma of wood smoke, but with this wedding he was turning his back on his native land, and now, in his fifty-eighth year, he had finally become an American.

So my father danced even more enthusiastically than the bride and groom; he sang the wedding songs and balanced the glass of wine on his head. He was clearly the host of the evening, and the guests handed the envelopes of money not to the bride but to my father, as a tribute to what he had achieved.

It was a proud day for all of us, a passage from despair to hope, and we all rejoiced. But at some point when we were not observed, each of us mourned the absence of those we loved.

The Greeks agreed afterward that it was a strange wedding: the bride had no mother, the groom not a single relative to stand up for him. My father had to carry the burden for everyone. But like Abraham, he would soon be surrounded by his descendants and relatives, those engendered by his blood and those he would bring over from the old country. It was a small wedding, little noted in the annals of Worcester society, but it was also the beginning of an epoch.

Just as Olga's wedding marked the end of our settling-in period and the beginning of our life as real Americans, for me fifth grade marked the beginning of acceptance by my classmates. My grades were among the best in the class, even though our fifth-grade teacher introduced us to fractions, which left Fotini completely bewildered. Outside the classroom I was enjoying even greater success as I became the boxing champion of the neighborhood.

Some of my friends had received boxing gloves as gifts, and we began to stage formal boxing matches of three three-minute rounds each in a clearing hidden within a wooded lot near my house. Three boys would time and judge the rounds as two of us went at each other like tigers. I handily beat everyone in the neighborhood, including several boys larger and in higher grades than myself. There was one boy named Don Muskovin, small, weak, and fearful, who only watched these matches, and we treated him with contempt, refusing to let him box but sometimes condescending to let him referee.

I became more convinced than ever that my future lay in boxing. Rocky Marciano, from the nearby city of Brockton, was featured in the newspapers nearly every day, with astounding tales of the astronomical purses he won and his glamorous female companions. This was the life for me, I concluded, and I saw no need to work hard in school. Sometimes Steve Zilavy and I played hooky and hitchhiked to the White City Amusement Park in Shrewsbury. The next day I would come in with some elaborate tale of sickness or injury and explain that no one in my family could write me a note of excuse because no one knew English. But despite my cavalier attitude toward school, my grades just kept getting better.

Olga plunged into married life with the joy of someone who has at last discovered her destiny. On the day after the wedding ceremony, Father drove the newlyweds through a snowstorm into Boston and left them at the Bradford Hotel for three days, then drove back to pick them up after this brief honeymoon.

Within two weeks, Olga began to suspect that she was pregnant — the ultimate fulfillment of a woman's role in life — but she kept the secret to herself, wandering around the house with an expression of smug self-satisfaction that the rest of us found a bit irritating.

One day I rushed into the house with the best report card yet, filled with E's for "Excellent."

"Here, sign it," I ordered, shoving it at Olga, who was the only adult at home. She bent over the card, the tip of her tongue protruding from her teeth, and laboriously printed "Mrs. Olga Bartzokis."

I looked at her signature in disgust. "No, no, you have to write 'Olga Gatzoyiannis'!" I complained. "Otherwise it won't be any good. It has to be signed by someone from my family, with the same last name as me."

But Olga would not be moved. She was Mrs. Olga Bartzokis, and not even when signing a report card for her only brother would she return for a moment to her unmarried state.

As Christmas came and went, I was much too busy with the adulation of my friends and my success at school to take any notice of Olga's swelling figure. I was forced to sleep on the couch in the living room, but I was hardly home enough to be concerned with the crowded state of our household. When I wasn't besting other boys in our neighborhood boxing ring, I was making the rounds of every spa, variety store, and cigarette shop within miles to add to my collection of baseball cards, which was already the envy of Greendale School. I followed the fortunes of the Red Sox more avidly than any native-born American boy and memorized such a staggering number of baseball statistics that the other kids used me as a reference library for settling arguments. All in all, I felt I had assimilated well to my new country and was convinced I had a brilliant future ahead of me as a boxer and baseball expert.

Then one day in March, just as the first buds on the apple tree heralded the approach of the baseball season, Father came home from work and toppled my comfortable universe like a tower of cards.

"We're moving," he announced. "With Olga pregnant we need a bigger place, and I found just the thing on Lincoln Street, across from Doctors' Hospital. It costs fifteen dollars more a month, but it's got four bedrooms, so you and I can each have our own, Olga and Dino will share another with the baby, and the girls will get the fourth."

Father beamed at this coup as I stared at him in horror.

"Lincoln Street — that's practically a slum!" I cried. "And I'll have to change schools!"

"Yes, you'll go to Harlow Street School — it's close enough to walk," he replied.

"But you're not going to take me out of Greendale in the middle of the year, are you?" I cried. "What about all my friends in the neighborhood?"

Disappointed at my lack of appreciation, he glared at me. "Don't talk back to your father!" he roared. "This is for the good of the whole family, including you. We're moving in two weeks."

9

The family in 1952. Christos is holding his first grandson, Spiro.

TESTS
OF WILL

Hearken to your father who begat you.

— Proverbs 22:23

In 1767 Judge Timothy Paine, a loyal subject of King George III, bought three hundred acres of Worcester that would later be called the North End. In 1774 he built his imposing estate, "The Oaks," there, on what was known as the Great Road to Boston. The townspeople were so hostile to the Tory judge, however, that work on the mansion couldn't be completed until 1778.

On March 31, 1952, when my family moved into the third floor of an ugly, squat, gray three-decker just a few doors down from Paine's estate, the road had become Lincoln Street, a busy artery into the heart of Worcester. The once distinguished neighborhood had deteriorated into a grimy industrial area, even though "The Oaks" still stood in decaying splendor just a few doors up the street, behind its picket fence and circular driveway.

Our previous home, on Greendale Avenue, was in a residential area of skilled workers, primarily Scandinavians. The new house was in a poorer neighborhood of Irish and Polish laborers, many employed by the factories, coalyards, and lumberyards on Crescent Street, behind Lincoln. Instead of grass, cinders covered the handkerchief-sized yards of the three-deckers; there were graffiti on the walls, and broken windows were patched with squares of cardboard. The lanes of traffic churned past our front door night and day, an unceasing roar punctuated by the shrieks of ambulances wending their way to Doctors' Hospital across the street from us — the same hospital where Olga had undergone the operation on her neck.

Even though our new home was in a worse neighborhood than the old one and up three flights of stairs, it had four bedrooms instead of two, as well as a tiny windowless room off the kitchen where Fotini slept, enjoying her privacy, unless the summer heat drove us all out to sleep on the balcony, or piazza, overlooking the street.

Fotini and I were enrolled in Harlow Street School, a large red-brick Victorian building heated by coal. It sat four blocks up Lincoln Street and one block to the left, on the edge of a ravine overlooking the lumberyards and coalyards. In front of the school rose the massive yellow bulk of St. Bernard's Catholic Church, the nerve center of the neighborhood, dominated by its bell tower.

Before sending us off to school, Father delivered a lecture on the perils of our new neighborhood. "Lots of bums around here — divorced women and drunks," he said. "Be careful who you make friends with. As I always say, no one stays clean who plays with mud." He warned Fotini especially not to make friends with any Americans, but only with Greek girls who were brought up in "high-class" families like our own.

I bid a sad farewell to my cronies on Greendale Avenue, who were sorry to see the neighborhood boxing champion uprooted. "I'm going to take the bus back to Greendale two or three times a week and spend all day Saturday here," I promised them. I said the same thing to my teacher, Mrs. Brosnihan, who gave me a hug and replied, "No you won't, Nick. In no time you'll be just as happy there and have just as many friends as you do here."

Our new fifth-grade teacher was a tall, gaunt man who reminded me of Abraham Lincoln as played by Raymond Massey. The assistant principal saw me tossing a ball around the playground one day and drafted me for the junior varsity basketball team. After the first game, when I discovered I was the only boy on the court with a fleece of hair covering his legs, I insisted on playing basketball in my blue jeans. But despite the jeans and my small stature, I managed to sink a few baskets in the last game of the season.

Most of my new friends went to catechism classes at St. Bernard's, and on days when I didn't have to walk into town to Greek school, I'd go with them. The panoply and ritual of the Catholic church reminded me of our village church in Greece, also the center of the community. Sometimes, without my father knowing, I even attended Mass with my friends on holidays, going up to the altar to receive the wafer on my tongue from the Catholic priest, then, on the same day, receiving communion at St. Spyridon's from the large chalice full of wine and bread spooned out by Father Rizos. I would go home afterward feeling doubly holy.

There were two kinds of boys in Harlow Street School, the well-behaved, serious students and the young toughs, most of whom had been kept back at least once. At the beginning I gravitated toward the first group, who came from working-class Catholic homes to the north of our house. Every evening before dinner their families would sit around the radio listening to the Catholic program and I would sit there with them, reciting the Hail Marys and crossing myself backwards, the Catholic way — left to right. My friends took their religion seriously, and we would have long debates on issues such as mortal and venial sins and whether the communion host really was transformed into Christ's flesh and blood.

I envied the unity of these Catholic families. My own was becoming more fragmented each day as we went our separate ways, Kanta and Glykeria working at Table Talk, Father and Dino keeping late hours at Putnam and Thurston, Fotini spending time with her new girlfriends, and Olga totally absorbed in her pregnancy.

Dino, despite his efforts to control his temper, found it irritating to have me and Fotini underfoot, and his lack of financial success did not sweeten his disposition. Not only was his salary only $28 for a forty-hour workweek, but Charley and John Kotsilimbas-Davis docked him eighty cents for Social Security. When he asked for a raise, they started deducting an additional dollar a day — allegedly for the food he ate during his dinner break — but Dino protested so violently that they capitulated and let him take home $27.20 a week. How could he ever get rich, with a baby on the way and only $27.20 take-home pay? Dino raged. Nevertheless, he controlled his temper around Olga, who was transfigured by marriage and pregnancy.

She gloried in her swelling belly. On days when Dino worked a split shift, with three hours off after the lunchtime rush, Olga promenaded downtown to meet him at the restaurant. In the cool green park behind City Hall they would sit together on a bench, holding hands and watching the people go by until it was time for the dinner shift.

Olga loved the way the traffic cop in Lincoln Square, where all the streets converged, nodded at her in recognition, then stopped the traffic in all directions as she waddled across the intersection. He told her not to hurry, to take all the time she needed. Pregnancy made Olga feel important, sanctified, almost like a modern Madonna, and it was only right that all of Worcester should halt in tribute as she passed by on the way to meet her husband.

It was during those first days of adjustment to our new home and school that Fotini and I drove Dino beyond the breaking point one Sunday afternoon. Jimmy Tzouras was visiting, and he, Father, and Olga were sitting at the kitchen table listening to one of Dino's long, complicated monologues delivered in his rapid-fire manner. Suddenly Dino noticed that his listeners were distracted from his eloquence by the sound of the radio from the bedroom. Fotini and I were in there listening to the Lux Radio Theater's dramatization of a successful movie.

"Turn it down!" shouted Dino from the kitchen.

"No, we won't!" Fotini shot back. "You didn't pay for this radio."

Suddenly Dino burst into the bedroom, picked up the plastic Emerson radio — the only one we owned — and smashed it to the floor.

Fotini and I and the onlookers from the kitchen froze, staring at the wreckage of tubes and shards of plastic. Dino turned on his heel and slammed out of the apartment.

Olga, who became even quieter and more solicitous when Dino lost his temper, eventually managed to coax him out of his black mood, but Fotini and I avoided him for days afterward, scuttling into our rooms when he appeared, secretly hating him for spoiling the only recreation we had in this grim, unfamiliar neighborhood.

Then one day Dino came home beaming with good will, carrying a huge box. With a theatrical flourish he opened it and pulled out a twelve-inch black-and-white television set. Fotini and I enthusiastically forgave him as he set the TV up in the den, where we could gather to watch *I Love Lucy* just like real American kids.

The small TV was just one more American temptation seducing us away from the rules and customs of our native land. Sometimes Father must have looked at us gathered around the flickering light of the screen and envisioned us slipping out of his grasp, transformed into foreigners without roots or self-respect. Of all his children, only Olga stayed home and honored the traditions of our village. Fotini and I already seemed half American, and Kanta and Glykeria were swiftly being molded into modern working women through their jobs at the bakery.

He fought hard to protect my sisters from the encroachments of this loose moral climate, even refusing to allow Kanta to go to the Christmas dance that the owners of Table Talk gave annually for their employees. "I don't care if it's free!" he thundered at her. "That doesn't make it all right for you to let some lecher put his hands on you."

Learning of his interdictum, Ismene Matsos, a middle-aged Greek woman who worked with Kanta, took pity on her and came over to our house to speak to Father. "Let the girl go, Christos," she coaxed. "My husband and I will pick her up and drive her there and bring her back, and the whole time I'll watch her like a mother. I guarantee you, I won't let anything happen to damage her reputation."

Eventually Father reluctantly bowed to Ismene's pleas. In a flurry of excitement Kanta bought a new dress for the occasion: black with a white collar. Some of the girls at work volunteered to do her hair up in bobby pins so she would have a headful of curls for the party. That evening Kanta was ready long before Ismene Matsos and her husband drove up in a car that also contained Ismene's sister Aphrodite Ghikas — another Table Talk employee — and her husband, Christos.

In the festively decorated ballroom of the Aurora Hotel, Kanta sat quietly at the table with the two Greek couples who had brought her. All the male Table Talk employees — the Greeks as well as the Italians, Rumanians, Scandinavians, and just plain Americans — were familiar with Kanta's oft-repeated warning, "Don't speak to me or my father will kill you," so no man ventured to ask her to dance.

Finally Aphrodite returned from a spin around the dance floor with her husband and whispered to him, "Ask the poor child to dance, Christo! No one else is going to."

Obediently, Christos Ghikas led Kanta to the floor. She had no sooner begun her first hesitant steps to an American dance tune than there was a commotion by the door. The conversation on the dance floor faded away to silence as everyone turned to see what was happening. Kanta looked over her shoulder and found Father standing in the doorway to the ballroom, glowering at her ferociously. He seemed intent on incinerating her with the intensity of his anger. Kanta realized he had secretly followed her to the Aurora Hotel and had been sitting in the restaurant adjacent to the ballroom all evening, keeping an eye on her. When he saw her get up to dance in the arms of a man, his worst fears were confirmed, and he stalked into the ballroom, pausing dramatically with his hands on each side of the door. The entire ballroom turned to watch the silent tableau of outraged father confronting wayward daughter. Father said nothing aloud, satisfied that the terror inspired by his countenance was enough to cow his daughter into proper behavior.

The sight of her father making such a scene and the realization that he had been watching her all evening made Kanta so angry she began to tremble as she felt the blood rise to her temples. "I think we'd better sit down," she mumbled to the bewildered Christos Ghikas. When he led her back to the table, Kanta leaned over and whispered to the woman who had volunteered to chaperone her, "Ismene, I think you'd better go over to my father and talk to him, because if I do, I'm going to kill him."

Ismene did as Kanta asked. Eventually, launching a final glare of triumph at the chastened crowd, Father allowed himself to be led back into the restaurant.

For the rest of that evening, Kanta sat there, her cheeks burning, silently praying to all the saints to strike her father dead. When Ismene and her husband drove her home, she went to bed in silent fury. The next day, as she entered the factory, she was greeted with catcalls from the men: "Watch out for that one — her father's right behind her!" "You mean he let you come to work alone?"

After that debacle, Kanta never tried to attend another Table Talk function, even though the owners gave a beach party every summer and a dinner dance every Christmas. She decided it just wasn't worth the aggravation, and conceded this one victory, at least, to her father.

By the time Glykeria joined the ranks of Table Talk's employees, Kanta was experienced as a working girl, so she became her younger sister's protector as well as her social mentor and dietician. Every day Kanta prepared the bag lunches they carried, allowing Glykeria only a single sandwich with the crusts trimmed off, an apple, and a cup of coffee. Usually Father drove the two girls to work and picked them up afterward or sent Jimmy Tzouras to do it, but once in a while, when the weather was good, they would walk all the way back to Lincoln Street alone, stopping at Woolworth's to buy candy, which Kanta permitted because Glykeria had walked off the calories. Woolworth's was a paradise of inexpensive treasures — dimestore pearls, perfumes, rings, stockings, and lingerie — and just choosing what to buy with the few coins they had saved from their milk allowance made them feel like women of power and independence beyond anything possible in Greece.

While Kanta and Glykeria were busy at Table Talk, I, deprived of my neighborhood Greendale Theater, was exploring distant corners of Worcester in search of movies, which I now craved like a drug. I walked, hitchhiked, or rode the bus to the downtown picture palaces, like Loew's Poli on Main Street, where plaster cherubs and white marble columns supported the burgundy velvet curtains and arched ceilings painted with clouds. In more obscure corners of the city I found oases like the Elm Street Theater, where you could catch second-run movies, or the Family Theater on Front Street, a dusty, moth-eaten cinema specializing in revivals, where Fotini and I faithfully attended the Saturday matinees.

One Saturday toward summer, trying to scrounge the price of a ticket to the new film *Ivanhoe* at Loew's Poli, I approached my father, knowing that he was feeling flush on his payday, his pockets stuffed with his own pay envelope plus Kanta and Glykeria's weekly salaries: a grand total of over $200. Anticipating his regular Saturday night at the Greek coffeehouse, he would, I suspected, be feeling generous. I was right.

"Entertain yourself! Get an ice cream soda too," he said, peeling a whole dollar bill off a roll the size of a fist. "It's a nice night; we can walk downtown together," he added. "Vasili said the car's ready, so I'll give you a ride home after the show."

Our Studebaker, in need of a new transmission, was being serviced by the local Greek car mechanic on Green Street, but Father seemed unperturbed at having to make the trek into town on foot. I waited patiently as he brushed his new fedora and his chesterfield, folded a fresh handkerchief for his pocket, adjusted his bow tie, gave a final swipe to the wing tips of his shoes, and collected the umbrella that he carried like a walking stick, fair weather or foul. His attire complete, we headed down Lincoln Street, my father, as always, strutting to the beat of an imaginary brass band. I knew that these nights at the coffeehouse meant as much to him as the movies did to me, and I never saw him dress as carefully as he did when preparing for his weekly evening out.

I left my father by the unmarked door of the Hellenic Club at 112 Front Street. There was no sign to attract the eye, for strangers were not welcome. This was a fraternal club of compatriots.

After the movie was over, still aghast that Robert Taylor could prefer the charms of Joan Fontaine to those of Elizabeth Taylor, I wandered back through downtown Worcester to the familiar doorway between Crown Lunch and Howard Clothes, mounted the dingy staircase, and entered the door to the Hellenic Club.

Since the first wave of Greek immigrants had arrived at the beginning of the century, the coffeehouses of Worcester had served as a home away from home to the Greek bachelors living in exile. Because they shared quarters in squalid tenements, packed ten to a room, and moved often, they even used their favorite coffeehouse as their mailing address. It was a place to peruse Greek-language newspapers and to spin the dial of the radio perched atop the big refrigerator, trying to pick up Greek-language stations from Boston or New York.

Spiro Tsefrekas, a thin, pale, white-haired immigrant from the Peloponnesian province of Elis, had owned the Hellenic Club coffeehouse for as long as anyone could remember, and he looked after his regulars with paternal solicitude. With the help of two cooks, he produced a good simple Greek meal every day for about fifty cents: typically a plate of lentil soup (*fakes*), yellow-eye bean soup (*fasoulada*), or stew (*yiahni*), accompanied by cheese and a round loaf of bread. Every Saturday night Tsefrekas used the roomy ovens of the restaurant downstairs to cook up eighty pounds of roast lamb and potatoes. This big meal of the week cost his clientele ninety-five cents, and fifteen cents more would buy a dish of the *cafenion*'s homemade yogurt. Another dime procured a cup of Greek coffee boiled to order in any of the thirty-odd variations from black to extra sweet.

Tsefrekas kept his coffeehouse open as late as necessary, depending on demand. If the cards were hot at three A.M., he would hand the keys to the players and go home to get a little sleep before he had to come back in the morning to start the ovens and the hundred pots of yogurt that mellowed atop the cast-iron stove all day. The Hellenic Club was open 363 days a year. Only on Good Friday and Holy Saturday did Tsefrekas hang the black jacks from the lamp cords over every table to indicate the tables were closed. Then he had to shove his customers out the door, telling them to go to church to mourn at Christ's bier and not to come back until Easter Sunday. That was the busiest day of the year at the *cafenions* (except for New Year's Eve, when it is practically a Greek's patriotic duty to gamble in order to sample his luck for the coming year).

Every Easter, Tsefrekas' wife made the braided cookies called *kou-lourakia* and dyed the ruby-red eggs at home. On Easter Sunday each customer would receive, along with his ten-cent cup of coffee, a free *koulouri* and a red egg as an expression of appreciation from the proprietor. Tsefrekas gave away 120 sets each Easter.

No women were tolerated within the coffeehouse — not even the owner's wife and two daughters, although his three sons, all my age or a bit older, scurried about between tables working like hyperactive ants. If a wife or daughter wanted to summon one of the gamblers home before his pockets were empty, she would stand in the hall outside the main room and tap a coin on the nearby steam pipe until someone took notice of her presence and called through the smoke, "Hey, Stavro, your old lady's here — hide your winnings!"

Despite the home-cooked food, the numbers runners collecting bets for "nigger pool," the joking and storytelling and arguing over politics, the main attraction of the Hellenic Club was gambling. This distinguished it from the other Greek coffeehouse in Worcester, known as Kritikos — its owner's nickname. That *cafenion*, located on Mechanic Street, was considered the coffeehouse of the bourgeois Greeks and the frivolous gamblers, because it served several functions. The premises were divided by thin partitions into a regular restaurant, a gambling hall, and an office in the back, where a versatile fellow advised Greeks on immigration and citizenship problems and served as their travel agent and real estate broker.

Unlike Kritikos, Tsefrekas at the Hellenic Club made his money only from the gambling tables, because the food afforded no profit. And he made a good living for his family of seven, even though gambling was illegal and he had to pay off the vice squad, which made periodic visits to collect its cut. (Liquor was also illegal, because he had no liquor license. Tsefrekas, a self-taught student of human nature, made sure to sell rye disguised in coffee cups only to customers who had demonstrated their ability to hold their liquor. Drinking to excess is not common among Greeks, and the occasional troublemaker who got drunk, pulled a knife, or smashed one of the bentwood chairs over an opponent's head was firmly ejected from the premises and never allowed to return.)

Tsefrekas charged his customers five percent of every pot, although there was no charge for sitting and kibitzing or just drinking coffee and gossiping. He and his sons would move around the room, monitoring the size of the pots. The players kept score on school slates with special slate pencils. When a game was over, they would call Tsefrekas or one of his sons to collect the fee and wipe the slate clean with a damp cloth.

In exchange, Tsefrekas made sure the big gamblers were kept supplied with fresh packs of Bicycle playing cards. Using up to eighty packs a week, he filtered the worn cards down from the poker tables to the "*koltsina* crowd" — the old men who sat at small tables for two, playing just to determine who would pay for the next round of coffee.

Poker was the choice of the hard-core gamblers, but *koltsina* and *tavli* (backgammon) were the games for older men who came to the coffeehouse to pass the time. The "fine gentlemen" at the coffeehouse seemed to gravitate toward medium-stakes gin rummy and pinochle, where $20 might be won or lost in an evening but the emphasis was on card-playing skill and sportsmanlike behavior rather than making money.

Pinochle was my father's game of choice, and he counted himself among the well-dressed, well-mannered crowd who played for moderate stakes along with John Kotsilimbas-Davis, his boss at Putnam and Thurston, and Peter Bell, the lawyer who had warned him against writing the letter Dino had requested, lest he be cheated out of all his money. Bell had the demeanor of a judge, a fine thatch of silver hair to match the silver frames of his glasses, and a deep, mellifluous voice worthy of a BBC announcer. Such elegant gentlemen playing pinochle, their silk vests unbuttoned for comfort, expensive suit coats draped over the chairs, fine cigars clutched in their teeth, seemed to me a magnificent sight.

The less refined gamblers, ready to lose or win hundreds of dollars in a night, gravitated toward the poker games at the round, claw-footed oak tables, which could accommodate up to ten players. Occasionally they were also allowed to play *barbout* (craps) in the back room. These men always filled me with a mixture of awe and fear. Prominent among them was Stanley Adamowicz, a blond Polish cop who played poker nightly in full police regalia, his uniform jacket on the back of his chair and his gun at his side. Other non-Greeks, including Armenians, Syrians, Albanians, and Rumanians, might also be found at the poker tables, although the majority of the Hellenic Club's patrons came from our northern Greek province of Epiros or from Elis in the Peloponnesus, with a few Cretans and Macedonians thrown in to spice up the mixture.

On that Saturday night after seeing *Ivanhoe*, I entered the Hellenic Club and inhaled the perfume of this male sanctuary: acrid smoke, pungent goat cheese and olives, bay rum aftershave, sweat, and the underlying odor of linseed oil, which Tsefrekas' sons spread on the bare oak floors every month to absorb the cigarette ashes, the dust, and the saliva that missed the spittoons. A cloud of yellow smoke hung over the suspended lamps and the slowly revolving ceiling fans, fed by silver curlicues drifting up from each player. The walls, once bluish green, had become a tobacco yellow, and the pressed-tin ceiling, fifteen feet above the floor, was the same jaundiced color. The tall windows overlooking Spring Street were masked by stained brownish shades so that the break of dawn would not distract the gamblers.

The murmur that filled the room that night was as hushed as the chanting of the priest before the altar on Sunday morning. It was the hour of serious gambling, and the dealers softly intoned their litany as the cards wafted from their hands to fall around the perimeter of the large tables. Everywhere there was the soft *tick-tick* of worry beads flicking through the nervous fingers of the players as they meditated on their cards. In the stale air of the long, narrow room, the only people hurrying were Tsefrekas and his sons, who seemed to be everywhere at once, collecting fees, wiping slates, selling cigarettes and cigars, taking orders, and balancing foamy cups of coffee on swinging round metal trays.

I searched the room for my father, expecting to see him at the square pinochle table with Peter Bell. With apprehension, I spied him at one of the big round poker tables, the overhead light glistening on his bald pate, his bow tie undone as he studied the cards. He didn't look right surrounded by the scruffy, perspiring cardsharps and factory workers, many of whom chewed tobacco and spit expertly into the spittoons.

I walked over and stood behind him, noticing his impressive pile of cash on the table. Harry Petralias, a former wrestler, glanced up and said to me, as he always did, flexing one mammoth arm, "Hi, kid! Wanna see my potatoes?"

"*Ande, rixe* — c'mon, play!" snarled Stanley Adamowicz. I always marveled at the way a Polish cop had picked up such a perfect mastery of poker Greek. "What is this anyway, a bridge game?" he continued. "Stop flexing your biceps and bet!"

The game was seven-card stud, and the dealer for the hand was Yiannis tis Grias, "The Old Lady's Yianni," a cadaverous young man so nicknamed because he was famous for abusing his mother. Softly he recited the cards as he dealt: "Ten, deuce, seven, possible straight, pair of fours," he said, as he dropped a second four on my father's hand.

I stood there watching as my father rode the pair, betting aggressively, finally winning a pot close to $70. He glanced up at me with a look of self-satisfaction and I muttered, "The movie's over."

"Already?" exclaimed Father, pulling his gold pocket watch out of his vest pocket. "Very short movie!" He smiled apologetically. "Can't leave now, just when the cards have fallen in love with me. Isn't there another cinema around here?"

"The Elm Street Theater is showing a revival of *The Best Years of Our Lives*," I admitted.

"Perfect! You deserve another movie," he said, reaching into his pocket. He pulled out Kanta's pay envelope and took out a dollar. "Have a good time!" he said. "Come back when it's over. Buy yourself some popcorn too."

He turned to the player on his left, Spiro Garoulis, who was as permanent a fixture at the Hellenic Club as the cast-iron radiators. Spiro and the other players waited impatiently as my father handed me the dollar. "What can I do? He's my only son," he said, grinning at the watching gamblers, their skin as pallid as the ash of their cigarettes. "I spoil him too much, but he's an orphan, lost his precious mother."

I stood and observed as my father won another hand, bluffing the entire table with nothing more than a pair of twos. "Too bad you weren't on my route when I was selling fruits and vegetables," he teased Stanley Adamowicz, who was becoming visibly annoyed by his glee. "I'd never get stuck with bruised bananas or wormy apples if I had you as a customer."

Father scooped up the pot and waved for one of Tsefrekas' sons. When he got the boy's attention he scattered a handful of coins across the floor with a dramatic gesture. "*Kerase teen parea!*" he called out. "Treat the house! I can't enjoy my luck unless I share it."

I could see that Father's evening was far from over, so I took his dollar and his advice and headed for the Elm Street Theater. When I returned to the Hellenic Club after eleven, I found him in quite a different mood. There was no longer a pile of money in front of him; in fact, he was no longer playing, just watching.

"What took you so long?" he growled when he saw me. "I was on a roll, but you lollygagged so long my luck turned bad. Movies are just a waste of good money anyway. Teach youngsters bad manners."

"Don't chew the kid out, Christo," said Harry Petralias, in a jovial mood as usual. "You'll get a chance to win your money back tomorrow."

"You won't see me here tomorrow," grumbled my father. "I'm a family man with responsibilities, not like you low-lifes who waste your days gambling as if you're never going to die." He turned to me. "Let's go," he muttered. "This place stinks of unwashed flesh and greed."

Out on the street I reminded him, "Aren't we going to pick up the car?"

"Garage is closed by now," he snapped.

"Then let's take a bus," I pleaded. "I'm too tired to walk back."

"Take a bus?" he exploded. "You think I'm made of money? The old years, kids walked everywhere, let their parents ride the mule. Kids today are all soft. The fresh air will do you good."

As we slogged home through the midnight silence of the streets, my father no longer swung his umbrella like a sword. I knew he didn't have even thirty cents left for bus fare. I was furious that he had gambled away my sisters' salaries as well as his own — all the money we had to live on for a week — and I was even angrier that he was trying to make it look like my fault. For the rest of the way home, I didn't speak to him and took no pity on his flagging steps, but kept walking so fast, to prove

I wasn't soft, that he became breathless and had to stop several times on the three flights of stairs up to our door.

The next morning, after the girls asked for coins to pay for some candles at church, I could hear through my bedroom door the sound of Kanta yelling at him. "You mean to say you don't have anything left from our paychecks?" she shouted. "You lost the whole thing in a poker game?"

"I was four hundred dollars ahead at one point," he protested. "My luck was unbelievable! I was going to take your salary and triple it. I could buy you a dowry plus the best bridal gown in Worcester. I was doing it all for you, and instead of being grateful, you yell at the father who slaves six days a week in a sweltering kitchen, being insulted by men who should be working for me!"

I noted that he was still trying to distract us from his own irresponsibility in losing our money by turning the blame onto others. I was guilty for dawdling too long at the movies, Kanta was at fault for not recognizing Father's generous intentions to win money for her, and his employers were culpable because they insulted him and deprived him of his rightful place. The only one who wasn't guilty, to hear him tell it, was Christos Gatzoyiannis.

I kept all these thoughts and my growing resentments locked inside me as we ate beans for a week and walked everywhere because we couldn't afford the bus. I noticed that our tribulations did not prevent Father from returning to the coffeehouse the next weekend, as soon as he had a new paycheck.

While Father was working and gambling at the coffeehouse, I was exploring the underbelly of our new neighborhood. Although in our fifth-grade class I hung out with the more studious and well-behaved boys, when summer came and school ended I found myself attracted to the rowdier element in the neighborhood. These were boys who lived in the run-down three-deckers toward Lincoln Square, in rooms with curling linoleum on the floor, furniture draped with sheets to hide the torn upholstery, dirty dishes in the sink, and, sometimes, an icebox instead of a refrigerator. I was drawn to these boys not only for the aura of danger and sophistication that surrounded them but also because many of them had been held back and like me were older than the other fifth-graders.

The oldest of the neighborhood gang, Jackie Walsh, didn't seem to go to school at all. When I asked him why, he always replied offhandedly, "You don't need school to be a success. Look at Jimmy Durante, you think he ever went beyond sixth grade?"

Walsh, although small and thin, was nearly sixteen, compared with the rest of us, who were twelve or thirteen. He walked with a swagger, chain-smoked, wore his pack of cigarettes rolled up in the sleeve of his T-shirt and his brown hair in a slicked-back ducktail, and talked with thrilling vulgarity about girls and the most lurid details of sex.

The other spark plug of the gang was Al Berry, only twelve but ready to accept any dare. Berry was fast and light like a ferret, full of nervous energy, always laughing and pacing in circles around the rest of us, who moved too slowly for his taste. Richard Joubert was the slick, good-looking member of the gang. The one I felt closest to was Jerry Kahn, because, as a Jew in this Catholic neighborhood, he too was an outsider. We both cultivated a chameleon-like adaptability which made us fit in with the whole spectrum of our classmates, from the straight arrows and teacher's pets to the delinquents and hoods.

From our back piazza, I could glimpse the neighborhood gang of adolescent punks hanging out on Henchman Street in the warm summer dusks. Henchman Street, named for Captain Daniel Henchman, a renowned Indian fighter among Worcester's earliest settlers, was a quiet side street off Lincoln, little traveled except by those headed for Ritz's Market, a grocery store in the ground floor of a three-decker at the corner of Henchman and Moen.

Ritz's Market was a good place to buy Popsicles, Fudgsicles, baseball cards, ice cream sandwiches, and (my personal favorite) Chunky candy bars. Just next to it stood an ornate Victorian cast-iron street lamp with a cross arm branching out of the main pole about fifteen feet above the sidewalk, ending in a lamp shaped like a flower bud. This street lamp inspired the neighborhood boys to devise a daredevil acrobatic routine intended to impress girls passing by on their way to Ritz's Market for a sweet dessert in the early evening.

The trick, perfected by the lighter and more agile members of the gang, was to shimmy up the height of the lamppost, sit on the crossbar, suddenly fall backward so that you were hanging by your knees upside down, and then — the ultimate display of devastating cool — unroll the pack of cigarettes from your T-shirt sleeve, light up, and casually smoke while hanging in this position, where a slip meant certain death, the skull crushed like an eggshell, the brains splattered on the pavement.

The first time I saw this routine performed by Al Berry, who scrambled up the lamppost with the speed and agility of a monkey, I could hardly believe it. But the way Al did it, it looked almost easy, and it always made the girls scream in horrified admiration.

Most of the corner gang mastered the trick sooner or later during that summer, when the girls they fancied were within sight. Naturally I dreamed of performing this feat of skill myself. I could imagine the whole thing clearly. I would time my ascension to the arrival of a long-legged girl in my class named Nancy Flynn.

Nancy lived just a few dozen yards from Ritz's Market, at 2½ Hench-man Street, an old three-decker set back from the road with room for a tree and a swing in the front yard. She was a nubile twelve-year-old who often wore short shorts that displayed her shapely legs to considerable advantage. Although she came from a strict Catholic family and was not "loose," Nancy's innocently flirtatious manner, her pouty lips parted like a half-opened flower, and her firm emerging breasts set me on fire. I was sure that once she saw me hanging by my knees from the lamp-post, Nancy Flynn would be mine for life.

Many other girls passed down Henchman Street to the market, and Jackie Walsh, our leader by virtue of his superior age and sexual expe-rience, fancied a lanky sixteen-year-old known for her tendency to climb into the cars of passing boys. "Would you look at the way she licks that Popsicle!" Jackie muttered as she sashayed past. "I'd like a little of that."

I wasn't quite sure what he was talking about, but I knew it had to do with sex. I always tried to keep from revealing my ignorance of fe-male anatomy and biology. "I'd like to buy Nancy Flynn a Popsicle myself," I responded knowingly.

All alone I practiced my ascent on a lamppost around the corner on Crescent Street, which was pretty much deserted once the workers from the lumber- and coalyards went home at night. To my surprise it took me weeks just to master shimmying up to the cross arm; it looked so easy when Al Berry did it. I spent another week or so sitting on the side bar, just thinking about hanging by my knees. When I finally managed to shut my eyes and hang upside down, I felt ready to make my debut before the audience on Henchman Street. Keeping a pack of cigarettes rolled up in my T-shirt sleeve was out of the question, because my sisters would tell my father if they even suspected me of smoking, but I decided it would be enough just to swing casually, suspended high above the heads of the admiring crowd, and to skip the cigarette.

While I was practicing lamppost-hanging, I was also learning to play poker from the Henchman Street gang. We gathered at one or another boy's house; unlike my friends to the north on Lincoln Street, these friends rarely suffered the inconvenience of having an adult at home during the day, so we were at liberty to relax and do what we pleased: smoking, gambling, drinking beer (if we had any money), and lying about girls and sex. Many of the allusions in the conversations went over my head, especially frequent references to visits to the "underpass" by Jackie Walsh and Al Berry. I assumed they did something unmen-tionable there with girls. They talked in veiled terms about many things they didn't want me to understand.

On hot days we might hike over to Bell Pond on Belmont Street, not far away, which because of its shape had originally rejoiced in the name of Bladder Pond, until the Worcester city fathers decided to change it to something more elegant. What I liked about going with my new friends from Henchman Street was that they couldn't swim either, so we passed the time roughhousing, splashing each other, and eyeing the girls in their bathing suits.

Olga's baby was due by the end of July, and on Saturday, August 1, just after she had finished giving the whole house its thorough weekly cleaning, she went into labor. In the village, babies were assisted into the world by the local midwife while the neighborhood women helped and the men and children gathered outside the door. There was no question of doctors or hospitals. But Father insisted that Olga have her baby the proper American way, aided by Dr. Seidenberg, and when the contractions began he told her to get ready to go across the street to the hospital.

Olga had terrible memories of that hospital and the operation on her neck, when she hadn't been able to eat any of the hospital food and had waited miserably every day for Father to bring Greek food from home. Now she looked longingly at a large pot of beans and lamb bubbling on the stove, and despite the urging of the rest of us, she said, "I'll just sit down and have a bite to eat before I go. Who knows when they'll feed me at the hospital?" As we all gathered around the table, watching her nervously, Olga put away two huge helpings of the stew, a meal she would have ample opportunity to regret during the next twelve hours. Then she gave in to our pleas and let Father lead her out the door to Doctors' Hospital.

Once Olga was safely checked in and delivered to the maternity section, Father went to Putnam and Thurston, where Dino was working the late shift, to inform him that he would soon become a father. The rest of us sat at home reassuring each other that Olga would be fine — look what a good appetite she had — and waiting for the phone to ring.

In the hospital, Olga spent the night laboring alone, without anyone from her family beside her for moral support. The American way of having babies far from the family hearth seemed to her cold and impersonal. She screamed so often and so loudly that she was sure we would hear her all the way across the street. The staff of the hospital remembered her cries for years afterward with awe. A nurse was assigned to her bedside. "Please don't scream so, my dear," she begged constantly, as Olga launched into another crescendo of ululating cries and operatic wails. "Just tell yourself that tomorrow you'll be a mother with a beautiful baby, and try not to scream so loud."

But Olga knew that woman was destined to bring forth children in sorrow and lamentation and that it was a woman's prerogative —

almost her duty — to scream as much as possible when giving birth. She remembered how she had heard her own mother scream as she crouched outside the door of our house while *Mana* gave birth to Fotini and, sixteen months later, to me. During childbirth, Mother had stood, clutching a rope that the midwife had suspended from the beams. Supported by other women, she had pulled on the rope and screamed with each pain while the midwife pulled and coaxed the baby out of the womb into her waiting apron.

While the rest of the family kept vigil in the parlor, I fell asleep that night, until the ring of the telephone shattered the silence of our house about three A.M. It was Dr. Seidenberg, telling my father that he was a grandfather — of a great strapping boy.

"It's a miracle!" Father shouted, first to Dr. Seidenberg and then to the rest of us. "A miracle baby! A boy! After the way my poor wife was cursed with four girls before a son — and her mother only girls, most of them born dead! I never thought Olga would have a son! It's a miracle! My first grandchild, and a boy!"

I remember Dino waking me out of a sound sleep, nearly incoherent with joy. Little Spiro Bartzokis, heir to a noble, ancient line, had been born. There was never any question about his name: like every dutiful Greek couple, Olga and Dino had to name the first boy for the paternal grandfather. (Unfortunately, Dino's father, who gave silver coins to half his neighborhood in Kastoria when he heard the news, did not live to see his namesake.)

Dino and my father were at the hospital door by dawn, waiting to meet this prodigy before they had to go to work. When they entered Olga's room, the nurse put the infant in my father's arms.

"No, give *him* baby!" cried Olga, pointing at her adored husband, who was trembling with awe. "He father! *His* baby!"

"But your father is so excited — look at him," replied the nurse. "Let him hold the baby first."

My father took the infant, who seemed to resemble him most of all since both were fair, fat, and bald, and his tears fell on the blue blanket.

We all welcomed this husky boy home like the miracle he was. Never had anyone seen hands so fine, cheeks so rosy, eyes so intelligent. No child had ever had so many admirers to applaud his every gurgle and hiccup. We all waited on him as if he were a princeling, trying to anticipate his wishes before he knew them himself. To us he was more than the first baby in our family; he was the living proof that our mother's sacrifice had not been in vain. She had given up her own life to protect and preserve her children and get them to the safety of America. Now this small lump of flesh was testimony that her death, like the grain of wheat that falls to the ground, had borne fruit. Our mother was dead, but her children had begun a new generation of life in a new country, and this coddled baby was the demonstration of immortality for her and would eventually be our immortality as well.

We all vied to walk, dress, feed, and amuse little Spiro. Olga wheeled him around the neighborhood in his baby carriage, displaying him to all passers-by with the pride of a Greek wife who has pulled off the greatest achievement of any woman: producing a son. Olga suspected that this child of hers was special — destined for an extraordinary life.

One hot day, shortly after Spiro joined our family, I happened to be poking around Olga and Dino's room when I heard her approaching with the baby. On an impulse I hid behind a large, low bureau which was topped with a mirror and two table lamps. Olga sat down in the rocking chair and began to give the baby his late-afternoon bottle, crooning to him the kind of lullaby that Greek mothers save for their sons:

> My warrior, my little king, my treasure,
> The fates will always smile on you.
> You'll grow up tall as a mountain,
> Straight as a cypress tree,
> And cast a giant shadow
> From Rome to Constantinople.

I was feeling mischievous and perhaps a bit weary of all the fuss over the baby, so I decided to play a trick on Olga. As she bent to put the nipple into his mouth, I reached over to the electric outlet behind the bureau and removed the plug for the two lamps, then stuck it back in. The lights flickered, and Olga looked up, aware of some change in the illumination of the room.

She searched all around her, but spied nothing amiss, so she turned back toward the baby, cooing, and stuck the bottle back in his mouth.

Again I pulled out the plug and replaced it. Again the lights flickered and Olga looked up in surprise, trying to see what was causing the room to go dark. Peering from behind the bureau, I could see her eyes widen. "*Panayia mou!*" she whispered, as she crossed herself with her free hand. "Holy Mother of God!"

Looking worried now, she gazed around the room, even over her shoulder, out the window, and up to the ceiling, but she saw nothing. Brow furrowed in puzzlement, she turned her head back down toward the baby.

As soon as the bottle entered his mouth, the lights flickered again. Olga let out a piercing shriek. "Kanta, come here quick!" she screamed, loudly enough to be heard on the street below. "It's the baby!"

Kanta dashed into the room, her hands dripping with dishwater. "What is it? What's happened?" she cried as she saw Olga's face.

"It's the baby!" Olga screamed. "The Blessed Virgin has come to me and given me a sign! He's not just an ordinary baby, he's the Messiah, come back. I've given birth to the Messiah!"

From my hiding place I stifled a snort of laughter. Kanta fixed Olga with a skeptical look. "What do you mean, the Virgin Mary has given you a sign? I don't see the Angel Gabriel in here."

"It's true!" insisted Olga. "Every time I go to feed him, there's a flash of heavenly light. It's the Virgin Mary, I tell you! Watch!"

She bent over little Spiro and put the nipple back into his mouth. Nothing happened.

"I'm not imagining it — it happened three times!" Olga insisted. "Every time I put the bottle in his mouth, the lights flickered."

"Those lights, you mean?" asked Kanta, pointing to the bureau. She pondered a moment, then strode over and pulled the bureau away from the wall, revealing me doubled up, purple in the face from trying to hold in my laughter.

For decades Olga refused to forgive me for my trick on her, and the rest of us never stopped reminding her of her claims that the birth of her son Spiro was the Second Coming.

Summer was winding down, twilight was coming earlier every day, and I knew that school would soon be starting, Nancy Flynn would be exchanging her short shorts for pleated skirts, and I would have lost my chance to win her heart with my derring-do. I was ready to lay my life on the line to earn her admiration, and as we lingered around Ritz's Market each evening I coached my cronies carefully in their roles. As soon as one of them saw Nancy starting out of her front yard toward the market, he would warn me and I'd start climbing the post. By the time she reached us, I would be high above her head, ready to flip into the hanging part of the routine.

One evening I waited nervously, afraid that the light would vanish entirely before her appetite for a Popsicle drew her out of the swing in her front yard. Earlier in the evening I had saluted her with an impeccably cool and casual "Hey, Nancy!" as I swaggered by, and now my palms were starting to sweat as I waited for her to follow. Mentally I rehearsed my moves, remembering the hard, cold feel of the iron beneath my legs.

"Here she comes. Get going!" hissed Jackie Walsh, and I lunged for the rusty lamppost. I could hear footsteps. The image of Nancy approaching through the dusk, her white shorts and blouse shining phosphorescent in the purple twilight, filled me with superhuman strength. I shimmied up the slippery post in record time, triumphantly swung my legs over the cross bar, and pulled myself into a sitting position, with my back to the sidewalk below.

Just as Nancy reached the foot of the pole, I would tumble backward, appearing to fall for one heart-stopping moment so that she would cry out in fright, just as the audience at a circus moans when it seems the trapeze artist is falling to his death in the split second before he saves himself. Then I would catch myself, insouciantly hanging by my knees, grinning at her in victory, high above her head. I could already imagine Nancy standing there, her mouth open in fear, her hand to her heart, astonished at my courage.

"Hey, Nick, look who's here!" called one of my friends with a strange undertone of warning. Nancy was right below. I took a deep breath and casually fell backward, catching myself just as planned, so that I swung like the clapper of a bell upside down above the pavement. There was a most gratifying scream, and then another. By the second scream I suspected something had gone wrong.

Hanging by my knees, I surveyed the audience below, not getting too good a view from my inverted position. Then my vision cleared and I saw, screaming, her hands covering her mouth . . . not the lanky, shimmering white form of Nancy Flynn but the stocky, black-clad figure of Glykeria, who had slipped out of our house when Kanta wasn't looking to purchase a forbidden ice cream sandwich.

"Cursed devil, you'll kill yourself!" Glykeria was screaming up at me in Greek. "Get down from there! God save him! He's going to die. If you fall down and break your neck, your father will murder you."

I grabbed the pole, righted myself, and slid to the ground fireman-style, searching in bewilderment for Nancy Flynn, wondering how my plan could have backfired so badly. Finally I saw her in the lighted door of Ritz's Market, giggling at the scene my sister was making as she stood there, hands on her hips, calling upon every saint in the Greek calendar to curse me for my sins.

It was even more mortifying, if possible, when Glykeria dragged me away from my gleeful cohorts and berated me in Greek all the way back to our house. Father was just coming in, and she gave him an inspired description of what she had just seen me doing on the corner by Ritz's Market, with my hoodlum friends egging me on.

"Is this why I brought you out of Greece?" roared my father. "Why your mother died to get you out, why she struggled to keep you alive through the famine and the war, so that you could kill yourself falling from a lamppost?"

I flushed with anger at hearing him invoke my mother's name against me. He was the one who had failed to save her in time. But I knew I was in no position to lash out at him now, so I tried to bring myself under control and then offered a mild protest. "All the other guys do it," I said weakly.

"Those bums you hang out with — I know about them," he shot back. "Besides hanging around street corners, they smoke and drink and steal and chase whores." He spoke with such conviction that I began to suspect he did know more about our activities than I thought.

"I work like a *hamal* at an age when most men are retired and your sisters slave on an assembly line nine hours a day so that you can hang out on street corners with low-lifes?" he went on. "Back in Greece, boys your age are doing a man's work. How old was I when my mother apprenticed me to a cooper?"

"Eight years old," I muttered, groaning inwardly at the prospect of hearing this story once again.

"That's right, eight years old! I was so little I couldn't bend the hoops with my hands, and he beat me. So they apprenticed me to a tinker. He would put me in the big pots with rags on my feet and sand underfoot and make me dance to polish the insides. I traveled with him to Crete, to Asia, to Constantinople, sleeping on the ground, shining pots. And how much did I get? One English pound a month, and I took it all home to my mother to feed my fatherless brothers and sisters. Do you think I had time for hanging from lampposts when I was your age?"

"No," I mumbled, hoping that my penitent expression would make him cut the story short. Then, recklessly, I added, "But there's nothing else to do around here in the summer."

"Damn right, nothing but Satan's business!" shouted my father, angrier than ever, but at least distracted from the tales of his underprivileged childhood. "I should have put you to work for Tzouras the minute school got out. Unloading fruit crates might teach you a little sense. You're just lucky school's starting next week, or I'd do it first thing in the morning. From now on, you're going to school and you're going to be home every night for dinner at five o'clock and you're not going out afterward. And if I catch you hanging out with those delinquents on the street corner again, I'm going to have a word with Stanley Adamowicz at the coffeehouse and get the police to look into their after-school activities. And don't think he wouldn't do it for me!"

The idea of spending the rest of my life coming home at five o'clock every night was nearly as bad as being sent to jail, but I could see there was no point in protesting his decision now, with Glykeria standing by, eager to embellish her lurid tales of my acrobatic feats. Sullenly I went to bed, plotting how to change Father's mind about this impossible curfew.

A week after Fotini and I started sixth grade, our portly principal, Miss McKenna, introduced us to square dancing. Every afternoon she would bring a phonograph into the cafeteria, direct us to push back the tables, and form us into squares of four couples each. Miss McKenna demonstrated the steps with vast enthusiasm and agility despite her girth. Square dancing held great appeal for me, because it was an opportunity to have physical contact with the opposite sex without all the stress of close dancing, and the intricate steps reminded me of the Greek line dances of our native province.

One day, as Nancy Flynn do-si-doed past me, she said coyly, "I haven't seen you around Henchman Street much. We've all missed you."

My pulse quickened at the thought that she had noticed my absence, but I answered, with a shrug, "Been pretty busy lately." Nancy's remark redoubled my determination to find a way out of my father's despised curfew.

That afternoon I ventured down Henchman Street, hoping to run into Nancy before five o'clock. She wasn't around, but my pal Richard Joubert arrived with a new BB gun he had just received for his thirteenth birthday. We all pooled our nickels and dimes to purchase a box of ammunition, then half a dozen of us headed toward Crescent Street, the industrial area of depots, warehouses, and factories, to do some target practice in a vacant lot.

As we trooped along Crescent past Wood's Lumberyard, four workmen standing near the summit of a pile of wooden planks saw us, a pack of thirteen- and fourteen-year-olds trailing behind Joubert and his rifle like rats behind the Pied Piper.

"What're you gunning for?" taunted one of the workmen, so far away we could scarcely hear him. "Elephants? That's the only thing you could hit with that popgun!"

The rest of us laughed, but Joubert, enraged at the insult to his marksmanship, aimed in the direction of the workers and let fly three pellets. It was meant only as a gesture of defiance, but some perverse demon led one of the BBs directly to the heckler's skull. He let out a howl and slapped his forehead.

With a great roar, he and his friends launched themselves downward in our direction — four huge workmen in pursuit of half a dozen terrified boys. They had to clamber down from atop the pile of lumber and cross the lumberyard to the street. We meanwhile ran like rabbits up Crescent Street. As we approached its end, we fanned out, scattering among the warehouses and slag heaps.

Too scared to think clearly, I kept running straight ahead, right for a pile of coal dust that blocked my way like a miniature mountain. I started to scramble up the barrier, not realizing how soft it was, and immediately began to sink in. The black powder rose above my knees like quicksand. I was firmly lodged in place, doomed by my encounter with the coal pile like Br'er Rabbit when he attacked the Tar Baby.

Two workmen converged on me, since I was so conveniently fixed in place, while the other two pursued the rest of the culprits, disappearing over the horizon. The men started beating me, hitting me with open palms and screaming oaths. Since my legs wouldn't move, all I could do was try to protect my head and face with my arms, meanwhile wailing, "Not me! I don't do it! Not me!" Each time one of the men knocked me down, I would turn to him to plead my innocence, bobbing up like a rubber punching bag only to be knocked down again.

Finally, after they had finished splitting my lip, bloodying my nose, closing my eyes, and gashing my head open on rocks, the pair decided they had punished me enough — clearly I wasn't the one with the gun anyway. They left me there with grime, blood, and tears coursing down my face and headed back toward Wood's, shouting over their shoulders threats of what would happen if any of us "goddamn J.D.'s" were seen in the neighborhood again.

When they had gone, I managed to extricate my legs from the coal pile. I made my way home by an alternate route, more frightened by the prospect of my family's reaction than by my wounds. As I climbed our stairs, I tried to brush the coal dust off, but it was mixed with blood and tears into a grisly coat of mud.

Through my swollen eyelids I saw Olga grow pale at her first glimpse of me. Then she regained enough strength to start screaming. She shrieked and cursed and tried to tend my wounds, but I wouldn't let her touch me. In martyred silence I went into the bathroom, bathed myself as best I could, and put on my pajamas. I could scarcely recognize my reflection in the mirror. In an attempt to hide the purple bruises, black eyes, and red gashes, I borrowed some of my father's talcum powder and dusted myself liberally, but it only made me look worse.

When I emerged from the bathroom, Olga started in again: how it would have been better for me to stay on the streets with my delinquent friends and let them kill me first, because Father was going to finish the job; how the whole family was disgraced by my behavior and she could never hold up her head at St. Spyridon's because of me. . .

I slammed my bedroom door, got into bed, and tried not to think about what Father would do when he got home. Eventually I heard him on the stairs and then Olga's shrill diatribe as soon as he was inside the door. Typically, she alternated between condemning my misdeeds and pleading for him to go easy on me. "His face is like raw meat from the beating!" she shrieked. "Can't find decent boys to hang out with. Don't kill him, *Patera*! He's lost enough blood already! The reprobate! Not a brain in his head! Why couldn't he just once walk away from a fight? Don't take your belt to him! He's just a baby!"

Olga fell silent as Father came into the darkened bedroom where I lay with my eyes closed. I heard him walk over to study me, could feel his breath on my face. Finally I couldn't stand it any longer, and opened my eyes to see him looking at me sadly.

"Why wouldn't you listen to me when I warned you about the bums in this neighborhood?" he said softly. "No matter what I say, if you go out for even an hour after school, you get in trouble with those devils. Well, from now on you're not going out at all. You're coming straight home from school. You go Home–School–Home. No more loitering, no more hooligan friends. Do you understand me?"

I began to wish for his usual routine of threatening me with the belt. This new decree sounded to me like a life sentence in solitary confinement.

"It wasn't my fault," I muttered sullenly.

"I don't want to know about fault," he shouted, suddenly turning savage. "I just want you home here, three-fifteen every day, and if you're not here, your sister is to call me at the restaurant. Do you hear? Answer me!"

"I hear," I said in an undertone, feeling my freedom slipping away with those words.

After this scene I came directly home from school, with Olga checking me in like a warden. Every day my rage against my father grew. Other kids were allowed to play and have friends, while I was being treated like a prisoner, and for what?

I spent a lot of time fantasizing about my father suffering a fatal heart attack or figuring how long it would take him to die of old age. I was thirteen and he was fifty-nine, I calculated, so he certainly wouldn't last more than another five or six years. Surely by nineteen I would be free of him.

This hope kept me going for a while, but after several weeks of Home–School–Home, I realized I couldn't wait around for him to die. In fact, I couldn't spend another week without seeing my friends. I decided to force the issue to a showdown.

I picked a Tuesday, because that was Father's day off and he always spent it in the coffeehouse. Instead of coming home after school, I stayed out until long past sundown. When I came in, Olga was frantic. Any other day, she said, she would have called Father at the restaurant, but now he was at the coffeehouse and there was no phone there — one of its many virtues in the eyes of its habitués.

Olga tried to stay awake to report to my father when he got back, but by midnight she was too exhausted. When I got up the next day he was waiting for me in the kitchen.

"I told you to come home straight from school, and last night you disobeyed me," he announced like a judge.

I was ready for him and immediately took the offensive. "I can't live here like a prisoner!" I said. "I need to go out and spend time with my friends, just like you do. As soon as you have time off, you go to the coffeehouse — one day, two days every week. *I* need a chance to relax with friends too! At least I don't gamble away our money while I'm doing it. I'll tell you what," I announced calmly, man to man, "if you'll stop going to the coffeehouse, I'll come straight home from school every day."

He flushed, and I could see I'd drawn blood.

"What do *you* know — a child who has everything handed to him?" he thundered. "A man who works seventy hours a week, who has five children to feed and take care of — children who drive him crazy — doesn't he deserve to relax one day a week? I don't get drunk, I don't go with women, I don't abandon you or go on welfare, and you're blaming *me* for playing cards with my friends once in a while?"

"I wasn't blaming you," I said evenly. "I was just explaining that everyone needs friends and time to relax — me as well as you."

"I don't *need* the coffeehouse; I only go once in a while to pass my time," he snarled. But I wasn't going to let him get away with that.

"You've wasted your whole life in that coffeehouse!" I said righteously. "And all your money too! You used to be a rich man — that's what everyone says. Where'd it all go? In 1945, when you could have gotten us all out between the wars, you didn't have the money. Now we're forced to live in a neighborhood like this and you go blaming *me* for the kids I hang around with! If you hadn't squandered your money at the coffeehouse, we could be living in the best neighborhood in Worcester. And if you had sent for us before the guerrillas came, the way *Mana* begged you to, she might still — "

"Enough! Not another word!" he screamed. He could see where my accusations were leading, and he couldn't bear to hear me say it. "You spew that garbage at me, your father?" he ranted, his face a dangerous shade of red. "All right! Go where you want, when you want! Ruin your life with bums and thieves! I wash my hands of you."

He grabbed his hat and umbrella and rushed out the door. I could hear him muttering all the way down the steps: "Talk to his own father like that. Insolent bum!"

I sat there stunned, filled with an intoxicating sense of triumph. I was free! He had caved in, and I could stay out as long as I wanted. I had never expected it would be that easy to make him capitulate. I had instinctively gone for his soft spots — his guilt about gambling and his failure to get us out of Greece in time — and I had broken his oppressive authority over me. Never again would he intimidate me with threats and whirling belt buckles.

He had cut me off before I finished all that I wanted to say to him, but I decided to hold my peace for now, because I had won the immediate concession I wanted: the curfew was over. One day soon, however, I intended to make him face the issue of my mother and his culpability in her death. I wanted him to admit his responsibility for her fate out loud, to me. I suspected now that I was strong enough to do it.

I ran to school, and waited anxiously all day for classes to end so I could return to Henchman Street and the company of my friends. After school I found Jackie Walsh hanging out with Al Berry outside Ritz's Market. "Look who's turned up like a bad penny," he greeted me. "I thought maybe you died from the beating Wood's gorillas gave you."

"It wasn't nothing," I said manfully. "My old man got mad, locked me up, but he won't bug me anymore."

"Then you can come with us," interjected Al Berry. "We was talking about hitching a ride to White City. Smash up a few bumper cars, cop a feel in the funhouse, see how far we can spit from the Ferris wheel."

White City had been a beacon to bored youth ever since its opening in 1905 on the shores of Lake Quinsigamond, site of nature camps, band concerts, and the sculling races still held there today. The eight-acre amusement park with its famous ten thousand electric lights was one of the wonders of New England. A two-mile narrow-gauge train track carried fun-seekers from Washington Square behind City Hall to White City, and on weekends the train would be so crowded that the iron wheels would spin in place and the conductor would have to throw sand on the tracks to get it going.

In its heyday White City was an enchanted spot where courting couples could enjoy the Ferris wheel, the tunnel of love, romantic rows in the lake, and candlelit dinners in lakeside restaurants seating up to a thousand. Pine-scented breezes ruffled the parasols and chiffon veils of the ladies dining on pickerel plucked fresh from the lake.

Billed by its developers as the "grandest and most talked about resort for hot weather entertainment and harmless fun in all New England," White City began to lose its luster when more and more people owned cars, which could carry them as far as Cape Cod in a day, and when Prohibition arrived. Hot dog stands and speakeasies sprang up where there had been nature camps for young lads to "get their bodies in good trim and their minds filled with good thought about the wonderful in nature," as the *Worcester Telegram* put it.

When Jackie Walsh and Al Berry suggested an outing to White City, they were much less interested in the wonders of nature than the stomach-turning thrill rides, the pitching and gambling concessions, the plentiful beer, and the promise of unescorted females. But such entertainment cost money, and my pockets were emptier than usual.

"I can't go, I've only got forty cents," I confessed unhappily.

Al looked at Jackie, who nodded and said, "Look, we'll treat you tonight. After all, you took the lumps for us from those bruisers at Wood's."

"Wood's will pay for it soon enough, don't worry," Al interjected, then stopped himself and glanced at Jackie.

Jackie didn't react. "Come on," he said. "Let's take a little trip to the underpass."

I flushed with pleasure at the prospect of learning what they did in the underpass that ran beneath the Providence and Worcester Railroad tracks off Lincoln Street. For a long time I had imagined all sorts of depraved pursuits taking place there.

What I didn't anticipate was that Jackie Walsh would reach up beneath one of the iron girders supporting the tracks, remove a large rock, and extract a metal box full of cash from its hiding place. He withdrew a $20 bill and handed it to me.

"Jesus Christ, where'd you get that money?" I exclaimed as he returned the box to its hole and replaced the rock.

"Here and there," he replied calmly. "These little stores and spas around here always leave some dough in the till at night. We think of it as a challenge." He turned to look at me intently. "Nobody knows about that box except me and Al and now you," he said. "So if word ever gets around, even a whisper, I guess you know who's going to be sorry."

I nodded, swallowing.

"Both of us are on probation already," Al said. "We can't take another bust."

"What's probation?" I stuttered. They looked at each other and laughed.

"I forgot what a D.P. you are!" Jackie replied. "Probation is what a judge gives you on your first offense instead of locking you up. Especially if you're under sixteen."

"It just means that we have to report to some tight-assed cop once a week and tell him again how sorry we are for being bad boys," Al explained. "It's a pain. If they catch us violating probation, like, for instance, breaking into Wood's, they'll put us away."

"But *you're* not on probation," Jackie pointed out. "And you're only thirteen. Nobody's gonna put you away no matter what you do, even if you were seen in Wood's some night."

"You mean breaking in?" I quavered.

"We figure they owe us," interjected Al. "Especially you, since you got the shit beaten out of you by those gorillas. Don't worry, we've got it all set up. It's a cinch."

"No kidding," I mumbled, trying to hide how I felt at the thought of ever setting foot in Wood's Lumberyard again.

"That twenty is just small change — you'll see," added Jackie. "So let's head for White City, check out the action."

As I followed the two boys up Belmont Street toward Shrewsbury, I tried to recapture my earlier exhilaration at being free, able to go where I wanted and return at any hour I pleased. But the $20 in my pocket seemed heavy against my leg, and I had a foreboding that it was one gift I would have to pay back at a high rate of interest.

The house on Chandler Street, which Christos bought in 1953

AGAINST
THE WIND

Where the lion's skin will not reach,
You must patch it out with the fox's.

— Plutarch, *Lysander*

LIFE AS AN EMANCIPATED thirteen-year-old was not going as well as I had anticipated. At home my sisters treated me like a juvenile delinquent. My father and I were on a cold-war footing from the day I shamed him into ending my curfew. He wouldn't risk issuing direct orders that he knew he couldn't enforce, but contented himself with dire warnings of what would happen if I continued my reckless habits, ranging from going out in the rain ("The boy is going to be in the hospital with galloping pneumonia by noon tomorrow") to coming in well past midnight ("One of these days he'll come home feet first on a police stretcher, the company he keeps"). In the best tradition of the Greek chorus, my sisters would nod and click their tongues in sorrowing accord and repeat his grim predictions in a rising arpeggio of disapproval.

I chose not to reply to his warnings, except to mutter an occasional snide remark. These were carefully calibrated not to push him over the edge, for I feared that if we embarked on another verbal showdown, I would lose control and attack him with all the anger and hatred collecting inside me. I didn't want to do that until I was ready to risk a complete break with him, so I limited myself to sarcastic mumbles and scalding looks.

With Al Berry and Jackie Walsh grooming me as their front man for the Wood's Lumberyard heist, I was reluctant to hang out on Henchman Street for fear they would set a date for my debut in crime. This kept me from pressing my courtship of Nancy Flynn. To ease my troubled mind in the fall of 1952, I sought out my usual refuge, the movies, using the change from the hot $20 bill that Walsh and Berry had given me before our outing to White City.

I went to the Plymouth Theater on Main Street to see *The Quiet Man,* a film that resonated with personal significance. I watched John Wayne, a former boxer from America, trying to make a new life for himself in Ireland and encountering obstacles at every turn. I knew how it felt to be an outsider. My life had become much more complicated since my year as the champion boxer of Greendale Avenue, which now seemed an idyllic interval.

It was almost like wish fulfillment when I encountered one of my pals from the old neighborhood, Steve Zilavy, on the way out of the theater. He was just as gangly and shy as ever, and I was surprised how glad I was to see him. "Hey, Steve!" I shouted. "Over here!"

"Hey, Nick," he replied. "How you doing? How come you never came back to see us like you promised?"

"Maybe I will," I said, meaning it. "How're all the guys?"

"They're okay," he said. "They still talk about you. We had some good times when you were around."

"Sure did," I said wistfully. "Who's the champ now? Marty?"

"No way! It's Don Muscovin."

"That little shrimp?" I burst out. "He was so weak, we don't let him fight, only referee!" I couldn't believe it. I remembered Don Muscovin as the most scorned boy in our neighborhood, a general nuisance in his pathetic eagerness to be included. It was impossible that this weakling had taken my place as the boxing star of Greendale.

"Don's not a shrimp anymore," said Steve. "He's got some good moves, too."

"Good moves! Muscovin? You gotta be kidding," I scoffed.

"I'm telling you, he hasn't lost a fight this year," Steve answered. "He made mincemeat out of Joey, me, even Marty. He took on all the guys and beat 'em."

"He don't beat me," I bragged. "You guys forget about me, but I make you remember. Set up a match for me next Saturday, and I come over on the bus and you can all watch me cream him."

Steve was not impressed by my bravado. "Maybe you better come up first and see Don fight," he cautioned.

"I don't need to see him," I told him. "You set it up."

"Sure, Nick," he agreed finally. "Everybody'll be really glad to see you back."

"Don't forget, Saturday," I said. "I'll be there. You make sure Muscovin is too."

That weekend I took the number 30 bus back to my old neighborhood, feeling like Achilles riding out to meet Hector on the battlefields of Troy. The old three-deckers on the sleepy, tree-lined streets of Greendale looked like home compared to the grim environs of Lincoln Street, and the boys gathered in the yard next to Don Muscovin's house looked just the same too — all except Don himself. Like the ninety-seven-pound weakling in the Charles Atlas ads on the back of my comic books, Muscovin had grown in the last year and was now big enough to kick sand into any bully's face. At five feet two inches and 105 pounds, I was the one who looked like the comic-book weakling.

"Hey, Greek, you haven't changed a bit!" Don greeted me cordially. "It's great to see you!"

"*You've* changed!" I muttered, silently rationalizing that despite his size, I could still beat him with my fast footwork and my strong right hook. All the old gang were there as spectators, including some neighborhood girls who seemed to have matured as well in the past year.

Joey Doyle acted as timekeeper, Marty Akerson was referee, and three other guys were the judges. As always, the match was three three-minute rounds. In the first one I discovered that my fancy footwork and right hook were not much help, since Don Muscovin's arms were now so much longer than mine I couldn't get close enough to land a punch. Every time I moved in against him, my face connected with his fist, which felt hard as an anvil despite the boxing glove that covered it. By the end of the first round I was out of breath and had acquired two black eyes.

"You okay, Nick? You wanna stop?" asked Don, with concern so sincere that I longed to murder him. I couldn't shake the memory of him tagging at our heels like a puppy.

"I'm fine," I gasped, gritting my teeth. "Just got to get my wind."

During the second round he cut my lip, and during the third he bloodied my nose. The worst of the whole debacle was everyone's kindness and concern. They kept asking if I wanted to quit, but I doggedly fought on to the end. There was no need for the judges to announce their verdict; we all knew that Don Muscovin, the former pariah, had met the challenger and was still champion.

The boys in the gang all begged me to come back to Greendale more often and I promised I would, but as I uttered the words through bruised and puffy lips, I knew I would never set foot again on the scene of my humiliation. I insisted my wounds didn't hurt; I shook everybody's hand, accepted Steve Zilavy's offer of a soiled handkerchief to hold against my gushing nose, and limped off the field toward the bus stop, convinced that the happy, carefree days of my youth were ended.

The ride back to Lincoln Street was a long and momentous one, because I revised my entire life plan on that bus. It was clear that my body had let me down: my growth was slowing, while the American kids were going to grow even bigger and stronger, thanks to superior diets and genetic programming. It seemed unlikely now that I would ever achieve my dream of winning fame and prosperity for my family in the boxing ring. I had to discover another path to success and choose different role models from Jimmy Cagney, Rocky Marciano, and John Garfield.

In the movies, which I used as my textbook, there were indeed small men like me who triumphed over their enemies — Bogart, Cagney, Alan Ladd — but these types prevailed through violence, using guns and knives as an equalizer. Al Berry and Jackie Walsh were the picaresque heros, the Cagney and Bogart, of Lincoln Street. Like the gangsters in the movies, however, they had only themselves to answer to. They didn't seem burdened with families and relatives, hovering clans of kinfolk, who had a personal interest in their good behavior.

I was further weighted by a growing sense that my life was not my own to squander. My mother had died to get me to America. She had battled for nine years before that to keep me from being killed by starvation, land mines, and artillery fire. Now, in America, my every failure and success was followed with obsessive interest by my sisters and the entire Worcester Greek community and reported in exaggerated terms to my relatives back in Greece. I couldn't help feeling that I owed it to my mother not to waste the life that had been so dearly won. I didn't have the right to self-destruct with the dashing élan of a Jimmy Cagney crying from the top of a gas tank just before it exploded, "Hey, Ma! Top of the world!"

If I couldn't conquer the world by brute force, I finally realized as the bus rumbled over Gold Star Boulevard toward Lincoln Square, then I would have to succeed through brainpower. I felt certain that my native Greek ingenuity was not inferior to that of my American classmates, whatever vitamins they had consumed with their pablum. I gazed at the white limestone majesty of the Worcester Memorial Auditorium, with its huge portico of Doric columns, a first cousin to the Parthenon I had left behind, and suddenly an inspiring figure strode onto the stage of my imagination, a man cloaked in an aura of integrity and glory: Paul Muni!

As I knew from my visits to the cinema, Paul Muni had begun his career as a callow punk in *Scarface* — a young hood relying, like the rest, on the power of the fist and the gun. But he had undergone a startling metamorphosis as he matured; he had given up crime for the life of the intellect, and developed a strong will, a noble character, and selfless humanity. He had become Emile Zola, the heroic journalist and author who defied society to demand justice for the oppressed; Louis Pasteur, risking his life to save the world from disease; Benito Juarez, the Indian revolutionary and champion of the poor who freed Mexico from French colonialism. All the world marveled at Paul Muni's keen

mind and noble character in these films; even tough guys like John Garfield in *Juarez* were in awe of him. An additional dividend, I mused, was
that Paul Muni's characters enjoyed a longer life and more personal
satisfaction than the gangsters and boxing champions of the silver
screen.

At Lincoln Square I descended from the bus with my battered and
bleeding features arranged in a beatific expression of conviction. I was
going to become Paul Muni and win renown with my keen intellect and
iron will.

My first hurdle was to get off the hook as the advance man in the
Wood's Lumberyard caper. Instead of going home to scandalize my sisters with my battle-scarred appearance, I walked directly to Henchman
Street. When I arrived at the corner of Ritz's Market, lurid in my bloody
shirt, black eyes, and purple bruises, Jackie Walsh and Al Berry were
gratifyingly impressed.

"Holy shit, who did that to you?" asked Jackie admiringly. "Your old
man pound the crap out of you for something?"

"Naw, it was them guys at Wood's again." I shrugged. "They catch
me chasing the place last night and let me have it."

"They caught you what?" they exclaimed in unison.

"Checking out the place like you guys said," I answered, looking hurt.

"You mean they caught you casing the joint?" interrupted Al.

I made an apologetic gesture. "Sorry, fellas. They caught me and they
beat me up, and then they took me to the cops."

"What did they ask you? What didja tell 'em?" Jackie demanded in a
threatening tone.

"I didn't tell 'em nothin', I ain't no canary," I shot back in my best
Marlon Brando imitation. "They grilled me about stores being robbed,
some as far up as Malden Street."

"We never went that far," Al protested.

"Shut up, moron," Jackie snapped, then turned on me.

"I pretend I no speaka da English," I joked, hoping I sounded convincing.

"Thataway, Greek!" exclaimed Al, and Jackie looked somewhat relieved.

"They let me go," I went on, "but when I got up this morning, I see
this guy standing in the doorway across the street watching my house."

"And you came here, you dumb fuck!" exploded Jackie.

"I go out the back way," I protested. "What you take me for?"

"Go back the same way and stay there," Jackie commanded. "Don't
come around for a while. You're no good to us now."

And that was how Paul Muni and I brought my budding career as a
thief to an early conclusion. Jackie Walsh and Al Berry, however, went

on to more challenging adventures. Though I lost track of Jackie, I often read about Al's exploits in the Worcester papers: several decades of convictions for bad checks, disorderly conduct, and petty larceny.

As a newly consecrated gladiator of the intellect, I marched with redoubled fervor onto the academic battlefield and, in the second half of sixth grade, did so well that I was placed in the advanced reading group in Miss Diggins' class, on track for prep school.

Sixth grade was a critical year in the Worcester public school system, for that was when the academically superior students were chosen for the special college preparatory middle schools that fed the city's elite high schools, Classical and North, while the less gifted students were eventually relegated to less prestigious "comprehensive" high schools.

While I sat on the left side of Miss Diggins' sixth grade, my sister Fotini, who had been a better student than I had in Greece, sat on the right side, because she did not make the cut. This meant little to either of us at the time, but it had serious consequences for Fotini's future.

By the time sixth grade neared its end, Fotini was finding school increasingly humiliating. Her maturing fifteen-year-old body made her look incongruous among a class of twelve-year-olds. When Miss Diggins sent home a note about an end-of-year excursion to a farm, advising parents to sign the permission slip and have their daughters wear trousers, Father firmly refused to let either Fotini or me participate in such a silly and wanton waste of time. Miss Diggins begged him to relent, promising to be personally responsible for our safety and emphasizing the educational aspects of the jaunt. Finally our father grudgingly signed the permission slips, but he made it clear that under no circumstances would his daughter be allowed to wear slacks.

For days Fotini fretted about the prospect of being the only girl wearing a dress, then she took desperate steps and borrowed a pair of slacks from a girlfriend, changing in the bathroom at school. But she was so nervous about her immodest attire, and afraid of Father's learning of her disobedience, that she couldn't enjoy the field trip, and she greeted the end of sixth grade with relief.

On the afternoon of June 9, 1953, as my sisters and I were sitting on our front balcony seeking relief from the breathless heat, a tornado struck Worcester, killing ninety-four and injuring nearly two thousand people. It was the third worst tornado in the history of the United States. Our old neighborhood of Greendale was one of the worst hit, but from our balcony on Lincoln Street we heard only a great explosion like a thunderclap from the north. Soon we saw hundreds of bloodied pedestrians, some carrying dead bodies, streaming toward the hospital across the street as sirens wailed. Olga, convinced that war had broken out, became hysterical, and all my sisters wept as police cars, ambulances, and civilian vehicles unloaded bodies at the emergency entrance.

When Father arrived home, after walking all the way from the restaurant, and explained what had happened, we realized how lucky we were to have been spared. An hour earlier I had failed to catch a bus to a golf course where I sometimes caddied. If I had succeeded, I would have been in the very center of the damage. Missing that bus seemed to me further evidence that I was being protected and watched over by the spirit of my mother.

We all lit candles the next Sunday in thanks for our escape, but the sight of the injured brought back to us vivid memories of the wartime terrors we had left behind. For many nights after the tornado, we slept fitfully and awoke screaming with nightmares.

Once school was out, Fotini discovered a new interest in life; Jimmy Tzouras hired her to work for him temporarily at Standard Fruit while his accountant underwent surgery. Fotini answered the phone and recorded the bills and shipments, and periodically she and Tzouras took the books to the accountant in the hospital to check. Fotini proved to have a keen business mind and an eye for good investments. On one of these trips, as Tzouras drove up Chandler Street, she spied a three-decker for sale. She investigated, and learned that because it was somewhat rundown, the large home in a residential area was selling for only $14,000. Fotini decided we should buy it.

Ever since I had become involved with the Henchman Street gang, Father had been talking about moving to a better neighborhood. With four salaries coming in, he had some savings at last, and each of the three older girls could help finance the house as an investment in her future. (In Greece a bride's dowry often includes housing for the newlywed couple, with the understanding that the real estate remains the bride's property in case of divorce or other disaster.)

We all piled into the Studebaker to see the three-decker at 369 Chandler Street and concluded that Fotini had made a wise choice. Kanta, Glykeria, Olga, and Father each contributed $1000 to the purchase and we took a mortgage for the remaining $10,000.

I had mixed feelings about leaving Lincoln Street. It would be a relief to escape Jackie Walsh, Al Berry, and the Henchman Street gang, but it would also mean adjusting to another school (the sixth one for me in as many years) and a new set of classmates — not an easy task for anyone on the threshold of adolescence, even without the additional burdens of being short and foreign.

While Fotini spent the summer working for Jimmy Tzouras, Father put me to work fixing up the empty four-bedroom first-floor apartment of our new house, where all of us would live except for Olga and Dino, who would get the smaller three-bedroom apartment on the top floor. The second floor would continue to be rented to the resident family of five until Kanta found a husband and needed it for herself.

My assignment was to repaint and rewallpaper our quarters while a newly arrived Greek immigrant, Stavros Michopoulos, did the necessary carpentry work: fixing up the floors, ceilings, and window casings. Father said he would pay me $20 a room for papering and painting. It seemed like a good deal until I learned that I had to soak and scrape off multiple layers of old wallpaper with nothing more than hot water and a knife. Nevertheless, I began to take pride in the work, learning to hang paper with professional precision and to paint so neatly that I didn't need masking tape to make a clean edge around a window.

Father, for the first time an American home owner, came around frequently to check our progress, and greeted his upstairs tenants with the *noblesse oblige* of a Daddy Warbucks. I sensed that he was pleased to see me working so hard instead of holding up banks or hanging from streetlamps, but his praise was inevitably mixed with criticism. "Nice job," he would say judiciously, "but you missed a spot there, and on this window you should have scraped better. Here it's dripped. How many times do I have to tell you to wipe your brush first?"

I never responded but would pick up my paint and move to the farthest point in the room, letting my silence express the cold hostility I felt. He would stand there watching me for a while in puzzlement, then retreat to where Michopoulos was working and start chatting with him.

Despite the heat and fumes and long hours, I derived a kind of satisfaction from seeing the house transformed by my skill. It was a summer when my body and voice were changing alarmingly and disturbing hormonal tides suffused me, especially when the teenaged daughter of the family next door walked by in short shorts. But the rhythm of the work and the discovery that I could do the job of a grown man gave me new self-confidence, except on the days when Father came by to find fault with my labors.

Our new school, Chandler Junior High, was a sprawling, brand-new building spread out on one level, and a dozen grade schools fed into it. I was assigned to the prep section while Fotini was put in the nonprep division, where she took classes in cooking, sewing, child care, music, and art in addition to academic subjects.

My schoolmates at Chandler were not like any I had seen before. They were expensively and conservatively dressed, the girls demure in Pendleton pleated skirts, penny loafers, Peter Pan collars, and virginal circle pins, the boys preppy in crew cuts, khaki pants with Ivy League buckles, and button-down shirt collars. I didn't own clothes like these, but decided to create my own style by dressing like the gangsters in the movies: Tony Curtis, John Derek, Humphrey Bogart. I put my sartorial image together with shiny white-on-white shirts, pants with razor-sharp pleats, and a ducktail haircut, long on the sides. I decided I looked sinister but fascinating.

It was an unsettling experience to change classrooms every hour in a school so large that I couldn't hope to know all my classmates. Like every newcomer, I kept quiet and watched carefully to learn the dynamics of the new school. I quickly learned that in the prep division I was surrounded by very smart kids — perhaps smarter than I was.

A week after my arrival, I was mystified when our home-room teacher announced that it was time for each of us to join a club. Every Friday during fifth period, she explained, we would be released to attend meetings of the club of our choice, to pursue our favorite hobby. This meant nothing to me, because the entire concept of "hobby" was incomprehensible to someone from a Greek village. When the teacher reeled off the list of choices open to us, I was even more perplexed: photography, chess, cooking, debate, Latin, astronomy . . . Some of the subjects might be useful, I thought, but most sounded like a total waste of time, and I had no intention of expending my energies on them.

I discovered, however, that I had to choose a club whether I wanted to or not. The only "interest" that occupied my mind in those days was girls, so on the appointed Friday, fifth period, I walked out of the room behind Judy Olander, who had caught my eye from the very first day with her buxom, precociously mature figure, her swaying ash-blond curls, her dancing blue eyes, determined chin, and exuberant zest for life. The daughter of the minister of the prestigious Trinity Lutheran Church, Judy was the most popular girl in the seventh grade, and whatever she chose would be my club as well.

Hard on her heels, I passed doors labeled for the occasion: photography, glee club, cheerleading, French, cooking. None of these drew Judy's eye. Suddenly she stopped, and together we entered the door marked "Newspaper." I was surprised to find a number of students already there — many of them the brightest of the prep-school division — but if Judy wanted to work on the school newspaper, I decided, then I would too, no matter what the competition. Thus are fateful lifetime decisions often frivolously made, especially when one's goals are dictated by a clamoring horde of adolescent hormones. Many times since that day I have offered thanks that Judy was not interested in sewing instead.

The milling group inside the room was called to order by the teacher-adviser to the newspaper, a steely-eyed woman of ample girth with a nasal Boston accent who clearly intended to tolerate no nonsense. This was Miss Hurd, the English teacher for the other half of the prep division, not mine.

"What are all you goof-offs doing here?" Miss Hurd bellowed. "Looking for a party? This is the newspaper club! What are we going to do? We're going to put out a newspaper! And the ones who are going to do all the work are *you*, not me. So if there's anybody in this room who doesn't like work, I suggest you leave right now and go across the hall to Glee Club, because you're going to work your tails off here. Now, just to see if you're literate enough to work on a paper, we're going to do an instant essay, and I'm going to eliminate anyone I think is better suited for the stamp-collecting club."

Soon I was more captivated by Miss Hurd than by Judy Olander. I liked the teacher's abrasive, humorous manner, and she seemed to return my esteem. She taught us every step of producing the *Chandler Echo*, from writing the articles and typing up the mimeograph stencils to collating each copy.

At first my literary muse expressed itself in poetry: doggerel in the manner of Ogden Nash, lampooning various activities at Chandler Junior High. I was so gratified by Miss Hurd's encouragement and praise that I went to the assistant principal, a jovial man named Mr. Ryan, and requested a transfer to Miss Hurd's English class, which he willingly granted because he thought highly of her as well.

Miss Hurd drilled us constantly on grammar, making us diagram sentences until I finally began to understand the intrinsic logic and structure of the English language, although prepositions — slippery little things that kept getting muddled in my mind — still tripped me up and revealed my foreign roots. But after a semester in her class my choice of words no longer provoked glee in my fellow students, although my Greek accent with an overlay of flat Bostonian vowels and missing *r*'s would stay with me for life.

Until the seventh grade I excelled in arithmetic and had vague intentions of becoming an engineer if I ever went to college. But Miss Hurd made me fall in love with literature. I was fascinated by the way she could read a story to us, then open it up like a fan, displaying its varied facets, colors, and meanings. I had considered stories to be simply the recounting of adventures, but she made me see that they could express feelings as well: pain, frustration, anger, and loss.

Miss Hurd also bequeathed me a love of my Greek heritage. I had considered Greece a small, poor, war-ravaged country of little importance compared to the rest of the world, but Miss Hurd seemed purposely to pick out stories and lessons that emphasized the literary wealth of the Greeks. She taught me that my country was the touchstone of Western civilization, and each time she made a reference to Aeschylus or Plato or Sophocles she would wink at me and say, "Another plug for your people, Nick!" From an outsider and a D.P., I was being transformed into part of a noble race of artists, philosophers, poets, and founders of democracy. Soon I could hardly wait to get to school for Miss Hurd's English classes and the Friday afternoons in newspaper club.

Miss Hurd was exactly the kind of humorous, tactful, but noninterfering maternal figure I needed at that stage. She revealed to me both the wealth of my ethnic background and the value of my intelligence. While I quickly forgot my infatuation with Judy Olander, who became a crony and eventually a co-editor, I never lost my initial ardor for Miss Hurd.

During seventh grade, as I was discovering literature, journalism, and girls, Fotini was becoming more and more uncomfortable, surrounded by classmates three years younger than herself. Whenever a teacher asked her why she had failed to do some assigned task, Fotini was so frightened she became mute and didn't answer. In gym class she was too shy to change into the required one-piece gym suit in front of the other, less developed girls, so she snuck into the locker room before the rest to change, then waited after class until all had left to change back into street clothes. She always arrived late at the next class, but she was never able to explain her tardiness.

As a student on the lower academic track, Fotini had classes like sewing, cooking, and music. When she was assigned to sew an apron as a class project, she was afraid to tell the teacher that she had no sewing machine at home. She tried to be accepted in the glee club, but was turned down and had to settle for the cooking club instead.

Our father's surreptitious visits to school to spy on her made her feel even more conspicuous. She would often look up from writing at her desk to see the teacher and the other students staring curiously at the small glass partition in the classroom door, which framed Father's face peering in, watching his daughter. He liked to leave work early to catch her by surprise. Frequently, as she walked home with friends, Father shadowed her from a distance in the car. The other girls would say, "Look, Tina, there's your father back there," but Fotini would only toss her head and pretend she didn't care.

Shortly before Fotini and I finished seventh grade, our family attended an event that was a milestone for us and the entire Greek immigrant community in Worcester: the consecration of the new Church of St. Spyridon, at Russell and Elm streets opposite Elm Park, on May 30, 1954. (After St. Spyridon's humble beginnings and the painful schisms caused by feuds between the royalists and republicans, the Greek religious community had united in the Orange Street church, which had been consecrated in May of 1925.)

The end of World War II brought a new wave of immigrants from

Greece: the wives and children of the "bachelors" as well as whole families who could find someone to sponsor them, all desperate to flee the devastated homeland. For the first time, the Greek restaurant owners, fruit peddlers, and factory workers of Worcester realized they would not end their days in luxurious retirement back in their native villages; they were in America to stay.

The consecration of our new church on Russell Street, near the most exclusive section of the city, was an announcement to the world that the Greeks of Worcester had finally entered the mainstream. To replace the dark, overcrowded edifice on Orange Street, the Greeks built a glistening yellow brick church that was considered one of the finest examples of neo-Byzantine architecture in America. The nave was in the shape of an equal-armed cross with a huge white dome in the center; there was a belfry, eighty-six feet high, as well. Inside, the church shimmered with white Carrara marble imported from Italy; priceless mosaics and icons; a mammoth chandelier of Bohemian cut glass; a white marble altar screen with vigil lights held in the beaks of bronze doves, eternally illuminating the long, solemn faces of the saints; and thirty-one stained glass windows, donated by the wealthy families of the congregation in memory of their dead.

The largest contributors to the new church were the owners of Table Talk Pies, Angelo Cotsidas and Theodore Tonna. In addition to paying personally for many of the interior furnishings, they were the powers behind the church's completion. Tonna headed the building fund committee, and Cotsidas was in charge of the consecration albums, paying off all the outstanding debts by selling pages in lavish gold-and-black souvenir albums at $1000 a page. These albums included the history of the church, pictures, and congratulatory letters from such dignitaries as President Dwight D. Eisenhower, Massachusetts Governor Christian A. Herter, and leaders of the Orthodox church.

Those members of the community who paid for a page in an album chose to fill their allotted space in a variety of ways. Some pages were illustrated with a photo of a favorite child or a beloved son lost in the service of his country, along with the family's congratulatory message on the consecration. For his page, our constant visitor Jimmy Tzouras was photographed with his shoulders back, straining his plump pouter-pigeon body to its full height in front of a painted backdrop of a terrace and formal gardens.

"Look at Tzouras puffed up like the frog in the fable who burst from self-importance," muttered Father, paging through a copy of the album. "You'd think he owned Standard Oil instead of Standard Fruit. Makes himself ridiculous."

We knew that Father longed to have his own portrait among those of the pillars of the community — most of them men who came to America after he did and originally looked up to him as one of the first and most prosperous Greeks in Worcester. But now, as the others posed in their finery to be photographed and recorded for all eternity in the same volume with President Eisenhower and the archbishop, Father couldn't even afford $250 — almost a month's wages — for a quarter page.

It had taken three years to complete the final touches on the church building, and Father Rizos, our patient and humble priest, had driven himself to the edge of a breakdown. But now the consecration had come at last — three days of ceremonies and festivities. There were to be dinner dances and balls, which we couldn't afford to attend, but I was present at all the church services as an altar boy captain. I was excited and nervous at finding myself standing on the same *solea* as Greek prelates from all over the world, resplendent in their magnificent robes. I was fairly splendid myself in my white garments edged in gold, as I swung the censer and supervised the younger boys with their candles, fetched the bread for the *antidoron*, and held a huge, heavy gold cross near the front of the great procession.

The real heart of a church's consecration, Father Rizos explained to us, was the consecration of the altar. That was done by entombing inside the altar the relics of three saints, and then anointing the altar with holy chrism, a mixture of olive oil and balsam. Just as the earliest Christians, hiding in the catacombs, prepared the Eucharist atop the tombs of the martyrs who died for their faith, so we too would prepare the flesh and blood of Christ every Sunday atop the bones of Christian martyrs.

I loved the pomp and ritual of the church, which had been so important when we lived in Greece. It made me feel part of a strong, flourishing, and important community. The years of being an outsider — first as a non-Communist in the village, because of my grandfather's royalist sympathies, then as a refugee and a D.P. in America — finally seemed behind me as I swung the censer and Archbishop Michael, head of the church in America, intoned: "Accept our prayers; grant us remission of our transgressions; hide us under the shadow of Thy wings."

Father had bragged about the new church for months to anyone who wasn't Greek: "You know, they took pictures to put in an encyclopedia — very important church, very beautiful." But when we entered the already crowded nave and saw that the entire front had been roped off for the dignitaries and VIPs, such as the members of the building committee, who would be the first to come forward and kiss the archbishop's ring, I could see how angry Father became; he considered the first pew rightfully his and every Sunday strode down to the front with a proprietary air. Now he had to content himself with sitting in the forwardmost pew behind the velvet ropes, while his card-playing chums sat with saintly mien right behind the black-robed prelates.

Once again I felt a growing resentment against him. After forty-four years in Worcester, he had failed to earn a place of honor in the Greek community, and his name appeared nowhere in the consecration albums. At least *I* was pictured twice, as an altar boy and Sunday school member, but my father might never have existed. If he hadn't squandered all his money, I reflected, things might be very different. Like Christ the Pantocrator, weighing souls from the apex of the huge dome, I judged my father from my vantage point on the *solea* and found him unworthy.

The archbishop lifted the golden plate containing the relics of the martyrs and slowly began the great procession out of the church, the hierarchs first, the clerics in order of rank, me and the other altar boys carrying the golden crosses and icons, then the congregation, in order of importance. Everyone filed out and marched three times around the building, then the bishop, representing Christ, knocked on the great doors, as on the door of paradise, and demanded to be let in.

Once inside, the bishop placed the holy relics in a small gold box, poured holy chrism over them to represent the presence of Christ, and intoned, "Eternal be the memory of the builders of this holy church." At that moment, all the philanthropic gentlemen in the front rows sat up a little higher, and my father slumped a bit lower in his place.

After the bishop ceremoniously cleaned the altar, he prayed for the new church: "Let Thine eyes be open upon it day and night, and let Thine ears be heedful of the prayer of those who shall enter . . ." We all stood straighter, united by our shared pride, but as I looked at my father, he appeared more miserable than ever. Finally I realized what was bothering him: the hour was approaching for the dedication banquet that evening, the climax of the weekend, when the notable members of the church would gather at Putnam and Thurston's restaurant. For my father it would be the final humiliation; while his old friends were sitting on the dais, making speeches congratulating each other, he would be back in the kitchen, sweating and cooking in his white uniform, waiting on them like a serf.

I could see that Kanta, in a stylish blue suit and matching pillbox hat, wasn't listening to the bishop either. Her eyes were searching the faces of the congregation. It seemed that like my father, she was thinking unhappy thoughts.

Kanta was now twenty-two years old, approaching the age when she would be labeled a *yerondocorie,* or old maid. She had to find herself a husband soon, before she was considered too long in the tooth to wed, but as she looked around the sanctuary, filled with the entire Greek community of Worcester, she realized there was no man among this throng who would satisfy both her father and herself.

Outside our community, America was being stirred by the first rumblings of the sexual revolution. A year before, the Kinsey report on female sexuality had revealed that 50 percent of the women in America had sex before they were married and 25 percent were unfaithful to their husbands after marriage. *Playboy* magazine, the explicit celluloid sexuality of Marilyn Monroe, and the blatant eroticism of the new rock 'n' roll had all become a part of everyday life in America, while in our Greek community dating was unthinkable, arranged marriages were commonplace, and a woman who wore slacks or danced European-style with a man not her husband would be considered brazen and condemned.

Our tight community of immigrants retained its almost medieval strictures on behavior for many reasons. The immigrants who settled in Worcester had almost all come from the remote mountain villages of the Mourgana range, an area so isolated by its geography that many customs had remained unchanged since the dawn of Christianity. People from the Mourgana mountains had little opportunity to marry or even to meet people from the outside world, and had become like the isolated pockets of hillbillies tucked into the Appalachian mountains, who were discovered in the twentieth century to be still speaking Shakespearean English.

The immigrants who had come to Worcester since the turn of the century had come directly from such villages, with no intermediary stops to introduce them to modern civilization. When they arrived, their medieval customs became frozen in time. While back in Greece, in places like Athens and Salonika and even provincial centers like Yannina, customs changed and evolved rapidly, in our immigrant world they were preserved like family heirlooms.

The mores that the Greek community of Worcester protected so fiercely would not permit any abuses of the code of behavior — especially not a marriage to a person who was from any other section of Greece, for the Mourgana villagers considered themselves the keepers of the flame, whereas someone from, say, the Peloponnesus might have had an immoral upbringing. Kanta had to marry a man from our own villages. Marrying an American-born Greek was beyond consideration. One of our Gatzoyiannis cousins had actually married a virtuous American-born Greek girl, and the community had reeled in shock.

Kanta looked around the church and saw that all the young and attractive men would be unacceptable to my father because they weren't from our villages, and most of the men who *were* from our area were approximately the same age as Father. Kanta had always vowed that she would not let herself be betrothed to an elderly man who wanted only a nurse for his old age. She knew she was attractive, intelligent, and sensible, but she feared that with only those men she saw before her to choose from, she would end her days a spinster.

Then, as the archbishop intoned his blessings on the newly consecrated church, Kanta had a brilliant idea. She knew that anyone returning from America to Greece, which was still desperately poor, could have her pick of hundreds of eligible mates. Any man in Greece, faced with earning a living in a country devastated by a decade of war and revolution, would leap at the chance to go to America. Kanta could stay in Worcester and marry an old man, she reasoned, or she could go back to our mountains, and pick the finest groom in Epiros; her father would have to accept her choice because he came from our own villages.

What she wanted in a husband, most of all, Kanta reflected, was a man of patience, with an even disposition. Our grandfather was infamous for his evil temper as well as his flagrant adultery. Our father, of irreproachable moral character except for his gambling, nevertheless was a stern, old-fashioned, and oppressively strict parent. And Dino, the husband whom Olga adored, was in Kanta's opinion nervous and temperamental. As Kanta watched the bishop place the appointments on the altar — the icons, the book of gospels, the candlesticks, and the receptacle for the holy sacraments — she promised herself that she would find a good-looking man with unflappable patience and calm, one who would not oppress her but would value her for her intelligence even though she was not educated.

She crossed herself and breathed a silent prayer to St. Spyridon, the simple shepherd whose miraculously preserved body lay, 1600 years after his death, in his church on the island of Corfu and was said to wear out a pair of slippers every year from walking about at night performing miracles. (One pair of those worn slippers was among the treasures of our new church, dedicated to his name.) As the archbishop motioned to the congregation to rise for the benediction, Kanta gazed at him with a rapturous smile, thinking that by sending this idea into her head, St. Spyridon may have already created his first miracle in this church.

Father rejected Kanta's plan before she finished telling it. No daughter of his was going gallivanting around the world on her own, he shouted. But Kanta could be very persuasive. She had already saved enough for the ship's ticket, she explained. And after five years, it was disgraceful that *Mana* had never had a memorial service read over her grave. Our grandfather could meet Kanta at the boat and chaperone her everywhere. Father knew she was too sensible to do anything that would compromise the family name.

Finally she produced her trump card: "You know the store in Yannina you have half-interest in?" she said. "You should sell it! With the Greek rent-control laws, you're only getting ten dollars a month, but if you sell it, you'll make back your investment plus a profit. I can find a buyer when I'm there, and that will pay for my trip and the wedding ceremony in Greece, if I have one, and I'll come back with money left over."

The thought of finding a suitable husband for Kanta and making a profit at the same time, without having to pay for a dowry, was so stunning that Father fell silent for several minutes while he mulled it over. If she met a man and married him in Greece, there would be no expenses for a big wedding, reception, and honeymoon. Her grandfather would protect her virtue with the puritanical strictness found in any compulsive philanderer put in charge of the morals of a female relative. And if, God forbid, Kanta made an unfortunate choice, no one could blame *him*. But she was a sensible and clever girl, after all, and would make an advantageous price on the store in Yannina.

Finally Father held out his arms to Kanta. "My daughter!" he announced. "I've taken the decision that it is time for you to wed. You have my blessing. I'll write your grandfather and tell him to meet you at the dock in Piraeus."

From that moment, Kanta devoted herself to shopping every day after work, putting together an appropriate wardrobe for her triumphant return to Greece (and perhaps for her trousseau as well). Meanwhile Fotini and I finished our last days of seventh grade and were released for the summer.

Even before school was over, Father called me into the kitchen one night for a serious discussion of my future. He complimented me briefly on the good grades I had been bringing home from school, then pointed out that so far I had been putting a drain on the family finances without contributing any income. He, in contrast, had started working at the age of eight.

I groaned inwardly at this familiar theme. If he had just saved his money instead of squandering it, none of us would have to work, I reflected as he lectured on.

"I've let you coast for this long," Father was saying in the righteous manner that annoyed me so. "But it's time you started pulling your own weight, contributing to the family income. Did I ever tell you how many years I supported my own brothers and sisters and mother?" I rolled my eyes and he snapped, "Don't give me that look — you learn from my example! And if you have any intention of going to college — which is what I hope for you, so you can become a man of importance in this world — then you had better start saving for your education now."

"My friends don't work," I muttered.

"Their parents don't have five orphaned children to raise," he retorted. "You should be grateful that I have good connections, so I can get you a good job. Every Greek in Worcester owes me a favor, because I helped them all get on their feet when they came over."

"Then why aren't *their* kids working for *you?*" I snapped.

Father gazed heavenward with infinite sorrow. "Always the poison dripping from your tongue," he sighed. "Just like your grandfather — and look at him, does he have any friends in his old age? Everyone hates him! I, on the other hand, can call every Greek in Worcester my friend."

"Which friend am I going to work for?" I said, tired of the whole subject.

"Ted Kiritsy," he answered. "You know Ted's market sells to all the big-shot families on the West Side. Of course his produce can't compare with what *I* used to sell, you can't find fruit like that anymore. But Ted's agreed to take you on part-time, teach you the business, let you help out his son. I want you doing a good job. Don't embarrass me. Ted's only hiring you as a favor."

So I embarked on my first paying job, for the princely wage of sixty cents an hour. Since I had no choice but to work, I decided to show up my father by being a better worker than he ever was. But I had hardly begun when it became apparent that my talents did not lie in the fruit-and-vegetable trade.

Kiritsy was a slight, balding, dark-complexioned Greek from northern Epiros with a cigarette permanently affixed to his lower lip. He was good-natured but meek. The real power at Ted's was his wife, Helen, equally small, thin, and dark, who stood guard at the cash register and watched the operation of the store with a steely eye.

Ted was an artist manqué — he delighted in selecting the most perfect fruit and then arranging it in displays to dazzle the eye, pyramids and cornucopias of jewel-like colors reflected by the mirrors he had mounted on the walls. In a creative frenzy, he arranged the fruit each morning: the royal purple of the eggplants enhanced by the emerald green of the curly romaine; the red Delicious apples, polished like rubies, set beside the yellow-green plums bursting with juice. The one thing that Kiritsy and his wife could not bear was for the customers to handle the fruit, possibly bruising it or destroying the perfect symmetry of the displays.

My job was to approach each customer with an open paper bag in one hand and say, "May I help you, please?" If the customer persisted in pawing the fruit, we assistants were supposed to say politely but firmly, "I'm sorry, but only the store personnel are allowed to handle the produce." We were instructed to find out the customer's selection and then measure it into the bag so swiftly that she could not wander off to start pinching the tomatoes.

From the beginning, Mrs. Kiritsy found me woefully lacking in both sufficient speed and firmness with customers. I even tripped on the curb one morning while carrying fruit to a car, and spilled an entire order.

Day after day I repeated my line about store personnel, and the irate customers always snarled, "This is ridiculous. I always choose my own tomatoes! Where's Ted? He knows me."

I would throw a look of supplication toward Mrs. Kiritsy at the cash register, but she would be gazing out the window to avoid any risk of offending a customer. By the time I arrived at the register, laden with brown paper bags to add up, her glare would make it clear that I had once again failed to uphold the standards of Ted's market.

Kiritsy felt sorry that I was not cutting it as a produce seller, so every night he went out in back and filled a paper bag with damaged and overripe fruit and pressed it on me for my father and sisters. I always refused his charity, but he insisted: "Your father was a good friend to me when I first came here. Please take it home — do it for me!"

As I made the long hike home, crossing Park Avenue past the old Harrington-Richardson gun factory where my father had once been a crackerjack gun maker (so he told me), then slogging up Chandler Street, past the athletic field where other, more carefree boys were playing stickball, the malodorous bag of damaged fruit — my personal albatross — got heavier with each step. All the while, I cursed my father for inspiring Ted Kiritsy's charity and forcing me to return every day to a job where I was so unhappy.

Because I had to work, I couldn't go to the train station to say good-bye to Kanta when she left for New York on July 8, 1954, to sail on the steamship *Nea Hellas*. She had packed her suitcases with bright flowered frocks and tailored suits (many with matching hats), elegant shoes, evening shawls and wraps, and, for gifts to relatives, dress-fabric lengths, headscarves, and nylon stockings. Last of all she had carefully packed the beautiful creamy lace wedding dress she had bought for $100, complete with a long train and long sleeves, the bodice embellished with pearls and sequins. She had bought a veil to go with it, for Kanta knew such things could not be found in Greece, and she had parried the friendly questions of the salesgirls, not wanting to admit that she was choosing a wedding dress before she had even met her groom.

It upset me to see her go. Since Olga's wedding, Kanta had been the only one of my older sisters to take an interest in my life, and sometimes she slipped me money from her pay envelope. Olga was totally wrapped up in her husband and baby, and now she was pregnant again. Kanta, I suspected, would probably come back from Greece months from now with a new husband and be just as daft and starry-eyed as Olga and never pay attention to me.

It also bothered me that Kanta was going to our village and our mother's grave without me. I often dreamed that I was walking the familiar mountain paths again, on the way up to our house where *Mana* was waiting. I always awoke filled with joy, until I realized that I was still in America. I hadn't forgotten my mother's warning that she would curse any of us who returned, but I still wished that I could go along.

It was bad enough working at Ted's, but it was even worse when Stavros Economou, the twenty-year-old son of Nassio, my father's erstwhile partner, pulled up at the curb to show me the new red Buick Skylark convertible with wraparound windshield and whitewall tires that his father had just bought him. When Stavros and I had both been living in Greece, Nassio had sent him wind-up airplanes and toy cars, whereas my father had sent me only clothing and a bookbag. Nassio had sold Terminal Lunch in 1950 and opened a very successful restaurant on the main road connecting Worcester and Boston. Now he could afford to buy his son that sporty little red convertible, while *my* father forced me to suffer the scorn of Mrs. Kiritsy in exchange for pennies. As Stavros leaned on his horn to get my attention, I couldn't help thinking that if Nassio hadn't sold the fruit truck and then reneged on the promise to make Father a partner in Terminal Lunch, things might have been very different now.

I would have sold my soul for that car. In a year I would be old enough to get my driver's license, and the craving to drive filled me like a fever. Owning a car was beyond my wildest fantasies, but I hoped to earn enough at least to pay for driving lessons. A driver's license, I thought, would be proof to the world of my maturity and my masculinity. With a car like Stavros', I was sure I could get any girl in Worcester.

Since Ted Kiritsy could use me only part-time, I was making about $15 a week. After giving half to my father, I could save only at an agonizingly slow pace. Then one day in August, Mrs. Kiritsy said, "Nikola, all our customers are going on vacation. We don't need so much help here, so we're going to have to let you go."

She handed me my last pay envelope and refrained from mentioning my general incompetence on the job. I could see that Ted was feeling guilty about firing me, because he packed an extra large bag of damaged fruit that night. I tried even harder than usual to refuse it, but he insisted, and when he shook my hand as a parting gesture I found a $5 bill in it. Ted winked furiously so I wouldn't reveal the gift to his wife, and said, "Give your father my best, Nick. He was always good to me in the old days. He deserved better, poor man."

I walked home that day burdened by the weight of the fruit and my shame, and vowed that I would never again take a job at which I wasn't capable or appreciated.

When I got home I discovered that Ted had already called my father, who rubbed salt on my wounds by saying, "I told you how hard it is out there. Only the tough make it. When I was ten years old, I had calluses on my hands so thick, I could take the pots out of the fire without a glove."

Without a word to my father I studied the classified ads and found a new job in a shoe factory behind Main Street, boxing and packing shoes. This one paid better than Ted's — eighty cents an hour — and I liked it better because the employers were pleased with me. The only problem was that I had lied and said I was sixteen. Every payday the secretary of the company asked me to bring in a Social Security card or a birth certificate, but I told her that all my papers had been burned in the town hall of my village when the Germans invaded. Then she asked for my passport, which I promptly brought, because I was listed as a minor in Olga's care, and there was no birth date for me.

Finally one day the secretary called our home and spoke to Olga, who told her I was born in July 1939. Thus, by the time I entered eighth grade, I had been fired from my second job. At least I had managed to save nearly $70 over the summer. Father never let me forget, however, that I had failed to cut the mustard as a workingman. I tried to avoid him so as to be spared his lectures on the need for fortitude and self-discipline.

By the time I entered school in the fall, we had received a frustratingly uninformative letter from Kanta in Greece. She had arrived safely, she wrote, had been met by our grandfather, and with him was spending two weeks in Athens seeing relatives there. Greece was even more wretched and poor than she expected, she said. Wherever she went in the capital she created a sensation with her American looks and clothing. She was getting dizzy from all the attention and didn't know what to do. "I tell everyone the same thing — first I have to go to the village and do the memorial service, and then, after that, if I want to see them again I'll come back," she wrote. "I hope to have everything settled so that I can be back by Christmas."

This letter depressed me. Considering how hard I was finding it to live in the same rooms with my father, the last thing I wanted was another male authority figure to push me around.

Kanta and Angelo posing in the village after their engagement

KANTA'S
CHOICE

We know the truth, not only by the reason, but by the heart.
— Blaise Pascal, *Thoughts*

WHILE KANTA WAS searching for a suitable husband 7000 miles away, I entered eighth grade at Chandler, a pulsing mass of fifteen-year-old longings. Although I had succeeded in making my mark academically, with the help of Miss Hurd and the school newspaper, I was still short, slight, and handicapped with an accent that made it difficult for me to compete for the popular girls.

Employing the tough-guy manner borrowed from my movie heroes, I often made *sotto voce* comments in class, to the amusement of the kids around me. I may have appeared short and unimpressive to the teachers, but I cut them down to my size with retorts muttered under my breath in the accents of movie villains.

"Nicholas, why are you standing up during study period?" Miss Mullaney might inquire, and as I sat down, I would mumble with Peter Lorre's voice, "I can't help myself! I haven't any control over this evil thing that's inside me — the fire, the voices, the torment!" Of course I was careful that the remarks weren't audible in the front of the room.

One day the art teacher, Miss Shamgochian, called my bluff. She was a rather bohemian and glamorous figure to us in her tight black skirts, spike heels, and jewel-toned silk blouses unbuttoned just enough to reveal a hint of cleavage. As we were busily wielding sticks of charcoal in an attempt to reproduce a still life of fruit that Miss Shamgochian had arranged at the front of the room, she asked rhetorically, "I wonder if I'll ever succeed in making you people understand about perspective."

From behind my sketchpad I muttered, in my Bogart *persona*, paraphrasing my favorite line from *Casablanca*, "You want my advice, kid, go back to Armenia."

This provoked an outburst of giggles from nearby students and drew Miss Shamgochian's attention to me.

"What was that you said, Nicholas?"

"Nothing."

"If it was nothing, why was everyone laughing?"

"They weren't laughing at what I said, it was the way I said it."

"Well, how did you say it, Nicholas? Why don't you come up here to the front of the class and show all of us?"

Miss Shamgochian's challenge provoked me to walk up to the front with a tough-guy swagger and declaim, with all of Bogart's shrugs and twitches and a curl of my upper lip, "You killed Miles, baby, and you're going down for it!"

This earned an even bigger burst of laughter from the class, but Miss Shamgochian did not seem amused. "I'll see you after class, Nicholas," she said.

My already pathetic rendition of the bowl of fruit deteriorated as I waited for class to end and the axe to fall. After the other students left, throwing gleeful looks my way, Miss Shamgochian called me up to her desk.

"Tell me, Nicholas," she said conversationally, "can you do any other impressions besides Bogart?"

I looked at her sharply to see if she was setting me up, then mumbled, "I do 'em all — Cagney, Edward G. Robinson, Jimmy Stewart, Marlon Brando."

She made me show her my entire repertoire, and seemed entertained at hearing all these famous personalities reproduced in gesture, voice, and manner with an overlay of my Greek accent. I didn't try to explain to her that these imitations were the way I had learned English in the first place.

Miss Shamgochian leaned toward me in a confiding manner, and I tried not to look down the neck of her blouse. "You know, Nicholas," she said, "every year each teacher is in charge of producing one assembly program, and my turn is coming up. I've got some dance solos, a couple of singing numbers, a piano player, but I need something funny to keep everybody from falling asleep. Do you think you could work up a monologue using your imitations?"

"I guess so," I mumbled, so relieved at not being punished that I didn't consider what I was saying.

Thus it came to pass within two weeks that I made my debut as a performer at Miss Shamgochian's fifth-period assembly. I had racked my brain and put together a little story of the funny-thing-happened-on-my-way-to-school variety. The monologue portrayed me being dragged out of bed by my father, who spoke with the heavy Italian accent of

J. Carrol Naish in "Life with Luigi." I left the house, my story continued, only to be stopped on the street by a policeman who spoke like Jimmy Stewart, telling me that a theft had occurred at school. The plot thickened as I encountered the leather-jacketed hood of the eighth grade, Roland Pickard, who protested his innocence in the mumbling voice and manner of Marlon Brando. Our assistant principal, in the accents of Karl Malden, tried to convince Roland to talk to the authorities, but Roland protested he was no stool pigeon. Our head principal entered my monologue, speaking with the psychotic intensity of Humphrey Bogart as Captain Queeg, and demanded that we track down the fiend who had stolen the strawberries from the cafeteria kitchen. Wesley Perkins, the only black boy in the class, embarked on the hunt, speaking just like Nat King Cole. In the end, the perpetrator of the strawberry theft turned out to be none other than Miss Hurd, who sounded like Mae West in my portrayal. She was suffering on one of her perpetual diets and had been driven to commit the strawberry heist by the pangs of hunger.

The audience roared at my impersonations, and for the first time I tasted the heady wine of applause as admiration engulfed me in waves across the footlights. I became an instant celebrity in the corridors of Chandler Junior High, in demand for every variety show and assembly. "Oh, you're Nick Gage, aren't you?" girls would coo. "Come on, say 'You dirty rat' for me. I just love the way you do that!" Pretty soon I could hardly remember how to speak in my own voice.

As I was tasting fame and popularity for the first time, Fotini, now sixteen, was finding the eighth grade more unbearable every day. Eventually she refused to attend gym class at all because she was getting into so much trouble for her unwillingness to change into a gym suit in front of the other girls. Father got Dr. Seidenberg to write a note saying that Fotini's health prevented her from participating in athletics. Still, she longed to drop out of Chandler altogether; she was old enough to leave legally, and Father was agreeable, for he considered a coeducational school no proper place for an adolescent girl. But before Kanta had left for Greece, she had exacted a promise from Fotini that she wouldn't quit until Kanta's return, so Fotini continued to show up for classes, feeling awkward, out of place, and miserable.

The worst moment, in her opinion, was the day when a music teacher played a passage from Beethoven's "Eroica" symphony for her class, then called on her, asking, "Tina, what was the highest note Beethoven used, and what note did he end on?" Fotini, who was completely unable to read music, was so befuddled by the question that she became mute, as always when embarrassed, and sat like a stone. Finally the teacher snapped at her, "You think you don't have to work, don't you, Tina? You think it's enough to just sit there and look pretty, but it's not!"

Fotini's cheeks burned in mortification as the class smirked at her. She felt totally disliked by her classmates and her teachers and vowed that she would drop out the moment Kanta came back from Greece and released her from her promise.

I was too engrossed in school and my burgeoning popularity to pay much attention to Fotini's problems, or to the successes of Olga and Dino, who now lived on the third floor of our three-decker with baby Spiro. Olga was reaching the end of her second pregnancy, puffing up and down the wooden stairs all day, often sitting at our kitchen table chatting with Father and Glykeria. Dino, through hard work and a good deal of nagging at Putnam and Thurston, had managed to be promoted to underchef at $55 a week and to purchase a rickety blue 1950 Pontiac for $600. On Tuesdays, his day off, he would drive his growing family on a round of visits to other Greeks as Olga gloried in her pregnancy.

On October 25, 1954, Olga went into labor, and Dino drove her to Doctors' Hospital. This time she didn't make the mistake of eating a huge meal before leaving, but she still screamed with ear-shattering cries from the very first labor pain. By afternoon she had given birth to another son, an achievement that filled her with justifiable pride. Since the first son was named for the paternal grandfather, this one would receive the name Christos for the maternal grandfather, so Father had his first namesake and second grandson. Our nuclear family was growing into a clan, and my father took great joy in his grandchildren, propping them in his lap in front of the steering wheel as he drove on visiting rounds to Greek acquaintances to show them off.

While Dino would let anyone pile into his ramshackle heap of a Pontiac, my father coddled and cherished his '47 Studebaker as if it were a Rolls Royce. He made Dino wash and shine the car every Tuesday, and no particle of dust, much less gum wrappers or cigarette ashes in the ashtrays, was permitted to sully its interior. Father considered it a great favor when he arrived at the school door on chilly autumn afternoons to drive me and Fotini home.

But by the time Fotini and I had reached sixteen and fifteen, respectively, we had become increasingly reluctant to ride home with him. Fotini had the feeling that he was only spying on her, and both of us found it embarrassing to be seen entering the funny old car beside our voluble, round, foreign, sixty-two-year-old father, who looked more like a grandfather. "It's a nice day, we'll walk," we'd say, no matter what the weather. I could see that he was hurt and bewildered when we repeatedly refused his offer of a ride, but I cared more about my friends' opinion than about his feelings.

Eventually he must have figured out why I kept turning him down, because one afternoon he drove up to the school in a shiny green Plymouth I had never seen before. "Get in, I'll drive you home," he said casually as I stood there staring.

"Whose car is this?" I asked, just as Dino had when he first got off the boat.

"Mine," Father replied smugly. "I decided it was time for a change."

It wasn't really a new car; in fact it was three years old — a 1951 Plymouth — but it had been kept in pristine condition and shone like an emerald. Hoping my classmates were looking, I got in and proudly rode home.

My delight in the new car lasted until Father drove us to church on Sunday. During the latter part of the service, while the priest gave the sermon, the other altar boys and I were at liberty until our final cue, so I said, "Hey, guys, come outside and see something."

I led the group out to the parking lot, where the green Plymouth reflected the glory of the bright fall day. "That's my dad's new car," I remarked modestly.

"Aw, that's not so new," scoffed John Rizos, the priest's son. "Look, it's got a divided windshield. All the *new* cars have a wraparound windshield."

Before my eyes the splendid new car shriveled into a crummy old piece of junk. When Father emerged from church sometime later, after exchanging greetings with all his cronies, I told him that I had decided to walk home instead of riding. "It's a nice day, I think I'll stop over at a friend's house," I remarked offhandedly. I could see his puzzlement at my rejection of the fine new car, which he no doubt had bought specially to impress me, but with the cruelty of youth I never willingly set foot in the Plymouth, with its despised divided windshield, for the rest of eighth grade.

Early in the school year we received a telegram from Kanta in Greek, which had been transcribed into Latin letters by Western Union. "I have given my pledge to Evangelos Stratis," it read. "Wedding on September 19."

The name Evangelos Stratis meant nothing to me, but to my father and sisters it was a cause for celebration. In the village before the war Olga had attended school with Evangelos Stratis, and she pronounced him "a nice boy, not too great as a student, but that's all right, because he's a Stratis."

In our village, each individual was judged by the reputation of his clan, and all members of a clan were considered to share the same characteristics. The Stratis clan was one of the best in Lia, and two of our female Gatzoyiannis cousins had married male Stratis cousins. Now Kanta had chosen another.

All the Stratises, my sisters said, were home-loving, loyal, conscientious, hard-working, and responsible. Evangelos, Kanta's choice, would therefore make an ideal husband, for he would not be shiftless, irresponsible, or unfaithful. The only drawback, according to Olga, our ultimate authority on village matters, was that Evangelos was an adored only son of an extremely strong-minded mother. If Kanta lived in her mother-in-law's house, as was traditional in the village, she would be tyrannized by the woman. But Kanta had no intention of settling in the village, and in fact had promised to be back before Christmas.

I paid little attention to all the speculation about Kanta's choice of groom, aside from being pleased that she had chosen someone from the village. It meant nothing to me except that she would be moving up to the second floor, which would allow me to have a bedroom all to myself.

At the beginning of December, Father received a call from Kanta asking him to contact Table Talk to see whether she could extend her absence another month; she and her new husband were in Athens, and it would take at least two more months before his papers to emigrate were approved. Father went in person to Angelo Cotsidas, but was told the union rules were firm: five months' leave of absence was all Kanta could take; if she wasn't back by Christmas, he couldn't hold her job open for her.

A week before Christmas, Father told me that Kanta was flying back from Athens and would be home in a day or two. She was changing planes in Rome and arriving in New York, where he would go to meet her.

The next morning, December 19, I awoke to find my father sitting tensely in front of the television set in the small den off the living room. He never was one for watching the news, so I asked him curiously what had happened.

"Plane crash," he muttered, never taking his eyes off the screen. "Italian Air Lines, near New York. Only six survivors. Hush." He raised his hand as a grim broadcaster began reading off a list of victims. Then Father turned and looked at me. "Not a word to your sisters. We don't even know if Kanta was on it, but her ticket was for Italian Air Lines."

I could feel the hair on the back of my neck rise as a black-and-white image of smoking rubble and fire trucks came on the screen.

"I should never have let her go back!" Father muttered. "This is my punishment."

Instantly the memory of my mother's curse came into my mind — the curse on any of us who returned to Greece. As the horror of the crash started to seep into my consciousness, Glykeria came into the room, and Father abruptly snapped off the television. But she had heard enough.

"That's not Kanta's plane!" she cried. "Is Kanta dead?"

Father tried to convince her she was mistaken — there was no evidence that Kanta had been in the crash — but Glykeria couldn't be stopped once the keening began.

"It's not fair, she just got married!" she wailed. "She never had time to enjoy her husband. Why would God kill a new bride?" She paused and thought a moment. "At least she lived to wear the wedding crown," she mused, "so she won't be buried like a virgin."

In Greece, children and young adults who die unwed are buried in white, with white banners and flowers and a wedding crown of flowers placed on their brow, symbolizing that they died unspoiled, married to Death instead of an earthly spouse. Older, married people have purple banners and draperies around their coffins instead. Nothing was as heart-rending as a white funeral, with a child or fresh-faced youth lying in the coffin, dressed like a bride or groom.

Glykeria's wails and screams had just begun to draw the other tenants and Olga down the stairs when the telephone rang. We all fell silent, staring at each other, each afraid to answer it and learn Kanta's fate. Finally Father forced himself to lift the receiver, holding it as if it were a snake. Then, over the static, he heard the faint voice of his daughter, and exploded in a roar of joy. "My child! My soul! You're alive!" he cried. "Where are you? We were just sitting here, watching the television, listening for your name. The plane crashed, the plane from Rome."

We learned that Kanta and four other Greeks arriving on the flight from Athens had reached Rome ten minutes too late to board the ill-fated plane for New York. This had left Kanta in tears, stranded in a strange country, cut off from her husband and her family. But the airline had bused the five Greeks to a luxurious hotel to wait for the next flight to New York, two days later. Kanta was calling to tell us of her bad luck, unaware that the plane she was to have flown on had crashed. Her life had miraculously been spared by a ten-minute delay.

When Kanta finally did arrive at 369 Chandler Street and emerged from Father's Plymouth, it seemed to us as if she had been reborn. She was radiant, her usually pale cheeks flushed with happiness. She was delighted with her choice of a husband and with managing her money so well that she had a respectable sum to give to Father. When she ceremoniously handed it over, he began to weep. He embraced her. "My golden child," he cried. "No one else would do so well and bring me back money besides! You're too smart to be a girl! It wasn't until I thought we'd lost you that I realized how much we depend on you. Thank God for sparing you!"

I realized that he was right: of all my sisters, only Kanta could be relied on for common sense, logic, and good advice. Even though her health was fragile and she was so sensitive that she often fainted when upset, Kanta, with her innate intelligence, learned faster than my other sisters how to assimilate and to take advantage of the opportunities of our new land.

My admiration for her cleverness grew tenfold when Kanta told us the story of her odyssey in Greece. "Odyssey" was the right word, for Kanta had played the role of Odysseus, traveling from one hazardous adventure to another, as well as that of Penelope, who had to stave off persistent suitors to save herself for the man she loved.

When Kanta first left Greece in 1949, she was a seventeen-year-old peasant girl in black homespun, her hair in braids, her legs and feet encased in black knitted stockings and heavy black brogans. Now, returning to Greece five years later, she was a thoroughly modern American working woman, with a cap of curly light brown hair, discreet makeup highlighting her fine-boned features, and a wardrobe of brightly printed dresses in drifting, silky fabrics, with matching purses, gloves, pert little hats, and high-heeled, open-toed, ankle-strap shoes. Everything from her large leather handbags to her gold-rimmed eyeglasses and dazzling costume jewelry distinguished her from the drably dressed Greek maidens in their braids, homespun, and black kerchiefs.

During the fifteen-day cruise to Europe on the *Nea Hellas,* while Kanta shared a stateroom with a Greek woman returning home, she had plenty of time to ponder the sort of man she wanted to marry. She had always known that she would choose a husband who was not just good-looking but whose qualities complemented her own. He must be someone who could make the most of himself in America, be ready to learn and assimilate, not be the traditional domineering and tyrannical Greek paterfamilias who would treat her like a galley slave and make her the butt of all his anger and frustration.

Kanta's cruise across the Atlantic was like a voyage on a time machine, for she was traveling from the America of 1954, the year of the first polio vaccinations, kidney transplants, and atomic-powered submarines, back to Athens, which was still in the throes of postwar reconstruction, and from there to our village, which lingered in the Middle Ages. Like all of us, Kanta had become a citizen of two worlds. She watched liberated American girls from the sidelines and took care not to offend the strict mores of our Greek-American community in Worcester, but she engaged in small rebellions like saving her milk money, wearing colorless nail polish, and curling her hair. Nevertheless, she had been nearly grown when we left the village, and she remembered well all the strictures that must be observed by a maiden who hoped to be a bride. She would not outrage public opinion in Athens or in the village with behavior learned in America but would play the traditional game until she found a worthy groom. Because she was clever and intelligent, however, she was determined to find a man who would be ready to travel by her side out of the Middle Ages and into the twentieth century.

Kanta had told Father to make it very clear when he wrote to our grandfather that as a modern American girl, she had no intention of staying in the home of some relative or fellow villager in Athens. He must book hotel rooms. Once she agreed to be a guest in someone's home, Kanta knew, she would be not only crowded and uncomfortable but hopelessly indebted to her hosts, and perhaps forced to accept their choice of a groom. Meanwhile, her hosts would be spying on her every move and reporting on her habits, clothing, and behavior to the rest of the world.

But our grandfather was a famous tightwad, even with someone else's money, and he thought it only sensible to avoid a hotel when a relative's home was available. When he met Kanta at the dock in Piraeus, as weather-beaten, white-haired, and gruff as ever, he told her he hadn't bothered to book a hotel room.

"Then we'll just get in a taxi and drive around until we find one," Kanta informed him, and that's what she did, all the while listening to Grandfather bemoaning the cost of hotel rooms, although Athens was so destitute in 1954 that the best rooms in the city cost only a few dollars a day.

Finally Kanta settled on the Cypress Hotel, with a balcony overlooking Omonia Square. "I was determined to have a shower and some privacy," she told us as we sat in the living room where only days before we had been mourning her death. "Every time I went out on the street, people started following us, talking to me. I needed someplace to be alone and think."

The sight of the slender, stylishly dressed American maiden walking beside the white-haired old peasant with his mustache, village clothes, and gnarled walking stick inspired many strangers to come up and ask our *papou*: "Very pretty girl — is she American? Is she married? I have a very handsome son/nephew/brother she should meet."

In Ithaca, Penelope juggled one hundred eager suitors, and in Athens, Kanta had just as many — distant relatives, friends of friends, even strangers who accosted her on the street or in restaurants. She told us of one young man, a very good-looking college student, who came up to them in a restaurant, remarked on Kanta's beauty, and seemed so polite and personable that she told *Papou* to invite him to the table. The dashing, dark-eyed student confided to her his dream to go to an American medical school and become a doctor, and for a few moments Kanta was tempted. "But that night," she told us, "I thought to myself, what would I do married to a doctor? I'm not educated. I'd spend my whole life working in a factory, putting him through medical school, and when he finally finished he'd be ashamed of me."

Like Penelope, Kanta managed to stall all the suitors in Athens. Her excuse was "First I must go to my village and hold a memorial service for my mother, then, if I want you, I'll come back here."

With Grandfather, Kanta traveled twelve hours on a bus to reach Yannina, the capital of Epiros. Yannina is an ancient Turkish-style city, with storks nesting in chimneys and minarets projecting above the walled town where the Turks ruled until 1913. The town is built on the edge of a huge lake teeming with trout and crayfish, eels and tasty frogs. In this seemingly bottomless lake Ali Pasha used to drown the hapless concubines who displeased him, and the mists drifting over the pine-edged water are said to be the ghosts of his victims.

In Yannina, Kanta insisted again on staying in the best hotel, the Akropolis, although Grandfather nearly became apoplectic at the expense. "You stay where you like," Kanta told him airily. "I'm staying here."

During her week in the city, she negotiated a good price with the tenant of the store in which Father owned a half-interest. It was a tiny corner niche in the old city, hardly more than a *souk,* where lengths of fabric were sold. Kanta wangled all of $1500 from the tenant for our share, because assisting him in the store was an unmarried nephew whom he hoped Kanta might favor. She did not disembarrass him of this notion until she made certain the bill of sale was signed.

Every evening at twilight, Kanta and Grandfather sat at one of the outdoor cafés, often in the company of relatives. They watched the evening *peripato,* as the population of the city strolled up and down the main street to the lakeshore, where musicians, shadow-puppet shows, and dancing bears entertained the crowds. This evening stroll, as in many Greek towns, was the central social event of the day, a time to show off one's finery and conduct flirtations, business deals, and a variety of liaisons.

As Kanta sat there in her flowered summer frock, the cynosure of the passing parade, dozens of people came up to her table and asked to buy her ice cream or coffee. There was one young man whom Grandfather repeatedly invited to the table, afterward saying to her, "Now *that's* the man you should marry. A fine boy! You couldn't do better!"

"But he's ugly, *Papou,* and he's from Metsovo! Why would I choose *him?*" Kanta replied. Finally she discovered that the boy's parents had paid our grandfather a considerable sum of money to influence her in his favor.

Adding all the swains of Yannina to her string of hopefuls, Kanta traveled on to Filiates, the last outpost of civilization before beginning the ascent of the mountains toward Lia. Here again she and *Papou* visited relatives and friends and spent the evenings in an outdoor café watching the *peripato*. And again Grandfather had a favorite among the suitors, a prosperous merchant sixteen years Kanta's senior. "You should give him your word," Grandfather told Kanta after the wealthy shopkeeper had greeted them with flowery politeness one evening. "A goodlooking man of importance, wealthy, with a fine store — you couldn't ask for more."

"But *Papou,* he's too old for me, and besides, I'd have to live here in Filiates if I married him," protested Kanta. Then she added suspiciously, "How much did this one pay you?"

"What's wrong with both of us profiting from your marriage?" Grandfather shrugged. "It's only that I don't want to lose you to America again. We'd rather have you here."

"Stop introducing me to husbands," Kanta snapped. "First we have to think about what we need to buy for *Mana*'s memorial service."

In Filiates, Kanta purchased all her supplies, even to the individual small round loaves of bread to give out to mourners at the memorial service. There were two hundred people in the village, she reckoned, but she knew our eccentric Aunt Nitsa would steal about fifty of the loaves for herself, so Kanta bought three hundred breads to be safe, along with plenty of pastries: *baklava, kataifi,* Turkish delight, cookies, and candies to give as gifts. Then, with her purchases, she and Grandfather took the bus to the village of Aghies Pantes at the foot of the mountain, where the road ended. There they hired four mules for the ascent to the village — a mount each for Grandfather and Kanta, and two more to carry supplies. Kanta showed us a photograph of herself at the head of this procession, wearing her best flower-printed polyester dress with matching jacket, sitting sidesaddle like a well-bred lady, riding up the mountain like Cleopatra sailing into the port of Tarsus to dazzle Mark Antony.

The news of her arrival had preceded her and the entire village was out to greet her, our grandmother and our Aunt Nitsa weeping and wailing at the sight of the first orphan child to return after our family's ordeal. When we had escaped from Lia, our grandparents, Aunt Nitsa, and Uncle Andreas had stayed in the refugee camp in Igoumenitsa with us, and they had long since returned to our deserted village; but the civilians who had not escaped, who had been taken by force into Albania and then into camps in Hungary, had only begun returning to Greece six months before Kanta's arrival, and were now trying to scratch sustenance from the fallow soil. She was shocked at the gaunt, starved faces and ragged clothing of the returnees. The children, including two boys who had been my playmates, held out their hands like beggars pleading for food, and she filled them with sweets, which the villagers hadn't seen for six years.

Cleopatra on her perfumed barge with its gilded stern, purple sails, and silver oars could not have dazzled the Romans more than Kanta amazed the villagers with her American clothing and her largesse. The one bed in our grandparents' house had been prepared for her, complete with sheets on the straw-filled mattress, and there she slept surrounded by Grandfather and Grandmother, Aunt Nitsa and Uncle Andreas, on their pallets on the floor.

As soon as Kanta arrived, the normal population of Lia nearly doubled with the influx of young men returning to visit their ancestral homes from all over Greece, in hopes that the American heiress might choose one of them. "As if it were the national lottery," Kanta said. "They all came to take a chance."

Kanta had not returned to Greece with an entirely impartial mind, however. When she had attended the village school as a young girl, she had noticed a clever, handsome, dark-haired boy in her class. Kanta knew that this young man was now working as a waiter near Athens and that his parents had summoned him back to the village to renew their acquaintance. But for the moment, she refused to talk to any potential husbands. Her first priority was to carry out the memorial service for our mother.

The service took place on a Sunday in August 1954, almost exactly six years after our mother was executed. It was held in the church of Aghia Triada, just below the village square. Kanta couldn't bear to climb the path to our neighborhood in the upper village, called the Perivoli or "orchard," where our mother's bones now rested in a box in the ossuary of the Church of St. Demetrios, just below our family home. She stayed in the lower village, in our grandparents' house, and there Aunt Nitsa cooked the boiled wheat, the *kolyva*, in our mother's memory.

Dressed all in black for the service, Kanta carried the loaves of bread to the church and refused even to glance toward the front of the congregation, where a host of young men in their best suits were looking back at her. The eulogy for our mother was given by a schoolteacher from the village. In his mellifluous voice, he spoke of the tragedy of our mother's murder — how she had died young and never had the chance to see her children grow up, especially her beloved only son. She had given her life for our freedom, he said, and now one of her daughters had come thousands of miles across the sea to honor her memory.

Overwhelmed by a rush of emotions, Kanta began to weep, and then she fell unconscious to the floor and had to be carried out of the church. The memorial service continued, with our grandmother and aunt passing out the breads and *kolyva* at the end in our mother's memory and inviting all the congregation to our grandparents' house to eat. After Kanta recovered, she asked the priest and one of our male cousins to go up to the church where *Mana*'s bones lay and then all the way to the top of the mountain, to the ravine where she had been shot and thrown into a mass grave. Kanta wanted the priest to say the *trisagion* prayer over her remains and her killing ground and to sprinkle holy water to give her soul peace. She put the request to Father Nicholas, the lean, bearded village priest, who worked as a cooper to supplement his meager income. Even with this help, Father Nicholas and his wife, the good *papadia,* were so poor that they had been forced to send their only son to a state orphanage near Arta because they couldn't afford to feed him. Kanta handed the priest a $10 bill in payment for the *trisagion* services and the long walk up to the ravine, and Father Nicholas looked at it in wonder. "Ten dollars!" he exclaimed. "For ten dollars I'd walk all the way to Albania!"

Once the memorial services were over, Kanta felt a new sense of peace. At last she was able to concentrate on the question of the suitors. Every few minutes there would be a knock at her grandparents' courtyard door and her Aunt Nitsa would open it to find another villager there singing the praises of some young man. "I got dizzy from so many callers," Kanta said. Each visitor had to be given coffee, a glass of water, and sweets, and Aunt Nitsa was so upset at the sight of Kanta's generosity that she often snitched the pieces of Turkish delight off the tray and hid them in her apron until Kanta forced her to turn out her pockets.

The young waiter whom Kanta secretly favored appeared in the village with all the rest, and he was as handsome and well-mannered as she remembered, but she soon discovered he had a fatal flaw: he hadn't fulfilled his required three years of military duty, and there was no way he could emigrate until he did. That meant that if Kanta married him, she would be stuck in the village for three years plus the additional time needed to complete his papers to go to America. Kanta took the young man's father aside and explained the situation to him. "I told him, it wasn't that I didn't like his son, but I couldn't bear to stay in the village a week, much less four years," she said. "I missed telephones and showers. Also, the memory of my mother and what she suffered is too strong there. The village was bad enough when I left, and now it's worse. I didn't want to go back to cutting wood and scratching in the ground! After all, I had always been the one in the family who wanted most to leave and come to America, and I wasn't going to destroy my life for this man!"

So, without shedding a tear, Kanta gave up the beau she had intended to wed and decided to look over the other options. "A female cousin of ours told me to look for her husband's nephew, Evangelos Stratis, when I went to church the next Sunday," she told us. "He had come home for a visit from Konitsa, where he worked in his father's tinker shop. I saw him when I went to church. He was wearing nice sunglasses and a brown suit, but I thought at first he was too skinny. He had nice curly brown hair, but I didn't like his big mustache.

"Then, after the church service," she went on, "when we all went outside, he came up and introduced himself. He was holding his sister's baby, who was little and blond — just the same age as Spiro. It made me homesick and I wanted to kiss the baby, and while I was fussing over it, Evangelos said, 'Why don't you drop by my parents' house after church and have a coffee?'"

As was traditional, Kanta and her grandparents and aunt made the rounds of many village houses after church, having a bit of food and a cup of coffee in each. Finally they arrived at the Stratis house, on the very farthest edge of town. Evangelos was waiting there with his parents and his sister, her husband, and the baby. Their proudest possession was an old-fashioned hand-cranked gramophone which played the latest tunes from Athens when it was wound. Soon everybody but Kanta, who was still mourning our mother, was dancing in the tiny parlor which constituted half of the two-room house. But in the midst of the dancing, the gramophone broke down, and no amount of cranking would make it play.

"I noticed that Evangelos wasn't a very good dancer, and that put me off him," Kanta said. "But when the gramophone broke and he started to fix it, I decided to stay and watch. This was the perfect test, I realized, because what I wanted most in a husband was patience, not a nervous disposition like Dino" (with a glance at Olga) "or a bad temper like *Papou*. So I sat there for maybe three, four hours and Evangelos took the whole gramophone apart and he kept calm, never getting nervous. If it had been me, after the first hour I would have thrown the whole thing down the ravine, but he just kept working patiently, putting it together and taking it apart again, and in the end, when he had it working, I said to myself, 'This is the man for me!' And besides," she added, dimpling, "even if he was too skinny and not a very good dancer, under that mustache he was a very good-looking guy."

From the moment the gramophone was fixed, the courtship moved with dizzying speed. At the very next house she passed, Kanta encountered our first cousin Despoula, a Gatzoyiannis woman married to a Stratis man, who came up to her and said, "Evangelos likes you very much."

"Of course he likes me," Kanta replied matter-of-factly. "The question is, do I like him?"

"Well, do you?" Despoula persisted. "What should I tell him?"

"Tell him," Kanta said, "to bring his people to Grandfather's house tomorrow."

The next afternoon, Evangelos, in his good brown suit, arrived at our grandfather's door along with his parents, his sister and brother-in-law, and assorted cousins. They all crowded into the good room, and as soon as coffee, water, and sweets had been served, Evangelos' father said to our grandfather, "Well, Kitso, shall we begin to discuss the terms of the betrothal?"

"Not so fast," spoke up Kanta, startling the group, who were not used to hearing a bride enter the negotiations. "Before we decide anything, I want to have a talk with Evangelos alone."

It was hardly proper for a couple to be alone before their engagement, but no one was prepared to argue with this strong-minded young woman from America, so she was allowed to take Evangelos into the other room of the house for a private conversation.

Once alone with her suitor, Kanta did not waste time on sweet talk. "There are some things that you must understand before we talk of marriage," she said to the skinny young man, who was gazing at her with a look combining equal parts adoration and astonishment. "You may think that in America we're rich, but we're not. If you marry me, we'll both have to work hard all our lives."

Evangelos assured her that he would work as hard as any man in America, and even harder. Since childhood he had labored in his father's tinker shop, hammering copper pots, burned by the heat of the forge, sweltering in the summer, freezing in the winter. The whole family barely made enough to survive. In America, he assured her, with all its opportunities, he would work like Hercules himself.

"It's different there," Kanta continued. "Nothing at all like Greece. You're going to miss your parents and your friends and the life here. If we go to America together, I don't want to hear you saying you're lonesome and homesick. The minute I hear the word 'homesick' I'm going to send you back."

Evangelos insisted that with her for a bride, he could hardly long for his family and friends, even if he never saw their faces again. To go to America and to win such a beautiful, clever, and sensible wife — he could ask nothing more out of life.

"Well, then, if you're sure, we can tell our families," Kanta conceded. "But before we become formally engaged, I want us to keep company for a week. If, seven days from now, I feel sure that you're the one for me, then we'll announce our engagement and make plans for the wedding."

Choked with emotion, Evangelos, who had always found words more difficult than actions, reached for Kanta's hand and kissed it with the same devotion he showed the icons in the church. The touch of his mustache made Kanta pull her hand away.

"One more thing," she added. "That mustache. It makes you look like an old-fashioned Greek and too old. In America men don't wear mustaches, and I want you to look like an American. You have a very handsome face, but no one can see it. If you want to become engaged to me, that mustache has to go."

Evangelos assured her that his mustache would not see the light of another day. When the young couple finally emerged into the good chamber, they discovered that Evangelos' parents, unsure of what to do, had tactfully gone home to the other end of the village. Kanta and Evangelos told their news to our grandparents and aunt and received their congratulations. Then Evangelos headed for home, running as fast as he could along the steep mountain paths to the hut where his family and his sister's family all lived so close to the bone that they could hardly put meat on the table once a month. Breathless from excitement and exertion, Evangelos finally burst through the door, staggered, and gasped to the assembled family group, "She agreed! We're saved!"

The trial week passed even better than Kanta hoped, as the courting couple paid social visits around the village, attended church together, walked up and down the mountain paths, and talked long and earnestly into the night. Evangelos trimmed his bristling hedge of a mustache into a neat tuft and promised he would remove it altogether on the day of the wedding; he wanted to part with it by degrees. He did nothing that disappointed Kanta, and at the end of the week, their families concluded the formal engagement and Kanta set the date for the wedding: two weeks later, on September 19.

Immediately Evangelos set out for Yannina to buy the wedding bands and to order himself a wedding suit as well as a wardrobe, financed by Kanta, which she very carefully spelled out: dark blue suit, trench coat, black socks and shoes. When Evangelos came to America, she didn't want him looking like a Greek peasant in mismatched jacket and pants, droopy cardigan sweater, and soft cap. With his mustache trimmed, he already seemed more sophisticated. In fact, everyone said it was remarkable how much Kanta and Evangelos resembled each other, with their finely chiseled features, high cheekbones, straight eyebrows, and curly hair.

When Evangelos returned from Yannina, however, he was almost unrecognizable: his neck and cheeks were badly swollen and he was burning with fever. Somehow he had contracted the mumps. Like a forest fire, the rumor spread through the village: it was the evil eye. The rich American girl had chosen a groom, leaving all the other suitors gnashing their teeth in anger, and now the chosen man had the mumps and would be sterile, unable to give her children.

"I didn't let the rumors bother me," Kanta told us. "I had decided Evangelos was my *moira*, my destiny, and if God wanted us to have children we would, and if He didn't, that was all right too."

The engaged pair traveled down to Filiates, where the closest doctor lived, and there they booked rooms in the town's one hotel, which was owned by a distant relative of ours. It was really more of an inn or *hanni*, with only four rooms and one toilet, and their party, which included Evangelos' family and our grandparents and aunt and uncle, filled up the entire place.

The doctor visited Evangelos, who lay in a room with the curtains drawn, running a high fever and attended by his mother and sister. If he was very careful not to exert himself, the doctor announced, if he stayed in bed and faithfully took his medication, he could still marry on the nineteenth of September, but it would be best if the ceremony took place in Filiates, because he was in no condition to travel back up the mountain.

From the next room Kanta sent wires and made all the arrangements for the wedding. She noticed uneasily that every time she looked over her balcony toward the street she saw a certain jilted suitor from Filiates, a hulking young man with a drooping mustache, lurking outside, watching her. She knew that many of the hopeful suitors had taken her engagement very hard, including the young waiter whom she had originally favored. When he learned that she had rejected him because of his military duty and chosen Evangelos instead, he went into a period of mourning and refused to shave for two weeks.

The rejected young man from Filiates was even more angered by her choice, and refused to accept it. Eventually Kanta learned why he always seemed to be skulking near the hotel. A relative who lived in Filiates warned her that with the aid of his friends, he planned to kidnap her. "They figured, her boyfriend is sick in bed, too weak to defend her, we'll watch her movements and grab her when we have the chance," Kanta told us.

In Greece, kidnapping was the traditional way of winning a bride when the families couldn't agree or the bride was reluctant. Once a young woman had been kidnapped, she was considered defiled and no other groom would want her; thus the swain who seized his intended by force didn't have to worry about details like marriage contracts and parental permission. Sometimes Greek brides collaborated in their own kidnapping, other times they were taken very much against their will, but the result was always the same: a shotgun wedding. So ingrained was this practice that the traditional village wedding was a ritualized kidnapping, with the groom's party marching up to the bride's door and singing songs demanding that her parents hand her over before they take her by force. The bride's family then was expected to respond with songs of mourning, bewailing the tragic theft of their finest flower.

But Kanta, a spirited and strong-minded bride-to-be, had no intention of allowing herself to be kidnapped when she had already decided that her destiny lay with Evangelos. So she barricaded herself in her room, guarded by her grandfather and uncle, and did not leave the hotel. She arranged the details of the wedding by proxy, while in the next room the groom sipped chicken soup and moonshine to build up his strength.

On the appointed day, Evangelos, pale, shaking, and even thinner than he had been before, rose from his bed and allowed the best man and his other friends to shave off his last vestige of mustache and dress him in his wedding finery while getting drunk, according to custom. Meanwhile, in the home of a relative, Kanta was being arrayed by all the women in her exquisite American lace wedding gown and train. At the last moment before she left the house, her future mother-in-law handed her a sharp pair of embroidery scissors. "Hide them in your hand and then tuck them in among your flowers," she advised, explaining that scissors would cut the power of the evil eye, which would certainly be drawn to Kanta by the admiration and envy of all who beheld her.

On the arm of our grandfather, Kanta walked through the streets of Filiates to the church, her only attendants two children dressed in white, as all the village followed in her wake. At the church door a ghostly Evangelos was waiting, holding a bouquet of white flowers, which he presented to Kanta as he took her from her grandfather. When she tried to tuck the scissors into the bouquet they pricked her palm, and the scissors and flowers fell to the ground together as the crowd gasped, but Evangelos gallantly retrieved them, and when Kanta was ready, he gave his bride his arm to lead her into the church.

The couple stopped in the middle of the sanctuary as all of Filiates crowded around them and the ceremony began. The best man produced a large length of blue fabric, which he wrapped around the shoulders of the couple so that they would remain bound together. After the ceremony the fabric would be a gift from the *koumbaros* to the bride, to make into a dress. Then the best man exchanged the wedding crowns three times and the priest led the newlyweds up to the altar.

The rollicking feast after the ceremony was held in Giza's Restaurant in Filiates, where the two hundred guests danced, ate, smashed plates, and threw money, while the courses of food kept coming all night. Unfortunately, Evangelos, who was euphoric but trembling with the aftereffects of his illness, couldn't dance more than one *tsamiko*. Even worse, the doctor had forbidden the couple to have sex for at least a week after the wedding while Evangelos recovered his strength, so the newlyweds set out the next day by bus on a romantic but chaste honeymoon trip to Yannina and Patras.

After the specified week, they returned up the mountain to Lia, where

Evangelos' mother slaughtered two lambs and roasted them. All the village came to drink the couple's health and dance to the family's gramophone. Then the pair set out on their real honeymoon, to the enchanted island of Corfu, where Odysseus won the love of Nausicaa on the last leg of his long journey home. From Corfu they traveled to Athens, where they learned that it would take at least three months for Evangelos' papers to be cleared for his trip to America. So they returned to the village to pass some time until Kanta had to leave for America to resume her job.

On December 1, the day after Uncle Andreas' name day was celebrated, Kanta and Evangelos left Lia for the last time. They told everyone, however, that they were coming back again, because they wanted to avoid the keening, wailing, ripping of clothes, tearing of hair, and general lamentation that would take place if their relatives suspected this was the final goodbye.

After three weeks of taking in the sights and introducing Evangelos to relatives in the capital, Kanta bid a tearful farewell to her new husband and boarded the plane for Rome and New York. Evangelos planned to stay in Athens until his papers came through, for he was afraid that if he went back to Epiros, resentful acquaintances and rejected suitors might sabotage his attempts to get clearance by writing anonymous lies about him to the American Embassy. He didn't hear about it when his bride's scheduled plane from Rome to New York crashed. The first thing Kanta asked when she called home and learned of her miraculous escape was that Father call Evangelos in Athens to tell him his bride had been spared.

As soon as Kanta arrived home, she returned to the assembly line at Table Talk. Early in February 1955, Evangelos called her to announce that he was in New York, at Idlewild Airport. His papers had finally come through, and he had left Greece the same day, without even saying goodbye to his parents, whom he would not see again for ten years.

"Stay right there, I'll send Father for you," cried Kanta over the telephone. She couldn't go herself because she had to work, but my father and his new son-in-law recognized each other from photographs. That evening, when Kanta's groom arrived at 369 Chandler, he came up the back steps and kissed me on both cheeks — a gesture that surprised and embarrassed me, for I had been away from Greece so long that I had forgotten men kiss each other in greeting. My father and I certainly wasted no kisses on each other.

Nevertheless, I soon discovered that I liked Evangelos. He was quiet, polite, eager to please, and he had a wonderful knack for machines. When Kanta decided to marry him after watching him fix the gramophone, she discovered the true essence of Evangelos, for he loved mechanical gadgets above all things. His ambition was to own every new gimmick that American technology produced. Even when he had been nearly starving in the village, he had squandered a small fortune to buy himself a camera. Now he couldn't get enough: cameras, a television set, metal detectors, any toy that needed batteries. His ultimate goal, he told me, was to own an automobile. "You watch," he vowed. "In a year I'm going to know English and I'm going to buy a car."

Kanta had managed to get her new husband a job at Table Talk, although she worked the morning shift, from eight until four P.M., and he was given the afternoon shift, from one o'clock to eleven at night. Although they saw little of each other, their combined salaries brought in over $100 a week, and they were able to make a down payment on a handsome suite of furniture for their apartment on the second floor of our three-decker. Angelo, as everyone quickly began to call him, proved to be a sympathetic and good-natured addition to the household, and Father was so pleased by the respect and deference showed him by his new son-in-law that he kept congratulating Kanta on her wise choice. For his part, Angelo was so euphoric at his good fortune and so enamored of his new country that he never suspected that the prosperity which had escaped him for so long in Greece would not be easily won in America.

Dino and Olga with their children and Dino's brother, beside Dino's fateful car

COLLISION
COURSE

Great blunders are often made, like large ropes, of a multitude of fibers.

— Victor Hugo, *Les Miserables*

WHILE KANTA AND ANGELO were feathering their nest, I was busy being the sought-after MC of all the variety shows at school. I teamed up with a set of identical twins who were half a year behind me, Stu and Phil Rosenberg, and together we worked up blackout skits based on excruciatingly corny jokes. Our performances were a cross between vaudeville and the television show *Laugh-In*.

Sample joke: "Hey, Stu, when the king of a tribe of pygmies chooses his best men for an elite guard, what are they called?"

"I don't know, Nick, when the king of a tribe of pygmies chooses his best men for an elite guard, what *are* they called?"

"Selected short subjects!" (Drum roll, applause, blackout.)

The team of Rosenberg, Rosenberg, and Gage proved so successful at Chandler that our guidance counselor decided to produce a variety show at night for the parents, charging admission to raise money for school athletic programs. I was the MC, of course, and the Rosenbergs and I enacted a grisly skit based on the television show *Medic*, in which I played Dr. Steiner. But the highlight of the evening was my performance of "Casey at the Bat," lip-synched to a record sung by Jerry Colonna. I wore a red-striped jacket and straw hat as I stood at the plate waving a bat and proclaimed: "The outlook wasn't brilliant for the Mudville nine that day/The score stood two to four with but an inning left to play . . ."

All the parents attended the variety show, even my father, and I was tense throughout the evening, wondering what his reaction would be to his son performing slapstick comedy in front of an American audience. After the show, while I was still wearing my stage makeup, Miss Hurd cornered me, raving that I was a great hit: everyone had fallen out of their seats laughing. She followed me as I searched for my father and finally found him near the back of the auditorium, dressed as usual in his best three-piece suit, bow tie, expensive hat, and gold-headed walking stick. He looked at me askance, taking in the makeup.

"What did you think?" I asked him nervously in Greek.

"Well, I was sitting so far back, I couldn't really hear," he replied, also in Greek. "I didn't like your clothes — you looked like a clown. But everyone seemed to enjoy it. They clapped for you most of all."

This meant that he hadn't understood a word of what I was doing, but he was impressed at the reaction of the crowd of Americans. I had expected to astonish him with my skill as an entertainer, but I realized that bewildered acceptance of my act was the most I could hope for.

Feeling Miss Hurd hovering behind me, I introduced Father to my favorite teacher. She congratulated him warmly on having produced such a son, and he responded, as Greeks do when meeting an authority figure, with courtly deference, bowing as he shook her hand.

"Yes, my son, very smart boy," he said to her. "I tell him, nothing important like education. A man who works with his hands, he's no better than animal. I'm workingman myself — my biggest mistake, not getting educated. I tell him every day, grab the education! Here in this country, educated man can go anywhere, do anything. God bless America!"

Miss Hurd seemed charmed by this speech, and I sighed with relief that Father hadn't lambasted me for putting on effeminate makeup and making a fool of myself in public. I know how it must have seemed to him, but he evidently figured that if this was part of getting an education, he wouldn't object.

My dizzying rise to the peak of eighth-grade popularity got me invited to a number of parties at girls' houses. I went eagerly, but was astonished at what I saw. It was a good thing my father didn't know what went on at American teenage get-togethers, I reflected. The parents were generally invisible, except for putting out food now and then. Meanwhile, interlocked couples danced to slow records, grinding their bodies together. At some point in each party the lights would go out and all the dancing couples would commit as much of the sex act as they could manage while standing up.

To a Greek, all of this was incredible. In Greece, if an unmarried couple is left alone for only a few minutes, all the parents involved assume that they have done their worst and the girl is no longer a virgin. For American parents to turn their daughters loose in their own rumpus room or living room with lustful young men and the lights low, then to provide food and disappear, was incomprehensible to me. Even more depraved, in my opinion, was the father who kept popping into the room to take photographs of his daughter's party. "Not only do these Americans happily let their daughters be felt up," I thought, "but the parents take pictures to commemorate the event for posterity." Nevertheless, I eagerly attended all the parties to which I was invited, glorying in my new popularity.

Meanwhile, Miss Hurd was selecting more of my poems, articles, and essays for inclusion in the school paper, and I suspected she was grooming me to be the editor next year. One day in the spring of eighth grade, she said to our English class, "We've been discussing how authors draw their best material from their own lives. I want each of you to write me an essay based on your own experiences." She paused and looked at me. "Nicholas, I want you to write something about what happened to you in Greece during the war."

This was the last thing I wanted to write about, so, characteristically, I postponed doing anything about the assignment until just before the Monday it was due. Then I went into my room, shut the door, and sat at the bedside table with a pencil and yellow pad on my lap. It was one of the first fine days of May, and the chorus of birdsong outside my window and the perfume of grass freshly cut by our neighbor's lawn mower distracted me even more from this onerous assignment.

Finally I took up the pencil and wrote the first sentence: "To many people the coming of spring means different things — the end of winter, the first robin, a time when a young man's fancy turns to thoughts of love. Spring to me has a very different meaning because this was the season when I said goodbye to my mother for the last time."

After that I just kept going, writing one line after another. I told how in September of 1947, the Communist guerrillas, at war with the Greek nationalist troops, occupied our village, and how the men all ran away before they arrived to avoid being conscripted. I told how the guerrillas took our food and then our house for their headquarters and how they wanted to take Olga to be a guerrilla, but Mother burned her foot with a hot poker so she couldn't walk. Then they took Kanta instead, but eventually they sent her back because she fainted so often during training. Meanwhile, my mother and sisters did everything the guerrillas asked: daily work details, planting land mines, building pillboxes, burying the dead, carrying the wounded over the mountains, sowing and harvesting crops for their army. Finally, I wrote about how the guerrillas held a meeting to demand that all the children between three and fourteen be handed over by their mothers so they could be sent to camps behind the Iron Curtain, where they would be trained as Communist soldiers of the future. Most of the mothers refused, even though the guerrillas put a table of food before the starving villagers and promised that any children handed over would immediately be fed.

The turning point, I wrote, came one day when I was lying in our family's bean field, invisible between the bean rows, and two guerrillas rode by, talking about how they were going to take all the children by force. I ran to tell my mother, setting in motion the series of events that ended in our escape and her trial, torture, and execution for sending us away.

I told how *Mana* began to plan the nighttime flight out of Lia and down the mountains to the nationalist lines, and how she paid one of the few men left in the village to guide us between the land mines. I described how, on the last day, the guerrillas demanded another woman from our house to help thresh wheat in distant fields, and how my mother decided to go herself, telling the rest of us to escape as planned. She would try to get away on her own and join us, she promised, bringing my sister Glykeria, who had already been sent to the wheatfields.

I did not write down the things my mother said to me on that last day, when she took me by the hand up to the place where the women harvesters were gathering. I didn't say that she took me on her lap and told me that I must be very brave; that if we children reached America, we must never come back to Greece. Then she took a crude silver cross on a chain from her neck and put it around mine to protect me. I didn't describe how she kissed me for the last time and then walked away behind the file of women being led down into the ravine, or how she turned every few minutes to look back at me. All those things that passed between us in our last few moments were too precious to write in a school essay.

We escaped at night as planned, I wrote, and by the time the guerrillas' sentries began to pursue us, we were nearly in the mined no man's land. When the sun came up we were in sight of the nationalist lines, and we made a white flag out of Olga's petticoat and climbed the hill into their midst. They transported us — in the first motorized vehicle we had ever seen — to the refugee camp, where we eventually learned of our mother's execution. "I can still hear the screams of my sisters," I wrote, "when my grandfather told us that both my mother and my aunt were shot by the guerrillas for what they called treason — retaliation for our having escaped.

"I'm very lucky I came to America," I concluded, "and I know that my mother would be happy too. This is what she wanted for us more than anything. But still, whenever spring comes in Massachusetts, and everyone else is glad that winter is over, I always find myself feeling sad, remembering the day I saw my mother for the last time."

The remembering, and the writing of the essay, opened the floodgates of memory and filled me with sharp grief. I resolved never to speak of these events again. It was almost like living the pain all over. I didn't reread my essay but turned it in to Miss Hurd on Monday, hoping I had seen the last of it. Unfortunately, a week later she told me that she would like to read it to the class, if I didn't mind, along with some of the other essays. I mumbled that it was okay, but as she read my words aloud, I became drenched with nervous sweat, trying not to listen but to pretend it was the prose of a stranger.

As the teacher read, none of my classmates looked at me, and after she was done no one spoke, except for Miss Hurd, who said, "Very fine work, Nicholas." Later in the hall several of the girls said quietly, "I'm sorry about what happened to your mother, Nick." One of the boys from my class blurted, "That was really good, Nick! I mean, not good, that was really terrible! Well, you know what I mean." That same day the assistant principal came up to me and said in a voice that seemed too loud, "I read your essay, Nicholas. My God, boy! The things that go on in this world. I had no idea!"

When eighth grade ended, I was sorry to leave behind my newfound social prestige for the summer, but for Fotini the last day of school represented the end of an increasingly painful passage through America's public school system. As soon as Kanta returned from Greece, Fotini refused to attend classes anymore, but after several weeks one of her teachers, Miss Doran, called her at home and asked her to come in for a talk. In Miss Doran's office, Fotini poured out all her unhappiness — the teachers who mocked her, the embarrassment of being three years older than the rest and ashamed to wear a gym suit, the mortification of having Father spy on her, the total incomprehensibility of fractions and music. She burst into tears and said she was old enough to quit school legally and that was that.

Miss Doran spoke kindly and asked her just to finish eighth grade. "It will look much better on your record, Tina," she said. "Don't worry about grades or homework — I'll take care of that and speak to all your teachers. Just come to school until the year's over. Do it for me."

Grudgingly Fotini agreed to complete eighth grade, but she never again spoke in class or did any work. And at the end of the year, she disappeared from the corridors of Chandler and from the memories of her fellow students. In Greece she had been an outstanding student, but being plunged into classes in a foreign language, three years older than her classmates, and from a very strict society had combined to destroy any enthusiasm Fotini originally had for education.

Kanta was not sympathetic, since she would have given anything for the chance to get a high school diploma. "You have to do *something*," she lectured Fotini. "You're sixteen years old and you have to learn some kind of skill. You're always fussing with your hair — why don't you save up some money and go to hairdressing school and get a certificate?

If you become a beautician, you'll have no trouble attracting customers, because you're so pretty."

It was true that Fotini, who resembled the young Elizabeth Taylor, was the prettiest of my sisters. Boys were always approaching her, only to be abruptly rejected. That summer of 1955, Fotini took a job during the day at Table Talk and signed up to take classes at night at the Ollis Beauty School on Main Street. There, for the first time, she saw girls her own age who smoked cigarettes and wore makeup, and she was shocked. There was a handsome Italian boy in the hairdressing school, and he admired Fotini not only for her beauty but for her quiet, modest manner. Every night he asked her to go out with him, if only for a cup of coffee in the café downstairs during the class break, but Fotini was sure if she ever walked out of the school beside the young man, her father would be spying on her. She invariably replied, "I'd like to, but you don't know my father — he'd kill me and you both if I ever had coffee with you."

While Fotini was working at Table Talk and going to hairdressing school at night, I found myself a summer job by going from one Greek diner to another. Finally an Albanian Greek hired me to work behind the counter at his lunchroom on Pleasant Street for eighty cents an hour. My newfound performing skills contributed to my success there, for as I grilled hot dogs and hamburgers, I developed a repartee with the customers and often created special sandwiches for them. I would name my creations for the customers, and pretty soon they were asking for me when they came in. Seeing how popular I was, my boss increased my hours to fifty a week, and pretty soon I was bringing home a salary of $40.

My hard work at the lunchroom was part of a master plan. In July I would turn sixteen and be eligible to take my driving test. I hoped to use the money to finance driving lessons so that I could get my license that summer.

As the one-eyed man is king in the country of the blind, the ninth-grader with a driver's license was king at Chandler Junior High, where the oldest students were usually fourteen years old. I remembered what a sensation had been caused by the two sixteen-year-olds who had succeeded in driving to school during the past year. They were the class hoods, and had both been held back so often that they reached driving age while still in junior high. When they appeared at school behind the wheel of a car, they became celebrities and could each have had their pick of the girls.

I, too, would be sixteen in ninth grade — not because I had been held back, but because I had lost two years in coming from Greece. Behind my dream of driving up on the first day of school was an even more ambitious goal — to get laid. Once I had my license, I was sure, the second wish would be quickly granted, for what girl could resist a man with a driver's license who also does Humphrey Bogart impersonations?

One night, after I had saved some money from working at the lunchroom, I apprised my family as casually as possible that I was going to take driving lessons. Father didn't object to my suggestion. "I'm the best driver in Massachusetts," he told me, "and I could give you lessons, but you're probably right — it's better to learn from a professional teacher. He would have more patience." We both knew that with all the bad feeling between us, we would be at each other's throats the whole time, and the driving lessons would be a fiasco.

Father advised me to choose as a teacher a Greek-American friend of his named Peter Vusvunis, who owned a garage near Table Talk. "It's not enough just to learn how to drive a car," he said. "You must learn how the insides of the car work too. Peter will teach you that."

I nodded my head obediently, pleased at the success of my plan so far, but Glykeria interrupted. Since Olga had moved upstairs, Glykeria had taken over her function as Cassandra and doom-crier of our family. Now she admonished my father that he might as well let me have a gun as a driver's license — either way I was sure to kill myself or someone else. "He's too young to drive, has no sense!" she insisted. "Let a boy like that loose on the streets — it's homicide! Have you forgotten that he was hanging from street lamps and associating with juvenile delinquents only two years ago? If you let that boy get a driver's license, mark my words, he'll be dead or in jail within a year."

The force of her rhetoric could hardly fail to influence my impressionable father, and I sensed my opportunity for a license slipping through my fingers. I called on all my best arguments. I would be conscientious, a true chip off the old block in driving skill, I promised. A license would make me responsible and useful to the family. It was the proper role of a man to drive a car. Then I produced the clincher: I already had saved enough to pay for the lessons.

"You hear that — he's saved up enough to pay for his lessons!" said Father, for once leaning my way in an argument. "And he's right, every man should know how to drive a car, in case of emergency at the very least. Yes, Nikola, you have my approval, as long as you take lessons from Peter Vusvunis."

Vusvunis was an excellent teacher and introduced me to the mysteries of a car's engine. He even taught me the difficult trick of coming to a complete stop on a hill in his manual-shift car and then starting up without a jerk by slowly releasing the hand brake while gently pressing down and then up on the clutch to put the car in gear.

I passed my driver's test on a sweltering day in August, even though the examiner nearly failed me for forgetting to look back before pulling out from the curb. It seemed fortune was definitely on my side, and I could hardly wait to dazzle the entire student body on the first day in September.

That, of course, would require a car for me to drive, and I knew it was hopeless to expect my father to lend me his. Nevertheless, I asked him, and got the same reply he always gave anyone who wanted to borrow his car. "As the proverb says, 'There are three things a man must never lend,'" he intoned, "'his wife, his rifle, and his donkey!' And that car is my donkey."

That left me with only one alternative: Dino's beat-up 1950 Pontiac. I promised to wash and polish it faithfully every week if Dino would only let me drive it to school on the first day. Before he agreed, my brother-in-law insisted on riding with me several times to see if I was competent. Finally he said he would let me have it that first day if I would then bring it after school to the parking lot some distance from Putnam and Thurston where he usually left it.

My arrival at school was as sensational as I had hoped. All my classmates gathered around the ancient Pontiac, wide-eyed with admiration. At lunchtime I took a selected group of friends for a ride around town and then to the Coney Island Diner for hot dogs. If I had been popular before, I was now lord of the school. Surely it was only a matter of time before I scored with a girl, I congratulated myself. I had no particular girl in mind but planned to invite a group of promising candidates to ride along with male friends so they would feel at ease, and then to start zeroing in on the girl who seemed most approachable.

The first issue of the *Chandler Echo* that fall appeared with a front-page cartoon showing many members of the faculty and student body staring in amazement as they were nearly knocked over by a streak of exhaust blazing across the panel. "Watch out!" read the caption. "Nick Gage has his license!"

A week after this triumph, on a Tuesday — Dino's day off — I asked him if I could take the car to school again, in exchange for washing it for all eternity. Tuesday was his day for making visiting rounds with his family, so he grudgingly allowed me to have it if I promised to bring it right back when school let out at two-thirty.

I promised willingly, but when school was over, while taking my selected courtiers for a short ride, I realized that it wasn't going to be easy to lose my virginity if I only got a brief loan of Dino's car every couple of weeks or so. Inspiration struck, and on the way home I stopped at Woolworth's and had the ignition key duplicated in the key shop.

Leaving Woolworth's, I passed a Greek friend from church named Perry Eliopoulos, who flagged me down. "I can't believe you've got wheels, Gage!" he marveled. "This is perfect! We'll drive around the high schools and pick up some high school girls — they're all fast! You just drive and let me do the talking."

We cruised by all the high schools — North, Commerce, Classical — and Perry did indeed talk, but his come-on was so aggressive and vulgar that none of the high school girls even deigned to reply, much less get in the car and let us have our way with them. Finally, crestfallen, I drove Perry home and went on to Chandler Street. I found Dino standing in the driveway, shaking his fist at me in rage as I drove into view.

"I said be back at two-thirty at the latest, and it's five-thirty," he shouted, red in the face.

"You lent me your car but not your watch," I rejoined. "How was I supposed to know what time it was?"

"You've ruined my family's whole day," he bellowed, a vein pulsing in his forehead. "This is the thanks I get for lending my car! Well, you'll see mountains dance before you get your hands on it again."

That was what *he* thought. I now had a duplicate key to the Pontiac, and I also knew the schedule that Dino invariably followed. His shift at Putnam and Thurston was from two-thirty to midnight. When he went to work, he parked the car on Orange Street, a long way from the restaurant, in a lot where he didn't have to pay. After six, when the parking meters no longer required a coin and he got a break from the dinner rush, Dino would leave the restaurant long enough to move the car closer.

Because I got out of school at two-thirty, I had plenty of time to walk over to the Orange Street parking lot, drive away Dino's car using my duplicate key, pick up friends who had stayed after school for some activity, drive them around for a couple of hours, and get the car back to the parking lot before Dino came to move it. I managed to do this a couple of times without his catching on, because I was careful to replace the gas I used and to leave the car just as I found it.

I had narrowed down the chosen few who were allowed to accompany me on these joy rides, and on my third occasion of clandestinely "borrowing" Dino's car, I invited my friend Chuck Goldthwaite and two popular ninth-grade girls, Paula Farrell and Franny Munton. "We'll go for a drive and then I'll drop you back at school," I told them generously. First we stopped at the Newport Creamery for ice cream, and then I drove through the mansion-lined avenues where many of Worcester's richest families lived, around Salisbury Street and Notre Dame Academy.

Finally, heading back in the direction of Chandler, I drove up Zenith Drive and took a right at the May Street intersection, going through a stop sign. As I sped around the corner, a large station wagon was passing through the intersection, and I crashed into its left rear fender with such impact that the station wagon began to spin around.

As my passengers screamed, I wrenched our car back on course and gunned it, speeding up May Street in the direction of the school, praying that the other driver hadn't gotten a good look at me and that Dino's car wasn't noticeably damaged.

"Hey, Nick!" Chuck Goldthwaite yelled. "Where're you going? You have to stop!"

"Shut up!" I muttered through clenched teeth as I sped toward the junction of May and Chandler, desperate to get out of sight of my victim. The girls didn't scream this time, only uttered horrified yelps as I hit the intersection, shaking with fear. I took the right turn so sharply that I went over the curb, across the sidewalk, and up the embankment, finally coming to a halt in someone's front yard.

"We'll get out here! This is close enough," my three friends cried, tumbling out the doors. "We'll walk back to school. Thanks for the ride, Nick!" They were eager to escape the clutches of this maniac.

"Okay," I mumbled, trying to control the violent trembling of my body and look as if I *meant* to be parked halfway up the hillside. "See you! Listen, guys," I added, "I barely touched him. It was nothing, just a tap. No need to mention it to anyone, okay?"

"Okay!" they agreed, hurrying off toward school, relieved to be still alive.

Thoroughly chastened, I drove carefully back to Orange Street and parked the car where I had found it. Then I got out, praying to all the saints, and walked around to the front.

It was worse than I feared. Dino's front fender was totally caved in, his front headlights broken. Clearly I was in serious trouble. The thought that terrified me most was what Dino and my father would do. I didn't know yet that my luck was running even worse than I could imagine: the man I had hit and left behind was a lawyer, and his car had spun around so that he got a good look at the retreating license plate number of Dino's car, which he immediately reported to the police.

This was definitely the worst thing I had ever done in my life, worse than hanging from lampposts or fraternizing with petty criminals. I tried to think of a way out of the punishment awaiting me, but my mind went numb. So I did what I always did in moments of crisis: I went to the movies.

I knew Dino would be coming to move his car around seven, so I hurried off to Loew's Poli on Main Street with the vague idea that I would go in, never to come out into the daylight again. After I huddled in one of the back seats, I discovered that my wretched luck was running true to form — the feature film was *Kismet,* a dismal musical with an Oriental background starring Howard Keel and Ann Blyth. There was nothing on the screen to hold my attention or give me guidance. What I needed was the inspiring courage of a John Wayne western or the cynical "I don't give a damn" attitude of a Robert Mitchum film, but instead I got Howard Keel warbling about kismet while my own kismet was waiting for me at home.

Theatrically, things got worse, if possible. The second show on the double bill was *Joe Macbeth,* an abysmal update of Shakespeare's tragedy set as a gangster film. By comparison, *Kismet* looked like *Citizen Kane.* I had planned to stay inside the sanctuary of Loew's Poli forever, but by nine-thirty, when the second film was finished, even the prospect of going home to face the music seemed more appealing than seeing one of these dogs again.

With lagging footsteps I traced my way back to Chandler Street and cautiously approached the house. Things looked quiet; no sign of Dino. Even my father's car was absent. Very quietly I mounted the back stairs. As I pushed open the screen door, the three people waiting in the kitchen turned to look at me: my sisters Glykeria and Olga at the kitchen table, and a uniformed policeman who was standing up, from my perspective appearing to be about eight feet tall.

My sisters, of course, got in the first word, shrieking in Greek like two banshees. "Accursed wretch, what have you brought down upon our heads?" they chorused.

The officer of the law took over, talking just like they did on *Dragnet.* "Are you Nicholas?"

"Yes," I answered meekly.

"Did you take your brother-in-law's car without permission earlier today?"

"Yes."

"Did you proceed to hit another car at the corner of Zenith Drive and May Street and then leave the scene of the accident?"

"Yes" (very quietly).

"Come with me, please. I'm going to have to take you down to headquarters and book you."

As if on cue, my father appeared at the back door, out of breath. He had been driving around Worcester, looking for me. His reaction to my crime was all I needed to make my day complete.

I turned to face the onslaught of his fury and stared: his face was wreathed in a beatific smile, which shone on me and the police officer alike. This did not reassure me, however, for I recognized the Mediterranean smile that masks emotions too terrible to be revealed. In *The Iliad* Homer described the fear that spread through the Trojan army when Ajax advanced "smiling under his threatening brows." Seeing my father, I knew exactly how the Trojans felt.

"I'm taking your son in to book him," the cop told my father.

"Is that really necessary, sir?" my father asked. "He's good boy — never make trouble. To be arrested, a criminal, spoil his good name . . ."

"I'll tell you what," the cop said in a milder tone. "It's time for my dinner break. If, while I was at dinner, you and your son should go to police headquarters and he turned himself in voluntarily, it would look a lot better later in court."

"You very kind man," Father said. "I don't forget this favor. Perhaps another favor, if I may ask. Do you know the name and number of the man in the other car? We must call him and apologize."

"All right," said the officer, pulling a piece of paper from his pocket. "But you didn't get this from me."

The policeman left and Father went to the phone and dialed Peter Bell, the diminutive lawyer whom all the Greeks turned to when they needed legal help. He arranged to meet Bell at the police station and then motioned me out the door as my sisters shouted advice after us.

I entered the green Plymouth feeling like a condemned man and waited for my father's wrath to fall, but he just drove in silence, staring straight ahead over the top of the steering wheel, deep in thought. Then he looked at me and that eerie smile reappeared on his face.

"Don't worry, my child, Peter Bell will fix everything. He knows everyone in Worcester," he said. "It'll be all right. I'll call up the man in the other car and talk to him, make him understand. He probably has children himself. I'll talk to him man to man."

This was too strange for me to deal with. I decided he was just trying to reassure me so I would be calm at the police station, and I braced myself for the outburst that would come after I was booked.

In the station they booked me, took fingerprints, photographed me, then left us alone with our lawyer. Pete Bell shook my hand and greeted me like one recently bereaved, then began whispering to my father, who nodded sagely at everything he said.

Bell explained that if we could convince Dino to say there was a tacit understanding that I could use his car, then that part of my crime would become taking a car without permission instead of car theft — a misdemeanor instead of a felony.

"No problem at all," my father assured him. "Dino will say whatever I tell him to say."

I gathered that Dino had lost his famous temper when the police had arrived at Putnam and Thurston, demanding to see his car and then inviting him to the police station. Dino told them that unless they were prepared to pay his salary, he wasn't going anywhere. Finally the police appealed to Charley Davis, the owner of the restaurant, who said he would send Dino to the police after the rush hour. But as soon as Dino saw the damage to his car he had a pretty good idea who had caused it, and he told the police, who went to my house to wait for me.

After I was booked and became a sixteen-year-old with a criminal record, my father drove me home in the same unsettling silence that had so unnerved me on the way down. When we got in the door, he cut short the questions and condemnations of my sisters with a few terrifying roars of "Leave the boy alone!" Then we all sat at the dining room table near the cubbyhole that held the telephone, and listened as he dialed my accuser.

Ever since the accident, which seemed to have taken place in slow motion, my senses had been preternaturally sharp, and now I could clearly hear everything the man on the other end of the phone said, as well as my father's solemn voice.

"Mr. John, sir, I'm Christy Gage, Nick's father," he began. "I call to say we very, very sorry what happened. The boy panicked, made a big mistake. He's a good boy — never any trouble. Good student. Serious boy. Our lawyer say, if you don't press charges, it will save his life, not ruin his future and his good name."

"Are you out of your mind?" came the explosive voice on the other end, each word like the blow of a hammer. "Your boy left me on the street — I could have been bleeding to death! He might have killed me. He's a menace, and I'm going to do everything I can to see he's locked up for a goddamn long time."

My father's face suffused with color and the veneer of politeness crumbled. "What kind of man, you?" he shouted. "Want to ruin my boy's life. You must be sick person, to do that. He's only sixteen years old."

He slammed down the phone and turned to look at the rest of us with defeat in his eyes.

Instead of despair, I felt a surge of joy. This was the first time I had ever seen my father defend me. But then I realized that the words he had used were chosen to sway the man on the other end of the phone and influence him to go easy on our family's reputation.

A date was set for the arraignment and we all gathered in court: Peter Bell, my father, and me, feeling like a guest star in a *Perry Mason* episode. My father still hadn't punished me for my rampage of crime, and I was almost groggy from bracing myself for the first blow.

Peter Bell pleaded guilty on my behalf to taking a car without permission, reckless driving, and leaving the scene of an accident. Then he spoke in my defense: "Your Honor, this unhappy incident was the result of youthful immaturity, not malice. This young man panicked because of his inexperience. He arrived in this country a war refugee from Greece six years ago and has been a good boy until this tragedy: an altar boy, an excellent student, beyond reproach. He's never been in trouble before and comes from a very responsible family. His widowed father has been working in Worcester since 1910, struggling to support his family of five children, and is a model citizen. I ask you to take the boy's circumstances, his youth and good character into consideration."

The judge looked at me grimly. I was dressed in my Sunday blue suit and a tie and I hoped that my small stature and youthful appearance would sway him in my favor. "Is the boy's father here?" he asked, and my father stepped forward, clutching his hat, gazing in awe at the black-robed magistrate.

"I'm here, Judge," he said.

"Do you have anything to say about your son's actions before I pass sentence?" the judge asked.

"Mr. Judge, my boy is a good boy!" my father began. "He come from the worst of the civil war — nearly starve to death, escape with no shoes, guns and land mines everywhere, sent to refugee camp, lost his poor mother, murdered by Communist bastards. He come here to America, they put him in school with the dummies because he don't know the language. He have a hard time his first years, Mr. Judge. But this boy, he learn the English, he make fine grades, big success at school, work hard at the job, go to church at the altar every Sunday. It's my fault . . . I didn't get my childrens out in time to save my wife. My boy never know his father until late. I try, but I never was a father before. I know my boy, sir, and I know he don't mean to do bad things. He just forget what's right when he hit that car. But he's been through a lot and he's very, very sorry. Please forgive my son, Mr. Judge. I promise he will never do such a thing again. He's only learning about America now and this thing, if he go to jail, will ruin his life."

The judge was silent for several moments, thinking and studying me. I could see that my father's speech had moved him. As for me, I was shaken by Father's fervent defense of me. I had never known him to take my side before, and hearing him speak so emotionally about my problems when I had arrived surprised and touched me. Nevertheless, I still suspected that he was talking for the benefit of the court and in the end would show me the fury he really felt. I was so busy trying to figure him out that I hardly heard when the judge began to speak.

"Stand up, Nicholas," he said. "You know this is a very serious matter. What you did was not just a youthful indiscretion, it was a crime that could have led to serious injury, even death. Do you understand that?"

"Yes, sir."

"You must be made to accept your responsibility. When you commit a crime in this country, you have to pay for it. No one else, including your father, can do it for you."

I didn't like the direction he was taking and frowned under his gaze as he went on.

"I will put you on probation," he said, "on the condition that you personally work to make full restitution for the damage to both cars, which, I am told, comes to $234 for the complainant's car and $120 for your brother-in-law's car. Your father is working hard to support you and your sisters and doesn't deserve this extra burden. He must promise me in writing that you will earn the money yourself and he won't give you any." He turned to my father. "Do I have your word on this, Mr. Christy?"

"Oh yes, Mr. Judge, sir," my father quickly replied.

"Then it is understood, Nicholas, that you will be on probation until all these moneys are paid and that your driver's license will be revoked for the duration. You will report weekly to a probation officer and the damages will be paid to the court as you earn them. Do you understand?"

"Yes, Your Honor," I muttered, as anger at the severity of my sentence rose in me.

Although Father and Peter Bell seemed relieved, I felt that I had been given a harsher sentence than I deserved. All the juvenile delinquents, arsonists, and petty thieves who had come up to the bench ahead of me had gotten away with just probation, but I had to work to pay expenses besides. By the time I was off probation and got my license back, I suspected, I'd be too old to drive *or* to seduce girls.

Nevertheless, Peter Bell was feeling very pleased with himself. My father, no doubt contemplating what he would have to pay Bell in fees, was less jubilant.

"The good thing," Bell told us, "is that Nick is a minor, so his name won't appear in the papers, and once he completes his sentence the record will be expunged."

My father thanked him for what he had done, although I felt he deserved no congratulations. My depression increased when I headed for Father's Plymouth and braced myself on the retribution he had been saving up for so long. But in the car he only said to me, "I'm sorry I can't help you out with the money, but you heard what the judge said. I gave him my word I wouldn't."

"I'll earn it all," I said, spitting out each word. It seemed like a life sentence to me, but I was determined to do it.

At home, my oldest sisters, posed like the three Fates, were waiting to hear the sentence. When Father explained it to them, they all started shouting at once: it wasn't enough, it should have been worse . . . it was time to teach me a lesson . . . maybe if they locked me up, I'd grow into a decent man instead of a hoodlum who brings disgrace on his family.

"Let the boy alone — he's suffered enough!" roared my father, and I stared at him in astonishment. But nothing could stop my sisters once they became intoxicated by their own rhetoric, inspiring each other to greater and greater feats of condemnation. "It's impossible to plug them up!" Father explained to me in exasperation. "Come, Nikola. Let's get out of here."

He hurried out the door with me in his wake and my sisters screaming even louder at our backs. We got in his car and he began to drive while I stared at him in wonder. When I heard him defend me against my sisters, I understood for the first time that he was never going to unleash his anger on me.

The road began to climb through wooded, unsettled countryside, and I realized Father was driving up toward the airport. Worcester's tiny municipal airport, deserted at this hour, was on a high, sprawling hill to the northwest of the city, surrounded by woodlands and three reservoirs. My father parked in the empty lot next to the runway. From there one could look down in all directions and see no sign of a bustling industrial metropolis, only lakes and gently rolling hills. He got out of the car, and I did the same. In silence we walked to the edge of the rise and stood contemplating the world falling away at our feet. Then he turned to me and gestured, as if sharing a gift.

"I come up here a lot just to look at the view, the hills down below," he said. "It reminds me of the view from our house in the village. Of course, it's not so steep and so beautiful, but it's the closest thing I could find to Greece."

His words touched a sensitive spot in me. Something rose in my throat, and a question burst from my lips, oddly strangled by my warring emotions.

"Why did you leave us behind?" I blurted, and immediately regretted my words. I had planned to attack him for his betrayal at the perfect moment, in public, where others would hear my accusations and see his shame, but the words flew out of me unbidden.

There was a heavy silence. He stared into the distance. Then he pulled a handkerchief from his pocket and blew his nose. When he started to speak, his voice sounded odd.

"You know, at the beginning, when we first got married, your mother didn't want to go," he said in a thick voice. "She didn't want to leave her parents. Her mother said she'd kill herself. I let her stay — it's proper for a daughter to look after her parents. Then the babies started coming. I bought your mother the best fields, built the biggest house."

"But she wanted to go to America," I insisted, refusing to allow him this excuse. "Every day she told us stories — how wonderful America was, what a fine life we'd have there."

"The Depression came," he continued doggedly, not looking at me. "Hundreds of Greeks left Worcester. America became a frightening place. I lost my truck. . . . I could send you enough money to live well in the village, but not here. I always intended to bring you when things got better. And then the war started."

"But why didn't you bring us right after the war, during the peacetime, like other men did?" I demanded, trying to keep my voice from betraying me, the way it often did lately. "If you had brought us then, the way *Mana* begged you to, she'd be alive now. I remember the letter she wrote you, pleading, and I remember the letter you wrote back: stay in the house, protect the property; she had nothing to fear from the guerrillas, they were only fighting for their rights. All you cared about was your property, not us!"

Father took off his glasses, and I could see the tears shining on his cheeks. "I was stupid, a fool," he said, looking at the horizon. "I believed what I read in the papers. They never wrote about the murders, taking the children from their mothers' arms. They said the guerrillas were fighting for democracy. I believed it. I never thought Greeks could kill their own countrymen. When I lived there, it was always Greeks together, against the Turks, against the Slavs and the Italians . . . "

He stopped and spent several moments polishing his glasses very carefully, then he put them on and turned to look at me.

"I want you to know that I loved your mother very much," he said. "Not a day, not an hour goes by when I don't think of her and how I failed her. I failed all of you, and all I can say is that I never meant it to happen."

He turned to watch the last glow fading from the western sky. I waited. When he spoke again, he seemed to be talking to himself. "It's strange how, living day to day, you do some little thing that doesn't seem so bad at the time," he said. "You play a friendly game of cards and lose, so you put off sending the papers until next month. You like going back to the village and being the big shot. And then one morning you wake up and discover that what you did is a terrible thing and your wife is dead and your children hate you. Of course, if you had known it was going to end like this, you never would have done those things in the first place."

He made no reference to my own misdeeds, but I realized how much his words applied to me too. When I had borrowed Dino's car I had only wanted to impress my friends, but I had nearly ended up in jail with my future ruined. But Father wasn't lecturing me; he was speaking of his own transgressions.

"Every day I blame myself for your mother's death," he continued, "but that doesn't bring her back. A person who means well, if he doesn't think about the results of his actions, he can be as guilty as the most evil man."

I stared at him, unable to think of anything to say. I had always believed that nothing could justify his neglect of us, but now I wasn't sure that I would have acted differently in his place. The weapons I had been gathering for years to attack him and make him admit his crimes now seemed pointless. I no longer felt the desire to do battle with him.

He stood for a while longer, looking down on his adopted country, no doubt remembering the village he had left behind and the wife who was buried there. When he turned to look at me, his expression reminded me that everyone always remarked on how much I looked like my mother.

"Let's go home," he said, and we both turned back toward the car. But when we got to it, he went toward the passenger door.

"You drive," he said.

"Me!" I exclaimed. "Didn't you hear the judge say my license is revoked?"

"It's not until you get an official notice in the mail," he replied.

"It doesn't matter. I never want to drive another car for the rest of my life," I told him.

He smiled. "But you can't live without a car in this country," he said. "You have to drive again, and the best time to find out you can is now. So get in."

I couldn't believe he was actually encouraging me to drive the car he coddled like an infant.

"But you never let *anyone* drive your car," I reminded him.

"This time I take a different decision," he said. "I want you to drive it."

That night I drove the green Plymouth home with the care of Yves Montand piloting a truck full of nitroglycerine through the Latin American jungle in *The Wages of Fear*. My father sat beside me in silence. As I drove through the darkness, I turned the events of the afternoon over in my mind. I had discovered that my father had failed to get us out of Greece in time not because he didn't want us but because he was naive and fallible — weaknesses that I now knew I shared. Remembering my own disastrous blunder and how he had supported me through it all, I suddenly realized with the clarity of revelation that my father loved me, even though he had never said the words. Before my accident, when I showed all the signs of becoming a failure and a petty hood, he had tongue-lashed me out of his sense of duty. But once I did the deed and got into real trouble, his feelings for me took over and he fiercely defended me against all attackers, even my sisters, just as my mother used to defend me. I knew from her example that when you love someone, you stand by them no matter what, and that's what my father had done. Now I understood that he loved me after all, and the knowledge was like balm on the wound left by my mother's death.

The conversation we had at the airport faded into the far corners of my memory, and I didn't think of it again for the next three decades. I forgot it completely until one evening not long ago, when, sitting again in a theater, I was moved to tears by a scene in a film — something that had never happened to me before.

The movie was *The Trip to Bountiful,* starring Geraldine Page, and the people around me no doubt thought I was affected by the story of an elderly woman who runs away from her thoughtless family to return to her childhood home before she dies. But what triggered my tears was not the story, but the sight of the car her son was driving when he set out to find her. It looked exactly like the one that my father bought so many years ago to impress me — the car I scorned for its old-fashioned windshield, the cherished vehicle he never lent to anyone but that he made me drive home on the night that I first realized my father loved me.

Celebrating the arrival of some of the many relatives Christos sponsored in the 1950s

WIDENING
THE CIRCLE

Many shall run to and fro,
And knowledge shall be increased.
— Daniel 12:4

M Y FEELINGS for my father underwent a sea change beginning
on that evening of our drive to the airport. Never again would I feel for
him the fierce hatred I had nourished for so long, perhaps to protect
myself from the kind of pain that followed my mother's death.

While I couldn't completely absolve my father of blame for leaving us
behind, I now understood that his failings grew out of human weakness,
not intention, and that I might have similar weaknesses. Because I had
heard him admit his failings and had learned through my own experience how easy it was to make tragic mistakes, I began to understand
him. And because I had discovered his love for me beneath his gruff
patriarchal manner, I began to feel affection for him in return.

When I went back to school after my accident and the court hearing,
I braced myself for disgrace, but to my astonishment I found that no
one at school knew about my crime. The three students who had been
in the car with me didn't tell anyone, as if they somehow felt implicated.
As Peter Bell had promised, my name never appeared in the newspapers.
When the friends who had been with me asked what had happened, I
only shrugged and answered, "Not much. I'm going to pay for the damages."

The grapevine of the Greek community, however, was more efficient
than the Worcester press, and word quickly spread that Christy Gatzoyiannis' son had gotten in some kind of trouble with a car. Each Greek I
encountered at church, on the street, or in our parlor went through the
same ritual, first trying to elicit the details of my crime by asking prying
questions, then, when he saw he could learn nothing, delivering the req-
uisite edifying lecture. They all chose the same phrases: Was this why

my father brought me to America and my mother died to save me, so that I could crack up cars and cause my father and sisters more anguish? Hadn't they suffered enough? Wasn't I aware that driving a car was a privilege, a responsibility, that an automobile was a deadly weapon, blah, blah, blah. It was like Chinese water torture, and I began to wince every time I saw another Greek headed toward me. The end result was to make me heartily sick of the subject of driving and to quash any dreams of finding ecstasy in the back seat of a car.

Freed from such fantasies, I concentrated more on my schoolwork, and my grades improved dramatically. While my police record remained a secret from my teachers and ninth-grade classmates, my success increased during the last year of junior high. I was still in demand as the master of ceremonies for every assembly, and I was appointed editor of the school paper. At midyear I was elected the president of our class by a wide margin. The vice president was Judy Olander, the girl whose charms had drawn me into the newspaper club in the first place.

As spring approached, Miss Hurd insisted that I let her publish in the school newspaper the essay I had written about our experiences in Greece. I reluctantly agreed, dreading the reactions of the students, but they were mostly tactful and encouraging. In some ways it helped to have the painful secret of my mother's death become common knowledge. Revealing my family's tragedy — the past that made me different and foreign — didn't make my classmates think less of me. In fact, after reading the essay they seemed to respect me more. I was beginning to discover the power of the written word.

As ninth grade and junior high drew to a close in June 1956, I was required, as president of the class, to give a farewell speech. At the ceremonies it was announced that I had been chosen to receive the faculty award for progress and achievement, an inscribed Webster's dictionary. My speech and the award, unlike my escapade as a hit-and-run driver, were thoroughly reported by the Worcester papers, and I became a local celebrity, especially among the Greek community. The comments by Greeks who encountered me in church changed from lectures on reckless driving to paeans of praise. "Is this the Nicholas we read about in the papers?" the old men exclaimed to my father after Sunday services. "You can be proud, Christos! He makes us all proud." As I watched my father preen at the admiration of his contemporaries, I was startled to discover how much my success meant to him and how much I enjoyed his pride in me.

My accomplishments in school and our improved relationship induced Father to introduce me, in my sixteenth year, to a side of his life I had only vaguely suspected. I knew he sent money and letters to relatives back in Greece, because I had often heard my sisters complaining that his generosity was taking the food out of our own mouths, citing the Greek proverb "When your garden is thirsty, you don't water the neighbor's." But I had no idea of the extent of his philanthropies until he started showing me the letters.

Ever since I had arrived in America I had seen my father sitting every night after work at the kitchen table, reading and responding to letters from Greece, laboriously composing his replies, sometimes pausing to look up a word in the Greek dictionary, then signing each one with a flourish. He always had his breast pocket full of blue-and-red-striped air-mail envelopes with his return address neatly written in the upper left-hand corner, ready to be addressed and sent to some petitioner, perhaps with some American bills carefully folded inside.

Now, because he felt I was responsible and educated enough, he turned over to me the shoeboxes full of envelopes, and I learned that his fortune hadn't been entirely frittered away on card games. There were letters from distant relatives and acquaintances thanking him for secondhand clothing, money to buy medicine, seeds for their fields, or a gun for hunting game. Many of the letters were pitiful: "I have been diagnosed as having tuberculosis and must go to a government sanitarium in Kerkyra," wrote a woman from a neighboring village. "I have sent my two boys to the children's camp in Philipiada and Thessaloniki and will leave my fourteen-year-old daughter in the village to look after the house. But she can't feed herself on what we grow in our field, and I can't let her, a girl, work on road projects around the village. Mr. Christos, you have daughters of your own, please help keep mine alive until I get better or my oldest boy is able to start working and look after her."

From my reading I could see that Father had heeded all of these requests to some degree, even those from people he had never met. Many were sent by cronies from early days in Worcester who had returned to their native villages during the Depression and found the economy there even worse than in America. "Remember the times we had, playing pinochle in the coffeehouse?" one wrote. "What I wouldn't give now for a cup of coffee and a cigar! We're boiling wild chicory here for coffee. . . . There is no sugar, no meat, only wild dandelions and beans."

Each correspondent had been sent something, if only a few wrinkled American dollar bills or a box of cast-off clothing from my sisters. After spending an afternoon reading these letters, I looked at my father with astonishment and new admiration. "Why do you do it? How can you send money to these people?" I asked. "Don't you know each one of them will tell ten others about you, and there will never be an end to it?"

"In this life, we are all beholden, dependent on each other," he replied, starting to draw concentric circles on the plastic tablecloth with his fingernail. "First comes the smallest and most important circle, our family — then our relatives, then our friends, then those in our community, then our *patrioti* [countrymen from Epiros], then all other Greeks, then all Americans, and finally everyone else in the world. This is how our responsibilities are measured, with the greatest responsibility to the family and so on, outward."

I would hear this lecture and see him drawing those concentric circles many times again over the years, whenever one of his children complained; for example, when some young Greek sailor arrived at our door announcing he had jumped ship in New York and found his way to Worcester because my father's name was the only name he knew in America. Inevitably the sailor would be allowed to sleep on our couch while my father summoned Peter Bell to advise him on how to make his status legal and called friends to find the runaway a job and a place to live. My sisters and I were often resentful of these strangers who seemed to be constantly washing up on our doorstep, but when we complained to our father, we would get the same speech with the concentric circles of responsibility drawn on the tablecloth once again.

When the civilians who had been taken during the civil war began to filter back into the ravaged villages of Greece in 1954, the pleas filling my father's mailbox turned from requests for food, money, and clothing to petitions for sponsorship and boat passage to America. Someone had to be found to sponsor each immigrant, to testify on paper that he would not become a burden to the state but would be supported by his sponsor if he failed to support himself. Father often talked wealthy men like Angelos Cotsidas or Charley Davis into signing these papers, but all concerned knew it was not as risky a contract as it might seem, for it was unheard of for a Greek to go on welfare once he made it through the golden doors.

It became my responsibility to fill in all the official papers for the new immigrants and, when they arrived, to enroll their children in the public schools. Each time I could feel the terror of the children, plunged as I had been into a horrifyingly strange place where no one could understand a word they said. Of all the children I enrolled in American schools, the one most vivid in my memory is a thin, bright eight-year-old named Pavlos, the youngest son of Mitsis Stratis and his wife, Despoula. Despoula was my first cousin and had helped my mother care for us in the village; her husband, Mitsis, was a cousin of Kanta's husband, Angelo.

With my help, Father brought Mitsis to America in 1956, and eighteen months later we applied for his wife and four sons to join him. Soon we learned that the second son, Takis, had been refused permission because he was retarded. Despoula was heartbroken at having to leave him behind with relatives, who grudgingly agreed to feed him. But once we had the family settled in a flat on Piedmont Street, the success of her youngest boy, Pavlos, became a consolation. Pavlos rapidly learned English and excelled at both studies and sports. By the time he was in high school, he was one of the most popular students.

Then, one day in 1967, seventeen-year-old Pavlos noticed a lump on his neck while taking a shower. Within weeks he was dying of a fast-spreading cancer. I found doctors for the boy and tried to console Despoula, but as she watched her youngest slowly waste away and die, she nearly lost her mind with grief. She had the boy photographed in his coffin and hung enlargements of the scene, along with his photos as a high school basketball player, on the walls of their darkened apartment. She wore only black and refused to leave the house to go anywhere but the cemetery, where the family's savings were spent on an eternal light and a huge stone memorial to Pavlos. She refused to eat or cook or even to go to church on Sunday. Despoula's husband and sons were certain she would die of grief.

Finally I had an inspiration; I wrote to the junior senator from Massachusetts, who at that time was Edward Kennedy, and requested that he intervene on behalf of the bereaved mother to bring her retarded son from Greece. Kennedy contacted the embassy in Athens, and soon Takis arrived in Worcester and was reunited with his parents. Caring for the young man gave Despoula solace and purpose, and Takis found a place in the Worcester Greek community as a paid custodian at St. Spyridon's Church.

This was not the first time I turned to elected officials to help our relatives and friends with immigration problems. It began in 1956, when my brother-in-law Dino tried to bring over his brother Andreas. The doctor at the U.S. Embassy in Athens refused the young man a visa because as a child he had suffered from pleurisy, which was associated with tuberculosis and other lung problems.

Seeing how depressed Dino became at the rejection of his brother, I remembered something I had learned two years before in my eighth-grade civics class. My teacher had said that our elected representatives were there to serve us, the public, and he had made us memorize their names: Leverett Saltonstall, the Republican senior senator from Massachusetts; John F. Kennedy, the Democratic junior senator; and Maurice Donahue, the congressman from our district.

I decided to start at the top, with Saltonstall, and composed a letter in my father's name, beginning "Dear Senator, I have been living in Worcester since 1910 and have never written an elected official before on any matter, but an injustice has occurred to a member of my family that only you can correct . . ." I went on to describe how Dino, after working hard for five years in Worcester, had finally saved enough to bring over his younger brother, who had suffered great privations in Greece during the war, only to have all our hopes crushed by the doctor at the Athens embassy. I assured the senator that Andreas' childhood pleurisy had been a very mild case and he was now so completely recovered that he had withstood the rigors of three years' military service without a day's sick leave. My final brainstorm was to guarantee that Andreas would go to the tuberculosis sanitarium in nearby Spencer for an examination as soon as he arrived, and if any sign of the disease was found, my father would pay for his immediate return to Greece. We already had bought his return ticket in case there was any sign of tuberculosis, I concluded.

I had my father sign the letter with his usual flourish, and within a week we received in the mail a carbon copy of the letter Saltonstall sent to the embassy in Athens. A week after that Andreas was on the long-distance telephone wire, shouting that his visa had been granted after all.

My father was amazed at how I had persuaded this illustrious Yankee senator to intervene on our behalf when we had never met him. "I don't have influence with anyone higher than the cop on Mechanic Street who always gets free coffee and doughnuts," he said. "And even *he* refused to fix a speeding ticket for me!"

"It's called constituency relations," I explained. "We learned about it in junior high civics. These senators and congressmen are elected by the voters — that's you — and when they get a letter from a voter in their district who has some kind of legitimate complaint or problem, they try to fix it."

"This is like the *rousfeti* system in Greece," said my father, nodding with sudden understanding. "Every official has a special secretary just to handle all the relatives and friends who ask for *rousfetia*. Every postman, bank teller, college professor, or streetcar conductor gets his job because of who he knows, not his qualifications. But the officials who grant these favors keep careful track of them, because someday they will call in all those *rousfetia* and demand a favor in return. Who knows what this Saltonstall will ask of us? Perhaps he'll want one of your sisters as a bride for a relative, or I'll have to find a job for one of his layabout nephews in the kitchen at Putnam and Thurston!"

"It's not like that in America," I explained, trying to reassure him. "Here you don't have to know the man personally and you don't have to pay him back. Except maybe to vote for him, but there's no way he can tell whether you did. If you're a voter in his district, he'll work for you whether he knows you or not."

At first my father couldn't believe this — what Greek could, after growing up in a country where even the men selling gum and papers from the kiosks won their jobs through family connections? But after learning how easy it was, I used each one of our elected officials to help our family out with immigration snags, writing to all of them in turn, regardless of party affiliation, alternating my father's name and my brothers-in-law's names so that the officials wouldn't get tired of petitions from the same person. Democrat or Republican, they all came through for us every time. Seeing how my letters convinced politicians to cut through red tape was another proof to me of the power of the written word.

My success at influencing important men like senators with the eloquence of my letters made Father even more inclined to give the problems of the immigrants he sponsored into my care. "I told you, an education is more valuable than gold," he said with satisfaction. "Who would guess that a boy, a poor refugee from Epiros, could get big shots like Senator Saltonstall and Senator Kennedy to change the laws for us? Good thing you weren't asleep during that civics class! You're a smart boy, Nikola, and this is a great country."

As the arrivals from our village multiplied, my responsibilities mushroomed. The only American-educated member of our clan, I had to get their Social Security cards, find their children schools, coach them on driving laws, secure jobs and doctors for them when they were sick or lawyers when they were in trouble. I also did all their tax returns if they used the short form (which they usually did, since few of them made over $5000 a year). This was a lot of responsibility for a teenager, but it gave me self-confidence and satisfaction and made me happy that Father would entrust me with such serious matters.

Among the crowd of immigrants from our province who arrived in Worcester in the mid-1950s was a young man named Prokopi Economou, who caught Glykeria's eye. My feisty, strong-minded third sister, who had escaped from the guerrilla army on her own at fifteen, was now nearly twenty-one. Under the stern dietary supervision of Kanta, she had lost forty pounds and now was so proud of her tiny waist that she liked to stand with her arms akimbo, hands on her hips, to call attention to it.

During Glykeria's seven years of working at Table Talk, many young men were attracted by her vivacious manner and lively glance. She fancied first one and then another, although, being a well-bred Greek girl, she never spoke to them. One day, while walking on Green Street with a girlfriend from the factory, Glykeria stopped at the door of a palmist, who informed her that she would marry a man from far, far away. Glykeria scoffed at this idea, knowing that she had no intention of going to

Greece to find a husband as Kanta had done. There were too many attractive men in Worcester already.

Of all my sisters, Glykeria was always the one most concerned with the opinion of the Greek community and most careful of the fine points of proper behavior. She might defy the entire Communist army, but she would never defy village convention, even by crossing her legs in church or leaving a house by a different door from the one she had entered.

Whenever there was a gathering, Glykeria was always alert to the subtleties of social interaction. She would notice which sets of in-laws neglected to greet each other warmly and which young women glanced at which young men. If a new bride failed to offer water and spoon sweets quickly enough or forgot the proper protocol for serving them, Glykeria would not miss the gaffe. After each social event, she was the leader of long, impassioned conversations with my sisters and other Greek women, analyzing everyone's behavior, clucking over infractions of the rules, deciding who was feuding, who was flirting, and who was behaving in a manner suitable only to an *alitis,* a bum.

The telephone was Glykeria's lifeline. When she got a home of her own, she installed telephone cords of such length that she could vacuum, cook, iron, and attend to her other household duties all day without ever releasing the phone receiver, permanently wedged between her ear and her shoulder. When forced to leave the house for the market or church, Glykeria always took the phone off the hook to avoid missing a call. She couldn't bear the thought of a phone ringing unanswered, a tidbit of news unheard.

Glykeria became the social commentator and general switchboard for our extended family and then for the entire Greek community of Worcester. She spread each scrap of news, conversation, or opinion with the speed of the Associated Press. Americans might label her an interfering gossip, but she did (and still does) serve an essential function in the Greek immigrant community. Like the chorus employed by classical Greek tragedians, Glykeria represents the force of community opinion, the voice of Everyman. She provides the censure and the praise and, if necessary, the ostracism that staves off social anarchy and fills us all with fear of breaking the rules. This is the moral force that gives Greece one of the lowest rates of crime in Europe (except for crimes of passion, which are implicitly permitted by the community). "My clients' families usually greet them with, 'How could you bring such shame on the family?' not 'How have we failed you?'" a Greek lawyer once told me. "A response like that is the most effective deterrent there is."

Even at twenty, Glykeria was one of the leading arbiters of community standards — the Greek chorus of Worcester — so she found it doubly painful when her first romantic attachment conflicted with some important rules of Greek behavior and honor.

One day in May 1955, only months after Kanta's husband, Angelo, joined our household, Father's crony Jimmy Tzouras drove us all to the home of Leo and Chrysoula Tatsis to welcome a new arrival from our mountains. Prokopi Economou, twenty-seven, had been a young post office employee in northern Greece, and was originally from the village of Babouri, next to ours. He was brought to Worcester by his second cousin, Chrysoula, and her husband, Leo, the well-to-do grocery wholesaler who had first told us of Glykeria's escape.

Prokopi came to America in hopes of making more money than he could earn in the Greek post office, for he had many responsibilities, most notably two younger sisters who needed dowries, and two brothers, one of whom had obtained a place in college in Athens but needed help with the tuition. A dutiful son and brother, Prokopi was committed to helping his family. Chrysoula took him out the day he arrived to buy him a new suit, for, as she said, "You can't go to church on Sunday looking like this. You come from a good family."

When we got to the Tatsis home, Prokopi was taking a shower. Soon he came into the living room wearing a new white shirt and American slacks, his round face gleaming red with shyness and the heat of the shower. He was short and stocky, but handsome, with the wide Epirotic forehead and an ingenuous smile that made us feel we had known him forever. After we left that night, Glykeria remarked on his ruddy complexion and straightforward manner. "He seems innocent, not like most of the wise guys fresh over from Greece," she remarked. "He doesn't behave like a Romeo but talks to us naturally, like a member of the family."

Father agreed that Prokopi seemed a fine young man. Furthermore, he remembered Prokopi's father as a prominent member of the community, a former teacher and tax collector of impeccable reputation. But he warned Glykeria, with a significant look, that this was a young man with many responsibilities. He would not be free to decide his own future for many years. As Father talked, Glykeria realized that she had met Prokopi's father officially while obtaining her papers to leave Greece, and she remembered how his stern face and authoritative manner had frightened her.

Nevertheless, Prokopi was as beguiled by Glykeria's lively manner and round, pretty face as she was by him. Soon rumors were reaching us that Prokopi had an interest in Glykeria; but Father discouraged all attempts at matchmaking on the grounds that the young man, who was working in Brown's shoe factory in Worcester and making only $29 a week, was in no position to be thinking of romance, especially not with one of *his* daughters.

Prokopi shared a rented apartment on Piedmont Street with another "bachelor," Stavros Michopoulos, the carpenter who had helped me fix up our house before we moved in. Michopoulos' wife and children were still in Greece, refugees just out of Hungary. The two men lived frugally, but Prokopi occasionally put a nickel into the pay telephone in the hall to call Glykeria at our house. This did not escape Father, who did not approve of his daughters socializing with young men, even by phone.

Shortly after we met Prokopi for the first time, we celebrated the baptism of Olga's second baby, Christos, with a small party at our house. The baby's godfather, Stavros Michopoulos, brought his new housemate. Both Michopoulos and Jimmy Tzouras had taken a paternal interest in the young immigrant, and both encouraged his romantic attraction to Glykeria. Tzouras, who considered Glykeria almost like a daughter, often remarked, "This one's got guts, she's a real heroine!" as he puffed on his malodorous cigar. He was delighted that Prokopi found her an exceptional young woman too.

It was at the baptism party, noticing how Prokopi never took his eyes off her, that Glykeria decided, "He must be my *tychero,* from the gods." She was worried, however, that others might observe the way they were looking at each other. Father reminded her often enough that her prospects could be ruined if she were suspected of being romantically linked to a young man and then that man didn't marry her.

Every day it got harder for the couple to keep their feelings a secret. There was a Greek wedding at which Glykeria was a bridesmaid, petite and radiant in a full-skirted dress of pale blue. Prokopi danced every one of the European-style dances with her. Allowing a man to hold her in his arms on the dance floor when they weren't even engaged was certainly questionable behavior for a girl from a family as strict as ours, but the excitement of the wedding and the adoration in Prokopi's eyes made Glykeria behave rashly. If she had been observing some other girl acting like this, she would have been the first to criticize her for risking damage to her reputation.

During the weekend picnics at Davidian's farm, where the Greeks of Worcester liked to dance, sing, and roast lambs during the hottest days of summer, the romance deepened, although Prokopi and Glykeria both tried hard to be circumspect. Prokopi would dance the Greek line dances like a *palikari,* showing his agility and strength, and Glykeria, who sat modestly by her father's side, knew it was all for her. Her suitor might not have a heartbreakingly beautiful baritone like Prokopi Pantos, who made everyone cry when he sang the lament of the Souliote women, but on the way home, when Glykeria rode in the back seat of Tzouras' old car, wedged between Kanta and Angelo, her cavalier sat in front next to Tzouras and sang a lovely song about the almond tree: "I shake the branches of the flowering almond," he crooned, "so that all the blossoms fall upon your hair." He never looked back at her, but Glykeria's cheeks flushed even rosier than usual with joy that he was serenading her and fear that the others would discover she had lost her heart to a man who had two unmarried sisters and only $29 a week.

While Glykeria was trying without much success to be discreet, I was oblivious of her budding love affair, because I was so involved in immigration matters and my job as a soda jerk at the lunchroom. Despite my success with the customers, work was not going well. For one thing, my boss disliked my popularity with the patrons and felt I should manage a quicker turnover. "Don't talk to the customers so much," he kept warning me. "You talk to them and they hang around, tying up chairs. Feed 'em and get 'em out." He didn't realize that the stools were always full *because* I talked to the customers, creating special dishes for them and lavishing extravagant compliments on the women.

One day I arrived at the lunchroom to find a lanky, glum boy a year older than myself mopping the floor. This was Tony Deli, whose family had just arrived from Turkey. His father was an Albanian Greek who had opened a restaurant in Constantinople; Tony had lived in Turkey since he was four, but now the family had escaped, just ahead of the pogroms that the Turks unleashed on the Greeks of Constantinople in 1956. His family was saved thanks to the sponsorship of my boss, a distant relative.

Tony was a muscular, quiet fellow with a mournful expression who, despite a good education in Constantinople, could speak very little English, but was fluent in Albanian, Greek, and Turkish. He and I immediately became fast friends, drawn together by our heritage, our age, and our mutual resentment of our boss.

I would give my boss an argument every time he criticized me, but Tony couldn't talk back, since the man had saved his family. Instead, he got even every morning when he came in to open up, by making himself a huge banana split — his favorite American food — and gobbling it down. One day the boss arrived early and Tony barely managed to toss the sundae, dish and all, into the garbage before he was caught.

Meeting Tony began a new phase in my life, when I rediscovered my Greekness and started associating with Greek immigrant boys who were older and more worldly than I. In the fall of 1956, when I entered tenth grade at Worcester's Classical High School, the most prestigious high school in the city, I was still sought after by my friends from Chandler, but I was no longer part of the most popular cliques. For one thing, with my license revoked I couldn't drive, and most other boys could. Furthermore, money began to be essential to social success, and I couldn't afford to dress or entertain like the students who regularly gave parties in their luxurious homes or invited friends to the Worcester or

Tatnuck or (if they were Jewish) Mount Pleasant country clubs. I began to drift away from my American classmates, although I stayed involved in school activities, joining student political organizations and the staff of the high school paper, the *Argus*. But after school, after working at the lunchroom until about eight P.M. and on weekends, I found myself hanging out with Tony and other recent immigrants whom I met through him.

My new involvement with the Greek community through the immigration paperwork my father assigned me was one reason Greek friends began to appeal to me more. Even more intriguing was my discovery that these newly arrived young men — most of them several years older than I — might not know English but were well educated in sexual matters, while the boys at Classical High, despite a lot of petting in back seats and on rumpus room couches, rarely had any real sexual experience. The Greek arrivals also quickly acquired driver's licenses, and some even bought cars, while I was grounded, visiting my probation officer every week to hand over a few dollars of my fine.

One afternoon Tony and I were walking down Front Street to meet my father at the coffeehouse when Tony suggested we stop at Howard Clothes to see a friend of his. There in the back room we found Fotios (Fred) Malitas sewing, doing alterations. Tony was lanky and muscular, relaxed and good-natured, but Fred was small and excitable, wildly neurotic, and always spouting a nonstop litany of miseries that usually reduced me to tears of laughter. Catching a glimpse of himself in a mirror, he would stop and stare in horror. "Look at that!" he'd cry. "Do you call that a face? What kind of excuse is that for a body?" He would fling his open palm toward his face with the classic Greek cursing gesture, the *moujoura*. "God in His wisdom should have told my father, on the day he conceived me, to masturbate instead!"

The first time I met Fred, then nineteen, he did present a bizarre appearance, although he was actually a good-looking, dark, sharp-featured Greek with intense eyes. In an effort to seem American, he had cut his hair into a ersatz crew cut that projected from his scalp in uneven patches. Despite his training as a tailor in Greece, he wore a motley assortment of mismatched clothes.

Like Tony, Fred knew no English, but his rapid-fire Greek soon had us both laughing as he recounted his day's worth of humiliations and miseries in this confounded country.

"What a terrible waste!" he mourned. "I happen to be one of the best swordsmen ever to come out of Epiros, but in this damn country, because I can't woo the women with words, they scorn me. They have no idea what they're missing. Back in Yannina the women used to plead for my services. Here, you'd think I had the clap. It's been so long since

I've used my pistol it's going to shrivel up and fall off. Of course, it's not a great hulking cannon like Tony has. *He's* the reason all the women in Constantinople walk around bow-legged. But it's not size that counts, my children, it's skill, finesse, and I happen to be the maestro of the *mouni*. Believe me, when I left Yannina, all the women from fifteen to fifty took to wearing black."

As I was listening to Fred's tale of woe, another employee of Howard Clothes recognized me and began talking to me in English. Suddenly Fred's face lit up, and he threw his arms around me.

"Do you hear this boy?" he shouted to Tony. "He speaks the English language! It flows off his tongue like honey. He's the answer to our prayers! Our miserable celibacy is over! We'll be like the three musketeers — all for one and one for all. He'll do the talking, and once he's got them listening, we'll take over and do the screwing."

Despite Fred's wild enthusiasm, our mutual efforts did not immediately succeed at enticing American women into his clutches. Naturally we didn't even consider Greek girls as sexual partners, for none but a professional prostitute would sleep with a man before marriage. In the old country, young men like Tony and Fred were initiated by prostitutes paid for by their fathers or older friends as a rite of passage when they entered their early teens. In the United States this posed a problem, since few prostitutes could communicate with Greeks.

To tide himself over until his amatory abilities were discovered by American girls, Fred somehow made the acquaintance of a long-established prostitute on Park Avenue who, I gathered from his comments, was very inexpensive and very old. As the time between assignations lengthened, however, she would become younger and more attractive in Fred's memory.

"She's not really all that old," he would say after a month. "I mean, with the lights out, she's not bad looking at all. She never gives me any trouble. In fact, I think she's got a thing for me."

After talking to himself like this for a while, Fred would save up $5 from his pay, borrow someone's car, drive us both over to Park Avenue, and leave me waiting at the curb as he rushed into the dilapidated three-decker. Fifteen minutes later he would come out, striking himself on the forehead with the heel of his hand. "She's a toothless old crone!" he'd scream. "A face that would curdle milk! Why am I, the greatest swordsman in northern Greece, wasting it all on a grandmother?" But I knew that in a week or two he would start to remember her more fondly.

While Fred sewed away in the back room of Howard Clothes, plotting how, with my help, he would conquer one of the blond, long-legged American girls who reduced him to quivering lust, Tony and I were chafing under our boss's harsh rule at the lunch counter. My father, too, was having problems with his job, because Charley and John Kotsilimbas-Davis had gone on vacation and left the restaurant in the hands of Charley's son, Jimmy, who was fresh out of Harvard.

One night I heard Dino come home from the late shift at the restaurant and wake my father up. They sat together at the kitchen table while Dino recounted a conversation he had had that day with young Jimmy Davis.

"He was making small talk, joking around," Dino reported, "and then he said, 'I want to ask you something, Dino. If your father-in-law left us, would you go too? You know we'd hate to lose you.' So I just played dumb. 'Don't worry, Jimmy,' I said. 'My father-in-law likes it here. He has no plans to move.'

"Jimmy started squirming," Dino went on. "He said, 'Well, yeah, but what if he did leave? What would you do?'

"So then I put it to him," Dino continued. "'Are you telling me you want to let him go?' I saw him squirming some more. 'You know, Dino, the man's in his sixties now,' Jimmy said, looking embarrassed. 'And he's not so fast anymore. Our customers expect great service. We need people who turn out the orders fast, like you.'

"I told Jimmy, 'Everything I know, I learned from that man,' but he said, 'There's nothing he can teach you anymore, except how to slow down. So come on, what are you going to do if he goes?'"

I braced myself and then could nearly feel the explosion through the bedroom door as my father began to shout. "That smart-assed son of a bitch!" he roared. "I remember when he was shitting in his diapers and now he's trying to dump me! Wait till his father and uncle get back and I tell them how he's treating me. They'll skin him alive!"

"Don't be foolish," I could hear Dino say. "Jimmy wouldn't say those things on his own. He must have been told to do it by the old men. They probably told him to wait until they went on vacation."

There was a long silence as the truth of Dino's words sank in. I could imagine my father's expression as he realized that his old cronies had decided to get rid of him.

"But why?" he asked. "How could they do this to me? I've looked after their place like it was my own."

"That's part of the problem," Dino answered gently. "You know how the waitresses always try to sneak a couple of extra shrimps into the shrimp cocktail so they'll get better tips? And you always stop them. And I say, 'What do you care how many shrimp they take?' and you tell me we have a responsibility to the Davises as fellow Greeks. Well, all the waitresses have been complaining about you. They say you take too long to fill their orders and give them a hard time. And Charley and John are always complaining that you take an extra fifteen minutes for lunch."

There was a long silence. Then I heard my father speaking in a more despondent tone. "I should have known never to trust anyone from the Peloponnesus, no matter how sweetly they talk," he muttered. Then he turned on Dino. "So what did you tell the young Harvard-educated bastard?"

Dino stuttered a bit. "I didn't really answer him," he said. "After all, I've got two babies and four brothers and sisters all depending on my salary. I couldn't spit in his face, could I? I said to him, 'Look, my father-in-law has his own home and I have mine. We each make our own decisions.' So the kid slapped me on the back and said, 'Well, I just wanted to know. Now don't say anything to Christy.' But you see, I came right home and told you."

My father began to curse the Kotsilimbas-Davises, young and old. "May they live to walk through their restaurant and hear only the echo of their own footsteps!" he shouted. "May it collapse and fall into ruins around them!"

As he got louder, Glykeria woke up and came into the kitchen to see what was happening. When she learned the whole story, she cautioned Father not to do anything rash. "Listen, *Patera*," I heard her say, "John Davis has been your friend for thirty years. When he comes back from vacation, you go to him and appeal to his friendship. After all, he's the one who took you away from the Terminal Lunch."

"Appeal to his friendship?" my father roared. "I've got a mind to set fire to the whole restaurant, with the Davises in it! They're going to learn they can't treat Christy Gatzoyiannis like a used Kleenex! Never again will I set foot in that stinking kitchen."

"At least wait until you've got another job!" Glykeria pleaded. "You're sixty-three years old. It's not easy to get work at your age."

By this time I had entered the room to watch the drama unfold. My father had a look of grim determination on his face that I had never seen before. He seemed almost energized by anger.

"You don't understand," he said. "If we had the option of living forever, then it might make sense to compromise and avoid risks. But since none of us is going to outwit death, then the important thing is to live out our years with honor and dignity. I've never allowed anyone to humiliate me before, and I'm not going to start now."

The Davises had severely wounded my father's *philotimo* (literally, "love of honor"), and there is nothing a Greek holds more dear. The next day Father called in sick, but when it was quitting time, he drove up to the parking lot next to the restaurant and conspicuously waited to pick up Dino, sitting in the old Plymouth with the dignity of Hector turning to meet his death on the fields of Troy. Jimmy Davis looked out the window and said to Dino, "Your father-in-law is too sick to come to work but he feels well enough to come pick you up, I see."

"If you have any complaints for him, he's right out there," Dino replied nervously. "Go tell him yourself."

But Jimmy Davis stayed inside the restaurant, and my father continued to call in sick for a week. On payday Dino collected my father's check and said that Christos had decided to quit and wouldn't be coming back.

Nick with Glykeria and Prokopi at their wedding

BONDS OF
FATE

Fortune leaves always some door open.
— Cervantes, *Don Quixote*

WHEN MY FATHER weighed the security of a regular paycheck against the humiliation of an insult to his honor, he didn't hesitate but instantly left Putnam and Thurston with his self-respect intact. Despite Glykeria's admonitions, he chose to begin job hunting again, and eventually he managed to find another post: cooking for the lunch counter of Kresge's dime store on Main Street. Of course this was a big demotion from being chef of Worcester's finest restaurant, but the job at Kresge's paid more: $85, compared to the $75 a week he had been making. Furthermore, it was much easier. Every morning Father would go into Kresge's kitchen on the second floor and cook up a couple of pots of soup and some specials like meat loaf, turkey, and ham, and then send it all down to the lunch counter on a dumbwaiter. There was no need to deal with the waiters, who served it themselves. The hours were easier, too — eight A.M. to four P.M., so he no longer returned home exhausted late at night, the way Dino did.

My father's defiance of the Davises, his courage in walking out on his job at an age when few men would have the nerve to do so, impressed me more than anything else he had ever done. It showed me how much honor meant to him, and I began to understand why he was always lecturing us on the subject.

After he quit the job at Putnam and Thurston, I started to ask myself why I was still putting up with my boss's insults when my father, at sixty-three, refused to be insulted. I began stopping at every luncheonette on Pleasant Street on my way home from work, and finally I found an opening for a part-time short-order cook.

It was a spa called O'Connor's with a bar next door, both establishments owned by a pair of brothers named John and Charley O'Connor. John was usually in his office, but Charley liked to sit in the back of the spa and drink screwdrivers and talk to me. Both men left me alone to do my work and entertain the customers, many of whom had followed me to O'Connor's. Both men were generous, urging me to stop now and then to make myself a sandwich or a sundae, and they paid me ninety cents an hour — twenty cents more than I made at my previous job.

While my life was improving both professionally and socially, Glykeria's romance with Prokopi was hitting some snags — most significant, his parents' downright refusal to let him wed until his sisters were safely married. My father grumbled ominously every time the phone rang and it was Prokopi wanting to speak to his daughter. One night Prokopi called Glykeria with a note of triumph in his voice and said, "Tomorrow I want you to leave Table Talk on your lunch hour and meet me at Kresge's in front of the lunch counter. I have something to say to you and your father."

Glykeria was at the counter sitting on one of the stools fifteen minutes early, breathless with excitement, while Father glowered at her and arranged a huge sliced ham, a roast turkey, and several meat loaves behind the glass case, garnishing them to entice Kresge's shoppers to stop and eat. Finally Prokopi arrived and faced Father with resolution, ignoring the customers all around who were watching the drama with curiosity.

"Mr. Christy," Prokopi began nervously, "I want to marry your daughter. I know that a man with my responsibilities and with so little money should not think of such things, but I have talked to my granduncle, Nassio Economou, and discovered a way to earn enough so that I will soon be in a financial position to marry."

Father winced at the name of his old partner Nassio. Since selling their vegetable truck and then Terminal Lunch he had opened a successful restaurant on Route 9 in Westboro and was prospering. But Father didn't interrupt the young man.

"I'm going to live over Nassio's restaurant with him and his new wife and open the restaurant in the morning and clean up after eleven when I get in every night," Prokopi explained. "For this, Nassio will pay me ten dollars a week and give me room and board. And he found me a job working from three in the afternoon to eleven at night at Bay State Abrasives as setup man. That pays fifty dollars a week. So you see, with a total of" (he paused for maximum effect) "sixty dollars a week coming in, more than twice what I'm making now, I can soon get my sisters settled with husbands, and then I'll be able to ask for Glykeria with a clear conscience."

"It had *better* be soon," my father muttered, savagely dismembering a turkey with his huge knife. "There are plenty of other bees with more honey. She can't wait forever."

Glykeria was both thrilled and worried. "But that means you'll be living way out in Westboro," she cried. "When will I ever see you?"

"You don't need to see him," interjected Father. "First you get engaged, then you see each other."

Despite this warning and the pressure of working two jobs a day, Prokopi did manage to see Glykeria. He would ask Nassio's son, Stavros, to drive him over to Table Talk during Glykeria's lunch hour in Stavros' red Buick Skylark and the trio would drive around the block until it was time for Prokopi to start his job at Bay State Abrasives. Glykeria was always careful to sit in the back seat of the car while Stavros and Prokopi sat in the front, in case anyone saw them driving by. Since Stavros was her godfather's son, they were considered almost like brother and sister, so having him along lent a note of respectability to these outings. And whenever Jimmy Tzouras came over at night and offered to take Glykeria out for a ride, she would say, "Oh, let's drive over to Westboro to see Nassio at his restaurant. It's been so long since I've seen my godfather!" although it was the young man mopping the floor and working behind the bar whom she really wanted to see. Nevertheless, she and Prokopi managed to keep their romance a secret so well that when Prokopi's younger brother Chris came from Greece to join him at Nassio's restaurant, and Glykeria dropped by with Tzouras, Chris asked her, "When are you going to the village to find yourself a husband? All the men over there are waiting to marry you!" But Prokopi and Glykeria only smiled at each other knowingly over Chris's shoulder and said nothing.

Sometimes Prokopi would also visit Glykeria at 369 Chandler Street, although he always came secretly, after arranging it by phone. She slipped him into the parlor via the front door so he wouldn't be seen by people who might drop by, who always came into the kitchen through the side door. As the pair sat together in the parlor, it was always under the watchful eye of my father or older sisters, for Glykeria could hardly be left alone with Prokopi before their relationship was formalized.

One night, after Father was awakened from a sound sleep at eleven o'clock by the phone, only to discover it was Prokopi again, wanting to whisper sweet nothings to Glykeria, he ran out of patience. When Glykeria dreamily hung up the phone, Father roared, "It's time to forget about this guy! He's never going to get married! He's just stringing you along, and he's going to ruin your reputation. He's wasting your time — you're not getting any younger. Tell him it's over!"

This order kindled Glykeria's defiant nature. She shouted at Father that she didn't care how long she had to wait. "I don't want anyone else but Prokopi," she screamed. "I'm in love with him!"

Father turned pale. "What's this talk about love?" he cried in alarm. "You haven't been alone with him, have you? How could you possibly think you're in love with him?"

"I've danced with him, European style," Glykeria shouted back boldly. "I've talked to him for hours, right here in the house and on the phone. I've known him for a year. I love him!"

"Love? Rubbish! I don't want to hear such nonsense," said my father with a snort. "Tomorrow you tell him it's finished and that's that!"

"I'll do what I like," cried Glykeria, storming out of the room. "And I'll wait for Prokopi no matter how long it takes!" She slammed the door.

Despite her defiance of my father, Glykeria spent a sleepless night crying, because she knew he was right. The next day she called up Prokopi on the pay phone from work. "I want my photograph back," she said, calmly but with finality. "And I'll give you back your photograph. We're going to break up. I'm losing all my opportunities to get to know other men. You're never going to get married. We've been friends, that's all, and it's time to leave it at that."

"Wait!" cried Prokopi in horror. "What's the matter?" But Glykeria had already hung up.

That noon Prokopi arrived at Table Talk with Stavros Economou in the red Skylark. He begged Glykeria to go for a drive with them, at least one more time. "What's come over you? Who's been talking to you?" Prokopi pleaded. "Why are you acting like this? You know I'm working two jobs trying to save up enough money!"

"You'll never get your sisters married off, and that means I'll die an old maid!" Glykeria cried. "My father said so last night, and he was right. We've been seeing each other for over a year. I can't wait any longer. We're finished."

"Wait, I can't lose you," Prokopi begged, while Stavros tried to pretend he wasn't listening. "Listen, I promise you that next month, on my name day — July eighth — I'll give you a ring. We'll make the engagement, whether my parents like it or not. Tell your father and your sisters to prepare an engagement party for July eighth!"

Prokopi sent a letter to his parents, telling them of the pledge he had made. He and Glykeria went to Marcus Jewelers on Front Street, where he bought her a diamond ring for $95 and she bought him one for $150. The rest of the family began to prepare for the engagement party, while Glykeria waited tensely to learn what her future in-laws' reaction would be: would they send a telegram blessing the couple, or would they curse their son and the scheming woman who had made him forget his responsibilities to his sisters?

On a steaming hot July evening, all our family and friends gathered on the first floor of 369 Chandler to formalize Glykeria's engagement. She was wearing a red lace dress and had her curly brown hair pulled back behind her ears, and she felt beautiful. Prokopi had sent Chrysoula Tatsis to buy a gift for Glykeria, a dazzling gold cross on a chain with a diamond in the center, as a sign of his pledge in addition to the rings, which were formally exchanged while everyone applauded. Then Prokopi pinned a corsage of white roses and carnations on Glykeria. She would wear it to church the next day and walk next to Prokopi to show the congregation that they were engaged.

There was a knock at the front door and we opened it to find a Western Union boy with a telegram. Glykeria tore it open and a flush of joy spread up her neck to her cheeks. She handed the telegram to my father, who read: "Congratulations on your betrothal. We wish you a joyful exchange of wedding crowns. Fotios and Calliope Economou."

Now that she had her in-laws' blessings, Glykeria's joy was complete. Soon everyone was dancing around the heavy-laden dining room table, doing a spirited *tsamiko*. My father put an arm around Glykeria and Prokopi and said, "Blessings, my children. Now you can go out together and fall in love."

The next day, Sunday, Prokopi sat next to Glykeria in our church pew. She was wearing a tiny-waisted yellow-and-white-striped dress, which set off her engagement corsage. After the service, when the young couple went forward in their turn to receive the piece of bread that was the "aftergift," the entire congregation marveled at their joyful appearance. Many commented what a handsome couple they made, both with fair, ruddy complexions and faces round as the moon.

Shortly after the engagement party Prokopi learned, to his relief, that Polyxene, the older of his two sisters back in Greece, had found a groom. His parents wrote that Glykeria must have brought the family good luck. Glykeria was so delighted that she wouldn't be flouting convention and leaving Prokopi's sister an old maid that she rewrapped every gift she received at her shower and sent it all to her future sister-in-law.

Glykeria and Prokopi scheduled their wedding for November 11 — Veterans Day, when they both had a day off work. Father decreed that it was going to be the best wedding Worcester had ever seen. The reception would be held at Putnam and Thurston, no expense spared.

"But why go there after they treated you so badly?" I asked. "Why give your business to Charley and John Davis?"

"Why not?" he countered. "It's the best restaurant in town, isn't it? Glykeria is the daughter who was lost to me and was returned. She was dead and now she's alive. I'm going to give her the best wedding I can."

"But there are other restaurants," I persisted.

"But Puts is where my son-in-law works, and Charley Davis has written his name as sponsor for lots of people I brought over," he explained. "Putnam and Thurston is where I earned our bread for seven years. Why *not* give them our business? They may have made some mistakes — we all make mistakes — but there's no point in holding a grudge. We came out all right, didn't we? In fact, we came out better off, once I left them!"

As I looked at his face, devoid of guile or malice, I couldn't help thinking how different he was from my grandfather, Kitso Haidis, who was clever and cunning. My father showed all his emotions as soon as he felt them. If someone did him an injustice, he exploded in anger and made dramatic threats, but he couldn't sustain his anger or hide it, and soon forgot his grudges. When I saw how quickly he had forgiven the Davises, I realized that he was a hopeless innocent.

Although it seemed to me that Father had forgiven his former employers with unseemly haste, I soon realized that having the wedding reception at their restaurant was in fact his method of revenge as well as of bridge-building. To him, outward gestures were all-important. He ordered an orchestra, the most expensive roast beef dinner for three hundred guests, elaborate centerpieces, and a cake four tiers high. I began to understand that, while generously giving business to his old friends, he was also showing them that Christos Gatzoyiannis could get along just fine without their job. They might have discarded him, but on November 11 his former colleagues would be working in the kitchen at his daughter's wedding while he would be leading the dances, as befitted the man who paid for the party. This was another aspect of *philotimo*. Although it translates as "love of honor," the meaning is more complex. To a Greek, protecting one's honor takes top priority, even above staying alive, but it is also important, after you fight for your honor and win, to make sure that the rest of the world knows it.

Father insisted that Glykeria buy the best wedding dress available in Worcester. She drafted Chrysoula Tatsis to go shopping with her and advise her on this important decision. When they returned from their shopping trip, Glykeria showed us a gown the likes of which none of us had ever seen. It had a full hoop skirt to show off her tiny waist and was covered with miles and miles of lace in many tiers. And all that lace was embroidered with millions of tiny rhinestones (Glykeria called them diamonds), so that the whole gown sparkled whenever she moved. Friends and relatives came from miles away just to stare at the wedding dress hanging in glory from a doorway in the parlor. No one had ever dreamed such a lavish garment could be made. "So many diamonds!" they murmured. "So much lace!"

Whereas Olga's gown for her wedding five years earlier had cost only $55, this wedding dress cost an unheard-of $750 — nearly three months' salary for my father. Of course, he had Glykeria's savings to help pay the wedding expenses. "What the hell!" he kept telling everyone. "This is my miracle daughter, returned to me after she was lost. She only gets married once!"

The *koumbaros,* who would exchange the crowns, was a relative named Gregory Bokas, from Philadelphia. Bokas had once come to our home saying he had a perfect husband for Glykeria, a priest from his own parish. Father, knowing that his daughter was secretly smitten with Prokopi, had thanked the man for his efforts and promised that whenever a husband was selected for Glykeria, even if it wasn't the priest, he would allow Bokas to be the *koumbaros.*

In preparation for the nuptials, Bokas and his wife and three children arrived at our house from Philadelphia a week before the ceremony, and Glykeria exhausted herself entertaining them and getting everything ready. "I'll never live until the wedding day," she moaned. "I'm sure I'll faint walking down the aisle."

Glykeria and Prokopi's wedding festivities were the biggest party our clan had ever seen. The dancing, singing, and eating began the night before, as relatives descended on our house with huge trays of food. The wedding songs were sung, the gold coins were tossed on the wedding mattress, and the "embroidered" wedding breads were admired. The next day, Sunday, my father glowed with pride as he marched Glykeria down the aisle of St. Spyridon's Church. The three hundred invited guests greeted the sight of her fabled gown with a gasp of admiration. My sisters were bridesmaids in ruby-red dresses, and I was an usher, in a black tuxedo.

After Gregory Bokas exchanged the wedding crowns, Prokopi placed on Glykeria's finger an ornate gold ring his mother had sent from Greece — further proof of his parents' blessing. Then the entire throng headed for Putnam and Thurston. In the red-velvet–draped banquet hall we feasted and sang and danced all night, and no one was more nimble at leading the *tsamiko* than my father, balancing a glass of wine on his head and glorying in the success of his children in America.

After the wedding, Glykeria's famous gown eventually took on a career of its own. She wrapped it carefully in tissue, shedding a few tears, and sent it to her sister-in-law Polyxene to wear for her wedding in the village. After Polyxene, it was worn by every bride in Prokopi's family. Ten years later, Prokopi's mother gave it to the village church to lend to impoverished brides of the diocese who would not be able to afford a

wedding dress. Glykeria always mourned the loss of her beautiful dia-
mond-encrusted gown, but by then her silhouette had expanded to the
point where she realized that even if she still had it, she would never be
able to fit into it again.

If Father gloried in the panoply of Glykeria's wedding to Prokopi, his
pride reached even greater heights three months later, when the front
page of the *Evening Gazette* of February 22, 1957, featured a photograph of me above the news that I had won an award from the Freedom
Foundation at Valley Forge. Without telling me, my junior high English
teacher, Miss Hurd, had submitted my essay about our escape from
Greece. With the ardent patriotism fashionable in the mid-fifties, the
Worcester paper quoted my essay at length, along with remarks from
my employer, Charley O'Connor, that as a soda jerk I was "regular and
brainy, with a strong will." Nicholas Gage, the newspaper announced,
was a sophomore at Classical High School and the son of Christy
Ngagoyeanes, "a five-and-dime store chef."

The medal and the newspaper article created such a sensation among
the Greek community of Worcester that my father was beside himself
with pride. The ultimate satisfaction was when his former employer
Charley Davis came up to us after church on Sunday to congratulate
me.

"This is a very smart boy you've got here, Christy," Charley said,
putting an arm around my shoulder. "He's got a great future ahead of
him! You should be a doctor, son. That's what I told every one of my
children. Go to medical school. You think they listened to me? But
you've got too good a brain to waste. What do you say, Nick? Do you
think you might go into medicine?"

Until that moment, I hadn't really given any thought to my future,
but at Charley Davis' question, everything suddenly fell into place, and
I surprised myself by answering, "No, I want to go into journalism."

I had become more and more impressed by the power of the written
word. When I saw all the excitement over my essay, the seed of an
ambition sprouted in me: one day I wanted to write my mother's story.
That would be a way to preserve the memory of how she gave her life
for us. Perhaps through journalistic investigation, I might even discover
the identities of those who killed her, so that she could be revenged.
When I spoke the word "journalism" to Charley Davis, it suddenly
seemed as if I had known my future all along. I enjoyed being editor of
both the junior high and high school papers, but the Freedom Foundation award clinched my decision.

"Good luck to you, son," Charley said, clapping me on the back.
"Whatever field you go into, I know you'll make a success of it." He

turned to my father. "You've done a good job with this boy, Christos. I envy you."

When my father turned to look at me, there was new respect on his face. "Journalism," he said. "That means working for a newspaper, right? Do you have to go to college to learn to do that?"

"I'm afraid so," I answered.

"If that's what you want, you'll have it," he exclaimed with sudden resolution. "I always say, education is worth more than gold. I was thinking about retiring next year, when I hit sixty-five, but I'm going to keep on at Kresge's until you're through college so I can pay for your tuition. Charley was right, you've got too good a brain to waste. Doctor, newspaperman, whatever you want to do, I'm going to see you get the college you need."

I was touched that my father, who had no real idea what I was talking about, was willing to put his retirement on hold to give me psychological and financial support. His encouragement made me feel closer to him than before.

As I completed my first year of high school, my father's fortunes prospered until he began to feel favored by the gods. In May of 1957 Olga gave birth to a third son, whom she named Thomas, and Kanta also became pregnant, despite the fears that her husband had been rendered sterile from his bout with mumps. Having secured excellent husbands for his three oldest daughters and installed all three couples in our three-decker, one on each floor, my father was becoming the patriarch of a dynasty.

In back of our house there was a stretch of cement, a scraggly piece of grass, and two large garages with room for a total of ten cars. This was much more than we needed, and we had rented garage space to some other Greek families in the neighborhood. But that summer Dino suggested that we tear down one of the garages and make a garden in its place. All the rest of the family agreed.

I couldn't have cared less about a garden, although I noticed that every Greek family arriving in Worcester, even if they had only a square yard of dirt in back of their tenement home, would soon have it planted with tomatoes and green beans and edged with pots of basil, chamomile, and geraniums, usually planted in empty olive-oil tins. There seemed to be an atavistic need to till the soil among Greek immigrants, and my family was no different. "There's nothing like the taste of your own tomatoes," my sisters agreed, and they were soon planning all the dishes they would make out of the flat fava beans we would grow — the kind you can't easily find in American supermarkets.

One day in August I arrived home from O'Connor's to find my father climbing a ladder to the roof of the condemned garage while Dino and Angelo held it steady. "What are you doing up there?" I called to him. "You're going to break your neck!"

"You think I'm a useless old man, don't you?" he called back. "But if I don't teach these young pups how to take down the garage, they'll make a holy mess of it."

I went inside to find Fotini, now nineteen, all in a tizzy because some Greeks from New Jersey had phoned earlier in the day to say they were in Worcester and would like to drop by and introduce a fine young man who might make an ideal husband for her. She was fussing with her hair in front of the mirror. "I wonder if he's good-looking," she muttered, teasing her bangs. "Do you think it would make me look better if I let the bangs hang over one eye, sort of like Veronica Lake?"

"I think it would make you look better if you let the bangs hang over your whole face," I answered helpfully. Fotini was about to throw her brush at me when we both froze at the sound of wood splintering and then Kanta's and Olga's screams.

Both of my sisters had been watching Father work from the vantage point of their back porches, Olga on the third floor, nursing her new baby, and Kanta on the second. As soon as I heard them screaming, I knew instinctively what had happened, and I rushed for the back door. Dino, Angelo, and Prokopi were all standing as if turned to stone. My father was nowhere to be seen; there was now only a ragged hole on the roof where he had been working.

"He fell right through," cried Prokopi.

"Quick!" yelled Olga from above. "Go to him! See if he's still alive!"

All three of my brothers-in-law hurtled toward the garage door, but I stood rooted in place as the scene before me seemed to go out of focus. I felt dizzy, and about to fall, the way my father had just fallen twenty feet onto a cement floor.

Back in the refugee camp, when we had learned that my mother was dead, my sisters had cried out in grief and I had run away into the ravine, trying to block out their screams with my hands over my ears. Now I had an overwhelming urge to run again, to run so far that I wouldn't have to see what had happened to my father. In that frozen moment of suspense I felt the same panic of loss that I had felt that earlier time, watching my mother walk away. As I held my breath, terrified of what my brothers-in-law would find, I realized that I had let down my guard and at last had come to love my father.

Only five years before I had been fantasizing about him dying of a heart attack and leaving me free of his tyranny, but since then I had discovered facets of his character that had won me over. He had defended me against the world when I was at fault and confessed his guilt in my mother's death. I had learned how many people he aided over the years and had seen him quit his job rather than compromise his honor. But I knew he didn't hold grudges and was fiercely loyal. He delighted in my successes even when he couldn't understand them. Little by little I had come to understand and care about him, and now I couldn't bear the prospect of losing him.

All those thoughts crowded through my mind in the few seconds before a great bellow of pain told me that my father was still alive. His screams released me from the panic that had turned my legs to stone and I ran into the garage to find Dino, Angelo, and Prokopi all kneeling beside him.

Father was lying on his back, twisting his head from side to side, his jaw clenched to suppress his groans. At least his neck wasn't broken, I thought.

"We've got to get him to the hospital," cried Dino, wringing his hands.

"Maybe moving him will make it worse," worried Angelo.

"He's probably bleeding internally," Prokopi interrupted. "We can't waste time. We've got to lift him."

My father weighed over two hundred pounds in those years, which was one reason the rotten roof hadn't supported him. Even with four of us, each taking an arm or leg, it was a struggle to carry him to the car, especially since he was bellowing with pain at each step. Finally we got him into the back seat. I was alarmed at the color of his face, gray as a corpse, but he was still conscious. Dino got behind the wheel and ordered me in next to him. "You've got to do the talking at the hospital," he said.

As we drove Father cried out at each bump in the road, and I kept looking back at him in fear, wondering where he was wounded and how badly. Each time he saw my face, he would grimace, trying to smile reassuringly, then dissolving into another cry of pain. At last we reached the emergency entrance of City Hospital. The orderlies rushed out with a gurney and wheeled him into a treatment room. I tried to explain to the intern what had happened. When the nurse cut away his clothing, I fell silent in horror, seeing that Father's leg, his side, and his back were all as purple as ink.

Seconds after we drove away toward the hospital, Olga, wailing and clutching her baby, rushed down to the first floor where Fotini was watching the whole scene from the porch, like me too frightened to go near Father. Both sisters jumped when the front doorbell rang. As Olga went to answer it, Fotini remembered the young man who was coming to call.

Fotini hung back in the kitchen as Olga opened the door, saw several

Greeks standing there, and began to scream hysterically: "My father just fell off the roof! He may be dead! They've taken him to the hospital! I have to go to him! You can't come in. You'll have to leave!"

Unnerved by her cries, the visitors quickly backed off, apologizing for the interruption and leaving profuse wishes for our father's well-being. As they hurried away, Fotini ran to the window, driven by curiosity, and saw with a sinking heart that the young man was handsome. But with typical Greek fatalism, she shrugged and said to herself, "I guess God just didn't intend it to happen."

In the hospital, my father had to endure a barrage of painful tests and x-rays, but finally they wheeled him into a room and the doctors came in to talk to us, addressing their remarks to me since I was the one who understood English best.

"There are some fractures that will take time to heal," one doctor said. "What concerns us most is that he has developed a blood clot. If it moves to his heart or lungs or brain, the consequences could be very serious. Your father has to stay absolutely flat on his back and be treated with blood thinners until the clot dissolves. If he's very careful for the next several months, the danger will pass."

The doctor asked if my father worked and what he did. When I told him, he said, "There's no way he can go back to a job where he has to stand on his feet all day. A single slip or fall at his age and weight, and he could break his hip. These things don't mend very well in older people. He's old enough to retire, and I urge you to persuade him to do it."

After the doctors left, I went over to my father, lying in the bed, as pale as his hospital gown. For the first time I realized he was an old man. He had always seemed tough, vital, and ageless to me, but now he looked old, weak, and vulnerable. I felt almost betrayed to discover his mortality.

"You heard what the doctor said," I told him. "It's all going to be okay if you take it easy. You were really lucky. I told you that was a crazy stunt — up on a roof at your age!"

"It was all *your* fault," he said, managing a weak smile. "When you said that, you gave me the evil eye. Good thing I'm a tough old donkey or I'd be dead by now."

Awkwardly I reached out and patted his hand. "The main thing is that you're not," I replied. "You just have to take it easy and watch out."

"But he said I can't go back to work," Father fretted. "If I can't go to work, how are we going to pay for you to go to college?"

"You nearly break your neck and you're worrying about me going to college!" I exclaimed. "You concentrate on staying still so that blood clot will go away."

I could see he wasn't as badly hurt as I feared, because he soon started complaining and wanting to get up. "That young doctor's full of it," he muttered, shifting painfully. "I want to go home. Dr. Seidenberg wouldn't give me this kind of hassle. I want you to call up Dr. Seidenberg and get him over here right now."

Seeing him complaining alleviated the fear that had gripped me since his fall, because it proved the fight wasn't knocked out of him. But later that night, when I went home and surveyed the damage, I realized that the rotten roof had taken my future plans down with it, for there was no way I could afford to go to college now.

Fred Malitas looking cool   Tony Deli and Nick in 1956, dressed to thrill

LOST AND
FOUND

Without hope we live in desire.

— Dante, *The Divine Comedy*

M Y FATHER'S CONVALESCENCE was even slower than the doctors predicted. He chafed at being bedridden and made me transfer him by ambulance to Doctors' Hospital so he could be under Dr. Seidenberg's care, but the verdict was still the same: he must stay in bed until the blood clot dissolved. He considered the words of a doctor to be pronouncements from Mount Sinai and accepted the sentence that he could never work full-time again.

While his life was in danger, I could think of nothing but the risk that I might lose him, but by the time he was allowed out of bed I was distracted by other concerns. With the final year of high school approaching, I became obsessed by two problems that crashed down on me like the rock of Sisyphus every morning when I awoke: how to find enough money to go to college and how to lose my virginity.

I knew I couldn't get college money from anyone in our family, because our financial situation was at an all-time low. Only Dino was making a good salary; Father had talked him into taking over the well-paying job at Kresge's lunch counter, and he stayed on as a chef at Putnam and Thurston too, working from five to nine after he finished his eight-to-four shift at Kresge's.

Dino's dream of wealth was proving much more elusive than he had anticipated. Olga had given birth to three sons in five years, and the arrival of Dino's siblings one by one from overseas had further strained the family budget and crowded Olga and Dino's small apartment to bursting. All these responsibilities and worries frazzled Dino's already volatile temper, and he often took out his frustrations on Olga, who meekly tried to keep the overcrowded household in harmony. Since Dino's two jobs kept him away fourteen hours a day, most of the domestic problems fell on her shoulders, despite her frequent pregnancies, so she couldn't help nurse my father — a chore that fell to Glykeria, who became pregnant shortly after marrying Prokopi and left her job at Table Talk. Kanta, too, had left Table Talk at the beginning of her pregnancy, which was so difficult she had to be hospitalized for the last three months.

After losing the salaries of Father, Kanta, and Glykeria, we could barely afford to eat. I knew my only hope of going to college was to raise the money myself, so I increased my after-school working hours at O'Connor's Spa from two-thirty to eight-thirty and worked all day Saturdays. I also redoubled my efforts to get good grades in high school, hoping to win a scholarship. I excelled in most classes during the first semester of my junior year, and Miss Shaunessy, the formidable head of the English Department at Classical, chose me to be the editor of the school paper, the *Argus*.

Outside of school and my working hours at O'Connor's, I spent most of my free time with my fellow Greek immigrants Tony Deli and Fred Malitas. Fred was constantly inventing new schemes to meet and seduce one of the long-limbed, fair-haired American beauties who obsessed him — plots that usually cast me in the role of his John Alden. To improve his chances of scoring, Fred had poured all his savings from his work at Howard Clothes into the down payment on a ramshackle old 1953 Ford, but so far his romantic conquests had not expanded beyond the venerable prostitute on Park Avenue.

I had acquired a following of female classmates from Classical and Chandler who regularly dropped by O'Connor's Spa after school to sit at the counter and talk to me. I practiced my line — my "nightingale's song," as Fred called it — dishing out extravagant compliments to every woman who walked in. "You are the star for whom all evening waits," I would announce to some startled middle-aged woman as I placed a menu in front of her. "The lights dim by comparison when you walk in the door." I thought these mature customers would realize that I was just kidding, but some took my flattery seriously. One older woman in particular began coming around to pour out her marital problems to me, until I wondered how to discourage her.

It was among the crowd of girls who regularly dropped by O'Connor's after school that Fred Malitas first discovered Debby, a young woman whose beauty distracted every man whose field of vision she crossed. She was a tribute to her Scandinavian ancestors: statuesque, fair, graceful, with a mane of titian hair and an innocently flirtatious manner. When Fred saw her, he staggered. Debby was the epitome of what he longed for — the ultimate American girl. As soon as she left the spa, he began hissing to me in Greek: "That's the one — the one in the tight pants! I'm in love! You have to fix me up with her. Get me a date with her and I'll never ask for anything else."

"Listen, Fred," I cautioned. "Just because American girls flirt and smile and lean close when they talk, that doesn't mean they put out. These girls may act like tarts, but almost all of them are virgins."

"I promise not to come on too fast, I'll be a perfect gentleman," Fred stuttered, gesturing wildly. "All I want is to have a date with her, just to touch her skin, look in her eyes, listen to her voice. Then I can die happy."

"But you *can't* talk to her," I reminded him. "You can barely say hello. You don't know English!"

"*You'll* do the talking," he insisted. "Just get us together. I'll take care of the rest."

Fred was so persistent that in the end I agreed to talk to Debby about him. We'd double-date, and I would convince Debby that Fred was a college exchange student from Greece and keep the conversational ball rolling.

Debby was a friendly, extroverted girl who had been a good friend for years. Eventually she gave in to my pleas that she would go out with Fred as a personal favor to me.

"But I don't even know him," she protested at first.

"Yes you do — you met him right here in O'Connor's," I insisted. "A dark, good-looking guy. Don't you remember? You gave him a big smile."

"I did?" she asked, puzzled. "Funny, I don't remember him at all. You said he's a college student?"

"Yes, from Athens. A really bright guy. He's starting Penn State in the fall. Probably pre-med. Come on, it'll be fun! What have you got to worry about? I'll be right there in the back seat."

"Well, I guess it's all right," she said finally. "If you say he's a nice guy. But he has to come in and meet my parents first."

On the appointed evening, as Fred drove toward Debby's house in Tatnuck Square, I coached him. "Don't say a word," I advised. "Just let me do all the talking and you smile and nod and keep quiet. I told them you're going to Penn State in the fall, you're going to be a doctor, you got great grades, you're a personal friend from Athens."

Fred combed his hair back nervously. I had convinced him to buy a gray sports coat for this evening and to wear it with matching gray slacks. He wanted to unbutton his shirt, European style, and spread the collar over the coat, but I made him button it and wear a tie, and he kept running his fingers under the uncomfortable collar.

Debby's parents greeted us warmly. As soon as we got in the door I started talking nonstop, deflecting any questions directed at Fred. He just stared besottedly at Debby, who was wearing a blue dress that emphasized all her curves.

"And when did you arrive on our shores, Fred?" asked Debby's mother.

"Oh, he's been here two months now," I said quickly. "He's starting Penn State in September on scholarship."

"That's nice," she said. "Do you come from a big family, Fred?"

"Four brothers and a sister!" I interjected. "Fred's kind of a role model for all of them."

As I talked, Debby smiled at Fred and he grinned back, sitting in uncharacteristic silence, shooting glances at the expensive beige decor, the huge TV screen, the piano in the corner. Finally, exhausted from keeping the conversational ball in the air, I looked at my watch and said, "Well, we'd better go if we're going to make the movie. I still have to pick up my date."

"It's been such a pleasure meeting you, Fred," said Debby's mother as we headed out the door. "Good luck in college. What school did you say you were going to?"

Emboldened by his success, Fred, who had caught the word "school," decided to venture an answer on his own. "State Pen," he replied, bowing as he took her hand in farewell.

"He's just kidding," I blurted into the puzzled silence. "He meant Penn State, of course. Fred's such a card!"

After this initial misstep, the evening deteriorated further. When the movie ended, Fred drove us all out past the airport. Debby leaned over and whispered something in his ear. Suddenly Fred pulled sharply into a dirt path and brought the car to a squealing stop. "Get out of the car!" he hissed at me in Greek.

"What do you mean?" I exclaimed.

"Don't ask any questions, just take your girl and go for a walk. Get out of the car! Now!" he snarled, even more emphatically.

We had gone hardly twenty yards when I heard Debby's screams, Fred's curses, and the sound of a struggle. We hurried back to the car to find Fred and Debby sitting as far apart as they could get, amid an icy silence. Later, when Fred stopped at Debby's house, I could tell by the way she slammed the car door that there wasn't going to be a second date.

After we took my girl home, I turned on Fred. "All right, what happened?"

Fred slapped his forehead with the heel of his hand. "I'll never figure out American women," he moaned. He then explained that he had thrown us out of the car because he thought when Debby whispered in his ear that she was propositioning him. After further inquisition I learned the titillating phrase Debby had uttered that had convinced Fred he had finally hit a home run. "What I'd really like now," she had murmured, "is something to eat."

I realized it would be a long time before I succeeded in educating Fred about the sexual mores of American girls of the late 1950s. Nevertheless, his optimism was unquenchable, even after this debacle. One day he arrived at O'Connor's stammering in excitement and told me that we were going to take dancing lessons.

"When you dance with a girl, you don't need to talk," he explained. "You seduce her with the language of the body, not the tongue. Just imagine the scene: dim lights, liquor, sexy rhythms — the tango, the rumba, the mambo! She'll be ready to do it right on the dance floor."

"But can you *do* the tango, the mambo, the rumba?" I asked. "Can you even do the two-step?"

"Not yet, but I've found a professor of dance," Fred said with a chortle. "He's promised to give us a special price if all three of us sign up together: you, me, and Tony. Pretty soon we'll need a stick to beat off the girls."

Fred had somehow met the surviving member of a former vaudeville dance team, a tall, dignified, white-haired man who resembled Clifton Webb and was now the owner and entire faculty of a dance studio on Mechanic Street. For $2 a lesson, he promised to make us dancing fools in only ten weeks.

Tony and I reluctantly let Fred drag us up the three flights of stairs to the studio. The old hoofer was the soul of patience, teaching with gestures when words didn't suffice. He danced the part of the girl, although he towered over all of us. Tony and I, however, proved to be hopeless at the terpsichorean arts, deaf to the rhythm, stumbling over our feet. I was mortified to dance with a man — a tall, bony skeleton who danced backward in my arms, whispering, "*One* two three, *four* five six, now dip and turn and . . ."

Fred, however, turned out to have a flair for fancy footwork, especially the Latin beats. He was small and agile, and soon he and the tall, skinny instructor were moving around the floor like a bizarre Rogers and Astaire. Tony and I dropped out of the lessons shortly after the fox trot, but Fred kept going, and liked to demonstrate his latest steps anywhere: standing at a bus stop, waiting in a movie line, walking down the street, cha-cha-chaing along behind us like a perspiring caboose.

Since Fred was deficient in English small talk, the teacher coached him in polite conversation. "May I have this dance?" he prompted Fred. "What's your name? You dance divinely. Would you like to go to dinner?" which Fred invariably delivered as "You dance divine, you like go for dinner?"

When Fred felt he was at last ready to go public with his art, he picked us up one evening in the old Ford and we cruised down Southbridge Street until he pulled up in front of the Musical Café, an ancient Irish watering hole where several middle-aged women were sitting in the window.

"Let's go in and ask them to dance. I can amaze them with my cha-cha-cha," Fred said eagerly.

"Those women are old and drunk," Tony pointed out.

"All the better — they won't know if I make a mistake!" Fred replied.

While Tony and I sat at a table watching, Fred put a quarter in the jukebox and selected "Cherry Pink and Apple Blossom White." Then, as the music began, he sidled over to the women sitting in the window and asked one, "May I have this dance?"

She looked at him blearily, seeing a dark, intense youth, young enough to be her son. Eagerly, if somewhat unsteadily, she accepted and rose to her feet.

Tony and I were treated to a remarkable *pas de deux* as Fred tried to demonstrate his most elaborate breaks and spins before the fascinated audience of Irish millworkers, while his dancing partner tried drunkenly to fold him to her ample bosom. Finally Fred shouted to us in a panic, "Get me out of here!" Once back in the car, he said that the reek of his partner when she held him close was enough to put him off women for good, or until tomorrow at least.

Our luck improved with the addition of another Greek immigrant, Ulysses Mitsopoulos, to our team of lovelorn Lotharios. Ulysses, at twenty-three, was older than all of us, and he had two major advantages: he lived in his own home and drove a brand new, pink-and-white Ford Sunliner convertible.

Ulysses had escaped from the part of northern Epiros that now lies in Albania, walking over the border through the mountains above my village in 1947 when he was twelve, leaving his mother and sisters behind. In 1955 he was brought to America by his three uncles, who owned a factory in Oxford, Massachusetts, that made summer furniture. They gave him a job and lodgings in a house near the factory.

On our hunting expeditions, Ulysses drove, Fred and Tony sat in the back of the car, and I was positioned in the front passenger seat in order to entice the girls into our car with my silver tongue. We four stallions would cruise Worcester in the evening when the night schools, secretarial schools, and clubs were letting out. Whenever we saw a likely-looking group of girls, Ulysses would slow down to a crawl and Tony and Fred would pound me on the back, hissing in Greek: "Talk! Talk! Talk!"

It was hard to be persuasive under this sort of pressure, but I developed a few serviceable opening lines. "Hey, Carol," I'd call.

"I'm not Carol," she would reply.

"Oh, sorry, you look like a girl who sits in front of me in history at Classical," I'd apologize. "Hey, wait a minute. We won't bite you! My friends and I are headed over to the Highland Diner to get something to eat. Want to come along?"

Another basic gambit was to ask where the girl was headed and offer to drive her there. We often hung around the Greyhound Bus Station on Front Street, drinking coffee at the counter, trying to look cool and convince girls headed home to let us chauffeur them.

"Excuse me, miss, but do you speak English?" I would begin slyly.

"Of course I speak English! Whadaya take me for?" she'd snap, surprised.

"It's just that you look so sophisticated, sort of foreign," I'd reply. "I thought maybe French or Swedish. You have more style than most American girls, the way you dress and all. You're really not from Europe?"

"No, I'm from Rutland" (or Webster or Uxbridge or Dudley).

"Is that where you're headed now? Because it so happens that my friend here lives out that way, and he's got that two-toned Ford convertible that you might have noticed outside. Why don't you let us drive you there?"

(Righteously) "I'm not getting in no car with no strangers."

"Well, whatever you like," I'd reply casually. "But they just announced your bus is delayed, and it won't be here for hours."

Perhaps one out of thirty attempts to get young women into Ulysses' car succeeded. They usually traveled in pairs, and as soon as we lured a couple of girls into the car — one in front between Ulysses and me, and one in back between Fred and Tony — my less fluent friends would vie to capture their affections.

Ulysses was usually the most successful because he had a dark, Byzantine face and exuded an air of desperate need. He would move in inexorably, flirting with the girl sitting next to him. "You like to drive the car?" he'd suggest. "Don't be afraid. It's easy!" He would pull her onto his lap and put her hands on the steering wheel. "See! You drive good!"

In the back, Fred and Tony were not competitive. "Who you like, me or my friend?" Fred would ask. "You like him better, that's okay! No problem! I don't mind." The girls usually did go for Tony first because of his muscular physique, but sometimes they were attracted to Fred because he was quick and funny.

"Tell her she reminds me of the first girl I had in Greece," Fred would mutter to me in Greek. "Say she killed herself over me."

"She'll never believe that!" I would shoot back.

"Sure she will. Girls will believe anything," he'd insist.

Inevitably the girl would listen to this dramatic story and then remark, "Jeez. I'd never kill myself for no guy!" But she would smile at Fred with new interest.

I had no success with these pickups, partly because at five-foot-eight and 125 pounds, I looked more like fifteen than seventeen. Furthermore, my grandiloquent literary asides and compliments went straight over their heads.

After we drove for a while I would announce, "My friend Ulysses here has a house in Oxford, that's right on the way to Dudley. It's too early to go home. Why don't we stop by there to have a drink first, listen to a few records?"

If the girls agreed, as they usually did, we would settle in with Ulysses' records and a bottle of Scotch, and soon he would entice the most compliant one into his bedroom. ("You like to come see my bed? Very big bed. Very clean!") Then either Tony or Fred would lead the other girl into the other bedroom, and I would end up playing gin rummy with the loser. My friends never suggested that *I* should get the girls, because they knew I was young and inexperienced. And Ulysses, unlike Fred and Tony, was fiercely protective of his conquests, although he often stole girls from the others.

One Saturday afternoon Ulysses came by to pick me up after work at O'Connor's, with Tony and Fred. I got into the front passenger seat and we set out on the hunt for female company. We drove past Elm Park, each making his cross as we passed St. Spyridon's Church at the intersection of Elm and Russell. Driving down Russell Street, Ulysses slowed at a vision that drew gasps and shouts. A tall girl with honey-blond hair and shapely brown legs beneath tight white shorts was pushing a baby carriage down the street. We shouted out a chorus of greetings and praise, but instead of acting insulted, she laughed. Heartened at our success, we pulled over down the block from her and got out, arranging ourselves along the length of the car, each of us leaning nonchalantly against the Ford in our best James Dean imitation.

"Hey, I know who that is," Fred whispered excitedly as she approached. "She's the girl who demonstrates things in Woolworth's and Newbury's. You know, vegetable peelers and spot removers and mixers. She's a knockout!"

"What a body!" muttered Tony. "I wouldn't mind going a couple rounds with her."

"You haven't got a chance, worm," said Ulysses. "*I'm* the only one here who's man enough to consume that piece of Turkish delight."

When the fair Aphrodite reached us, she laughed again at the mangled compliments shouted at her. She paused, smiling and rocking the carriage with one hand, and answered our questions without hesitation. Her name, she said, was Angela.

"An angel, or if not, an earthly paragon!" I exclaimed. She rewarded me with a look and laughter like crystal prisms in a breeze.

No, she wasn't baby-sitting, she answered Ulysses' next question. This was her own baby. Yes, she was old enough to have a baby.

There followed a chorus of admiring remarks about what a remarkable baby this was, a virtual paragon of a baby. Tony inquired as to the whereabouts of the lucky husband and father.

"I'm not married," Angela replied without a flicker of shame. "I was, but we're separated."

"What's that mean?" my friends all asked me in Greek. When I explained, Ulysses said in English, "This man, he must be crazy!"

"Not crazy, just too dull and boring to deserve us," she replied. "I want to fly and he just drags me down."

I nodded and quoted Balzac in a world-weary voice: "There is no object heavier than the body of someone we don't love." This time she gave me a long, quizzical look before favoring me with a smile that came out like the sun.

"This man, he was not worthy of you," Fred declared. "Come out with me tonight. I will show you what is a man."

"I'm afraid I'm busy tonight," Angela said.

"Then we drive you home," piped up Ulysses, pointing to his car.

"Thanks, but I live right down the street," she said, pausing significantly. "With my parents."

"So give the baby to your mother Friday, Saturday. Go for dancing with us," pleaded Fred. "You give us the number, we call you."

"But I don't have a pencil and paper," Angela replied coyly.

There was a flurry of activity as Fred fished a pencil out of his pocket and Ulysses ran to the car to rip a scrap of paper off a road map. We all gathered around as Angela wrote down a telephone number, bracing the paper on the roof of the baby carriage. Then she straightened up, looked from one eager face to the next, and walked all the way down to the end of the line. Folding the paper carefully, she gave me a glance weighted with meaning and slipped it into my shirt pocket. Then, ignoring the exclamations, shouts of dismay, and whistles from my cronies, she tossed her head and strode off, pushing the baby carriage before her. The others immediately gathered around.

"Can you believe that?" Ulysses fumed. "She picked Nick over a *palikari* like me? An inexperienced child!"

"She was just kidding," Tony grumped.

"No, she goes for you, Nick!" exclaimed Fred. "Must be a little crazy, but what a body! She's hot for you. This is your big chance. You just won the national lottery!"

"You've got to call her. Tonight, before she comes back to her senses!" Tony urged.

That night, each one of my friends called me to find out if I had phoned Angela, but I hadn't yet worked up the courage. By the next evening I decided I had better follow through before she forgot my existence entirely. When Angela came to the phone, her voice was warm and friendly and she sounded as if she'd been expecting my call.

"I'm sorry, I can't go out tonight," she said. "My baby's got a temperature, and my mother's too tired to stay up with her. But come on over after dinner for coffee and dessert. We can sit around and talk."

I walked from O'Connor's to the small wood-frame house nearby, and Angela opened the door wearing an angora sweater and a full skirt puffed out with crinoline petticoats. She looked like a high school girl, although I knew she must be at least four or five years my senior. We sat in the kitchen and her mother offered me coffee and chocolate cake. Soon her father came home. In answer to her parents' questions, I lied that I had just graduated and was going to college in the fall — Princeton. This seemed to please them.

Eventually Angela's mother and father went into the living room to watch television, leaving us in the kitchen, where Angela played with the baby and told me about her ambitions. Her dream, she said, was to go to New York and work in the theater. She believed her job demonstrating appliances was good training for the stage as well as a way to earn money. But while working at a dime store demonstrating Mouli graters, she had started going out with the assistant manager, and he had eventually made her pregnant. He was a nice boy, she told me, and he had offered to marry her, but "I can't spend the rest of my life married to a man who comes home and talks about the turnover in women's girdles, I'd go crazy! I need someone who can talk about theater, books, life! I feel bad being a burden on my parents, but I know one thing: I'm not going to die in Worcester."

"What about the baby?" I asked.

"I'll figure something out," she said. "For now I can leave her with my mother, and when I get a place, even if it's one room, I'll send for her. I'll take her to rehearsals with me."

Finally the baby fell asleep and Angela put her to bed. We sat in silence until her mother came in to clear up the last of the dishes. Angela said impulsively, "This is the best time of night, right after the sun goes down. Let's go sit out in the yard in the swing."

Angela's mother tried to force another piece of cake on me, then put the radio on the windowsill over the sink so we could hear the music out in the yard. Angela led me to a wooden porch swing suspended from a branch of a huge maple tree in the back of the yard. In the perfumed twilight, we sat side by side, listening to the Penguins sing "Earth Angel" and to the clatter of dishes. We could see Angela's mother, framed in the rectangle of light of the kitchen window, looking out our way now and then and smiling.

Keeping one eye fixed on her mother, I put an arm around Angela, and she moved close to me, slowly inching up on my lap. She had on so many petticoats that they billowed over me, hiding what was going on underneath. I was startled when Angela took my free hand and put it under her petticoats, and I nearly jumped when I discovered she had nothing on under them. The next thing I knew, she had unzipped my fly, all of this clandestine activity screened from her mother's view by the layers of petticoats.

Things started to move very fast. As we sat demurely on the swing, Angela, facing the house, deftly adjusted her many layers of petticoats so that from the kitchen it looked as if she was just sitting on my lap. As the swing slowly rocked, I was drenched with sweat, experiencing a variety of sensations I had never suspected were within the reach of mere mortals. There on the swing under the maple, with the crickets stitching up the darkness and the sound of *The Milton Berle Show* faintly audible in the distance, I entered the gates of paradise under the guidance of my ministering angel.

When I left Angela's house that night, I didn't walk, but capered like the young mountain goats that leap from crag to crag above my village. I swung from tree branches, kicked tin cans, and occasionally let out a whoop of triumph.

As soon as I got home, I called Fred, Tony, and Ulysses in turn to announce my initiation. They were full of envious compliments and couldn't wait to see us together. The next night, the four of us arrived at Angela's door in Ulysses' Ford and drove to his house in Oxford, where for once *I* was the one who went into the bedroom while the others played gin rummy.

By then I had stopped asking myself how such a prize — the most beautiful, sexiest, and most intelligent of all the girls we had ever approached — had fallen to me, the youngest and most inexperienced of the gang. Evidently I had some quality that appealed to Angela, and I wasn't fool enough to question such a windfall. I moved through the daily routine of school and work like a zombie, physically present but mentally reliving the sweet moments I had passed with her and fantasizing about what we would do when we were next together.

On the third day of our affair, I called Angela and my euphoria vanished as she told me that she wouldn't be able to see me that night.

"In fact, I won't be able to see you any night, Nick," she said softly. "I'm really sorry, but Charley came over today and I've decided to go back with him."

"Who's Charley?" I asked, as my heart thudded into the pit of my stomach and electric currents of fear radiated to my fingertips, making it hard to hold the receiver.

"The baby's father. The guy from Woolworth's." She explained, "We're going to get back together. He talked to me and my parents and I guess it's for the best."

"But what about New York? I thought you said he dragged you down and you wanted to fly," I reminded her, frantically trying to keep the best thing that had ever happened to me from escaping.

"I said a lot of things, but it's time for me to grow up and face reality," she replied tonelessly. "That's what my folks say, and I suppose they're right. I'm really sorry, Nick. I liked the way you were always quoting poetry to me. It made me feel like someone special."

"You *are* special, Angela," I pleaded. "You can't just give up and marry him!" But I didn't argue much. I could hardly protest losing something that had been such an undeserved gift in the first place. I never saw Angela again, but whenever I went into Woolworth's, I always looked around, wondering which employee was Charley, the man who had clipped my angel's wings.

The loss of Angela did not send me back to the sexual desert from which she had plucked me, however. I soon learned that I had more to thank her for than just my initiation. After Angela, women somehow seemed to know instinctively that I was experienced, and responded to my overtures. I rejoiced in the sudden flood of female society where before there had been only drought. Although my amatory activity would seem mild to those who climbed the barricades during the sexual revolution, it was certainly gratifying enough for me to turn my attention to my other obsession during that period of my life: finding a way to go to college.

Unfortunately, as I finished my junior year, my prospects of raising tuition were bleaker than ever. My father had filed for Social Security, since he could never work full-time again. Dino had had to give up his second job at Putnam and Thurston because a full-time chef was found to replace him, so he was now supporting his growing family on the $85 a week he made at Kresge's. Kanta's husband, Angelo, had been through a sequence of ill-starred jobs from Table Talk to a Greek candy-making firm to Bay State Abrasives, but in each case he was either laid off or the company was sold from under him, so he was reduced to picking apples seasonally for $10 a day. Fotini had found a job as a hairdresser at a beauty shop on Main Street, but she earned a pittance, and complained bitterly and long about the work. Since Glykeria and Kanta had both quit their jobs at Table Talk when they became pregnant, Prokopi, still working at Bay State Abrasives, was the only one in the family earning a decent salary: $125 a week. From the $40 I was making at O'Connor's, I had to contribute $15 a week to help with my room and board, and I was still paying off the expenses of my accident, so there was no way I could save a penny.

Even though we were all struggling to get by, however, there were consolations in our poverty. Each of my three oldest sisters had a son during that year; Glykeria quickly followed the lead of Olga and Kanta, who both had sons in 1957, by giving birth to her first child, Fotios, in May 1958. That made five grandchildren for my father, all boys and all living like brothers in our three-decker.

As I watched Father with his grandsons, I realized that he was happier than he had ever been, even though his health prevented him from working. He loved overseeing the babies, taking them to Green Hill Park to play on the swings and visit the small zoo, where he taught them about the buffalo, deer, goats, and ducks. Every day he would walk them to the spa on the corner to buy ice cream or candy, or take a small grandson in his car, tucking him between his left arm and the locked door while he drove on his visiting rounds, with the baby peering happily over his shoulder.

We were poorer than ever, but this was one of the best times for our family. It was like life in the Greek village, where extended families live next to each other: a mixture of grandparents and babies, newlyweds, aunts and uncles. In our three-decker, we had a vertical version of the village clan, with the cousins growing up like siblings, my sisters and brothers-in-law providing company and support for each other, and my father presiding over it all.

Although we had no money for luxuries, each Sunday Father would put all his culinary skill into cooking a hearty noon meal: chicken and rice in a lemon-and-egg sauce, or lamb shanks fricasseed with herbs and greens picked from the garden in our back yard. After church we would all eat together in the first-floor kitchen and afterward pile into two cars and drive out to Purgatory Chasm in Sutton, where the strange, towering rock formations and deep ravines made us feel as if we were back in Epiros. My sisters would pick dandelion greens while the babies rolled down the slopes and threw stones into the waterfalls and streams. We were secure and happy in each other's company then, never thinking that prosperity, if it came, might fray the ties that bound us together.

None of the Greeks in Worcester were making much money at that time except for a balding, moon-faced young man named Nick Karagounis, from northern Epiros. Karagounis had hit on an innovative idea that puzzled and amused his fellow countrymen but would eventually transform the lives of hundreds of Greek immigrants in New England.

My friend Fred Malitas was a distant relative of Karagounis, and one day Fred told me how his cousin was renting a little run-down store on Pleasant Street and converting it into a pizza house.

"Nick's selling pizzas for seventy-five cents each, and if you buy three, you get one free," he said.

"How can he make any money that way, after he pays the waitresses, busboys, and overhead?" I asked.

"That's the genius of his scheme," Fred explained. "There *aren't* any tables: no waitresses, no plates, no busboys, no overhead. It's all take-out. He makes at least forty percent profit on each pizza."

"But pizza's not a dessert and it's not a meal," I said, unconvinced. "How often will a family eat pizza?"

"You haven't tasted Nick's pizza!" Fred insisted. "It's not thin and skimpy like the Italian kind; it's got a thick crust like bread and another inch of stuff on top — cheese, pepperoni, very spicy. A seventy-five-cent pizza can make a meal for three or four people."

Most of the Greeks in Worcester ridiculed Karagounis, and I was skeptical too. The idea of fast food was still a novelty in 1958, when McDonald's was charging 25 cents for a hamburger. I was surprised when I saw how much business Karagounis was doing just down the street from O'Connor's, where we offered a full menu at the lunch counter. He was selling pizza-to-go the way street vendors in Greece sold take-away shish kebabs and gyro sandwiches. But when I told my brothers-in-law, they explained to me that when a family goes out to dinner, they want to sit down, be served, and have a choice of entrées.

For a while I considered going to work for Karagounis myself, but I was dissuaded by the hellish heat from the pizza ovens every time I went in to watch Nick expertly sliding pizzas out of the ovens with a broad wooden paddle. But I had to find something that paid more than O'Connor's, if I was ever to have any hope of going to college.

Luckily I would be finishing high school a semester early, in January of my senior year, because of the extra subjects I had added in my junior year. If I did find a good job, I could work full-time for nine months until college began. Meanwhile, a good job remained so remote that I just kept working at O'Connor's and fantasizing about what I would do *after* college, when I would earn so much money that I could support all my clan. I'd build a compound of five houses surrounding a big swimming pool, and just as we all lived together now in the crowded three-decker on Chandler Street, we would all live together into old age.

But my sisters had their own dreams, especially Fotini. Tina, as we all called her by now, had been unhappy ever since we arrived in America. Even in Greece she was the most melancholy of my sisters, always weeping and complaining of slights, and there were reasons for her discontent. Born in a society where a female child is considered a curse and a lifelong burden, because she must be trained, rigorously guarded, and finally sent off to her husband's family along with a large dowry, Tina was our mother's "fourth calamity," as my grandfather would put it, and had felt unwelcome from the beginning. She was hardly more than a year old when *Mana* had me, the long-awaited son whose arrival set off forty days of celebration, and Tina had felt ignored from then on.

As the most beautiful of my sisters, Tina never lacked for male admirers, but she had been so thoroughly cowed by my father's insistence on virtue and his habit of spying on her that she wouldn't speak to any man. Besides, there were no young men among the Worcester Greeks whom she found appealing.

By the spring of 1958 I began to realize that we were going to lose Tina to a groom from a distant city. She was approaching her twentieth birthday, and Father had decided it was time to find her a husband. The previous fall, when Glykeria had married and traveled on her honeymoon to visit her best man's home in Philadelphia, she had discovered many likely-looking bachelors there, all immigrants from our part of Epiros. She told my father about them when she got back.

Because immigrants follow their kin, it happened that the people leaving our small mountain region on the northern border of Greece settled in either Philadelphia or Worcester. There was much travel and intermarriage between the two colonies, and now Gregory Bokas, Glykeria's best man, could serve as a matchmaker for Tina. January 25 happened to be the feast day of St. Gregory the Theologian, and every year Gregory Bokas threw himself a big name-day party, so in January Father decided that he and his youngest daughter would travel to Philadelphia to pay their respects.

If Tina was the prettiest Greek maiden in Worcester, Minas Bottos, twenty-six, was one of the handsomest Greek bachelors in Philadelphia. He had recently arrived along with a brother and sister from the village of Finiki, only twenty miles down the mountain from Lia. The three Bottos siblings had been brought over by a kind aunt and uncle because they were part of a huge family of eleven children and their parents were hard pressed to put food into all those mouths. Minas and his brother had been trained as cabinetmakers in Greece, and everyone hoped they could earn money in America to help the rest back in Finiki.

Just as Tina had always felt lost in the shadows of her older sisters and younger brother, Minas had been swallowed up by his crowd of siblings, and he too longed for glory. He nurtured dreams of becoming an actor and joined a theatrical troupe in Philadelphia which performed melodramas in Greek. Small, dark, handsome, and intense, Minas talked passionately about his hopes for the future, which included making a fortune with his woodworking skills. Like Tina, he was clever, and at night he created his own projects: hand-carved wooden radiator covers which resembled fine furniture and ornate household altars for displaying icons in the eastern corner of Greek homes. He sold these creations to supplement his income from installing cabinets in Philadelphia stores.

It was Minas' aunt and benefactor, a pillar of rectitude among the Greek community of Philadelphia, who first picked Tina out as a potential wife for him. All the women were gathered in the kitchen of Gregory Bokas' house, putting the last touches on the lavish St. Gregory's Day buffet. Tina sat quietly, pretty as a flower, but when she offered to help, her culinary skills quickly became apparent. "A pretty orphan girl from Epiros and a wonderful cook as well!" the old lady told her nephew that afternoon. "When you go to Gregory's this evening, you must get to know her."

Tina had been similarly appraised of Minas' good looks and advised to notice him when he arrived. That evening, with so many people in the crowded house observing them, the young couple scarcely exchanged a dozen words, but they were pleased with what they saw.

Not long after Father and Tina returned to Worcester, Father received a call from Minas' uncle and aunt, saying that they would like to come up to pay a visit on us. Glykeria immediately shot off a letter to her in-laws demanding background information on Minas and his clan. The answer came that the family was virtuous and hard-working but huge and therefore poor.

By the time Minas and his aunt, uncle, sister, and brother were formally escorted into the parlor by our father, we were rabidly curious to meet this suitor from Philadelphia. We all stared with an intensity that would have intimidated most young men, but Minas proved charming and talkative, properly deferential to my father and gallantly attentive to Tina.

When Tina went into the kitchen to get the tray of coffee and sweets, my sisters hurried in after her to hold a whispered conference. He was indeed good-looking, they said, and he seemed nice, but she shouldn't commit herself until she got to know him better. She was still young, and there was the problem of the houseful of siblings back in Greece — a lot of people needing financial assistance and tickets to America. This could put a strain on any marriage. She should think it over, they advised, before giving her hand to the cabinetmaker from Philadelphia.

These warnings were a challenge to Tina. While the aunt and uncle were chatting with my father, Tina, who had never been alone with any young man, asked permission to walk around the block with Minas to show him the neighborhood. When they came back in the door, she announced to the thunderstruck group in the parlor that she had given her word to marry Minas.

Engagement parties were held in both Philadelphia and Worcester, at one of which Minas formally presented Tina with a diamond ring that cost him several months' pay. Although the handsome pair seemed passionately in love, there were some rough spots in the courtship, such as an incident at St. Spyridon's during Sunday services when Tina began to point out to her fiancé some of the young men in the congregation who had admired her. Minas, not to be outdone, countered with tales of the many young women who had pursued him. The claims of disappointed admirers escalated until the discussion climaxed with Tina taking off her precious ring and throwing it in Minas' face.

Like all their disagreements, however, this one was quickly patched up. Later, in private, I suggested to Tina that their stormy courtship might indicate that she and Minas should reconsider marrying, but she burst into tears and replied, "I'm in love with him! You don't understand what true love is! Someday you'll know." She had her mind made up, as usual, and all our advice was no more effective than making holes in water, as the Greek proverb puts it.

To Tina, marrying Minas meant that she would move to the great cosmopolitan city of Philadelphia and a whole new circle of friends and relatives. She would reign over her own home like a queen with a handsome and adoring husband, and be free at last of the stultifying atmosphere of Worcester and the overbearing presence of her siblings.

Minas, meanwhile, could hardly wait until their honeymoon trip to Greece, when he would walk into his parents' crowded home in Finiki with this stunning girl who spoke English as fluently as she spoke Greek — a stylish, modern, clever American wife who nevertheless would fulfill his every need, waiting on him and adoring him like a concubine while his brothers and sisters stared in envy.

I watched the progress of Tina and Minas' courtship with reservations, secretly glad that I had not yet encountered something as tumultuous as true love. My most pressing problem was finding a good job so I could save money for college. My benefactor turned out to be the same person who had served as Glykeria's best man and Tina's matchmaker, Gregory Bokas.

One day in May, Bokas called long distance from Philadelphia to congratulate Glykeria and Prokopi on the birth of Fotios. Bokas talked to each of us in turn, quizzing Tina on her wedding plans. When he learned I hadn't been able to find a job, he offered me $75 a week to manage his restaurant in Ocean City, New Jersey, for the summer, and a room in the back of it where I could sleep. It didn't take me long to accept. Free of the need to pay my family for room and board, I could save all of my earnings, and the chance to leave O'Connor's lunch counter to spend a summer on the beach was too tempting to refuse.

In 1958, before the days of drugs, race riots, and protest movements, Ocean City was the perfect American family resort. Liquor was prohibited on the island, and there was a strong Christian moral emphasis, bolstered by the many churches. Gregory Bokas' restaurant was called Ocean View, and, like all the other restaurants on the boardwalk, it did such good business during the summer that customers had to wait in line outside the door during rush hours.

Gregory, his wife, Sofia, and their three small children lived in rooms behind the restaurant next to the one I occupied. Gregory ran the kitchen, while I handled the dining room from seven A.M. through the dinner hour, which usually finished by eight-thirty, so I could lock up by nine. Whenever things got quiet in the afternoon I could sneak off for a swim.

Sofia couldn't work out front because she couldn't speak English, and Bokas was very insistent that no Greek be spoken in the hearing of the customers. "They don't like foreigners around here," he warned me, and it was true that on several occasions arriving customers turned away when they heard me speak to Sofia in Greek.

After closing up the restaurant about nine every night, I would head across the bridge to Somers Point, along with every other restless youth in search of a lively evening. Somers Point was a noisy collection of nightclubs where thirsty residents of Ocean City could find a drink, musical entertainment, and congenial company. The main attraction was a huge club called Tony Mart's, where an immense rectangular bar surrounded a raised bandstand and the customers were jammed body to body against the bar. At Tony Mart's, fledgling musical groups singing and playing the hot new sound of rock 'n' roll got their start in those summers of the late 1950s.

It was a clean-cut, collegiate kind of clientele who frequented Somers Point in those years, the men in Bermuda shorts and crew cuts, the girls with sun-bleached hair and tanned legs. Their main goal every evening was to get falling-down drunk and then to spend the next day bragging about the size of their hangovers.

Since I never was very interested in drinking, this was not my idea of a good time. If I didn't manage to pick up a girl in Tony Mart's by eleven, I would take a taxi back to the Ocean View and be asleep by midnight. But at least a couple of nights a week, I would manage to convince some young woman to accompany me back in the taxi and would sneak her into my room.

Those three months in Ocean City were the golden summer of my youth. I had it all: money, authority, sun, sand, and sex. I'd spend steamy nights nursing a screwdriver and listening to "Fever," "Blueberry Hill," and "Hard-Headed Woman," while wedged into a throbbing, screaming mass of tanned bodies perfumed with cocoa butter, and then ride back to the edge of the sea to embrace one of those smooth golden girls in my single bed with the crash of the surf in the distance.

My summer idyll ended with a jolt after Labor Day, when I returned home with $600 in my pocket, proudly paid off the last of my court fines, and then discovered that because of the recession, I couldn't find a job anywhere. I had given my place at O'Connor's to a Greek friend, thinking that when I got back, with my new experience in management, I could land a much better position. The unpleasant truth was that I couldn't even find work as a soda jerk.

Before I learned the futility of my job hunting, there was the pleasant distraction of Tina's wedding to Minas on September 7. Despite our straitened finances, we managed to put together a respectable party in Putnam and Thurston, using Tina's savings. So many compatriots arrived from Philadelphia that the Greek houses of Worcester were overflowing with guests. It was a melding of the two great expatriate communities from our province, and my father reigned over it all like a king, breaking dishes, dancing, and balancing wine glasses, while Tina, in her white lace dress and long train, looked like a vision from the movies. Minas was so proud and excited, he never stopped talking and toasting his bride with ouzo.

Hardly had they boarded the plane for their honeymoon when rumors began filtering back to us of disagreements between the newlyweds. She wanted to go to her village first, to introduce her groom and to weep over her mother's grave. He was afraid she'd upset herself too much with mourning, and besides, he wanted to visit his own village first, to show off his bride. There were reports of shouting matches and tears and of Tina setting out from Minas' village one day, on foot down the dusty mountain road, until he caught up with her and convinced her to come back.

When they settled in Philadelphia, the disturbing reports continued. The argument over which one had rejected more admirers came up frequently, always ending with shouts and tears. Tina didn't seem to find Philadelphia as gratifying as she had expected. My father and Kanta went down several times to resolve conflicts, and Tina's in-laws also tried to smooth the rough spots in the marriage. Finally everyone concluded that Tina, who had suffered the tragic loss of her mother under such terrifying circumstances, probably needed to live near her sisters to feel secure and happy, so Minas and Tina moved to Worcester and rented an apartment not far from Chandler Street.

Now the battles were so close we began to feel shell-shocked. Once I came home to find my father sitting at the kitchen table, weeping over his inability to make his daughter's married life a happy one. My sisters counseled her to have a baby — that would settle everything — but it didn't, although Tina and Minas produced both a daughter and a son. In the end, after fifteen tumultuous years, they decided to part. We all felt saddened but were also relieved that the agonizing arguments were over and they would have a chance to find peace separately.

As Tina and Minas set off for Greece on their honeymoon, I returned to the discouraging rounds of job hunting. After a month of fruitless searching, I gave up and took a part-time job that made my days at O'Connor's look like a paid vacation. I began working as a short-order cook on the lobster shift at a White Tower hamburger shop, from midnight to eight A.M., for ninety cents an hour. Working all night, I finished the final semester of high school like a zombie, completely out of synch with the rest of the world. I would come home from school at two, sleep until eight, do homework until midnight, then work at the White Tower until school started.

Working nights in one of the seediest parts of Worcester introduced me to the underbelly of the city. After two A.M., when the bars closed, the serious drinkers came in for something to eat, and often vomited on the counter or dozed off into their hamburgers while I had to clean up after them. Every morning I headed to school more disgusted than the day before.

During the slow hours of the night shift, I filled out college applications, daydreaming about how my life would change if I could only get a scholarship. I applied to every college within two hundred miles, counting on my good grade point average and awards to win me something. Finally, by Christmas, unable to stand the White Tower any longer, I gave notice and quit.

That Christmas was one of the worst I remember. I sat around the house contemplating my bleak future. In only a few more weeks I would be finished with high school and unemployed.

"I've got to raise money for college somehow, but I can't go back to the White Tower," I confided to my father in despair.

"Why should you be a short-order cook?" he asked sharply. "That's okay for me, but you're smarter and better educated. You said you wanted to work for a newspaper, so go do it."

"There's only one paper around here, the *Telegram and Gazette,* and they'd never take me without a college degree or experience," I replied.

"We'll see about that," he mused. "I'm going to talk to Charley Davis. All those big shots from the *Gazette* eat at his restaurant every day."

"Don't go asking Charley Davis for any favors!" I exclaimed. "Why should you be obligated to that guy when he threw you out after all those years?"

"A man with no job and no prospects can't afford to ride a high horse," Father replied. "Charley has always taken a personal interest in you. Just let me talk to him. After all, it's the Christmas season. I'll pay him a little holiday visit to wish him *Chronia polla.*"

Shortly after the new year, Charley Davis called me and told me to come to Putnam and Thurston the next afternoon, bringing the clippings of my stories from the high school paper and my academic records. Like my father, Charley was a short, stocky man who walked with great dignity, swinging an umbrella like a walking stick. With the grandeur of a lord, he led me out of his restaurant, across Worcester Common behind City Hall, and into the portals of the *Worcester Telegram and Evening Gazette,* the city's commonly held morning and afternoon papers.

Charley was greeted with deference by everyone and passed straight up to the imposing offices of the editor-in-chief, who welcomed him like an old friend. He eventually sent us on to the executive editor, who, after reviewing my clippings, offered me a job in the promotion department, starting at $60 a week. I accepted at once, even though I had no idea what "promotion" meant. It was a foothold in the newspaper business, and that was my dream.

Afterward, on the pavement, I thanked Charley Davis for getting me the job.

"Don't mention it, Nick," he said kindly. "I like to see a young man, especially a Greek, who knows what he wants and will work for it."

I quickly discovered that "promotion" was another word for public relations. The head of the department, a short, excitable man who scurried about the offices constantly blowing his nose, had three young women and me working for him. As the junior member of the team, I was assigned jobs like going to merchants for testimonials ("I sold my car in the *Telegram and Gazette* classifieds") and writing ads promoting upcoming features.

I loved working for the paper, feeling the tension all around me as reporters raced to meet deadlines, and the wire-service machines clattered to life with another news bulletin. But it was frustrating being sidelined in the promotion department when I longed to be in the newsroom, where reporters chronicled the important events of the world beneath a permanent haze of cigarette smoke. Whenever there was a lull in my promotional duties, I would sneak into the newsroom and try to coerce the lean, laconic city editor, Steve Donahue, into assigning me something — anything — to write. Sometimes he shooed me away, but other times he threw me a crumb: articles about the weather or city high school activities, or obituaries of Greek immigrants.

My first break came one day in March when a freak wind blew the roof off a large warehouse in Auburn. All the reporters were out on the street, and in desperation Donahue called me over. I grabbed a taxi and rushed to where a number of workmen were standing, scratching their heads at the sight of the decapitated building. Just like a real reporter, I asked all the right questions, and that night I was thrilled to see my prose on the front page of the *Evening Gazette*. I was deflated, however, when I realized there was no by-line. The next day I asked the city editor why.

"I'm really sorry, Nick," Donahue replied. "I wanted to give you a by-line, but the problem is that unpronounceable name of yours. 'Nicholas Ngagoyeanes' just won't fit in a single column of type. You're either going to have to get a shorter name or remain anonymous."

One Sunday I was sitting on the floor of the parlor with two former schoolmates, the Rosenberg twins, reading the Sunday *New York Times,* which I bought every weekend. I was studying the entertainment section, as usual, when I saw an article heralding the opening of the annual Shakespeare Festival at Stratford, Connecticut.

"Look at this cast!" I exclaimed to my friends. "*Othello* starring Alfred Drake and Earl Hyman! God, I wish I had a car. I'd give anything to see that — it's my favorite Shakespeare play."

My father, sitting nearby, overheard me and asked, "Who is this Shakespeare?"

"The only dramatist who can stand beside Aeschylus, Sophocles, and Euripides without shame," I answered.

"Then of course you must go," he said. "I'll drive you and your friends to Connecticut."

It was an odd group that set out in my father's seven-year-old green Plymouth, but I was exhilarated at the thought of seeing the performance, especially since Donahue had given me permission to write a review for the *Gazette*. "It'll give us a little class, reviewing the Shakespeare Festival," he had said, smiling.

My father sat silent throughout the performance. As he drove us back toward Worcester afterward, I asked him, "Did you understand it at all?"

"Not all the words," he replied. "But the story, yes. That Iago was a bastard."

"Did you like it?" Phil Rosenberg asked him.

"Yes, Shakespeare is a great man," he answered. "The movies, the good people win in the end, but Shakespeare tell the truth. In life, the bastards always win."

I labored over my review almost until morning, and when I was finished, I typed at the top a new version of my name, borrowed from the nickname given to my father by his cronies: Dr. Gage. The next day, the *Evening Gazette* appeared with a review of *Othello* by the paper's Shakespearean correspondent, the previously unknown Nicholas Gage.

Donahue complimented me on the review and congratulated me on my first by-line. Then he asked what I planned to do with my life. I told him about my dream of working on a newspaper, my lack of money, and the college acceptances I couldn't afford.

"It's important that you go to college, Nick," he advised. "It doesn't have to be Princeton. I went to Boston University, and they've got a first-rate communications school and they cost a lot less."

"But it's too late even to apply," I said.

"Not necessarily," he replied. "I'll give them a call and see what I can do. Meanwhile, you call everyone who might have scholarship funds: your church, Greek organizations, your high school, the Chamber of Commerce."

Steve Donahue called his alma mater, sang my praises, and guaranteed me a job as a reporter on the *Gazette* during my summer vacations, and suddenly I was accepted by Boston University with a scholarship of $500. Then I was awarded $400 by AHEPA, the American-Hellenic Educational Progressive Association. Tuition for a year at B.U. was only $950, so if I added in the $600 I had saved, I figured I could just manage to pay for room and board. And next summer, according to Donahue, I would at last be able to sit in the city room, a real reporter.

By the time the summer was over, I could hardly wait to pack my dime-store footlocker and get on the bus for Boston. I couldn't afford new clothes or luxuries like a typewriter, but what I lacked in material goods I made up for in anticipation of this new world which would educate me so I would never need to earn my living flipping hamburgers or selling fruit.

On the first day of September, when Father drove me in his Plymouth to the bus station, scene of so many assignations between my Greek friends and the girls of Worcester, he followed me to my bus, then handed me a $50 bill.

"This is all I can give you for college," he said, with an expression I had never seen before. "I'm sorry you weren't lucky enough to have a rich father." Then he turned to walk off with the stiff gait of an old man.

"Goodbye, *Patera*," I called after him. "I'll be back for Thanksgiving." But if he heard me he didn't give a sign.

On the bus I alternated between admiring the landscape along Route 9, which seemed to have taken on a new brilliance since my high school days, and counting the money I had in my wallet. I had to find an apartment and a job in the city, and even with the most stringent economizing, I wasn't sure if I could stretch my funds to last until Christmas.

Nick receiving the Hearst prize from President Kennedy in 1963

HIGHER
EDUCATION

Man . . . can learn nothing without being taught.

— Pliny, *Natural History*

As SOON AS I arrived at Boston University and found my way to the College of General Education, I left my luggage and went out to find a room. All freshman were expected to live in a university dormitory, but that cost $855 a year — more than I could afford. I walked the side streets near campus and finally found a sign in a window on St. Mary's Street, in a once-patrician brownstone that had been turned into a boarding house. The room, facing the street, cost only $8 a week, less than half what I'd have to pay in a dorm.

Pleased that I had accomplished so much so fast, I returned to the campus to collect my things. I unpacked sheets for the bed and a large photograph of my six small nephews and one niece lined up against the back-yard fence on Chandler Street, their arms around each other's shoulders. It made me homesick for the commotion of our three-decker. I placed a sack of Greek coffee and the copper *briki* for boiling it on the bedside table so the pungent aroma of the coffee would remind me of home. Then I took out bottles of Metaxa brandy and clear ouzo that I had brought as well, in case anyone ever came to visit me.

Despite my homesickness, I soon made friends at B.U., most of them from blue-collar families who couldn't afford Ivy League schools. But when classes were over, I would go back to my room and find the silence unbearable. If I went to the library it was worse. It was so quiet that I couldn't concentrate, after years of doing my homework on the kitchen table surrounded by the comforting chaos of my family, as an unending stream of relatives and visitors came and went.

I looked for the office of the college paper, the *B.U. News*, during the first week of classes. There I found the city editor, Jim Savage, who asked to see the clippings of articles I had done for the *Evening Gazette*. When he read the review of *Othello*, he stuck out a hand and grunted, "Congratulations, you're the new drama critic."

I attended every campus theatrical production and interviewed the occasional theater or film personality who visited the campus to speak. Unfortunately, there was no budget to pay for tickets to legitimate theaters in Boston, but as university critic, I was one of the first to praise the thespian skills of a talented drama major in the School of Fine Arts, a plump brunette named Faye Dunaway who later became a slender blond film star in *Bonnie and Clyde*.

The *B.U. News* staff were a group of bright, funny, compatible students who like me were smitten with journalism. We tended to gather after classes in the newspaper office, polishing stories, studying, and hanging out until a group went on to the nearby Peter Pan Restaurant for hamburgers (I ordered coffee, mindful of my budget). It was tempting to linger with them, but I knew I had to find a paying job if I was going to remain in college.

I looked in the Boston phone book for every firm that began with the words "Greek" and "Hellenic" and discovered a newspaper called the *Hellenic Chronicle* in downtown Boston. Certain that Providence was leading me, I took the subway to Copley Square and met the publisher, Peter Agris, a tall, husky Greek-American World War II vet who had gone to B.U. on the GI bill and then pursued his dream of founding an English-language newspaper for the American-born sons and daughters of Greek immigrants.

"I know there's a large number of educated, prosperous, second-generation Greeks out there who are interested in Greek affairs but better at reading English than Greek," he told me. "A lot of them are forgetting their heritage, but we're trying to find them and remind them what they're losing."

I immediately liked Peter's enthusiasm and dedication. He explained that the weekly *Chronicle* was basically a family operation: he was the publisher and chief ad salesman, his wife and sister ran the business side of things, and his brother-in-law, an editor of a Rhode Island newspaper, wrote the *Chronicle*'s articles and editorials in his spare time. I was hired to come in after school on Mondays, Tuesdays, and Wednesdays to help with the writing, and on Thursdays I would go with Peter to the printer to oversee production. For this I would receive $1 an hour, or about $15 a week (before I subtracted the cost of subway tokens).

The job at the *Chronicle* gave me an opportunity to practice real journalism and write about Greece, but I still wasn't making enough to eat on a regular basis, so I went to the university's placement service and found a second job, working Saturdays and Sundays at the counter of a Howard Johnson's in Cambridge. I could get there by walking across the bridge over the Charles River, so I saved the cost of public transportation.

As winter erased the fiery palette of fall, turning Boston into a charcoal drawing, the rowing teams disappeared from the Charles and my resolution began to wear thin. It seemed that I was always hurrying through the bitter cold toward one job or another, fighting the wind as I crossed the bridge toward Cambridge or emerging from the MTA station to enter the dark offices of the *Hellenic Chronicle*. Often I would find myself staring at the picture of my nephews and niece, imagining what was happening on Chandler Street. "Now Glykeria's clearing the table and Jimmy Tzouras is arriving with his cigar to sit and talk politics with Father," I'd think. "Olga's nearly got the babies to bed and then she'll come downstairs and bring *koulourakia* to go with the coffee."

My longing for home was eroding the energy I needed to get through each week, but there was no way I could go back to visit Worcester while spending every Saturday and Sunday behind the counter at Howard Johnson's. On Saturdays I worked there from three o'clock until eleven-thirty, and then I had to be back by eight A.M. on Sunday to work until four-thirty in the afternoon. Sundays were the worst, because it seemed that everyone in Cambridge went out for a walk in the afternoon, then stopped at Howard Johnson's to order a snack.

One day, in the cold heart of winter, I was frantically serving the counter, running back and forth and thinking wistfully about the Sunday afternoon scene on Chandler Street: my father sitting in the parlor with his belt loosened after the big Sunday meal, passing the string of amber worry beads through his fingers as the grandchildren played at his feet. Suddenly I heard a sound out of my fantasy, the rhythmic *click-click* of the *koumboloi*, and I looked up, startled, to see my father sitting at the end of the counter, watching me intently and fingering his beads over a cup of coffee.

It was so busy we couldn't do more than smile at each other as I rushed past, but he sat there all afternoon, watching me work until my shift was over. When I was finished, he drove me in his old green Plymouth back across the river to my room.

"I brought you some *koulouria*," he said. "I thought I'd take your dirty laundry home to clean. Anyway, I wanted to see how you're getting on."

I took the demitasse cups and the *briki* down the hall to the kitchen to make us Greek coffee, then brought back the foaming cups, handing him one as he sat on the wooden chair. Father looked around the room, which seemed to grow smaller and tawdrier under his gaze, and neither of us said anything. Then he spoke.

"When I first came to Worcester, seventeen years old," he said, "I went with some other greenhorns over to Reed and Prince, trying to get work. It was a day like this, below zero, and we stood outside the gates and waited while the foreman picked workers out of the crowd. First he picked the Scandinavians — the Swedes and Finns and Danes — and then he picked the Germans and Irish. Then he looked at the rest of us standing there with our collars up and our hands in our pockets and he said, 'You greasers can go on home!' I couldn't understand all his words, but I figured greasers, Greece — it was the same thing. So he went away, but we stood there longer, thinking maybe he would need a couple more men or feel bad seeing us standing outside in the cold. We Greeks were very persistent in those days; had to be. After a while the foreman came out again, up to the gate carrying a bucket of water, and he said, 'Didn't I tell you to leave?' He threw the freezing water right at us. It was like being hit in the face with an axe."

He stopped speaking and we both heard a rattling sound: his coffee cup shaking against the saucer as he held it. Carefully he put the untouched coffee on the table beside the bed.

"That's all I could think of when I saw you working today — running like that behind the counter," he continued. "I always thought, my son, he won't have to live like I lived, scrambling for work in order to eat. Now I don't know. My only son, and what have I ever done to help you?"

He dug into his pockets and took out every crumpled bill he could find — $63 in all — and placed them next to the coffee cup. Then he picked up my bag of dirty laundry without another word and left, walking down the hall with that same old-man's gait that I had first noticed on the day I left for college.

My first impulse was to go after him, because I could see how much pain he felt at being unable to help me after years of saying how important it was for me to get an education. His shame and disappointment were so palpable that I wanted to reassure him that it didn't matter, but a great weariness held me back. The truth was, it *did* matter. I couldn't help wishing he had managed his life better so that I wouldn't have to work so hard now to pay for college. Whatever I said to comfort him, Father would know I was lying.

As his footsteps faded away, my eyes fell on the pile of money on my bedside table and I realized that although he could never give me much, he always gave me all he could, just like now. I was sorry I hadn't managed to thank him. But I knew he had left this money to make me feel better, not worse. Suddenly I knew what I'd do with the windfall. I had been longing to see some of the touring Broadway companies performing in Boston, especially Henry Fonda in *Silent Night, Lonely Night* by Robert Anderson, at the Colonial Theatre. Now, I rashly decided, I was going to buy myself a ticket. The thought of actually seeing a first-run play energized me, and I walked all the way down Commonwealth Avenue with my coat collar turned up over my ears until I reached the theater, just off the Boston Common.

I bought a single ticket in the balcony for $4.50, then I realized there still were two hours until curtain time. I strolled across the Public Garden and caught sight of the Ritz-Carlton. I still had over $58 left, so I decided to splurge and have dinner at the Ritz.

That evening I discovered the Ritz's famous lobster in whiskey sauce while sitting in solitary splendor beneath the cobalt blue and crystal chandeliers, sipping a glass of white wine and exchanging companionable smiles with the Boston Brahmins around me. After coffee, feeling totally satiated for the first time since I left Worcester, I walked around the corner of the garden and stopped at Peretti's on Park Square to choose a good Havana cigar. (Peter Agris had introduced me to the habit by rewarding me with one every time we put the *Hellenic Chronicle* to bed.)

Puffing on my Partagas, I continued on to the Colonial Theatre. Reserving half the cigar for later, I settled in to watch Henry Fonda with the eye of a seasoned theater critic, imagining myself in the same league as Elliot Norton, the *eminence grise* of the *Boston Record-American*. I would review this production for the *B.U. News*, I decided, and bestow on Fonda some neatly phrased praise for his deceptively casual style of acting.

After the performance, I left the theater, inhaling the icy night air and surveying the Boston Common, white and silver in the moonlight. The world seemed a much lovelier place than it had that morning when I had been struggling over the Charles River toward Howard Johnson's. Relighting my cigar, I strolled back toward Boston University and my solitary room, feeling as prosperous as press lord William Randolph Hearst, the subject of my all-time favorite film, *Citizen Kane*. My one Lucullan night of luxury had cost me $15.25 — $4.50 for the theater ticket, $9.50 for dinner at the Ritz, and $1.25 for the cigar — but it had revived my spirits enough to keep me going for weeks. I resolved that I would set aside my father's gift and any Howard Johnson tips I could hoard, and once every month I would treat myself to this kind of evening.

The monthly outings became my salvation. Naturally I couldn't afford to take a date, but just knowing that one evening out of thirty I could put on my shiny blue suit, sit in a real theater, and watch the world's finest actors perform in first-run plays after dining on the Ritz's ineffable lobster in whiskey sauce gave me the strength to spend the other twenty-nine days working, studying, and dining on tomato soup or leftover Howard Johnson's hamburgers.

Christmas break was my chance to return to Worcester and my family at last. The tumult of my niece and nephews at 369 Chandler Street, the aromas of spinach pie and the buttery Greek Christmas cookies, were as sweet as my homesick fantasies had painted them. But once I had been home for a few days, I realized that financially my family was doing even worse than before.

Dino was the most ambitious and the most overburdened of my sisters' husbands. His and Olga's daughter Eleni, named for my mother, had been born in 1958 — their fourth child and the first granddaughter. In order to feed his family and help support his siblings and parents back in Greece, Dino was now working three jobs and making himself sick with exhaustion and stress. From eight in the morning to four in the afternoon he worked at my father's old job at Kresge's lunch counter, sneaking out fifteen minutes early to get to his next job, cooking from four to midnight at a nightclub restaurant called Bronzo's. And on Sundays, Dino worked from eleven in the morning to midnight at Adam's Steak House, owned by a fellow Greek.

Olga and Dino hadn't planned to have so many children so fast, but Dino adored his brood. One day, when he walked into Worcester's Greek grocery store, the Olympia on Main Street, holding two toddlers by the hand, an old Greek bachelor asked him, "These both yours?"

"These and two more at home," Dino replied proudly.

The old man rolled his eyes and said to the patrons of the store, "Well, what else do poor people have to do but make babies?"

Dino flushed scarlet, grabbed the man by the throat, and nearly lifted him off the floor. "I have a wife, children, a home, and a good name!" he shouted. "What do *you* have after forty years in America, you old shit?"

But despite his protestations that he was satisfied, Dino still dreamed of making a fortune. As he worked around the clock in other people's restaurants, he talked of opening a place of his own. My father, however, like all men who were young during the Depression, insisted it was foolhardy to give up the good jobs he had for a risky venture.

Angelo and Prokopi were having an even harder time than Dino supporting their families, because of the sagging economy in Worcester. After picking apples, Angelo had obtained a low-level job at Bay State Abrasives, where Prokopi was working two consecutive shifts and worrying about the health of his wife. In the two years after her first baby was born, Glykeria suffered two miscarriages. Dr. Seidenberg treated her both times and advised, "You should wait a while, build up your strength and then try again." But Prokopi was impatient.

Glykeria decided to take her problem to a higher authority. She had originally agreed to her father-in-law's insistence in a letter from Greece that she name the next baby Vasili, but after two miscarriages she concluded the name was bad luck. She went to church and invoked the aid of our region's patron saint, famous for the miracles accomplished by his mummified corpse in Corfu. "Dear Saint Spyridon," Glykeria prayed, kneeling before his icon, "if you help me have a baby, I'll name it Spyridon, or Spyradoula if it's a girl, and I'll light candles to you every Sunday." She returned home feeling better, but when I came back from college that first Christmas vacation, I was shocked at how pale and exhausted she was.

Despite my family's worries, they all pampered and praised me, and when I went back to Boston, I felt my spiritual batteries recharged. Until I left Worcester I hadn't understood how much of an advantage my family's love and emotional support gave me — a strength and self-confidence that many of my American classmates lacked. While I spent my days at school longing to be home, I was amazed at how many classmates hated returning to their parents and seized on any excuse to postpone it.

Whenever classes were suspended for the pre-exam week of cramming, I took the opportunity to go back to Worcester, but I still did well enough in my courses so that in June my $500 B.U. scholarship was renewed. Another financial break was my appointment as city editor of the *B.U. News* for the next year, succeeding Jim Savage, who became executive editor. The post would pay half my tuition, which was now $1150, so I could give up the weekend job at Howard Johnson's and still get by. This meant that on weekends I could hitchhike back to Worcester and see my family more often.

My run of luck faltered when I went back to the *Worcester Gazette* that spring to begin the reporter's job that the city editor had promised. My nemesis was the executive editor, who told me that no matter what Donahue said, I would have to start by serving in a suburban bureau before I could work on the metropolitan staff. He offered me a job in far-off Gardner, but I protested that I would need a car to get there every day and I didn't have one.

"Then buy one," he said.

"But I can't afford a car," I explained. "I can barely afford to pay for college as it is."

"Well, then have your father put the down payment on a car and you pay him off from your salary," he replied.

"My father can't afford to buy a car any more than I can," I answered irritably. "He's sick and out of work."

The editor shrugged. Rules were rules, he said. There was no way he could let me skip to the city staff without serving my apprenticeship in the suburbs, no matter how much Steve Donahue wanted me.

I called up Gregory Bokas in Philadelphia and asked if he could use me to manage his Ocean City restaurant again. He agreed and offered me even more than I'd made two years before: $100 a week.

That summer of 1960, while a young senator from Massachusetts waged a new kind of media-wise election campaign against Richard Nixon, I enjoyed three months on the boardwalk that were even better than those in 1958. Now I was as old as the waitresses I managed, and my social life was even more stimulating than it had been when I was a high school boy. The sun, the surf, and the rock 'n' roll at Somers Point seemed better too — probably because that summer was the end of an era.

After three months of hedonism in Ocean City, I had almost $1000 saved. The only flaw was that I had been cheated of the chance to spend time with my family, and now I had to return to the lonely grind of college. I couldn't even go home on weekends, because Glykeria, who had become pregnant again, was confined to bed by her doctor, and her husband asked me not to visit so she wouldn't insist on getting up to cook for me.

Being forced to stay in Boston, concentrating on my studies and the newspaper, proved to be to my advantage. As city editor of the *B.U. News* I learned a lesson from the editor in chief, Joel Elman, that would ultimately be more useful to me than anything I learned in the classroom.

Joel was an original, a former high school dropout, trapeze artist, and battery commander in the air force who was now an honor student of Slavic literature. He insisted that all of us on the staff look for a fresh perspective on every story and never take anything for granted.

The first time I saw Joel's method at work was when he assigned a series on the parking violations given to B.U. students by the Boston police. "Maybe the police are being unfair. Are they as tough on VIPs and public officials?" Joel asked the staff. "Let's see if we can find out."

We staked out expensive downtown hotels, civic buildings, and the statehouse and found dozens of public officials flagrantly ignoring parking rules while the police left them unmolested. At the climax of our coverage, the *B.U. News'* roving photographer snapped the car of the registrar of motor vehicles triple-parked in a no-parking zone outside a luxury hotel. Our story and pictures were picked up by the Boston newspapers and the registrar issued a formal protest, but in the end he was forced out of office. Meanwhile the police patrolling the periphery of the campus became more evenhanded with students, and I learned the value of Joel's warning: take nothing for granted. It was my first lesson in investigative reporting.

As city editor I also inaugurated a page devoted to dissenting opinions and tried to get a variety of students and faculty to write on both sides of current issues. One of the most difficult assignments was the presidential election of 1960. I couldn't find anyone on campus willing to write an essay supporting Richard Nixon, since the students and faculty were all for John F. Kennedy. I finally assigned a bright political science student to *pretend* he was pro-Nixon and write in his defense. When Kennedy won by the smallest plurality of the century, I learned never to consider Massachusetts college voters a microcosm of the country.

Kennedy's inaugural speech in January 1961 was the finest speech I had ever heard, as he appealed to a "new generation of Americans" to help him "light our country . . . and the glow from that fire can truly light the world." Perhaps even more than my classmates, I considered Kennedy to be *my* candidate. Since I had come to America, Kennedy had been the first presidential challenger from Massachusetts, and as an Irish Catholic he was an outsider in this Yankee stronghold, just as we Greeks were.

My sophomore year came to a close, and I learned that the *B.U. News* staff had recommended me for the post of editor in chief, although this position traditionally went to a senior, and that the administration had approved their recommendation. I would be editor during my junior year — and the position carried with it payment for full tuition.

The night of the official announcement, the staff of the *News* retired to the nearby Dugout Bar to celebrate. After a few congratulatory toasts, I decided to call my father from the lounge and collected enough change to pay the toll to Worcester. When he first heard my voice, he thought something was wrong, but I reassured him.

"It's good news — great news, in fact," I shouted. "I'm the new editor of the school paper next year!"

"This must be an important honor at your college, from the way you sound," he replied.

"It's the first time the position will be held by a junior," I boasted.

"Ah, it's a position as well as an honor," he said.

"Yeah, of course. I'll have more than forty people under me," I told him. "And it pays full tuition. I'll be able to make it through another year."

"That's wonderful news. I'm proud of you," he responded somewhat uncertainly. "Are you sure it won't be too hard for you . . . this being editor?"

"Not at all," I assured him. "I know exactly how I want to change the paper, and I have a good staff."

"You have the education, you know best," he said. "But tell me something so I can explain to your sisters. What does an editor do?"

I told him as best I could and he listened attentively, never reluctant to ask for more explanation when he didn't understand something.

"Yes, now I see," he said finally. "I'll tell your sisters."

As I returned to my friends, I found myself wondering somewhat apprehensively how much my education and the new opportunities it brought me would create a gulf between my life and my family's.

That spring I returned to the *Evening Gazette* armed with the news that I was the first junior at B.U. to be chosen editor in chief. I managed to make the *Gazette's* executive editor relent and give me a job on the city staff even though I hadn't served in the suburbs. This meant that I could live at home at last.

When I reported to the *Gazette,* I made a friend, another reporter who also began work that day: Dave Mulholland, a tall, lanky graduate of Tufts with a blond crew cut, spectacles, and protruding ears. I soon discovered that Dave burned with the kind of social consciousness endemic among my generation. When President Kennedy established the Peace Corps on March 1, 1961, it was as if he issued a personal summons to Dave, who immediately applied to join the new volunteer army for peace and was just marking time at the *Gazette* until he received word.

In July Dave learned that he had been accepted. He couldn't wait to get started, but I tried to temper his idealism. "Since I come from one of those underdeveloped countries you're going to save," I said to him one day over lunch, "I think I should warn you what you're going to find. People will look at you with suspicion: 'Why does some rich, blond American college boy think he can tell me how to cultivate my field or raise my children?' Their governments are crawling with corruption, nepotism, and political feuds. You're going to get frustrated, angry, and discouraged at the way the people you're trying to help will resist being saved."

"So what should we do, let them live in misery and die of malnutrition?" Dave replied evenly.

By the time he left for the training program, promising to keep in touch through letters, I was so distracted by problems at home that I could only wish him good luck. Glykeria was still in bed trying to bring her pregnancy to full term, and Dino feared he was dying.

Dino had always avoided eating at home because he could survive on the leftovers from the three restaurants where he worked, thus leaving more food for his children. But for some months he had been suffering agonizing stomach pains and vomiting whenever he ate. Dr. Seidenberg diagnosed it as appendicitis and operated on him, but as soon as Dino got back to work the same symptoms began again. Finally he concluded that he must have stomach cancer.

One day Dino confided his fears to Olga, saying, "When I die, I want you to have your father come up here to the third floor to live and take care of the kids. You're going to have to go out and find a job somewhere. You have to stay calm and strong, because if you fall apart, our children are going to end up living on the street."

Olga, never noted for her composure, instantly became hysterical, screaming, wailing, and keening loudly enough to rouse the whole neighborhood. We all learned the terrible news: Dino had the "bad sickness."

Greeks react to illness within the family in a manner that might seem peculiar to westerners. First they leap to the worst possible conclusion. A cold is diagnosed as pneumonia, a rash is probably leprosy; therefore Dino never doubted that he had cancer eating away at his belly. Already thin, he was now haggard, with black hollows under his eyes.

As soon as Greeks diagnose the illness that threatens their home, they begin fixing blame. "No wonder he's dying, your children never stop making noise so their father can sleep!" Glykeria volunteered from her own sickbed. "It's not the children, it's his accursed relatives, draining him of strength and money like vampires," Father retorted, his voice drowning out Glykeria's.

We all pitched in with our own suggestions as to who was responsible for causing Dino's cancer, but whenever an outsider approached, we all drew together into a wall of silence and denial; for the final reaction Greeks have to illness is to deny to the outside world that there's any sickness at all. Serious illness is a shameful secret, and we all insisted that absolutely nothing was wrong with Dino.

Glykeria, however, with her natural gift for spreading news, couldn't help whispering to a cousin that Dino was on the verge of death from the "bad sickness," but no one must know. Within days the entire congregation of St. Spyridon's was planning Dino's wake. The invalid himself, however, decided to consult another doctor, who concluded that Dino was only suffering from a nervous stomach caused by too many jobs and responsibilities. Dino decided to take the doctor's advice and quit all of his jobs except the one at Bronzo's.

Our other medical crisis, Glykeria's pregnancy, also ended happily, when she gave birth to a second son, dutifully named Spyridon for the saint who had brought about this miracle. Little Spiro, weighing nine pounds eight ounces, was born at ten A.M. on August 4, 1961.

I put the lessons I had learned from Joel Elman to work that summer as a reporter on the *Gazette,* and tried to approach each assignment from a fresh perspective. When the summer was over, Steve Donohue told me I'd done some good stories and he hoped I would come back to the *Gazette* full-time when I finished B.U.

Steve's words gave me a sudden inspiration. I said that I might be able to work full-time for him even *before* I graduated. If I fulfilled the main requirements of my journalism program in my junior year, then in my senior year I could choose classes that met in the afternoon. That way I could work full-time for the *Gazette,* because a staff reporter's hours went from seven-thirty A.M. to one-thirty P.M. If I had a car, I could leave a little early and drive to Boston in time for two o'clock classes.

Steve agreed to the plan and said he would pay me $85 a week — enough, I figured, to finance my last year's tuition and the payments on a used car (after all, I would be living at home without the cost of room and board).

I returned to B.U. and moved into a real apartment with kitchen and bathroom, which I shared with a friend from the paper. As a junior I began the two-year journalism program, but my experience at the *B.U. News,* the *Hellenic Chronicle,* and the *Worcester Gazette* had already made subjects like copy editing, reporting, and feature writing second nature to me, so I breezed through the required courses, scarcely having to study. I spent far more time at the *B.U. News* offices in the basement of a university office building than I did in my own apartment, and the staff became like my family.

In a university as large as B.U., everyone needs some sort of group for friendship and mutual support, and the *News* staff became insepa-rable. Monday nights were the climax of the week, when we sat up nearly till dawn getting the paper to the printer's. In the dark, smoky city room of the *News,* amid the clatter of our old Underwood type-writers, we became a team of colleagues and friends.

It was a bittersweet moment when I handed over the editorial duties at the spring dinner. I still had a year of college left, but I couldn't con-tinue on the staff if I was to work full-time on the *Worcester Gazette.* Because I couldn't just quit writing cold turkey, I continued to do some articles and columns for the *News* during the final months of the year, under my Greek name, N. C. Ngagoyeanes.

One Monday, sitting in the *News* office, I read a review in the *New York Times* book section praising a new biography of playwright Eu-gene O'Neill by Barbara and Arthur Gelb. Because theater was one of my passions, I went to the university bookstore, where I discovered the book cost $12.50; so over a number of visits I read it furtively, standing in the bookstore's aisle.

Eventually I came to a poignant scene from O'Neill's last days. His widow, Carlotta Monterey, related that when O'Neill realized he was dying, he decided to destroy all his unfinished plays so no one else would ever work on them. He had planned an eleven-play cycle, but only one play was finished, and the depressed and ailing O'Neill insisted that Carlotta help him rip up the unfinished manuscripts and burn them in the fireplace of the Boston hotel suite where they were living. "It was awful, it was like tearing up children," Carlotta told the Gelbs, describing one of the most terrible acts of destruction in America's literary history. Some months later, the book continued, O'Neill died at the age of sixty-five, shortly after gasping, "Born in a hotel room and . . . damn it, died in a hotel room!"

As I stood in the aisle of the bookstore, lost in the biography, I realized that this scene had taken place on the campus of Boston University, for the Shelton Hotel, where O'Neill died, was now a university dorm, Shelton Hall. I decided to write a story for the *News* about this local angle, but when I convinced the housemother of Shelton Hall to take me up to suite 401, I discovered that there was no fireplace. After knocking on all the walls and then tracking down the original blueprints in Boston's buildings department, I learned that there never had been a fireplace: O'Neill couldn't have burned his plays there.

Shortly after my piece describing what I had learned appeared in the *B.U. News*, it became the subject of a newspaper column by Elliot Norton, the famous drama critic. He cited my detective work and wondered if O'Neill's widow had perhaps lied to the Gelbs and still had the precious missing plays in her possession.

The story hit the Associated Press wire and appeared all across the country. I received a frantic telephone call at the *News* office from the biography's co-author, Arthur Gelb, who was then the chief cultural correspondent for the *New York Times*. The *Times* calling the *B.U. News* seemed as unlikely as the White House calling the president of our student body. I took the receiver nervously from the hand of an awed reporter and heard Gelb's intense, rapid-fire voice asking: What had I written? How had I learned it? What were my sources? How could this be true? He and his wife, Barbara, had checked every fact in the book's 970 pages, he insisted.

"Did you go to the Shelton?" I asked.

"Of course I went to the Shelton," Gelb replied. "But there was some problem about getting into the room."

He assured me that he would question O'Neill's widow at once about the discrepancy and let me know what he found.

In the meantime, I continued my own investigation. I tracked down the man who had been manager of the hotel before B.U. bought it, and he eventually led me to a woman who had been a maid in the hotel when the O'Neills lived there. She told me that she and Mrs. O'Neill and a hotel floorman, since deceased, had carried the torn manuscripts down to the basement and burned them there in the incinerator.

Soon Gelb called me back and said Carlotta O'Neill had given him the same story. He said he would revise the biography in its next edition, and thanked me for catching the error. "That was a nice piece of investigative reporting," he added. "You should think about going into journalism."

"That's what I want to do," I told him.

"Well, if you ever get to New York, come and see me," Gelb concluded amiably. "Maybe I can help." The following week I received in the mail a copy of the biography *O'Neill*, which had been inscribed to me by both authors, "so that you won't have to read this standing up."

Getting praise from the *New York Times* was heady stuff for a college junior, but I knew that to work for a New York newspaper, I'd first have to get my college degree and some experience on a smaller paper. At the end of my junior year, I left normal college life behind to work full-time for the *Evening Gazette* and commute. That way I hoped to save enough to pay for my final year and perhaps have some left over for graduate school. Columbia's Graduate School of Journalism was the best in the country, I knew, and a short cut into New York journalism. But for the time being, I could hardly pay for my last year of college, much less graduate school.

I returned home to Chandler Street, where I received periodic letters from Dave Mulholland. His experiences working for the Peace Corps made my work for the *Gazette* seem trivial by comparison. The previous Christmas, Mulholland had arrived at his post in a *barrio* called Ilog in the southern Philippines to teach in an overcrowded school where the students had to provide their own chairs. To get to school every day he had to travel three miles, riding a bike through sugar-cane fields and paddling a dugout canoe across a river. When a student failed to come to school and David asked why, the other children would usually reply, "Oh, he died," Dave wrote.

Dave's tales of life in the Philippines reminded me how lucky I was, and I worked with redoubled energy at the *Gazette*. I was getting interesting assignments and searching the classified section to find a good used car. I was also encouraging Dino to buy his own restaurant. One summer day he showed me a place called The Crossroads at the junction of two highways in West Boylston — a small restaurant with a counter, a few tables, and a location on the corner of a pretty village green. I said it looked like a good investment, and Dino decided to combine his savings with Angelo's and buy it.

My life seemed all worked out when Steve Donahue told me one morning that I was being moved from the reporting staff to the county desk, where I would edit stories coming in from suburban bureaus.

"I don't want to be an editor working on other people's stories!" I protested. "I want to be a reporter."

"Sorry, Nick, you *have* to take it," Steve persisted. "Those are A. F.'s orders."

Ayton F. Smith was the managing editor of the *Gazette,* a flamboyant Sydney Greenstreet type who wore a Panama hat in summer and moved and spoke with a languid elegance rarely encountered in Worcester. I went to his office at once, but A. F. calmly and firmly told me I'd better transfer my things to the county desk.

I lost all enthusiasm for my work as I spent every day brooding over the suburban copy — town meetings, debates over water rights and dump privileges — trying to inject some life into the stories. Every day as I got off the elevator I would stop in A. F.'s office and beg him to put me back on the reporting staff. Pretty soon he would wince every time he saw me. Finally, one day in August, he said in his well-modulated accent, "Nicholas, my boy, I'm afraid that life offers options, not ideals. Your options at this particular moment in time are to keep on doing what you're doing on the county desk or to leave the paper."

"All right then," I said in less modulated tones. "If those are my options, I quit."

Suddenly all my carefully laid plans dissolved like a soap bubble. I had no job, no way to pay for my last year of college, no position on the *B.U. News,* and nowhere to live. In desperation I approached every newspaper in and around Boston during the rest of the summer, but they all insisted on a college degree before they would hire me. I paid a sentimental visit to the *B.U. News* office, and on the way out ran into a woman who worked for the university's press office. She offered me a position as the press officer of the School of Fine Arts, saying, "It doesn't pay much, but it might get you through."

The job meant spending about four hours a day in a tiny office in the School of Fine Arts, writing press releases about events happening there: art exhibits, concerts, theater productions. It paid only $800 a year, but combined with a *Wall Street Journal* scholarship of $500 I'd won the previous year, I thought I might make it. I found a tiny apartment on Park Drive with a Murphy bed that folded into the wall, and prepared to return to Boston.

At the nadir of the summer, just after losing my job, I learned that my old colleague and friend Dave Mulholland had died of dysentery in the Philippines. He was the first member of the Peace Corps to lose his life in its service. His parents told me that on his last day he was asking the doctors how soon he could return to Ilog, saying, "I have so much to do there."

Once I was settled in Boston, I hitchhiked to Quincy to visit Dave's parents. They showed me a collection of his photographs and letters, including one to a Filipino friend in which he wrote, "Try to do one little thing that's immortal. Perhaps then everything will seem worthwhile." I wanted to write about Dave and contacted my old city editor at the *Evening Gazette* about doing the story, but he said, "It would never get printed if you wrote it; A. F.'s still really pissed off at you for leaving." I finally convinced Dave's hometown paper, the *Quincy Patriot Ledger,* to print it, and they devoted an entire page to Dave's life and work in the Philippines on December 21, 1962.

Shortly after Christmas I got a call from the dean of B.U.'s Journalism School, asking me if he could submit the piece to a contest sponsored by the William Randolph Hearst Foundation. "We never win these things," the dean said to me, "but I liked your story on the Peace Corps guy so much, I thought we should submit it."

A month or so later, by the time I'd forgotten the contest, I got another call, saying that the story on Dave Mulholland had won me the first place national award for the month: the sum of $750! I was several months behind in my rent and I realized that the prize not only would save me from eviction, it would get me through the rest of the year.

"What else have you got that we can submit?" the dean inquired.

"What's the next category?" I asked.

"Let's see," he muttered. "For March the category is editorials."

I sent him a sheaf of editorials I had written for the *Hellenic Chronicle.* The dean was as excited as I was when he called me again, two months later, to announce that I had won eighth place in that month's competition — a prize of $100.

Winning the Hearst awards gave me the courage to do what several of my old friends from the *B.U. News* were doing: apply to Columbia's Graduate School of Journalism. It had a highly competitive program that accepted only eighty students a year out of some eight hundred applicants, and it provided working experience in New York and contacts on the big city newspapers.

By the time I went home to Worcester that April to celebrate Greek Easter, I was in sorry shape. All of my friends had received letters of acceptance from Columbia, and I hadn't. Furthermore, when I got home I learned that Dino and Angelo's restaurant was failing badly. "The place is eating up all our savings," Dino told me.

The roasted lamb, the dill-and-entrail soup, and the sweet braided Easter breads studded with red eggs were as delectable as ever, evoking past Easters in the village when meat had been only a faint memory, but I couldn't really enjoy myself, because I was worried about my brother-in-law's restaurant, the poor advice I'd given Dino, and my own problematical future. Then a letter arrived saying that Columbia had accepted me and furthermore awarded me a scholarship of $2500. This was wonderful news, but I needed at least $3500 to attend. I wrote back accepting, adding that I didn't yet have the full tuition but was optimistic I could make the additional $1000 I needed over the summer.

Shortly after returning to school from Easter vacation, I was in my office in the School of Fine Arts one afternoon when I received a call from Karen Gaines, the press officer who had given me my job. "Are you sitting down, Nick?" she asked.

With an instant vision of press releases gone wrong, I took a deep breath and said, "Let me have it."

"You're going to the White House," Karen said.

"If nominated I will not run, and if elected I will not serve," I replied.

"No, seriously!" she insisted. "You're the first-place winner of this year's Hearst National Journalism Award, and President Kennedy is presenting it to you on May fourteenth!"

First I was incredulous, then ecstatic. John F. Kennedy was a hero not just to Greek immigrants but to college students, Peace Corps volunteers, professors — everyone I knew.

As soon as Karen hung up, I dialed my father. "You'll never guess what happened!" I shouted. "I'm going to the White House. Next month!"

"You mean they've given you a job at the White House?" he exclaimed.

Somewhat deflated, I explained that no, it wasn't a job. It was an award for journalism that I would receive from the hands of President Kennedy.

"Well, that's pretty good for a greenhorn who just got off the boat fourteen years ago," he said cheerfully. "Is it going to be on television?"

"I don't think so," I admitted, my ego definitely reduced to normal size by now. "But it'll be in the papers," I added consolingly.

"Well, let's not tell anyone until we see if it really happens," he advised. "You know how these politicians change their minds."

My father evidently didn't follow his own advice, however, because the next time I returned home for a weekend, I was mobbed by Greeks on the church steps, all of them wanting a word alone with me. Women and men were tugging at my sleeve, grasping my shoulder, hissing in my ear: "You know my daughter's husband, the one who can't get a visa because he jumped ship once? Just a single word from you to Kennedy and I know our problems would be over." "My brother's passport . . . My son's application to college . . . My mother's heart operation . . . My father's pension . . ." — all these matters would be instantly resolved if I would only whisper one word into the president's ear.

I explained, at first patiently and then more irritably, that it would not be appropriate for me to request favors at the moment the president of the United States was presenting me with an award. It was a public ceremony, I said. We would not be alone together; there was no opportunity for such requests.

"Of course, I understand," they replied, winking and tapping a temple with a forefinger. "After all, we are both men of the world, are we not? *Naturally* you couldn't speak of such things while the president is conferring an award. But before the ceremony, or perhaps afterward, just a discreet word from you, as friend to friend, on the subject of my problems with the Internal Revenue Service . . . well, I know it would be nothing to a man of importance like yourself."

By the time the three-hundredth person had come up with instructions for the *rousfeti* that I must ask of the president on his behalf, I was no longer civil. Even my own relatives would not accept my statement that I couldn't carry petitions to Kennedy for them.

My father had no personal boon he wanted me to demand of Kennedy. Instead, he counseled me on how to make polite conversation with the president. "You tell Mr. Kennedy that the best customers on my vegetable route were the Irish — the cooks in the rich Yankee houses," he advised.

When the day came to fly to Washington, I went alone. I put on my one well-worn blue suit, white shirt, and narrow all-purpose tie, put another shirt and a change of underwear in a school satchel, and took the MTA and a bus to Logan Airport. I had never been on an airplane before, but I was so excited that it never occurred to me to be afraid. I was going to the White House to meet the president — God wouldn't let the plane crash now.

The Hearst Foundation had mailed me the plane ticket and the directions to the Mayflower Hotel, where the winners of the Hearst contest would be welcomed at a cocktail party. When I entered the hotel, I discovered that the other two winners to be cited by the president were from the University of Nebraska and had come with an entourage, while I knew no one. There were also many prestigious newsmen and -women and several members of the Hearst family, including Randolph Hearst.

The next morning we were escorted on a brief tour of the city and then to the Capitol, where we were honored at a luncheon hosted by our respective senators. Mine was Edward M. Kennedy. That afternoon, at the White House, as our credentials were checked and we were waved through the gates, I was overcome by the sense of being in a movie instead of real life, a feeling that recurred often before I got back home. We were ushered into a richly decorated waiting room and then joined by Kenneth O'Donnell, the president's director of appointments. Finally he said, "The president is ready to see you now," and led us into the Oval Office.

I blinked in the bright sunlight and saw the imposing figure of John

Kennedy standing in front of his desk, holding out his hands in greeting. Then I heard a commotion, and turned around to discover several dozen reporters with cameras and microphones pointed toward us. They were all shouting, flashing light bulbs, waving, and calling to me as if I were Cary Grant disembarking from the *Queen Elizabeth II*: "Look this way, Mr. Gage"; "Smile, please"; "How do you feel, meeting the president?"

After posing until the photographers were satisfied, Kennedy shooed most of them out of the room and spoke to each of us individually. He was relaxed and seemed to be enjoying himself, perhaps because his first job after leaving the navy had been as a reporter for the Hearst Corporation, and he enjoyed the company of journalists and Randolph Hearst. He obviously had been briefed on our backgrounds, and made much of the fact that he and I were both from Massachusetts. "You're getting a great start with this award," he said to me. "You're obviously a much better reporter than I was. I was pretty bad, wasn't I, Randolph?"

Hearst told him briefly how I had come to America as a war refugee and managed to learn English, enter journalism school, and work my way through college with a combination of academic scholarships and part-time jobs.

"And you're doing all this so you can become a reporter?" Kennedy asked. "Why do you want to be a newspaperman?"

"Just a masochist, I guess," I answered, because I couldn't think of any way to encapsulate all my reasons in a few words.

Everyone laughed as if this was a pearl of wit, and it was widely quoted in the newspapers the next day. The quarter-hour we spent in the Oval Office passed in an instant.

Back in the hotel, I immediately called my family to tell them about the president. They listened politely, but all they asked was whether he had offered me anything to eat. I was disappointed at their reaction, but the next day, when my picture standing next to Kennedy appeared on the front page of the *Worcester Telegram,* they called me, frantic with excitement. They didn't really believe I had met Kennedy until they saw it in the paper.

"No one I know, no Greek in Worcester or Massachusetts or all of Greece, for that matter, can say what I can say," my father proclaimed over the phone. "I am an uneducated immigrant and my son has been entertained by the president of the United States in the White House. I hoped for great things for you, but I never imagined glory like this."

My sisters told me later that Father went out and bought himself a suit in order to be properly dressed for his new status when he received the congratulations of the Worcester Greeks. From the haberdashery he went to the coffeehouse and spent the rest of the day buying drinks for the patrons — all those men who had bought full-page ads in St. Spyridon's commemorative album, whose names were immortalized in the church's stained glass windows, and who had dined with the archbishop when he came to town, but who did not have sons who went to the White House.

That day my father bought many copies of the Worcester paper and cut out the picture of me with Kennedy. He had one of these laminated in plastic, and then carried the plastic-coated newspaper photo in his breast pocket, producing it at the slightest excuse to show friends, relatives, and total strangers. Each time he told of his son's honor, he ended with the words "God bless America!" I found the much-worn, nearly unrecognizable photo still in his breast pocket on the day he died.

No one had told me that the award festivities would continue for two more days in New York City. I put on my slightly wrinkled suit once again and we traveled as a group by train from Washington, D.C. — my first train ride. As we sat in the club car, some of the Hearst executives and Randolph Hearst himself quizzed me about my future plans. I told them that I hoped to go to Columbia, if I could only manage to save up the extra $1000 I needed by next fall.

When we reached New York, we were settled in a midtown hotel and told to be ready at noon the next day to attend a luncheon in our honor at Toots Shor's Restaurant. I had never seen Manhattan, except for New York harbor on the day we arrived in 1949. The city seemed like a huge movie set, its canyons choked with people and traffic at the foot of improbably high skyscrapers.

On the morning before the luncheon I decided to call Columbia Journalism School. When I reached the assistant dean, Richard Baker, he asked me to come up for a visit. "I want to talk to you," he said, and described how to get to the Columbia campus.

Unlike B.U., Columbia looked like a college campus in a movie, with red brick buildings around a green quadrangle dominated by Low Library and the huge seated figure of Alma Mater. I entered the journalism school beneath the bronze statue of Thomas Jefferson, and met Dean Baker. He told me that I had been accepted in a special International Fellows program that took qualified students from each graduate school. I would have an additional six hours of classes a week in foreign relations, and my scholarship would be increased to $3500, enough to get me through the year.

I stammered my thanks. I was so excited by this unexpected bonanza that I could hardly find my way back to midtown. I was already late for the Hearst Foundation luncheon, so I went directly to Toots Shor's. When I was welcomed by Shor himself and a gaggle of television and media stars, I began to think I had stepped from the seats of the Greendale Theater into some Noel Coward film. In a fog of excitement I ate and drank and chatted with the celebrities, and hadn't the slightest idea what I was eating or saying.

The only clear memory I have is of the aftermath of the luncheon, following the speeches congratulating the winners and the jokes by "America's toastmaster-general," George Jessel. Randolph Hearst, the son of America's archetypical press lord (and later known as Patty Hearst's father), stood up to make an unscheduled presentation. With a smile in my direction, he announced that the trustees of the Hearst Foundation had just voted to confer "surprise fellowships" on the two student prizewinners, "in the sum of five hundred dollars to Miss Harrington and one thousand dollars to Mr. Gage."

As we rose to accept our awards, I looked around the room at the trustees of the Hearst Foundation. I realized that they had probably taken pity on me after seeing the same threadbare suit draped on my undernourished 134-pound frame for three days.

"Now you'll be able to go to graduate school," Randolph Hearst said as he shook my hand.

"Yes, I will, sir," I mumbled. "I never expected anything like this."

Later that day, as my plane took off from La Guardia and circled Manhattan before heading northeast toward Worcester, the sun was sinking behind New Jersey. Its rays hit the skyscrapers and the streets of Manhattan below, so that for a moment they really did seem to be made of gold, just as my mother had told us back in the village. Whether such immigrant fairy tales are true or not, one day in New York had brought me two separate fortunes. Now I not only had enough to pay for Columbia next fall, I had a $1000 surplus! Two days before, I had been a student who couldn't pay his rent; now I was a capitalist who had to decide what to do with his extra money. But I knew the answer to that question the instant I received the second windfall. I would use the $1000 to go back to Greece.

The moment I heard Randolph Hearst announce my surprise fellowship, everything fell into place with a click, as if preordained. This summer after graduation I was free, because I didn't need to work. Then I would begin the year-long graduate program at Columbia and continue directly into my career. If I didn't take the opportunity now, there was no telling when I'd be able to do it. For a long time I had known that someday I had to go back to my village to learn the details of what happened to my mother after we escaped. If I waited any longer, many witnesses might disappear or die. Even my grandparents might die if I postponed my journey.

I realized it would be painful to learn my mother's fate, but I had left

Greece a boy of nine; now I was twenty-three and a man, and it was time to start asking questions. After all, everything good that had happened to me — our escape from the village, our voyage to America, even the essay for Miss Hurd that started me on the path to journalism — all these had been caused by my mother. I was becoming more and more convinced that the events of my life did not happen by chance, and these two unexpected awards were the latest evidence. The Hearst fellowship decided me that the time had come to return to our village.

At the Worcester Airport my father was waiting. I could see his green Plymouth in the parking lot as soon as we were low enough for buildings, houses, and then vehicles to pop up from the flat map below. When we were on the ground I spied him, wearing his best felt hat, waiting inside the small airport building. I walked across the tarmac, and when I got inside, he shook my hand gravely.

"Now you've seen the White House and the president and New York City and ridden in airplanes and sat at banquets with rich and famous men," he said. "Tell me all about it."

I told him, saving the best for the last. He drove out of the airport parking lot, the same place he had brought me to talk on the night after my day in court. He took the long winding road down toward the city. First I told him about the additional money from Columbia, and he smiled with pleasure.

"That means you won't have to worry and work so hard this summer," he said. "You can rest a little."

"I won't have to work at *all*," I said, and then I told him about the surprise fellowship from Hearst.

"A thousand dollars — as much as a workingman makes in months, and they give it to you for a surprise!" he marveled. "They must be very rich men! What are you going to do with all this money?"

I watched his profile as he drove.

"I'm going to use it to go back to Greece for the summer," I said.

He turned to look at me in alarm. "Why should you want to go back there?" he exclaimed. "There's nothing for you in Greece but painful memories. Your life is *here* now."

"I must go, *Patera*," I said. "It's this feeling that's been growing in me for years. I have to go back there to find out things."

"What things?" He was shouting now, and I could see fear as well as anger in his face. "Don't you remember that your mother told you never to return?" he demanded. "That her curse would be on you if you did?"

"I don't think so, Dad," I said. "This money falling into my lap, just at the right time in my life, when I can go — I think it was meant to be."

"Everyone makes his own life," Father replied grimly. "Sometimes we make the wrong decisions, the way I did. That's what we talked about the last time we came up here. You're a man now and that money is yours, so you have to decide what to do with it — I can't stop you. But I can advise you, and my advice is that you put Greece and everything that happened there behind you. Don't go back and open old wounds. You have a wonderful future waiting for you, but it's in this country."

"It's only for the summer!" I protested. "And I'll never have another chance like this one. If I don't go, I'll always regret it." I was trying to convince him of my resolution and win his approval. "I *have* to go, Dad," I said.

He didn't respond immediately, but when we reached the bottom of the hill and pulled up at the stop sign, he turned to look at me. "Yes," he said. "I can see that you do."

We drove the rest of the way home in silence. I was relieved that he wasn't going to forbid me or continue to argue, but I couldn't dismiss his warnings as easily as I pretended. In fact, I wasn't at all sure I really wanted to know the answers that were waiting for me in Greece, but I felt my mother had brought me to this point and I owed it to her to go back and ask the questions.

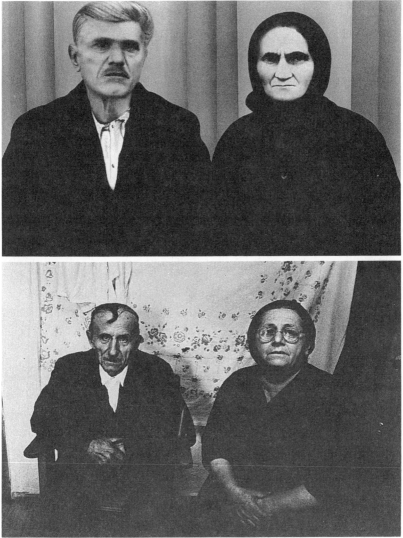

Top: Kitso and Megali. *Bottom:* Uncle Andreas and Aunt Nitsa.

RETURN
VOYAGE

Wherever I go, Greece wounds me.
— George Seferis,
In the Manner of G.S.

IT WAS EVEN HARDER to convince my sisters than my father of the wisdom of my returning to Greece. They were certain that I had come to America at such a young age and been so thoroughly assimilated that I was now a naive *Amerikanaki,* ready to be duped and victimized by the cunning Greeks.

"There are old ladies in the village who know all sorts of magic," warned my sisters, telling me their names. "They'll feed you a potion so that you'll fall in love with the first village girl you see and never return. Or, if they're Communists, they may even poison you! When you go to one of their houses, you must be careful never to eat or drink anything!"

"Even if you survive the magic of the village hags," admonished Olga, "you'll probably step on a guerrilla land mine and be blown to bits! They're buried all over the mountainside, you know. Just last summer a shepherd boy was out tending his flock . . ."

Their advice and warnings engulfed me, but in the end, when they heard my father defend my decision, mainly because he believed that the men of the family must support each other against the women, they realized that my trip was inevitable.

Father had his own barrage of advice. "When your grandfather and my ingrate brother Foto ask why I didn't come with you," he instructed, "you must tell them, 'My father fears that if he ever looks on your accursed faces, he'll fly into a rage and kill you, so he has decided not to return.' It's true, you know! I can never forgive either of them for abandoning my wife and children to the hands of the guerrillas, after all the years I sent money to those two scorpions."

He also warned me several times to be careful how I behaved with women. "In America, the girls are more free," he said. "In Greece, if you compromise a young woman . . . if you are even alone with her for very long, her father will feel you have dishonored her and take harsh action." Like my sisters, he seemed concerned that some village Aphrodite would ensnare me and I would be lost forever.

The final order he gave was that I must go every day to the village coffeehouse and treat all the patrons in his name. "I was always the big sport when I went back to the village — wasted maybe a thousand dollars every trip buying food and drink," he recalled with nostalgia, saying the phrase "big sport" in English. "They looked at me like a king and crowded around to hear my stories of America. I don't want them to think my son is less of a sport than his father, so you must show your generosity with a free hand."

On the day before I left, he gave me $50 of his own money to add to my assets. "And tell them these drinks are from Christos Gatzoyiannis," he reminded me.

My entertainment fund grew swiftly, because each of my sisters gave me $20 to help me make a good show and Jimmy Tzouras added another $50 with the instructions "Have a good time." But these gifts were only the beginning. I was showered with money that was meant not for me but for relatives of my relatives. In 1963 it was still fairly rare for an immigrant to return to Greece for a vacation. Only one or two of the Worcester Greeks would "go down" to the old country every summer. Therefore, the voyager must visit everyone else's relatives to carry them the good wishes of their kin in *xenitia* and to hand over a couple of dollars from that kinsman to show he still remembered the folks back home and was solvent.

I had to buy a separate wallet to hold all the singles and fivers entrusted to me for this purpose. In the wallet I kept a notebook with the names and addresses of the donors and recipients. These included farflung cousins and second cousins, all my brothers-in-law's relatives, and all my father's old cronies. When the small gifts were added up, my wallet of other people's money was stuffed with $714.

People also wanted me to take material gifts back to Greece, but I refused. The two suitcases I had borrowed from Kanta were already full with my own family's gifts: lengths of dress fabric for my grandmother and my Aunt Nitsa, a suit and shirts for my grandfather, more shirts and cartons of cigarettes for my uncle, *Barba* Foto (my father's older brother), and for Uncle Andreas, the husband of my Aunt Nitsa. I had bought myself a khaki summer suit to replace the old shiny blue one, as well as a whole new wardrobe of shoes, underwear, shirts, and casual pants. I paid $410 for a round-trip charter flight advertised in the *Hellenic Chronicle* that was to leave on June 10 and return September 2, just in time for graduate school.

My graduation from Boston University took place in June, but I was so distracted by my impending trip that the ceremony in the stadium at Nickerson Field was less exciting to me than to my four guests: my father, my two oldest nephews (whom I was trying to imbue with a taste for higher education), and Miss Hurd, my junior high English teacher.

After the ceremony, Miss Hurd took snapshots of me with my father and nephews and then stood beside me while Father took some more. Earlier he had told Miss Hurd the story of how my mother had been forced to leave school in third grade because village girls weren't allowed to associate with boys, but she had bribed a male cousin to repeat his lessons to her every day while she scratched letters in charcoal on a rock and thus had learned to read. Now Father took a picture of me standing next to my former teacher. As he handed the camera back to her, he said to me in Greek, "Think what it would have meant to your mother to be here today." He took off his glasses and polished them busily to hide his emotion.

To me, however, graduation was just an anticlimax, something I had to do before my odyssey back to the village. The entire clan came to see me off at Logan Airport on June 10, including the youngest nephews and nieces, who took a great interest in the airplanes. My sisters kissed me and cried and delivered more warnings and advice. When my flight was finally called, I kissed them all goodbye. Then I turned to my father, who had spent the entire drive from Worcester proudly describing what a success I'd be in the village. As he took my face between his hands and pulled my head down to kiss me, I was astonished to see his eyes also filled with tears. "My child," he said gruffly. His words suddenly brought back the sound of my mother's voice on the day we parted, and I felt a rush of fear that I wouldn't see him again, but it was too late to stop now. I walked across the tarmac to the plane, afraid to look back at him standing there.

Once inside the plane, I realized the passengers were nearly all Greeks. The prayers and cries of fear as we took off, the socializing and laughter in the aisles throughout the journey, and the applause, shouts of congratulation, and hands inscribing the sign of the cross when we landed reminded me of the differences between Greeks and Americans. Although we flew all night, no one slept, and the exuberance increased as we crossed the Gulf of Corinth toward Attica.

When the plane dipped toward the Athens airport with its small white Byzantine church and grazing flocks of sheep near the runways, I was struck by the vivid, unexpected colors, especially the sea, with its medley of blues, turquoises, and purples. The clay-red earth and roof tiles and the blazing white buildings dazzled me. After fourteen years of the dull grays and greens of Massachusetts, I had forgotten the colors of my native land.

When the plane landed and the passengers surged toward the door with typical Greek disregard for waiting one's turn, I saw that Athens' airport was hardly bigger than Worcester's. No one was there to meet me, because I had kept my visit a secret. I didn't want to be forced to stay in anyone's home, for the same reasons Kanta had insisted on a hotel room.

I collected my suitcases, passed through customs with my American passport, and hailed a taxi to take me into the city, an old rattletrap with woven rush seats and a driver who cheerfully whistled along to the cantatas on his radio while the worry beads, icons, and other protective charms hanging from the visor, swaying in the sultry wind through the open windows, chimed an accompaniment. As we passed rows of jerry-built five-story apartment buildings facing the seaside and approached the center of the capital, where dignified neoclassical mansions crumbled into the dusty streets among huge concrete apartment developments, I was astonished to see that Athens looked more like a midwestern town than the modern metropolis it had seemed fourteen years earlier. I was disappointed at how crowded and unlovely the city was, but when we came to the end of Singrou Street and I saw the Parthenon gleaming like white bones high above the city, I once again felt the awe that I remembered from my first sight of the Acropolis.

My hotel was the Amalia, right across from the walled park of the Royal Gardens, created by Amalia, the first Greek queen after the revolution, who used to wander among the trees, artificial ponds, peacocks, and rosebushes, weeping with homesickness for her native Germany. At the hotel I unpacked, took a shower, and asked the concierge how to get to Zonar's Restaurant, where two of my cousins worked as waiters. It was three blocks down the street, he told me, just past Constitution Square.

Everything I saw and heard in the streets fueled my excitement: the cries of the pretzel vendors, sponge peddlers, lottery sellers, and bootblacks; the old women in black kerchiefs and the smart Athenian matrons in Paris fashions. On my way, I paused only a moment to gawk at the towering guards in their white pleated skirts and pompommed shoes goosestepping back and forth in front of the Royal Palace, then I hurried on to the elegant restaurant and outdoor café where my cousin Yianni Gatzoyiannis worked. It was Yianni who had looked after us when we first came to Athens from the refugee camp in 1949. Yianni himself, handsome as a movie star, and his nineteen-year-old wife, Katie, the first woman we ever saw wearing lipstick, had been part of the wonders of the city, so cosmopolitan with their stylish clothes and polished manners.

Zonar's Restaurant was a meeting place for Athenians, where businessmen and intellectuals could argue over drinks and *pitas* and ladies of fashion could refresh themselves with elaborate ice cream concoctions after buying diamonds and gold jewelry at Zolotas across the street. I approached one of the waiters in his white jacket and black bow tie and asked for Yianni.

"What do you want him for?" he asked suspiciously, taking in my American clothes and village-accented Greek. I explained that I was a relative from America. This caused a ripple of excitement, and I was escorted into a back room, where the waiter telephoned Yianni at home.

My cousin insisted that I come to his house at once and told me how to take a bus from the center to his neighborhood of Kaisariani. It was an area heavily populated by refugees from Asia Minor who had fled the massacres launched by the Turks in 1922, arriving with little more than the clothes they wore. Now these streets were lined with grim stucco cubes of connected buildings, draped with swags of laundry and electric wires.

Yianni met me at the bus stop wearing American-style Bermuda shorts. He was as affable as ever, although a bit fatter. He led me to the two-room apartment where he lived with his wife and two children, across the hall from another two rooms that housed his wife's parents. Katie, who at nineteen had seemed a dangerous *femme fatale* in her lipstick, was now very pregnant with their third child, but she scurried about bringing food from the tiny kitchenette while Yianni pointed out all the improvements he had made in fourteen years. They had a toilet and a shower inside the house and no longer had to rely on the outhouse in the courtyard, he said proudly. They had even managed to acquire a telephone, and someday, he claimed, he was going to build a second floor on top of the present rooms to double the amount of living space.

I kept remembering how awestruck my sisters and I had been by Yianni's luxurious metropolitan residence on our first visit to Athens, when such novelties as telephones, toilets, and store mannequins had mystified and fascinated us. Now, despite the new conveniences, I couldn't help comparing the crowded two rooms to the way we lived in Worcester. Such luxuries as our car, television set, and big refrigerator made us seem like millionaires by Athenian standards.

The next day I visited the home of another relative, Foti Haidis, who was working as a trainee waiter at Zonar's. He lived with his wife and baby son in a crowded two-room home he had built on top of his father-in-law's small house in the section of Athens called Virona, for Lord Byron. Foti and I had been friends since childhood. He was about seven years older than I and had grown up in the other half of my grandparents' house in the village. His parents both died of tuberculosis when he was small, so his grandmother, Anastasia Haidis, raised him until the day in 1944 when she was murdered by the invading Germans, who set fire to our village and threw her into the flames of her burning house.

Finding himself all alone at twelve, Foti lived with a relative until the end of the occupation, then walked all the way across Greece to Lamia, where he had an aunt. He worked first as a tinker's apprentice and then on road gangs until he decided to walk down to Athens, a distance of 140 miles, to see if he could find work there. Athens was jammed with new arrivals like Foti, all fleeing their war-devastated villages, hoping to find jobs in the city. The boy nearly starved, sleeping wherever he could find a day's pay. Eventually he met the sixteen-year-old daughter of a baker and married her, and Yianni got him a job as a busboy at Zonar's. Every day as I ate in the restaurant and Foti hovered nearby, snatching moments to chat, I was reminded that my fate would have been exactly like his after the war if I hadn't had a father living in America.

In the ensuing days I visited relatives even more hard pressed than Foti. Some lived in shantytowns where they had bought tiny plots of land and erected illegal shacks of cinder blocks and corrugated tin, which were periodically knocked down by raiding police. My cousins simply rebuilt their shacks, hoping that one day the police might leave them standing. They were optimistic when I visited them because on the day I arrived in Greece — June 11, 1963 — the prime minister, Constantine Karamanlis, had resigned in a heated dispute with Queen Fredericka. Whenever new elections loomed, both parties tried to curry votes by promising to make all existing shantytowns legal if the inhabitants would vote for their candidate.

Despite the primitive conditions, every hovel I visited was immaculately clean. Tin cans planted with sweet basil and geraniums, embroidered doilies, and paper icons covered every surface. And when my relatives entertained me, they served me meals so huge that I knew the feast meant weeks of starvation after my visit. It was a point of honor to feed a guest far more than he could eat. Finally I began dropping in unannounced, so the mistress of the house couldn't spend the whole day cooking; but she still would run to the nearest butcher or wring the neck of the family hen and cook it for me.

I always came with boxes of Zonar's confections for the host, fifty-drachma notes for the children, and an American dollar or a hundred-drachma note for the old people, who were tucked into dark corners, grieving for their lost villages while their children worked in basements, factories, or restaurants and lived in slums. "I want to go home, I wish my bones were in the church of Panayia beside my father's, instead of rotting here in this cave," an old man mourned as I slipped a dollar bill into his yellowed hand. "Your father lives like a king in America and I'm left in a corner by my children like a piece of refuse."

Two days after my arrival I wrote a long letter to my father describing how much worse the conditions were than I had expected. I went to the post office on Voulis Street near Constitution Square to mail it, along with some postcards, and when I got back to my hotel I discovered that the wallet was missing from my pocket — the one with over $700 of other people's money in it.

The post office had already closed when I got back. I lay awake all night wondering how I could reimburse all those relatives; I'd have to give up graduate school and go to work. But when the post office's doors opened in the morning and I was shown into the manager's office, I learned that the wallet had been found and turned in by the janitor without a cent missing. All the post office manager wanted was a signed statement from me attesting to the honesty of the postal employees. I gave it gladly and demanded to meet the janitor, knowing that the wallet had held as much money as he would make in two years. He was brought in, wearing much-mended work clothes, and he refused my offer of a reward with dignity, saying, "I did nothing but what was right."

In the end I managed to slip a thousand-drachma note into his pocket and left the post office with a light heart and an improved perspective on Athens. The living conditions might be poor and the economy stricken, but the Greeks had many qualities Americans lacked, I realized. Like the janitor, they were scrupulously honest in their personal dealings. No matter how poor, they had an appreciation for life and a talent for enjoying themselves that a millionaire might envy. The relatives I visited went out every night, if only for a coffee at the neighborhood café. They teased each other, flirted, and argued with a playfulness that I quickly learned to imitate. Their hospitality could move me to tears. Greek men and women alike communicated better than Americans, with honest affection. I became used to seeing men kissing and hugging each other in greeting and teenaged children kissing their parents good-bye. I learned to catch and toss back the conversational jokes and barbs that filled every Greek conversation. I grew accustomed to staying up every night until long after midnight, savoring the banter, the political arguments and gossip. But after two weeks, I reminded myself that I hadn't come to Greece to spend pleasant summer evenings at Athenian cafés. It was time to go back to my village.

I flew from Athens to Corfu, taking a hotel room in the old Venetian-style city where my parents had stayed when my father saved my mother from a wasting disease by bringing her out of the mountains to the European-trained doctors. Her convalescence in Corfu had been the happiest time of her life, and the air, scented with the perfumes of the orange groves and the sea, still seemed to carry the memory of my parents riding in an old-fashioned landau to see the fabled beaches of Prospero's Isle.

I telegraphed my grandfather to meet me on the mainland the next day, and spent the morning visiting more cousins before boarding the ferryboat. Within two hours we were approaching the town of Igoumenitsa, built up like an amphitheater around the harbor. This was where my sisters and I had stayed for nine months after our escape, living in the corrugated tin huts of the refugee camp until our grandfather escorted us to Athens for our voyage to America. This was also where I had learned my mother's fate, when Grandfather returned from his journey to the village and described finding her body in a shallow mass grave.

While the boat was still at a distance from the harbor, I could make out the long road lined with plane trees where I had been walking when I got my first sight of the sea. Higher up the hill, the tin Quonset huts of the refugee camp still stood, now inhabited by soldiers. As the ferryboat neared the dock, I could finally make out the white-haired figure of my grandfather, looking just as he had on that final day in Piraeus, when the *Marine Carp* steamed away and he was the last person I saw, recognizable only by the way he waved his walking stick in farewell. Now it was as if he had been waiting for me for fourteen years, frozen in time.

As we docked, I saw that Grandfather had brought my father's brother Foto with him. My grandfather was eighty-three, and had worked as a millwright all his life. He was lean and tanned, with white hair and mustache and the muscular arms of an athlete. My Uncle Foto was eighty-one, a thinner, nearly toothless version of my father: completely bald, with a round face and glasses, but he moved with the strong stride of a mountain dweller accustomed to walking long distances in high altitudes.

My grandfather scrutinized me for a moment, then announced, "You left a child, and now look at you!"

I had always feared my grandfather, with his terrifying temper, cold silences, and unsettling glare. Both his wife and his two daughters — my mother and my Aunt Nitsa — had often felt his blows, although he had never hit me; the roar of his voice was enough to frighten me into obedience. In the village, Kitso Haidis was known as a tightwad, a vengeful enemy, and a compulsive philanderer, but he was even better known for his shrewdness, his miraculous skill at building and repairing mills, and the quick mind which made him one of the most respected men in the Mourgana mountains.

Until I sailed to America, my grandfather was the only male relative who influenced me. Now I saw that we looked very much alike, with the same lean, angular features, deep-set eyes under heavy brows, and abundant hair. My father and Foto and my sisters Olga and Glykeria all had the softer, rounder features and physiques of the Gatzoyiannis clan. But I had the Haidis features of my mother and her father. I wondered how much of my grandfather's nature was in me and how much of me resembled my father, who was in every way his opposite.

As Grandfather stared at me, perhaps wondering the same thing, Uncle Foto asked, "Did you recognize us?"

"Of course he did, idiot!" snapped my grandfather. "He wasn't a baby when he left!"

"Nine years old is a baby," Foto replied, smiling. "But in America he has become a man. The only trouble is, he looks just like you!"

"You'd rather he grew up bald and toothless like you?" retorted my grandfather.

"I may be bald and toothless, but I can still shoot out a quail's eye at a hundred meters and climb up to Prophet Elias while you're still struggling past Siouli's spring," teased Foto. It comforted me to hear them going at each other with the same competitive insults they had always used.

We hired a taxi to take us to Filiates, the town at the foot of the mountains where we would spend the night. During the bumpy half-hour ride, while the two old men bickered and quizzed me about everyone back in the States, I could feel my grandfather's eyes on me appraisingly. He hadn't yet passed judgment, but would reserve his opinion until I had been tested. It annoyed me that I cared so much about winning his approval. I had been free of his tyranny for so long, but now I found myself trying to sound clever and worldly so he would not think me a foolish *Amerikanaki*.

Glykeria had arranged for us to stay the night in her father-in-law's home in Filiates. Prokopi's father, a civil servant, had a large Turkish-style house surrounded by a wall enclosing a pleasant garden and a separate kitchen, where the women of the household — Prokopi's married sister as well as his mother — labored to cook us a feast in the beehive-shaped ovens.

I set about purchasing the sweets, pastries, Turkish delight, and staples like salt, sugar, butter, meat, and bread that my sisters had told me to take to Lia. That night I slept in one of the cool stone-walled rooms of the Turkish house and dreamed that I was back in the village, a boy again, setting traps for birds with my Uncle Andreas.

My grandfather had always scorned Andreas, the soft-spoken, self-effacing husband of Aunt Nitsa, because he was only a poor cobbler with almost no customers and no money. My eccentric aunt dominated him, never letting him interrupt her harangues, but he had been the kindest man I knew in my childhood. It was Andreas who taught me to make and shoot a slingshot, to set traps for birds and animals, to play checkers on a tree stump. He was the one who consoled me after the news of my mother's death by sitting silently nearby. When I left for America, Andreas was the one I most regretted leaving, except perhaps for my frail grandmother, who had also been one of my protectors.

In my dream I heard Andreas' voice telling me how to set the traps for the birds, and when I woke, blinking in the morning sun, I realized that I really had heard Andreas' voice speaking. He had sneaked out of the village before dawn to descend the mountain and welcome me. He also seemed unchanged by the years; he was still wearing his grimy shepherd's cap and had a hand-rolled cigarette tucked behind his ear, with one large curl combed from the sides and plastered over his forehead in a vain attempt to hide his baldness. He embraced me as shyly as ever and scarcely said a word beyond "You've come back."

We hired a taxi in Filiates to drive us toward Lia. When I had left the village, there had been no road beyond Aghies Pantes, but now the dirt ribbon twined back and forth up the cliffs between boulders and scrub pine, around cypresses and ruined chapels, all the way to Lia and Babouri, hidden above the clouds.

As the bone-jarring road climbed, every time a village came into view I was sure it was Lia. The road had changed everything and nothing looked familiar, although I once had known every stone of these mountains by heart. "That's it!" I'd cry, and my grandfather would snort with laughter and reply no, that was Povla or Tsamanta. I should show a little patience, he said. We'd get there soon enough. As the taxi climbed higher and my ears popped in the thin altitude, I realized that the memory I had considered flawless was now badly corroded by time. If I couldn't recognize my own village, I wondered, how would I retrieve all the details of the years when my mother was alive?

When we finally entered Lia, my grandparents' house was the first one we reached. The road had reorganized everything in the village — it passed just above the roof of the Haidis house, bisecting the vertical footpath, originally the main thoroughfare, that wound up past the house's courtyard and the spring just outside the gate.

My father, climbing that footpath toward the Church of Saint Demetrios in 1924, had looked into the Haidis garden and seen a seventeen-year-old girl with wheat-colored hair tilling the soil and had immediately decided to marry her. But now the taxi stopped on the road above the house, and I was looking down into the courtyard. My grandmother and aunt had hurried outside at the first sound of the taxi, and were staring up at me. Because the mountainside was so steep, I had to pick my way down to the door of the house, stepping from rock to rock. My grandfather, *Barba* Foto, and Andreas carried down my luggage and the many parcels of food from Filiates.

"Take that stuff inside before the neighbors see it," snapped Aunt Nitsa without any words of welcome, then she turned to look me over. "Took you long enough to come back to us, didn't it?" she grumped. "Let's go inside and see what you brought."

I expected my grandmother to burst into tears at the sight of me, for I had always been her favorite, but the tiny, shriveled old woman only stood with her hands clasped beneath her apron and stared at me in bewilderment. My grandfather had warned me on the way that her mind was beginning to fail.

"Is that him? It doesn't look like him!" my grandmother asked no one in particular.

"It's him! It's him!" Nitsa muttered. "Now come inside."

The Haidis house, where we had lived with my grandparents after the guerrillas threw us out of our own house up in the Perivoli, was just as I remembered it: two rooms on either side of a tiny hall, each with its own fireplace. The outhouse was in one corner of the walled courtyard, the goats were in the basement, and the only source of water was the mountain spring outside the gate. I could see that my relatives had hastily whitewashed the walls, no doubt to clean them for my arrival, but the job had been sloppily done, with white paint splashed on the windows and the green ceiling.

My grandfather proudly pointed out two cots he had acquired for the "upper chamber" — the good room reserved for guests. He and my grandmother, whom everyone called Megali, "the old one," still slept on pallets beside the fireplace in the other room, but now I would have a bed and even a set of springs that he had bought in Filiates and covered with a straw mattress. At his insistence I sat down on the mattress, for there was no other furniture except for the low table or *soufra* at which they ate, crouching on their haunches, and the *cassella* against one wall piled high with the blankets of my grandmother's dowry. The others sat on the floor and studied me, except for Andreas, who stood in a corner, as if not daring to take up too much space.

Nitsa immediately collected all the sweets, pastries, and foodstuffs I had brought and said she would store them in the pantry, a small nook at the back of the house. "And I'll just pack up a few things to take home with me," she said.

"I'm sure you will, but will you leave anything for us?" growled my grandfather. "She's fifty-nine and her husband's sixty-four and they're still eating my food," he complained to me, lighting a cigarette and not offering one to Andreas.

"Why don't Andreas and Nitsa live here with you?" I asked, thinking of the wretched hut they had at the opposite end of the village. "Then they could help you and Megali."

"Help us? Eat us out of house and home, you mean!" he shouted. "They're here far too much anyway."

It was the same old hostility I remembered: Nitsa complaining while my grandfather sniped at her. His oldest daughter, with her laziness and poverty, was a continual disappointment to him.

I passed out the gifts — the clothing and lengths of dress fabric and the dollars that my sisters had sent for all of them. My sisters had given me additional money to hand to Andreas and Megali in secret, for they knew that both Grandfather and Nitsa would immediately confiscate anything their spouses had. When I handed some dollar bills to my grandmother, I leaned over and kissed her on the forehead, and she looked helplessly at her husband. "Are you sure that's him?" she quavered. "I don't remember him."

Later, as I sat on the bed answering questions about my family, I was startled when my grandmother rose to her feet, silently walked over, and kissed my brow. "*Idia Eleni* [just like Eleni]," she said. The words and the sudden recognition in her eyes brought tears to mine.

Aunt Nitsa took the money I handed her, blessing me profusely and my sisters as well. "If it weren't for you, I'd be dead long ago," she said, glaring at my grandfather. "I remember in the summer of 1955, Andreas and I hadn't eaten for two days, and I wasn't speaking to your grandfather, as usual — the skinflint! I decided to go up to the ravine and throw myself off, but as I passed the *cafenion* they told me there was a letter from the United States. Glykeria had sent two dollars and you had put in five, so I went and bought meat and made soup and it saved our lives."

"Yes, you barely have enough to survive, that's why you're just skin and bones," retorted my grandfather, indicating Nitsa's rotund body. She pretended she hadn't heard him.

"What can I get you?" she asked. "Megali's too far gone to cook anymore. Would you like some coffee or some *raki*?"

"No, just cold water," I said with sudden longing. "But I want it from *matsala*, and I want to get it myself."

I went through the courtyard, out the huge wooden gate with the massive handles clamped in the teeth of iron lions' heads. As I had done a thousand times before, I knelt where the icy water bubbled out of a cleft in the rock, raised my cupped hands to my mouth, and suddenly I was a boy again. As I swallowed the water I was transported back to a moment during the war when I was drinking at the same spot and a mortar shell struck a few hundred yards up the mountain, showering me with stones and debris. I could hear my mother screaming from the doorway of the house, certain I had been killed.

The sound of a footstep behind me made me jump. I turned around to see Andreas, silently following me as he had in the old days. I stood up and tucked into his pocket the secret cache of money I had for him, knowing he would use it to buy bottles of *raki* at the coffeehouse to drink during the long days he sat high up the mountainside watching the sheep. He smiled and said with a conspiratorial wink, "You were always a devil."

Later, when I discreetly handed my grandmother her secret money from my sisters, she turned it over to my grandfather as soon as he appeared, having lost the little guile she once had. It made me sad to think that she no longer would have a hidden trove of ground coffee, her one luxury, to enjoy when her miserly husband was out of the house.

After I went back inside, Nitsa insisted that we all lie down for a siesta. Her own had been interrupted and she was getting sleepy.

"I'm not tired, I want to go up to the Perivoli and look at my house," I replied.

Immediately Nitsa began squawking. "People will see you! It's the siesta hour, after all! Why would you want to go up there anyway? It's all in ruins."

She made such a fuss, with Andreas and my grandfather chiming in, that I decided to wait. I lay on the new mattress until I could hear them all breathing evenly, my grandparents on their pallets in the other room, then I tiptoed out into the afternoon sunshine, gently closing the door with its latch and wooden bolt.

The footpath that climbed past the Haidis gate continued straight up toward our neighborhood after the interruption of the new road. I knew every inch of this path, even in the dark, because I had always climbed it barefoot. Above my grandparents' house there was a rocky stretch where you had to place your feet just so, almost like climbing a ladder. In the spring and fall it was carpeted with yellow crocuses and purple grape hyacinths, but now it was covered with wild chamomile and clouds of drowsy bees. A little higher the path curved toward the right, past a hayshed where I first learned about sex while exploring during the siesta hours, when I came upon a newlywed couple snatching a private moment of love in the shed away from the many relatives who slept in the same room of their house.

The road jogged back toward the left, and soon, beneath the spires of ancient cypress trees, I saw St. Demetrios, the neighborhood church where my mother had stopped to pray every day and where her bones now lay in the ossuary. In the cool purple shade beneath the cypresses was a tiny graveyard, each plot neatly enclosed by an iron fence and containing a corpse that would be unearthed and moved to the ossuary after three years so that a new body could take up residence. The reddish clay tiles of the church's roof peaked above a niche that held the ancient icon of St. Demetrios slaying a snakelike dragon, the painted colors as vivid as they had been hundreds of years before. I tried the door of the church but found it locked. There was a padlock as well on the metal door of the square ossuary, and I saw no sign of a caretaker who might have the key, so I continued up the path toward my house.

The next curve in the road brought me to the yard of the Makos property, the spot where I had said goodbye to my mother before she descended into the ravine behind a file of village women being led by the guerrillas to work in the threshing fields. As I had watched, she had disappeared into the vegetation of the valley far below, then reappeared, a tiny dot climbing the distant mountainside toward the chapel of the Prophet Elias, where the road wound out of sight. That had been a bright summer afternoon like this one. She had turned around, a tiny brown-and-black figure, just before disappearing from my sight, and raised her hand to me in a gesture of farewell. Now the heaviness of the heat and the drone of the cicadas pressed like a weight on my shoulders as I squinted toward the distant mountainside, and it seemed as if I could still make out her figure on the path, her hand raised in that final salute.

I turned my back to the ravine as the path took me again to the left and up toward our house. Our field was terraced into three levels below the house. As I approached the bottom level and looked up, I heard a scratching noise and saw a black shape moving among neat rows of beanstalks. At first I thought it was a goat or a sheep, but then it straightened up into the figure of a woman, her black kerchief draped around her face, dusting her hands on her black homespun skirt.

She looked straight into my eyes with her blue eyes and my heart contracted — it was my mother, waiting for me in our garden! Then she spoke and my mother's features blurred, finally resolving themselves into the face of Vangelina Dimitriou, a neighbor.

"But who are you?" she cried, rubbing her hands on her apron. "Not the son of Eleni! They told me you were coming back! Your grandfather gave me permission to plant here, you know. It seemed such a shame to let the land lie fallow. Of course no one would plant up by the house — they buried so many prisoners there. But I wanted to put in some rows of beans, tomatoes, and cucumbers. I hope you don't mind."

"Of course not, *Thia*," I said, still trembling from the shock of seeing my mother waiting for me in our garden. "You plant anywhere you want. I just came up to look at the house."

"What's there to see?" she asked, gesturing upward. "There's nothing left but the souls of the dead searching for peace. It's all changed, ruined! But go and look for yourself."

I continued up the path toward the wall-enclosed compound and the gate, still intact but hanging ajar. Many flat stones had fallen from the top of the wall where I had sometimes lain as a child, sunning myself.

Just inside the gate I found a stone structure built by the soldiers, a sentry hut, perhaps, or a storehouse. The windows of our house were still barred as they had always been, but the glass was gone. I went up to the front door, but it was locked and chained, so I just peered into the windows toward the kitchen, where we used to sleep in a row on the floor, and the main *kamera,* which had once held the iron bed reserved for my father's visits, the gramophone he brought, and the family iconostasis, where my mother crossed herself every morning and evening. The empty kitchen brought a quick image to my mind: my mother rhythmically churning the goats' milk to make butter while I lurked nearby, waiting for the foamy whey to rise to the top, because I loved to eat it with bread. But now all was silent; there was nothing but dust and the occasional swift movement of a lizard among the cracks in the stones. The kitchen wall built against the side of the mountain was damp and thick with moss.

Discouraged because I had been expecting to see more, although I didn't know what, I walked downhill to the side where there was an entrance to the basement. This had been the quarters of the sheep and the goats, dug into the slope of the mountain. It was a low-ceilinged, cavelike room with tiny barred windows high up, and when the guerrillas had taken over our house as their headquarters, they had made the basement their prison.

Here in her own cellar my mother had been kept, crowded in with dozens of other prisoners, until she was led with the rest of the condemned up to the ravine to her death. Here she was taken from the prison to be interrogated and tortured in the rooms above and then thrown back, unable to stand. I had been told that at least one of the prisoners, a young woman from the village of Mavronoron, tried to kill herself to escape the horror of the basement prison, stabbing herself in the stomach with a large nail she found protruding from a beam. But she didn't die of the wound, and was left to plead for water until she was taken out and shot.

As I approached the entrance to the dark basement, I could see the wooden door was ajar. In the white-hot afternoon sun I felt a claustrophobic fear of what was inside, but an equally strong force was pulling me into its depths. I couldn't stop walking toward the open door.

"What are you doing here?"

I spun around and saw it was Andreas, out of breath from hurrying up the mountain behind me. "Couldn't you wait?" he continued. "You had to come up here alone! Well, now you've seen it. Come back down with me. Your aunt and your grandmother are frantic."

I turned away from the dark basement, secretly relieved that he had stopped me from going in. I matched my steps to his as we descended the path, past Vangelina Dimitriou, who paused in her hoeing to study my face intently. To hide my emotion, I asked Andreas about the houses we passed, which all seemed shuttered and empty. He told me of former neighbors who had gone to Germany or Athens in search of jobs, or who had never returned from Hungary or Rumania after the war.

When we got to the Church of St. Demetrios we stopped, and he said, "Wait here." Soon he returned with the keys to the ossuary. I had been inside it many times as a child, when my mother had stopped to pray before the bones of her mother-in-law. Then, the rows of skulls and crude boxes full of bones had held no terrors for me. But now my mother lay in that same room.

Andreas unlocked the padlock and the iron door swung noisily open. Right in front of me was a small wooden box not three feet long standing on four legs, with a rounded lid like a coffin surmounted by a simple metal cross. Behind it on the wall, an icon of Christ, his body covered in hammered silver, raised his hand in blessing over the box, which my grandfather had fashioned to hold the remains of both my mother and her sister-in-law Alexo, Foto's wife. Hand-lettered in white paint on the side of the box were the words "Eleni C. Gatzoyiannis, 41 years, and Alexandra F. Gatzoyiannis, 56 years, murdered 28 August 1948 by Communist gangsters."

There was a small ornate oil lamp hanging from the cross, but it wasn't burning. "I came by here yesterday and lit the lamp," Andreas told me as he handed me a box of matches. "But every time someone opens the door, the draft blows it out." He left me alone and went outside to smoke a cigarette among the graves beneath the cypresses.

Inside the ossuary I lit the wick of the oil lamp, but there in that dank, musty storehouse of the dead I found it hard to believe that the small wooden box held any part of my mother. She seemed to be outside in the sunlight, pausing for a momentary prayer to Saint Demetrios, then hurrying up toward our fields leading our donkey, Merjo, or down the path carrying fresh-baked pita to my grandmother. As I stared at the burning lamp I wondered why all my memories were so rich and pleasant, when my childhood had been a decade of war and starvation. I realized that it was because my mother's love had wrapped me in an armor of security. Once she died, nothing ever seemed secure anymore, even our good life in Worcester. The great fissure in my life that opened when we were separated for the last time — me fleeing toward freedom and my mother being led toward her death — was a chasm that had grown until I wouldn't let myself become so attached to anyone or anything again, because I feared it would be suddenly taken away.

When Andreas and I finally descended to my grandfather's house, Nitsa and Megali were waiting. Nitsa immediately launched into a diatribe. "You couldn't wait, could you? You had to go up for yourself," she screeched. "Why go looking for pain? It'll find you soon enough. Wherever you go in this village, you should have someone with you. You don't know what these people are capable of!"

"All right, I'll go up again tomorrow and this time I'll take you with me," I said, trying to shut her up.

But Nitsa crossed her arms and shook her head stubbornly. "You can't expect me to climb up to the Perivoli anymore. It's too steep for me. I can barely make it over *here* on the flat road from my house."

"Well then, we'll go as far as St. Demetrios and make sure the lamp is still lit," I said placatingly.

"Even St. Demetrios is too far!" she complained. "My climbing days are over, now that I suffer this constant torture in my hips."

A suspicion took root in me. "When was the last time you climbed up to the Perivoli?" I asked.

"Last Easter, when Olga Venetis came back from Athens and I went up to welcome her," she answered.

"You mean you'll climb the mountain to visit strangers, but you won't go up there to light a candle for your own sister?" I shouted.

"What's the point?" Nitsa snapped. "I send Andreas to light the lamp every day when he passes with the goats. What good will lighting a candle do, anyway? I can't bring Eleni back by lighting a candle. Neither can you!"

I decided to drop the subject, but it upset me to realize that to my aunt and uncle and my grandparents, my mother's death was long past, while to me it was still a fresh wound. They had learned to live with the fact of Eleni's murder and go on with their lives, while I felt that her fate was too perverse ever to be accepted. I had to explore it and confront every detail of her suffering and death before I could go on with my own life. It enraged me to see the way my relatives calmly chose to put it in the past.

The news of my arrival had reached every corner of the village, and no sooner was the siesta hour over than villagers began arriving to get a look at Eleni's son. Nitsa grudgingly brought out trays of the sweets I had bought, ungraciously snatching them from the guests before they could take more than one, while Andreas hurried about making coffee and pouring shot glasses of *raki* for each newcomer.

"Where are the good pastries, the ones wrapped in gold paper?" I asked as Nitsa placed a few hard candies on a dish.

"You start serving those and we'll have every beggar in the village over here," she said with a sniff.

Soon the two rooms of my grandparents' house were filled to overflowing. Each time more arrivals knocked, earlier visitors were forced to leave. The old village women all remarked in wonder on my resemblance to my mother. They sat on the floor around me, and like storytellers recounting a myth or fairy tale, they told me of the last times they had seen her.

I learned that on the day after our escape, my mother and Aunt Alexo were arrested in the threshing fields, brought back to the village, and imprisoned in the guerrilla headquarters. But after eight days they were released, with orders that they were to speak to no one, especially each other. They were allowed to wander about at liberty until, a month later, the guerrillas came and arrested them again. After that came the trial and the executions. I gathered from what the women told me that the guerrilla leaders expected my mother and aunt to lead them to the other conspirators or to serve as bait for a rescue attempt by their relatives on the other side, but when this didn't work, they decided on more direct means of getting information about the escape plot.

Each old woman who visited me that night had memories of my mother in her blue dress wandering the mountainside like a lost soul while everyone feared to speak to her. One neighbor saw her sitting in the doorway, weeping and holding the brown bookbag filled with my small treasures I had left behind at the last moment. Another woman, one of our closest neighbors, told with shame how, when she saw Eleni ascending the path carrying a sack of beans from our garden as a gift, she whispered to her to toss it over the wall into the courtyard; she didn't want to be seen taking anything from the hands of the *Amerikana*.

One of the few people who had dared to speak to my mother during her brief period of freedom was Olga Venetis, a very tall woman who lived in the house just above ours in the Perivoli. "I went down to our field one day below the Haidis house and I saw your mother far below, carrying kindling on her back, coming up the path," she told me as the light from the fire played on the sharp, strong features beneath her black *mantilli*. "When we were close enough to talk, Eleni said, 'Come by the house, Olga, but stick to the back gardens so no one will see you.' When I got here, she pulled me inside and kissed me. She said, 'They watch me at night — every morning I find a pile of cigarette butts outside the gate — but today I've been as far down as the monastery of St. Athanassios and I saw no one. I could have just kept going and reached the other side.' I asked her, 'Why in God's name didn't you?' and she told me she couldn't leave with Glykeria still in the threshing fields, because they'd kill the girl. She was quiet, thinking, then she said, 'It's so hard, Olga! The other night I had a dream and saw my little Fotini, her hair all unbraided and knotted, and my Nikolaki, and he was calling for me.' Then she started to cry and said, 'Olga, bring me Dimitri once so that I can hold him for a little. He looks so much like Nikola.' The next day I did. I brought my son, and she held him and wept. She had such a weakness for you! Then, when August began and the fast for the Virgin, they came to the house and took her back into the prison."

I questioned Olga about the trial of my mother and the six other villagers. She said she had been there the first day, when the entire village was summoned to the central square to watch the people's justice in action, but the proceedings had been disrupted by mortar fire from the nationalist encampments in the distant foothills. The judges were forced to run for their lives, and they moved the trial far up the mountain to the *Vrisi*, a high plateau used for festivals, where overhanging cliffs gave protection.

"But by then I was too frightened to go," Olga told me, "because the main judge, a man with a voice like Death himself, told me, 'Your name is written in red ink,' and I thought that meant they would arrest me next."

"But I need to know about the trial," I insisted. "Who spoke against my mother? What were the charges? Who were the judges?"

"You should go ask Athena Charamopoulos about that," replied Olga. "She was there for the whole three days."

"When you saw *Mana* at the beginning of the trial, did she look like they had hurt her?" I asked, barely able to finish the question because my mouth was so dry. Finding out what my mother had suffered before her execution was what I dreaded most in coming to Greece. In my memory she was always beautiful, her golden braids hidden by her kerchief, her dress and apron immaculate, her face serene. I didn't want this image permanently destroyed by the revelation of beatings and torture, bruises, blood, screams of agony and cries for mercy. I wanted to remember my mother as strong and perfect as she had been when I had seen her last, and I recoiled from the fear of learning some different, terrible truth about her suffering. God knows I had imagined many horrors, but no witness had yet turned these nightmares into facts. Yet I had to learn all that she had endured, because she had done it to save me.

"No, it wasn't until *after* the trial that they really started to beat your mother badly," chimed in Vasiliki Petsis, a wrinkled old woman with an innocent, round face who lived near my grandparents' home. "I remember when they brought Eleni down the mountain on a mule and made her show them where she had hidden Olga's dowry. I didn't even recognize her at first, she was so badly beaten."

"Hush, woman. Leave it!" interrupted Nitsa. "What's the good of going over it all again? Why upset the child?"

The old woman lapsed into silence.

I didn't say anything, for I was horrified by what I'd heard already, and the heat in the overcrowded room was making me feel sick. But I resolved to go find Athena Charamopoulos, and to talk to Vasiliki Petsis later, when I could question her without an audience.

All that night people came and went, gobbling the pastries I had brought and exclaiming over how I resembled my mother. Several old women took me aside as they prepared to leave and inquired with friendly concern if I had fulfilled my military obligations in the United States. I told them all the truth — that I had an educational deferment until I finished graduate school.

When the last visitor was gone and my Aunt Nitsa was sulking over the depleted store of sweets, I asked her why there was such interest in my military record.

"The old hags know that if you haven't served your time in the American army, then the Greek army can conscript you while you're here," she said, pressing a forefinger to the side of her temple. "They're asking so that they can inform on you."

With a shiver I said, "But what would they get out of it? Would they be paid for the information?"

"No," replied Nitsa, chuckling. "They just like the feeling of power it gives them. They may not even inform on you, they just like knowing they can. You've forgotten how people are here. They still resent us because we were the prosperous family — your father and your grandfather. The guerrillas beat your mother because everyone said she had hidden a treasure of gold sovereigns, but what they dug up, after they beat her into confessing, was nothing but a pot full of rotted blankets and rugs — Olga's precious dowry! The water had seeped in until it was all moldy, but the guerrillas still spread it all out on the ground and called the villagers, shouting, 'See what wealth the fascist traitor has hidden!' And there it was, all rotting and green with mold!"

I felt exhausted from the evening's revelations, although I knew I had to keep asking questions if I was ever to discover how my mother died and who was guilty of her murder. But I had already learned more than I could stand that night, and my dreams, when I finally slept, were full of faceless monsters and shapeless things covered with rot, all of them waiting for me in the basement of our ruined home.

18

Nick dancing with Uncle Foto at the village festival, July 20, 1963

STALKING
THE PAST

On these mountains memory burns.

— Odysseus Elytis, *Axion Esti*

THE NEXT MORNING, my grandfather took me to the village coffeehouse on the central square near the giant plane tree. It was a small tavern run by a man named Yiorgios Venetis. Tables spilled into the square and a spit stood nearby, ready to roast chickens and goats' entrails for the plates of *mezedakia*, including tidbits of olives, cheese, and tomatoes, served with the drinks.

When we arrived the tables were filled with village men talking, drinking, playing cards, passing around the most recent newspaper, and waiting to see the son of Christos Gatzoyiannis. At our appearance the laughter and joking faded to a silence broken only by the clicking of multiple strings of worry beads.

Pointing his walking stick with authority, my grandfather selected an empty table. In a gesture borrowed from my father, I summoned the proprietor and announced, "Treat the house!" The bill that eventually arrived, scribbled on a scrap of brown paper, added up to less than a dollar, so I promptly ordered another round, determined to do my father's reputation proud.

Soon we were joined by two leathery old men, eager to test our skill at the game of choice in Lia, *kseri*. I looked around at the interested observers and again was astonished by how few faces I recognized. It bothered me that I didn't know which were friends and which were enemies — who had spoken against my mother and who had taken pity on her.

Like poker, *kseri* requires skill at bluffing and recalling which cards have been played. The stakes were no more than the price of the drinks we consumed during the game, but my grandfather's reputation as a cardsharp was also at risk. As soon as I shuffled the cards with the waterfall effect my father had taught me, I saw that our audience was impressed, and my grandfather began to preen.

As partners, we soon discovered we had an uncanny ability to bluff in tandem and to lay traps for our opponents. After a few winning games of *kseri* against different pairs of men, it was clear that I had succeeded in burnishing my father's and grandfather's reputations. Setting down the deck, I called again to the owner, "Treat the house, Yiorgio, and bring some more *mezedakia*, in the name of Christos Gatzoyiannis." I looked at my grandfather. "And Kitso Haidis," I added, and he beamed. Although my grandfather was a relentless miser to his family, he was obsessed with putting on an impressive show of hospitality to outsiders. The feasts he offered to those who came to pay their respects on his name day were legendary.

Besides endless rounds of *kseri,* the primary leisure entertainment for the men of the village was the display of competitive conversational wit. The itinerant tinkers, cobblers, and coopers of Lia spent long working journeys on the road, for six months to a year at a time, going from house to house to solicit business, sleeping on the ground at night. When they returned, during their well-deserved period of rest and recreation before setting out on another odyssey, they gathered daily in the coffeehouse to regale their compeers with tales of gossip overheard, women seduced, murders committed, family feuds begun, Olympian hardships and natural disasters endured — stories that improved in the telling. In a thousand coffeehouses like this one under a thousand plane trees throughout Greece, the tradition of Socrates and his symposium was kept alive.

My grandfather was the acknowledged sage of Lia, and his cleverness coupled with his prestige as a millwright was the reason he had been continuously re-elected to the post of village president before the war. As I sat watching him in the *cafenion,* I noticed that his technique was to listen while the others spoke, interjecting ironic comments now and then to indicate his amusement at the stupidity of the speaker. Then, when everyone had said his piece, he would stun the group with a verbal *coup d'esprit.* Many of his village cronies were so dull-witted, however, that they didn't realize they were being ridiculed, and it decreased my grandfather's enjoyment if he had no one there to appreciate his cleverness. This was my function.

Politics, hunting, border disputes, feuds, sports, and of course sex — these were the traditional topics. On the first afternoon of my visit, the subject for debate was what it takes to achieve success with women. Several listeners pulled their rush-seated wooden chairs over to our table to contribute their opinions, while my grandfather listened with a look of amused disdain.

"Money is what you need!" averred a tinker in his forties, his face and hands patterned with scars from stray bits of burning solder. "If you spend enough money on a woman, she's sure to give in. I remember this woman in Larissa —"

"Not the *good* women — they can't be bought!" interrupted a cooper. "But *any* woman can be won with praise. Tell her how beautiful she is if she's plain, or how intelligent she is if she's beautiful. Say she moves through the wheatfields like the summer breezes . . . women will believe anything! Pretty words, my friends, not drachmas, will storm the barricades of a woman's chastity!"

"All women aren't that vain and stupid!" disagreed another man. "The whole secret is just to be persistent and make them feel needed. If a woman believes you need her, that you'll die without her, and if you keep returning to the fray, even though she begins by saying no, in the end she'll say yes!"

Thus it went, with each man proposing his own theory about the secret of success with women. When they were all done, my grandfather leaned back in his chair, turned the full force of his frown on each man in turn, and announced, "You're all wrong! No wonder none of you could seduce a twenty-drachma hooker in a Piraeus bar!"

"Then tell us, *Barba* Kitso," they chorused. "What's the true secret?"

They asked eagerly, for everyone in the village knew that my grandfather had been a famous womanizer well into his seventies and perhaps later, yet unlike other men he had never been caught by an outraged husband or father. Rumors surrounded him like a seductive aura, but the women of the village kept their secrets and so did my grandfather. (More than once, however, my grandmother had gone after him with a fireplace poker on the basis of rumors that reached her ears.)

"The one quality you need to succeed with women, whether they be young or old, ugly or beautiful," my grandfather announced as we all leaned forward, "is the ability to recognize those who want it."

He settled back in his chair, smiling in satisfaction as the rest of the men sat stunned by the brilliance of this observation. That was of course what had made my grandfather such a successful philanderer over the years — he recognized the ones who wanted it. His mill lay in a ravine at the bottom of the village, by a waterfall. The village women would harvest their wheat, load it in sacks onto a mule, and carry it down to the mill to be ground into flour. My grandfather watched as they came, noticing which women allowed a hand to graze his as they unloaded the sacks together, which ones went over to the stream and splashed cold water on their faces, revealing a bit more throat than was necessary. "Why don't you come back later?" he'd say to such a woman. "I'm too busy right now, but I'll grind your wheat at noon, when I'm finished with the rest." And when she returned to the deserted mill, he would grind more than her wheat.

Village women in Lia and Barbouri had husbands who were gone for half a year or more at a time, so it was no wonder that many of his customers were attracted to my grandfather's muscular body, chiseled face, and intense blue eyes. Furthermore, he had that one essential for success: he could recognize the ones who wanted it.

As I admired my grandfather's cleverness that day in the coffeehouse, I couldn't help contrasting him once again with my father, who was naive and innocent, easily duped by those around him. My father was impulsive in his anger but quick to forgive, while my grandfather never got in a fistfight but would nurse his anger for months, eventually taking his revenge. He had a habit of rendering judgment on villagers who he felt had wronged him, casting himself as judge and jury. He might decide that the village storekeeper had cheated him and announce with cold anger in front of the customers, "You overcharged me two drachmas for the sugar I bought yesterday. I went home and weighed it myself. Therefore, I will not buy anything from this store for the next six months." And he would carry out his sentence to the day. This well-known behavior guaranteed that my grandfather always got the sweetest and softest *loukoumi,* the tenderest cuts of meat, and just a little extra sugar every time he made a purchase.

After our triumphant first afternoon at the *cafenion,* he and I returned to the Haidis house and found Megali asleep. I decided to make feta-and-onion omelets for the two of us, and as I cooked, Grandfather watched me with satisfaction.

"It's good to have your company," he said. "Most of the regulars at the *cafenion* are soft in the head from too much sitting in the sun. Today it reminded me of the old years, when your father was back on one of his visits, lording it over the coffeehouse like the pasha of Yannina in his fine American clothes, buying everybody food and drink. Of course, we all had to listen to the same stories every day, how he takes weekly baths, how clean habits and regular hours made him a tycoon and community leader. 'There are two basic rules to living a long, healthy life,' he would always say, like Moses passing out the Commandments. 'Never sleep on your left side and have a bowel movement every morning.'"

Grandfather laughed his hacking smoker's laugh. "I always enjoyed Christos' company, even if he let the locals take advantage of him," he reminisced. "Why didn't he come back with you this time to play the plutocrat again?"

His smug superiority annoyed me. As instructed, I repeated what my father had said, softening it a little because I feared arousing the full heat of his anger. "He doesn't want to come, *Papou,*" I told him, "because he's never forgiven you for leaving *Mana* and us alone when the guerrillas were coming, without even saying goodbye."

My grandfather's eyebrows drew together and his face darkened until I began to get nervous, but he didn't lash out. I knew he was remembering how he had stopped speaking to my mother at the end, because he insisted that my father owed him five hundred gold sovereigns for giving us enough leftover flour to avoid starving during the famine that followed the German occupation, when the mails from America were cut off. He and my mother had been bitterly estranged when he fled the village ahead of the invading guerrillas, leaving us to our fate.

"I fed you during the war and I felt I was owed something," he said finally, and I could tell he wanted to leave it there.

"But you knew the guerrillas were coming. We were trapped when you left us behind!" I plunged on. "They made us suffer and turned us out of our house and finally started taking the children, so *Mana* arranged our escape because you didn't, and they killed her for it."

"Who knew any of that was going to happen?" he said. "We thought the guerrillas would stay a few days and leave. That's what they had done in other villages. When it became clear they were dug in to stay, I worked out a plan to sneak back and get you all out."

"So why didn't you?" I snapped, my own temper flaring. "Nobody came for us. Ever!"

"You're wrong — I *did* come for you!" he retorted. "I came back with the nationalist troops in March of 1948, when they attacked the Mourgana. There were several of us from Lia and Babouri with them, hoping to get our families out. I got as far as Aghies Pantes and then I heard the shooting and realized that they would never make it into Lia. We were outnumbered and outfought. So I stayed in Aghies Pantes, but the others went on ahead with the soldiers and were captured, the fools!"

"While you stayed behind and saved your skin!" I said acidly.

"You'd rather I went ahead like those idiots and got captured?" he shouted. "Look what happened to *them*. Spiros Migdalis! He was caught, they arrested his wife too, and they lined them up in front of the church and shot them in front of their children. Is that what you wish I'd done? What did Migdalis accomplish? I tried to come back for you, but I'm not a fool. I knew when to retreat."

I turned his omelet out onto a plate with an angry gesture and we ate in silence. I knew he was right, as usual, and I couldn't help admiring his cunning, but part of me still wished that he had cared enough about us to risk his life, even though things might have ended as he said. Instead of conceding his guilt, he shouted and defended himself when I confronted him with my accusations. My father, far less culpable because he had been on the other side of the ocean when the guerrillas came, had reacted exactly the opposite: he had heaped all the blame on his own head. My grandfather was smarter, I mused, but I found it hard to like him.

The coolness between us lasted for a few days, but eventually dissipated in our daily visits to the coffeehouse, our card triumphs, and our mutual enjoyment of my grandfather's *bon mots*. Eventually a wary respect for each other replaced the bad feelings. He liked having me around, and I couldn't help taking pride in the way everyone looked up to him.

One afternoon when my grandparents were sleeping, I climbed up the path to the house of Athena Charamopoulos, who had attended all three days of the trial. She was a small woman with intelligent brown eyes who lived near the Church of St. Demetrios and had been one of my mother's friends.

"No, your mother didn't look like she'd been beaten when she came to the trial," Athena said, in answer to a question. "They beat her later. At the trial she just seemed sad and resigned. She thought from the beginning that they were going to kill her. She told me that during the period between her first imprisonment and when they took her in again."

I asked her who among the villagers had spoken against my mother, and she told me. A total of twenty-one witnesses had been called to repeat in public the testimony they had given in secret against the seven defendants from the village. "Most of the witnesses against your mother didn't say much that was incriminating," Athena said. "They told how Eleni made her daughters wear kerchiefs to hide their faces from the guerrillas, and how she hid valuables from them. But the one who really hurt her was Milia Drouboyiannis, because her mother and sisters were in the first two escape attempts and she described it in detail — how the group turned back once because of a baby's crying and again because of a heavy fog. She testified to save her mother, who was also on trial, but she didn't have to say that your mother organized everything. She could have put the blame on one of the people who escaped. Milia was wearing her guerrilla uniform at the trial, and she banged her rifle on the ground and shouted, 'I swear by the gun I'm holding —'"

"Where is Milia now?" I interrupted.

Athena shook her head. "She's in Czechoslovakia, I think, where many of the hard-core Communists ended up."

"Didn't anyone speak up for my mother?" I asked.

"The only ones who dared were the old people," she answered. "Old Gregory Tsavos said, 'I have known Eleni Gatzoyiannis all her life, and I know that she has done no injury to anyone in the village. On the contrary, she always shared whatever she had.' But the judge cut him off. Then Kosta Poulos stood up, and they thought since Poulos was a Communist and his son died fighting for them he'd speak against her, but Poulos said the same thing. The judge got furious and finally said only those with *evidence* should speak up, so no one else did."

"Which judge? How many were there?" I asked.

"There were three, I think. The main one, the one with the deep voice who was in charge, he was called Katis," Athena replied.

"But 'Katis' just means 'judge' in Albanian," I said. "That's not a real name!"

"I know," she answered. "They all had fake names, to disguise their true identity. Even the commander of the guerrilla army — the one who had his headquarters in Babouri and who told all the judges what to do. We all called him Pavlos Arvanitis, but later, when the guerrillas retreated behind the Iron Curtain, that man became the head of the entire Greek Communist party in exile. That's what he is today. His real name turned out to be Kostas Koliyiannis."

"But the others — the judges, the jailers; the ones who beat her — how can I find them if I don't know their real names?" I said.

"They must be on record in the army files somewhere," Athena suggested. "You could probably find that out in Athens."

Over the next few days I talked to several other women who had been at the trial and asked them the same questions: who were the jailers, who were the officers, who were the leaders? But they could give me only nicknames like "the Butcher" and descriptions. Several had good memories for the testimony at the trial, however, and I hoarded each bit of information like a piece of a mosaic so that one day I would be able to lay out all the pieces and fit together the pattern of my mother's last months of life.

One afternoon I went to the house of Vasiliki Petsis, the old woman who had started to describe the day the guerrillas brought my mother out of the prison to dig up Olga's dowry. After bustling about making me coffee and chattering about my sisters, the black-clad woman with the guileless face picked up the tale of her last sight of Eleni.

"At the trial she looked as always — calm, resigned, dignified, her hair covered with a kerchief," she said. "Then, sometime after the trial, I was in my house when I saw a procession: three guerrillas walking in front of the mule, one with a shovel, another with a pick, then the mule with a woman riding it slumped against the back of the wooden saddle, her chin on her chest. Behind her were two packhorses and lots of guerrillas. All the other neighbors were hiding behind their curtains and peeking out, but I was always too curious, and I came out of my yard and over to the Haidis gate, where they stopped. I heard her say, 'It's there, under the patch of dry beans,' but she spoke with an unnatural voice, as if it pained her to talk. And they left her and went to dig, *thump, thump, thump* with the picks. I went up close and I said, 'Eleni, my child. Is that you?' And slowly, slowly, she lifted her head and looked into my eyes and said something — I could hardly make it out. 'Go!' she said. 'Or they'll do the same to you . . .' Her lips were cracked and her hair was uncovered and all knotted. Her legs and feet were bare and terribly swollen — all black from the beatings —"

By this time I was on my feet, unable to hear another word. "That's enough, that will do!" I snapped, startling the old woman, who was just getting into the spirit of her story, clearly proud that she had been the only one brave enough to speak to my mother.

"But don't you want to hear the rest?" she asked.

"Not now, another time," I muttered as I headed for the door. "Thank you for the coffee, but I have to get back. They'll be looking for me."

I left the Petsis house far more discouraged than when I had left Athena Charamopoulos. The names of my mother's jailers and judges were eluding me, but I had hopes of finding them in Athens. But the sickening horror that filled me when I heard Mrs. Petsis so glibly describing my mother's pitiful condition was more than I could bear. I had cut her off because I couldn't stand to know any more. What she had already said would haunt me for years, and I realized I wasn't strong enough yet to learn any more of how my mother had suffered. Imagining the execution, the fatal shots that ended her life in a split second, was something I could endure, but to imagine her agony and her loneliness, cut off from everyone she loved without any hope of deliverance — that was still too painful.

I had purposely scheduled my visit to Lia to coincide with the three-day festival celebrating the feast of the village's patron saint, the Prophet Elias, because I knew that the far-flung villagers would return if they possibly could for the *paneyiri*. It would be the perfect opportunity to question those who had been in Lia during the last weeks of my mother's life. For days before the festival began on July 20, the bus from Filiates disgorged arriving Liotes returning to stay with relatives or in their deserted family homes.

I had been born on the third day of the festival in 1939. When my mother's labor began, she sent Olga up the mountain to bring the midwife and Aunt Alexo down from the festivities to assist at the birth. According to my sisters' accounts, as Mother labored in our house, pulling on a sash hung from the roof beams, my grandfather lurked outside, puttering in the garden. He had already suffered the disaster of four granddaughters, and if this was another girl he was prepared to hide his grief. But finally the midwife sent Olga out to ask for her grandfather's hat. When one has great news, the tradition is to snatch the hat of the lucky recipient and make him redeem it with gold. The moment Olga said the word "hat," her grandfather grabbed her in a gleeful bear hug — the only time anyone ever saw him show affection toward his grandchildren.

After my birth, my family celebrated the arrival of a boy for forty days, baking and serving hundreds of pastries as the villagers came to see the *Amerikana*'s son, while the mirrors of our house were covered to keep out the evil eye.

When I returned to the village, the celebration of the prophet's feast hadn't changed from the day of my birth. The inhabitants of the village still climbed to the chapel perched on a ledge high above the timberline, where the priest celebrated a service for the prophet.

On July 20, I awoke later than most villagers, as usual. I could see a dark line of people high up on the mountainside, wending their way toward the chapel.

"I wanted to go to the church service," I told Aunt Nitsa, who was bustling about, but she replied, "It's too late. By the time you got up there, it would be over. Let's just get our things and go up to the *Vrisi*, so we can get the best spot."

The *Vrisi* was a spring that flowed across a triangle of flat land tucked into the mountain above the Perivoli but below the chapel of the prophet. This natural plateau, set against sheer cliffs, included a narrow pond where the village women did their laundry, and here the festivities were always held. The space made a natural dance floor, and a raised area near the cliff was a stage where the itinerant, dark-skinned *yifti* musicians would stand. These mysterious nomads of Egyptian descent appeared every year to play for the festival with their clarinet, fiddle, and tambourines. The dancers, moved by the *kefi* of the music and drink, tossed money into a hat to pay them.

Above the *Vrisi*, the cliffs were pocketed with caves, where the people of these mountains had taken refuge from invaders since the days of Alexander the Great. Here the Liotes once hid from the Turks, and here my mother and sisters and I took refuge from the invading Italians when I was a year old. Below the *Vrisi* was where my mother's trial had been held after the nationalist troops had fired on the town's central square.

Nitsa and I hurried up the mountain past St. Demetrios' Church, our old neighborhood, and my ruined house, past the millpond where my mother used to beat our laundry on the rocks with tree branches, and up to the *Vrisi*, where people were already spreading rugs, trying to commandeer a spot with a good view of the dance floor and near enough to the pond to chill beer and watermelons.

My Aunt Nitsa was so eager that she reached the *Vrisi* ahead of me. When I caught up with her, panting from the steep climb in the thin atmosphere, I said, "I thought you were too sick to make it up the mountain. How did you manage to beat everybody else?"

"Well, I've been resting and regaining my strength," she mumbled defensively. "After all, this is only once a year! Come on, let's get something to eat."

The proprietors of the village store and the coffeehouse had been roasting lambs on spits since before dawn. They sold beer, wines, and *raki*, and meat from the spitted carcasses, charging by weighing each portion with a hand-held scale.

Soon Uncle Andreas and *Barba* Foto arrived, descending the mountain from Prophet Elias. With them was Leonidas Charamopoulos, the owner of the kiosk in the village and husband of Athena, the woman who had told me about the trial.

"I didn't see you up there," Leonidas said to me, extending his hand in greeting.

"I got up too late for the church service," I replied.

"Right behind the chapel is the ravine where they shot your mother and aunt," said Leonidas. "If you want, I'll take you up there now and show you where it happened and where they put the bodies."

"No, not now," I said, horrified at the thought of standing where my mother stood as she realized her life was over.

"Why do you say such things to the boy on a day like this?" cried Leonidas' wife. "This is a day for celebration, not painful memories!" She led him away.

People had returned for the *paneyiri* from Salonika, Kalamata, Athens, even as far as Germany. In the crowd I saw many of my own age, former playmates who had been taken in the *pedomasoma* as children and had returned as adults. Some came over to greet me, among them a young woman named Magdaleni Kyrkou, a few years older than I, who was in the last group of children taken from our village, days after my mother's execution and shortly before the nationalist troops attacked and the guerrillas decided to retreat into Albania.

"There were about thirty children in our group," Magdaleni told me. "Many mothers followed us, weeping and begging the guerrillas to give their children back. They followed us all the way to the border, then the guerrillas told them to leave or they'd be shot. One little boy — George Siopoulos, who was nine — was bitten on the way by a rabid dog, but the guerrillas kept saying, 'Don't worry, he'll be fine once he's inside. We have doctors to treat him.' But in Albania he went crazy. They shut him up in a room and tied him because he was biting his own hands. He died in terrible pain."

"We were starving by the time we reached Durazzo," Magdaleni continued. "A Russian ship stopped to unload wheat and we ripped a bag open and ate it, stuffing the raw wheat into our mouths. You can imagine how sick we got! In Durazzo they took out the older children to train as soldiers and loaded the rest of us onto trucks and drove us to Belgrade. Then they sent us on trains to Rumania — still in the same clothes, no baths, no food. They told us if we made a sound they'd shoot us. They didn't want the civilians to know it was a train of kidnapped children. When we finally got to the camps in Rumania, they decided that at fourteen I was old enough to fight, so they sent me back to Albania."

Hearing tales like this made me realize again what we had escaped through my mother's sacrifice. If I hadn't fled the village, I would have spent years of my childhood starving in camps behind the Iron Curtain, and perhaps would have been so thoroughly brainwashed that, like many of the 28,000 children taken in the *pedomasoma,* I would never return. Worse, our family would have been separated like so many from Lia, me in a re-education camp in Rumania, my sisters sent to fight in other countries, scattered like leaves across the Communist world.

The village women had told me that on the third day of my mother's trial, as the charges were being read against her, the judge Katis called for a recess so that parents could say goodbye to a group of children being led up the mountain toward Albania. The scene became pandemonium as the mothers took their children in their arms for the last time. As she watched, my mother smiled, knowing that even if she was killed, her children were safe. The nine-year-old son of one of the village's foremost Communists, a little boy named Sotiris Bollis, was in the group, and he asked my mother in front of everyone, "Where's Nikola? Why isn't he going with us?" She hugged him and replied softly, "Nikola's gone to his father." Then the children were led up the mountain and the trial resumed, to the sound of muffled sobs.

As I listened to stories of the last days of the civil war and the diaspora that followed, the plateau became crowded with revelers and the musicians began to play the mournful, slow dances of our mountains. Everyone moved back to clear the center for the dancers, linked hand to hand, moving sideways in a sinuous line with measured, stately steps as ancient as Greece itself.

As the line of dancers approached, someone reached out and pulled me into it. I was no expert, but I did know the steps to the *tsamiko,* the dance of Epiros beloved by the mountain fighters during the War of Independence. Although the dance is slow, dignified, and warlike, the man at the head of the line is expected to do acrobatic feats, supported by a handkerchief firmly grasped by the next dancer. When my turn came to lead the dance I wasn't skilled enough to do the aerial somersaults performed by the best *palikaria,* but I managed some spins over and under the handkerchief. Then I saw Uncle Foto, a renowned dancer even at eighty-one, come up and take the handkerchief to support me. Under his encouragement I managed some leaps and turns that drew hisses of appreciation from the audience, along with an occasional *"Opa!"*

My uncle took my place, relying on my strength to keep him from falling as he bent back, nearly letting his head touch the ground, and then crouched, doing a powerful kick-step. The onlookers cheered to see the patriarch of our family still outdancing the youths. Soon I noticed my relatives — Foto's children and grandchildren — all hurrying to take a place in the line, until the slow-moving serpentine of dancers was composed almost entirely of the Gatzoyiannis clan.

The musicians moved closer, playing their instruments in my uncle's ear to fill his body with the rhythms. I saw tears in the eyes of many of my relatives, for by this dance at the *Vrisi* we were bearing witness that the murders of my mother and Aunt Alexo had not destroyed our clan, despite the best efforts of envious villagers. We had been the dominant family in the village once, and now we were stronger and more numerous than ever. Even the son of the *Amerikana* had returned to these peaks to dance the dance of Epiros and prove that by her death, Eleni Gatzoyiannis had given her children life.

Sometime during that afternoon, as I was talking to a young woman from Babouri, taking care, as my father had warned, not to seem too forward, I noticed my grandparents staring at me quizzically with a look I had seen before. During the early morning hours, when I lay in bed and they got up to do the chores, I often heard them whispering about me in the next room, and when I went in they would fall silent, looking at me strangely. "What are you staring at?" I'd ask in irritation, but they would always change the subject.

One night shortly after the festival, I was sleeping in my grandparents' house when I was awakened by an eerie, almost inhuman moaning coming from outside. It continued, a terrible sound of pain, raising the hairs on my arms. I remembered how the Germans had burned this very house in 1944 and thrown Foti Haidis' aged grandmother into the flames because the old woman, who had refused to flee the village with the others, was screaming at them for incinerating her goats. After the villagers returned and found her skeleton in the coals, her voice could sometimes still be heard in the ravine, calling for her grandson: "Fotooo, Fotoo!" Even my sisters had heard her. Now I wondered if the moaning was the uneasy soul of old Anastasia Haidis.

After listening for a while longer, I decided the only possible explanation was that someone had fallen into the deep ravine nearby, broken some bones, and was calling for help. I woke my grandfather and whispered, "Listen!" He picked up the big flashlight I had brought him and went outside to investigate. I waited in suspense, but when he finally returned, he had a small smile on his face. He reached for a cigarette from the pack that sat on the mantle and lit it with a match scraped on the stone. My grandmother came into the room asking, "Why's everybody up? What's going on?"

I couldn't stand it anymore. "Tell me!" I implored my grandfather. "What is it that's moaning?"

"It's just a she-goat." He smiled.

"Is she dying?" I exclaimed.

"No, she's not dying, she's in season and she wants a ram. She's just frustrated."

"And she's moaning like that?" I asked. "How long has this been going on?"

"Oh, about a week," he replied.

"Imagine carrying on that way!" I said dryly. "I haven't been near a woman for five weeks now, and you don't hear a sound out of me!"

"Nikola!" My grandmother beamed. "And we thought you were a virgin!"

My grandfather's usually dour features broke into a huge grin of relief and pride. "That's a Haidis talking, not a Gatzoyiannis," he said with a chortle.

As July drew to an end, I knew it was time to go back to Athens, but I resolved to return to the village for the anniversary of my mother's death before leaving for America. I told my grandparents that I had work to do in Athens and some people still to see, but that I would be back. I also distributed most of my wardrobe to various relatives, to lighten my luggage but also because I had discovered how much my smallest possession would mean to people who wore the same clothes all year round. Even the handkerchiefs and small bars of soap I had with me were great luxuries to the old women of the village.

I had to go back to Athens to research the identities of the military leaders of the Communists in our mountains, but I also needed to return to civilization for a while. In college I had read Rousseau's romantic notions of the noble savage, but in Lia I moved back into the Middle Ages and discovered that while the landscape was magnificent, the life of the village was harsh, brutal, and squalid. There was no way to keep clean except for a rare sponge bath, because there was no running water, only distant icy springs. Everyone sat on the floor and ate from the same pot, and dishwashing meant a casual rinse in the stream. There was no electricity, no street lamps or light bulbs, so darkness fell with the force of a blow, leaving us with little to do but sleep. The hard, isolated life made people vengeful, suspicious, and superstitious. When I was a child, I knew nothing else and so never noticed the desperately primitive conditions, but now I was longing for a bath, clean underwear, and a meal at a table from a clean plate.

"I'll come back before I leave Greece," I promised my grandfather.

He looked at me hard and asked, "You're not deceiving me?"

"No, I'll be back, I promise," I said.

Nitsa scoffed. "Kanta promised, just like that, after her wedding," she said. "Did *she* ever come back? Did Fotini and Minas return as they promised? Don't be a fool, *Patera*, he's just saying that so we won't make a big fuss!"

"Shut up," snapped my grandfather. "If Nikola says he'll come back, then I believe him."

I took the daily bus out of Lia as my relatives gathered to wave me off, Nitsa wailing the ear-shattering *myrologia* or mourning songs of the village, which could be heard from one mountaintop to another. Soon I was back in the luxury of the Amalia Hotel. As soon as I had bathed, I went to the Greek Armed Forces Archives on a side street not far from the hotel. I told the uniformed military officer at the desk that I was a student preparing a research paper on the history of the Greek civil war, and I wanted to look up some information about the leaders of the Communist guerrilla army.

At first he seemed speechless at my nerve, then he found his voice and informed me, as if speaking to a child, that without authorization from the Ministry of Defense there was no way I could get access to their files. Realizing I had hit a dead end, I decided to try another tack.

I got in touch with Minas Stratis, a man in his fifties who had once been the respected schoolteacher in Lia, before his nationalist sympathies put his life in danger in the early years of the civil war. After being hidden for forty days in the cellar of a relative, the tall, gangly scholar had managed to escape and take up residence in Yannina, where he found a job as a schoolteacher and worked during the war for the Greek military intelligence service, Alpha Dio, as well.

Minas was a second cousin of my mother. Shortly before the invasion of the guerrillas in Lia, when Mother had traveled to Filiates in an attempt to fill out the necessary papers for emigration to America, he had encountered her and warned her to move out of the village at once, for it would be dangerous for the *Amerikana* and her children if the guerrillas came. But *Mana* was under orders from my father to stay put.

Minas was now a grammar-school teacher in Athens, and I knew he still had good contacts in the military. I called him and asked him to meet me at Zonar's one sweltering afternoon. Despite the terrible heat, he arrived dressed in his usual suit, high-collared shirt, and tie. He greeted me as if fifteen years hadn't passed since we had last seen each other, then reproved me for the casual slacks and open-collared shirt I was wearing. "It behooves you to set a good example by wearing a suit and tie," he chided me, in his formal Greek. "As an individual who has matriculated from the university and who has met the president of the United States, you should present a good appearance to others."

When I told him that I needed his help to find out the names of the guerrillas in our village because I wanted to write about my mother's trial and execution, he responded as a schoolteacher would, from an ideological and historical viewpoint. "You shouldn't focus on the individuals responsible for the crimes against your mother," he said. "That only distracts people from the guilt of the party leaders. These trials and executions were political charades carried out in every occupied village to terrify the civilians into obedience, especially at the end, when the guerrillas realized they were losing and would have to retreat and take the civilians with them to fuel future armies. Commissars like Koliyiannis made the decisions to execute certain individuals long before the trials. The guilt for your mother's murder rests squarely on the leaders of the Greek Communist party. Her judges and jailers were just puppets."

"The leaders may have formulated the policy, but why kill my mother?" I interrupted. "I need to find out the names of the villagers who informed on her. Who were the jailers who tortured her — that was a personal, not a policy, decision, wasn't it? To beat her until she couldn't walk? Individuals did that! I want their real names. I need to see the faces of the people who tortured and shot her. I can't settle for hating the entire leadership of the Communist party."

"Most of them left their bones to rot on the slopes of Grammos and Vitsi during the last months of the war," he told me. "The ones who survived are now scattered all over the Communist world, from Warsaw to Tashkent, beyond your reach. So what good will it do to know their names?"

"I want to write it down," I said. "I want to write all the details for me and my sisters and our children — Eleni's grandchildren. I want them to know what sort of a woman their grandmother was, how she suffered and died and who was responsible. I'm going to do it for my family and my mother's memory, nothing else."

In the end, Minas agreed to use his contacts in the military and try to learn the identities behind the nicknames I gave him. But a few days later, he invited me to his house for lunch and told me he had had no success.

"This is the wrong time," he said. "Because we have a caretaker government and elections are coming up, everyone's very nervous. I called someone at the archives, but they don't have listings by nicknames. Everybody's afraid liberals will win power, and they won't want to stir up the past. If you could come back with credentials from a news organization, you might get somewhere, but a student, and during a transitional government . . . I'm sorry, Nick, but I can't do any more. My advice is to leave it alone. The ones who are still alive, they'll get what's coming to them someday."

On the way back to my hotel I realized that Minas was at least partly right. I would have to postpone my research until I had the professional skills and credentials to enable me to track these men down. Just as I wasn't ready emotionally to face the whole truth about my mother's torture and death, or even to walk into the basement where she had suffered, I wasn't ready with the skills and experience to find her killers. The best thing I could do for now, I concluded, was to go to graduate school, hone my journalistic skills, and increase my professional clout until I could come back and follow her story to its end.

I returned to the village in mid-August, stopping in Filiates to fill my nearly empty suitcase with more pastries and sweets. When the taxi deposited me at my grandfather's house and he came out into the court-yard, he flushed with pleasure but said only, "You've come back."

When Nitsa arrived, out of breath from hurrying across the village to see what was happening, Grandfather snapped, "Now will you admit you're wrong? I knew he wouldn't lie to me."

I could tell that in fact he had doubted he would ever see me again. By returning, I had risen several notches in his estimation.

Our pleasant round of eating, sleeping, and idling in the coffeehouse continued as the villagers began to harvest a wealth of grapes, figs, to-matoes, corn, and walnuts, a cornucopia of delicacies that made it easy to observe the two-week fast preceding the Virgin's feast day on August 15. But as I joked, played, and ate, I was aware that during this harvest period fifteen years before, my mother had been rearrested and the last tragic events of her life had begun to unwind, culminating with a burst of gunfire.

My sisters had warned me not to attempt a full memorial service on the anniversary of our mother's death, for that required a week of cook-ing and complicated protocol that they felt was beyond me; only they, steeped in village tradition, could carry out all the rituals without risk of tarnishing our family's reputation. So on August 28, 1963, the anni-versary of her murder, I walked up to the Church of St. Demetrios ac-companied only by the gray-bearded village priest, Father Nicholas, an acolyte, my aunt and uncle, my grandfather and grandmother, and Un-cle Foto. We entered the ossuary and stood before the small box that held the bones of my mother and of *Barba* Foto's wife Alexo as the priest swung his censer and chanted the *trisagion*, the thrice-holy prayer for the dead, while the perfumed smoke drifted heavenward.

We were all silent with our memories; only my grandmother sobbed softly. I tried to sense my mother's presence: did she know I had come back despite her command, I wondered, and did she understand why I had had to do it? But I felt no hint of her spirit nearby.

Since my return to the village, my mother had appeared in my dreams several times. My sisters dreamed of her often, but theirs were always messages from the world of the dead. In mine, however, she was always alive, moving about our house and the village paths doing the tasks that used to fill her days, while I followed her.

When we returned to the Haidis house after the *trisagion* service, my aunt and grandmother lay down for the siesta. My grandfather went out on the veranda to smoke, and I followed him. I could tell he was still thinking about my mother. She had always been his favorite, because Eleni was the only one in his family with an intelligence to match his own. But their relationship had been volatile.

"You came back and I'm grateful, Nikola," he said to me now, and I could tell that every word was difficult for him. "I'd always hoped for a son to carry on the Haidis name, but it wasn't to be. God sent me all daughters, most of them dead as soon as they were born. Because Nitsa is barren, you're the only male to carry my blood."

Once again I couldn't help wondering how much I was destined to inherit my grandfather's nature along with his blood.

"I want to tell you something I've never told anyone," he went on, not looking at me but leaning on the railing of the house he rebuilt with his own hands after the Germans burned it. He gazed down at the clouds drifting like sheep over the foothills below. "I once killed a man," he said tonelessly. "A Turk. It was in 1916, and I was working a mill outside Yeromeri that I had rented for the summer. We were vassals of the Turks then, and this brigand started coming around, telling me I had to pay him a percentage of my profits or my mill might burn down. It was a common practice in those days, demanding protection money from any prosperous Greek. Well, one day, after agreeing to pay him his tithe, I started serving him *tsipouro,* and then, when he was good and drunk, I took an axe off the wall behind him and split his skull open. I buried him beneath the stones that line the channel of the millstream, redirecting the water into an emergency ditch while I dug the hole and then putting the stones back. The bones are still there, under the millstream at Yeromeri, and will be until the Second Coming.

"I was relieved I had solved my problems so easily," he went on. "No one ever did connect me with the Turk's disappearance. But your mother — she was nine at the time — had been visiting me, and was asleep in· the loft of the mill when I killed the bastard — or so I thought. She saw the whole thing. I could tell from the way she looked at me afterward. She never said a word about it to anyone, including her mother, but every time I looked at her, I could see her eyes accusing me."

He said nothing more, and together we stared southward at the gray leviathan humps of mountains in the distance — the farthest boundary of my world until the night of our escape.

My grandfather never again mentioned the man he had killed, but he had given me the key to his thorny relationship with my mother. She had known his crime, and had constantly reminded him of it through the fear in her eyes. Despite his cynicism, I knew that like all Greeks he believed the sins of the father are visited on the children. My mother had died violently, and he undoubtedly felt this was punishment for the blood staining his own hands. God had taken his favorite child in retribution for his secret crime.

Eventually I understood that my grandfather's confession to me was an overture of friendship and an attempt to win my absolution for what he had done. He felt responsible for my mother's death, and not just because he had left us behind in the village. But he didn't say any of this on that anniversary of her execution — only one more sentence, delivered in a tone of resigned irony. "You lost your mother," he said, "but I lost my Eleni, and God left me with Nitsa."

At that moment I felt closer to my grandfather than I ever did before or after. By confessing, he seemed to be asking for my love and forgiveness. My opinion of him by then was much higher than when I had first arrived in Greece. But shortly before I left for good, he demonstrated once again why I had feared him so as a child.

It was a few days after the memorial service when a relative came from the distant village of Vrisela to pay her respects to my grandfather, and he directed Nitsa to bring coffee and water. When she complied, Grandfather said, "Where are the pastries that Nick brought? Serve us some of those."

"They're all gone — the villagers have eaten them," Nitsa responded.

"The villagers! *You've* eaten them all, you greedy pig!" he thundered, rising to his feet. "Nothing is safe around here with you and your useless husband bleeding us like vampires! You've eaten my food for fifty years now, and I'm sick of it!"

With that he started throwing things, kicking over furniture and smashing dishes against the wall, screaming curses at Nitsa while the veins in his neck and forehead bulged to alarming size. Both the visitor and I tried to calm him while Nitsa and Andreas scampered to safety. My grandmother burst out crying.

"You've got to get hold of yourself!" I shouted. "Stop this! This is crazy." But it was as if he couldn't hear me. His temper had taken over and he was unable to stop, still swearing at the top of his lungs and trashing the room. Finally, after the visitor had gone out the door with undignified speed, I shouted at my grandfather, "If you don't stop this ranting, I'm packing my things and leaving." But he didn't stop, only glared at me as if he'd like to kick me the way he was kicking the furniture, so I threw my few belongings into my suitcase and walked out.

Once outside the door, I found Nitsa and Andreas lurking in the courtyard. "Come sleep at our house!" Nitsa whispered. "You know it's not safe when he gets like this."

"No, that would look like I'm taking sides," I answered. "I'll sleep at *Barba* Foto's."

As I walked down the road I could still hear my grandfather shouting and raving and my grandmother wailing and taunting him: "That's right, break everything we own! You've managed to drive Nikola away, now let's see what else you can do to ruin us!"

The next day my grandmother found me at Foto's and convinced me to move back: my grandfather's fury had passed and he had disappeared, as he often did after these tantrums, probably to sleep in his deserted mill until he could control himself. He and I were coldly civil for the remaining days of my stay, but when I left the village I understood better than ever why my mother had been so eager to marry and leave his house. Any man her father chose as her husband, she knew, would probably be an improvement on her father and his temper. She had been fortunate that Christos Gatzoyiannis, despite his faults, turned out to be a loving and generous man, often wrong-headed in his decisions but willing to admit his mistakes and not one to harbor anger.

When it was time for me to leave for good, Aunt Nitsa wailed just as loudly as before, but I sensed more emotion in the quiet goodbye of Andreas and in my grandfather's parting words. "I hope you will remember us kindly and come back before I die," he said. "It won't be the same after you're gone."

My grandmother, addressing no one in particular, complained loudly, "I wish he had never come back! I'd got used to life without him, and now I'm going to have to start all over again!"

On my flight from Athens to Boston I couldn't sleep, so I had plenty of time to ponder the differences between the two countries that had been my home and the two men who had served as my role models. During the summer I had learned to admire my grandfather for his cleverness, wit, and resourcefulness. No matter how bad things got in Greece, through war and famine he was never down to his last drachma. He was totally self-sufficient and had always managed to survive better than anyone else. No one ever took advantage of him or made him look like a fool, because he was always on guard, expecting the worst from everyone.

My father, in contrast, like many Americans, trusted too easily. He was guileless and naive in judging people, so he was easily exploited and he never managed to save any money. In fact, he always was swayed by the opinion of the last person who had talked to him. Nevertheless, I preferred my father's generous nature and innocent optimism to my grandfather's vicious temper and suspicious nature, and despite his bluster, my father never killed anyone. He would get angry and then forget his grievances within hours. My grandfather would hold a grudge for years, and everyone feared him.

Even though I resembled my grandfather more, I resolved on that flight back to America to find a middle ground between the two men and to emulate my father's good qualities as much as possible. If that made me an *Amerikanaki*, it was still better than ending up like my grandfather, lonely and bereaved of those he loved best, haunted by his memories of the people he had wronged.

I hadn't told my family exactly what day I was returning, because I wanted to surprise them. When I landed in Boston, I took the subway and then the Trailways bus to downtown Worcester and called the house, where Glykeria answered the phone. Suddenly, hearing the shrieks of my sisters and the ruckus of the children in the background, it was as if I had never left. After bombarding me with questions, Glykeria told me Father was at the coffeehouse. "Go over there and find him and he'll drive you home," she said. "And hurry up! We want to hear everything that happened."

When I got to the coffeehouse I found my father playing cards with an impressive pile of dollar bills in front of him, but when he saw me, he threw down the cards, saying, "No more gambling today, my friends! My son has gone to the mountains and come back to me. Well, Nikola, tell me what tidings you bring from over there and how they treated you and how this new country looks to you now, compared to the old world."

"Pretty good, *Patera*," I said. "I missed you."

"Is this the famous son, the one who has been to the White House and met the president?" asked one of the card players, a balding old man with a gold watch chain draped over an impressive paunch. "Perhaps this one will be president himself someday!"

My father switched into English to chastise the man properly. "Whatsa matter with you? My son born over across, so can't be president! Don't you know nothing, greenhorn? How you get your papers, anyway? Never mind, he gonna do pretty good, that's for sure. In this country, whatever he wants, he'll get it. But not president. He went back to the old country, and he come home to me. Educated son with college degree. Honors from the hand of the president. What more I want out of life? Don't care if I drop dead tomorrow, I'm satisfied!"

George Cocaine

Top left: Father and son at Nick's graduation from Columbia in 1964. *Top right:* Nick and Joan's wedding, September 6, 1970. *Bottom:* Some words of advice before Nick sets out on his honeymoon . . .

THE DANCE
OF ISAIAH

You have trespassed and married foreign women.

— Ezra 10:10

ALTHOUGH MY FATHER liked to express his satisfaction with life by proclaiming, "Don't care if I drop dead tomorrow," he survived for another twenty years after my return from Greece. Only at the end were we living in the same city, but we visited each other often, and each time I discovered something new about him and the bond that connected us.

At Columbia's Graduate School of Journalism, I was taught to cover the news of New York City by veteran journalists who ran the school something like Marine boot camp, berating and humbling us as we typed frantically against deadline, threatening and warning that many of us would drop out or suffer nervous breakdowns before the year was over. Among my classmates were a number of women from all over the world, including a blue-eyed brunette from Minnesota named Joan Paulson.

On Friday, November 22, 1963, she and I both had plans to go out with others, but when the news flashed across campus that President Kennedy had been shot, most of the J-school students instinctively gathered in the newsroom. All afternoon we stood around the clattering wire-service machines as fragmentary bulletins about his condition came in. When it was over and Kennedy's death was official, we were all so despondent that no one had any idea what to do or where to go. Eventually that evening a few of us wandered off to a nearby movie theater on Broadway — my usual place to take sanctuary when I couldn't cope with life — and I found myself sitting beside Joan.

After that, we began dating, although I still went out with other women, including some whom I had known since Boston University. There were many glamorous and exotic coeds at Columbia, students from many countries, and I had no intention of becoming involved with a WASP from Minnesota who was descended from six generations of Presbyterian ministers. Nevertheless, I was fascinated by Joan's honesty and complete lack of guile — a quality that was rare among Greeks of either sex. But I had very clear demarcations between the kinds of girls I kept company with: there were Greek girls, one of whom I would eventually choose as my wife, and there were non-Greek girls, whom I dated strictly for the purpose of having fun. Joan was a bit of a problem, because she was much less worldly than the other girls I knew, and I decided that a non-Greek innocent was not someone I should waste any time on. Unfortunately, she invited me to be her guest at a Christmas dinner given by her dormitory. There was a party at the J-school that same night. I told her that I would allow her to treat me to Christmas dinner, if she would promise not to hang around me at the party afterward and cramp my style with other girls. She agreed.

At the end of our year-long master's program, my father drove from Worcester to New York City to attend my graduation. It was a warm, sunny day, and we graduates of the journalism school were filled with optimism about the careers that lay ahead of us. We had covered murders in Brooklyn, riots in Harlem, trials in night court, corruption in Albany. We had interviewed Malcolm X and Henry Kissinger, teenage drug addicts and Madame Nhu. We had done features on New York's morgues and theaters and hospitals and celebrities. If we could make it there, we told ourselves, we could make it anywhere.

Before the ceremony I asked Joan to take a graduation photograph of me and my father standing beneath the bronze statue of Thomas Jefferson outside the J-school building — a snapshot that became one of my favorites, because it illustrates so well the bond between father and son. He's standing straight as a soldier, pulling himself to his full five feet five inches, beaming behind his wire-rimmed glasses, his shoes shined to dazzling brilliance, his AHEPA tie clasp glowing against his narrow blue tie — the picture of paternal pride. I, in my black robe, am humorously leaning with both arms on my father's shoulder, draped in an informal pose that suggests the constant teasing between us. It's clear from the photo that my father was exceedingly proud of my degree, but hardly too intimidated by my education to advise his son on any aspect of life. In fact, he proceeded to do so shortly after the ceremonies.

"That girl Jones you introduced me to," he said (he never mastered the name Joan). "She's a very nice girl, very modest and seemly. Doesn't wear makeup like most girls today." This was not true, but so it seemed to my father. "What a pity she's not a Greek!" he continued. "You find a Greek girl like that, you should marry her!"

The subject of marriage seemed to be still on his mind later that afternoon when I took him back to an apartment near Central Park, the quarters I was temporarily sharing with my old junior-high friend Phil Rosenberg. For most of the year I had shared a room in a residence hotel on Broadway — one step up from a welfare hotel — but my room-mate had disappeared, leaving me far behind in the rent, and Phil had offered to take me in.

In the years since my father had driven me and the Rosenberg twins to Stratford to see *Othello*, Phil Rosenberg had become a student of English literature, and he too was now attending graduate school at Columbia, working on a thesis about the obscure nineteenth-century playwright Dion Boucicault. Phil's living quarters were scarcely better than my cockroach-ridden hotel room. He rented a studio apartment on the first floor of a converted former brownstone, with every inch of wall space and table surface covered with scholarly books. But Phil kindly offered me free use of the trundle bed that unfolded from beneath his own bed for as long as I needed it.

"I want to thank you, what you done for my son," my father told Phil as he searched for a spot to sit down. "I always say, Jewish people nice people! You know, I almost marry a Jewish girl one time — before I meet your mother," he said, looking at me.

"You did?" we both exclaimed in amazement.

"That's right," he went on, pushing some books from a lopsided arm-chair and gingerly settling his considerable bulk in it. "She live near Ledge Street, where I live when I first come to America — all Jewish neighborhood, you know: Ledge Street, Water Street, Providence Street. She was on her family's porch one day and I see her and she smile at me and I like her right off. Later I see her shopping on Water Street and I introduce myself. Well, she like me back and pretty soon we almost marry, but her parents very against. She take it hard, get sick from worry, but her parents still against. Finally I tell her, if parents against, you must always respect parents, most important thing. Then her parents take her away and I never see her again. I don't know if she ever marry, but I hope she have a happy life. That's when I decide it's better, go back to Greece, marry my own kind."

"I never heard this story," I said, wondering whether it was true or had been created as a cautionary tale for this occasion, to remind me that marrying out of my ethnic group would be a mistake.

"You don't know everything about me," he said slyly. "Do I know everything about you?"

"I hope not," I answered, grinning.

After graduation my father returned to Worcester and I set about hunting for the job that would be the entering wedge of my brilliant career. Throughout the year at Columbia our professors had warned us to give up the idea of finding work in New York City; there was a hiring freeze on: "Go to a good paper in a small city, get some solid experience, then you'll have a chance at New York." We had heard it so often we could tap-dance to the refrain, but we didn't really believe it. We were the *crème de la crème* of journalism, as we had been told by the same professors. Columbia only took the top ten percent of the applicants and then forged them into ace reporters.

Joan dutifully prepared to go back home to find a job, but for some reason — I didn't want to examine it too closely — the idea of never seeing her again bothered me. A few weeks before graduation, on a sunny spring day, we went on a romantic boat ride around Manhattan Island and I said to her, "How can you leave New York? Give it two weeks — and I'll do the same. You could share an apartment with other girls from the J-school. Maybe we'll both find jobs, and then we could still see each other."

She agreed to give it two weeks, no more, and within that period she did find a job: writing a company newspaper for a soap-and-toothpaste conglomerate with a skyscraper on Park Avenue. She would make $75 a week and share an apartment with three other Columbia graduates.

Armed with my brand-new master's degree, I made the rounds of all the newspapers and wire services, especially those people who had met me at the Hearst awards ceremony a year before and offered me work. But now there were no jobs to be had, and I got nothing but apologetic turn-downs. I was down to my last $14 before I found a temporary job replacing a vacationing writer for a small firm that wrote feature articles containing hidden plugs for paying clients. These promotional features were circulated free to newspapers across the country, where they were often run as news stories by small-town editors with a hole in their pages that needed filling. I was told, for instance, to write about the exciting life of truck drivers, to boost the image of the American Trucking Associations; another story related how the French used pigs to find precious truffles, thus promoting the French truffle industry. For making such plugs interesting enough to be printed as a feature story, I was to be paid a weekly wage of $75 for the month the staff writer was on vacation.

This certainly wasn't the career I had dreamed of, unveiling crime and corruption in the pages of the *New York Times*. In fact, it was about the lowest form of journalism I could think of, except for making up lurid stories for supermarket tabloids. At night when I lay on the cot in Phil's room, I was horrified at where I had ended up after the glory of the Hearst award and the White House visit. But, I consoled myself, at least I could afford to eat for another month.

In the middle of that hot, dismal New York summer, I took the bus back to Worcester to attend the Liotes' *glendi*, the day-long picnic celebrated each year by the immigrants from our village in a wooded area beside a lake in Marlboro. My brothers-in-law started marinating the chunks of lamb for the shish kebab the night before. There would be a Greek orchestra, a lottery with the first prize of plane tickets to Greece, and lots of eating, drinking, dancing, and singing. This annual picnic was an event that no one in my family would miss, because my father was the patriarch of the scores of Liotes living in Worcester — the revered first immigrant, or *protoporos,* whose efforts had brought everyone else over.

As usual, Father was treated like a king at this event. Splendid in his light linen suit and new straw hat, he was seated in the place of honor while babies and children were presented to him and grateful relatives came up to greet him, many kissing his hand and addressing him as *Papou.* When the music began, he led the first dance, moving as always with a careful, stately step as he balanced a glass of wine on his bald pate. When he was tired of dancing he sat on his makeshift throne to watch the rest of the dancers with the satisfied smile of one who knows that everything he surveys is the result of his own sweat and toil.

This year my father insisted that a chair be placed beside him for me, as the community of immigrants came up to pay their respects. I tried to talk him out of it, for I felt like a fraud. The son who had been welcomed at the White House was now a penniless hack flogging dubious feature stories, but my father wouldn't let me slip away. "You must sit here and greet everyone," he said, "for someday I won't be here anymore and you will take my place."

These summer picnics were always times of drama — the heat, drink, and music heightened emotions until feuds erupted, flirtations led to altercations, and gossip rose like the smoke from the roasting pits. This picnic was no exception, for Dino once again announced he was going to strike out on his own in business and leave his job as a chef at Bronzo's nightclub. He had finally realized the wisdom of Nick Karagounis' pizza business and was determined to open a pizza restaurant of his own.

My father, like all the men of his generation who remembered the worst of the Great Depression, believed that leaving a secure job for an uncertain one was folly. "You're a king at Bronzo's; you run the kitchen like you own it," he told Dino. "Why risk becoming a beggar just so you can say you have your own place? Look what happened when you put your money into The Crossroads!"

I knew all Dino's arguments. The pizza business was different. With low overhead and no need for a staff, he and his brother could run the place alone. But Dino was beyond arguing with my father. He just glowered and tossed down the last of his ouzo and said, "I didn't come to America to work in someone else's kitchen. I came to America to make money."

I had always given Dino opposing advice to my father's: take a chance, the timid never win the prize! But now, thinking about my own efforts to find a job in New York, I wasn't sure that my father was wrong to counsel caution.

As we sat and people came up bringing food and drink, I tried to explain to my father that my work in journalism was not going as well as anticipated, but he brushed my anxieties away with a wave of his hand. "Ah, you worry for nothing. Every beginning is difficult," he said, then gestured toward the dancers in front of us. "Look at all those greenhorns. How did they start? No education, no skills, no language. But now they have cars, homes, businesses, money in their pockets. If they could do all that, think what *you* can do, with your brains and education!" He continued in that vein, sounding so sure about my future that for the first time since my graduation I started to feel I might have one.

My optimism grew as soon as I returned to New York. Although the writer I had replaced returned from vacation, my boss offered me a permanent place on the staff at $100 a week. On the heels of his offer I received a call from an executive of Cowles Communications, where I had applied for a job, saying he wanted to hire me for the staff of the *Insider's Newsletter* for the dizzying salary of $125 a week. I accepted at once.

The *Insider's Newsletter* was a small pamphlet mailed out weekly to subscribers who wanted inside information about trends in business, politics, fashion, marketing — the news before it hit the newspapers. I tracked down these nuggets in a variety of ways, including reading European newspapers. From my perusal of various Eastern European Communist publications, I scored my biggest coup at the *Insider's Newsletter* within a month of joining its staff, when I predicted the fall of Nikita Khrushchev.

The item was a stab in the dark, but it was noticed in the Cowles organization. Nine months later, when the editor decided to leave, I was offered his job, in the same week that I received a call from the personnel director of the Associated Press saying that he had a New York opening for me at last. After some vacillation, I decided to take the AP job, because this was the kind of journalism I was trained to do.

In my new job I covered several breaking news stories a day and phoned them in, composing them from my notes as I stood in the telephone booth. After several months of this I was promoted to night state editor, which meant working the night shift in the Associated Press Building at Rockefeller Center, consolidating all the state news and preparing the report for the morning. By this time Joan had found a job on the *Ladies' Home Journal* a few blocks away, and we would sometimes meet early in the morning in Rockefeller Center under the statue of Atlas and go for breakfast at Schrafft's as I was leaving work and she was coming in. I would tell her about the crises and stories I had handled during the night and she would tell me anecdotes about the glitzy world of women's magazines, and I'd think how pleasant it was to talk to an intelligent woman who also knew all about journalism. Now if only I could find a Greek girl like that.

My next promotion at the AP sent me to cover the United Nations, where I put to use what I had learned as an International Fellow. Finally I was assigned to the foreign desk, in line to be sent overseas: my first step in getting back to Greece in a position to learn the identities of my mother's killers.

But just then I received another job offer that seemed irresistible. A reporter from the *Boston Herald Traveler* called to say that his paper was putting together an investigative reporting team and he wanted me for it. At that time investigative reporting had not yet become a fad. Most editors felt that investigative stories took too much time and money and generated too many libel suits. But the *Herald Traveler's* editors had decided that important, exclusive exposés would give their paper an edge on the competition that it badly needed, and they were hunting reporters like me who liked digging through files, cultivating sources, and tracking down leads.

I jumped at the chance to practice the kind of reporting I had dreamed of and to suggest colleagues to add to the team, including my old friend from the *B.U. News,* Jim Savage, who was then working for the *Miami Herald.* Delighted to be living closer to my family, I moved from New York to a sunny apartment on Commonwealth Avenue in Boston with a wall-to-wall view of the Charles River below, and soon had a duplicate apartment key made to give my father. He always carried a huge, rattling chain of keys to all his children's and relatives' homes, cars, and places of business, for it made him feel like lord of the manor.

Of course I was sorry to leave New York and Joan behind, but then it was just as well, I told myself, because there was no point in leading her on when our relationship had no future. I did suggest that she might want to come to Boston now and then for a weekend, and I offered to show her the sights.

Joan did come to visit, and on one of these occasions I took her to Chandler Street, where she met my sisters. This didn't cause any excitement, for they were used to having me pass by with some American girl I was dating and they knew it didn't mean anything, for an American girl was just a diversion. They had never met one like Joan, however.

She was wearing a hat and gloves when I brought her into the first-floor kitchen. She sat at the oilcloth-covered kitchen table and talked to my sisters, asking about their families. She offered to show them around New York and to amuse their children if they ever came to the city. "What a nice girl," they all told me afterward, "and so modest and seemly in manner! She dresses like a high-born lady. You should try to find a Greek girl like that."

All four of us reporters on the new *Herald Traveler* investigative team were elated at the chance to devote ourselves to stories that other newspapers didn't have the time and skills to uncover. My first effort was investigating reports of abuses in the Fernald State School for retarded children, in Waverly. I posed as a student and took a job as an attendant in the building for severely retarded boys. During the days of feeding, supervising, and cleaning up after these children, I saw many examples of abuse, neglect, and overcrowding, and wrote a series of articles that eventually resulted in legislative reforms in the state's mental hospitals. The series brought both the *Herald Traveler* and me a good deal of publicity, including a commendation from a young Greek-American legislator named Michael Dukakis.

While my own career was prospering, my brothers-in-law were at last finding financial security in the pizza business. Dino opened a pizza parlor in Needham, twenty-five miles from Worcester, in partnership with his brother, and immediately began making a profit. Soon Angelo, Kanta's husband, who had been struggling at restaurant jobs, hit on the idea of outfitting a school bus as a traveling pizza parlor and selling pizza to the students of Boston University, who, I assured him, were a great untapped potential market. Angelo's peripatetic pizza parlor was eventually replaced with a stationary one in Waltham, and my other two brothers-in-law, Prokopi and Minas, after opening a fruit store together and failing, eventually struck out on their own with pizza restaurants in Westboro and Concord. Soon all of them were making more money than they had ever imagined.

Beginning with Dino, my brothers-in-law drafted their wives into the business, and that meant that my sisters had to learn to drive. Getting a license was a traumatic experience for women who could speak little English and had little experience outside the house, but eventually all four managed, although Glykeria failed the test five times and came home weeping after each failure.

As my sisters worked side by side with their husbands, something they would never have considered doing in Greece, they learned to deal with the American public and to speak better English. Eventually, as partners in the work, they began to have a greater voice in how the family's money was spent. Washing machines, color television, better clothes and jewelry: these were some of the fruits of the American dream that they could now afford.

My sisters and their husbands worked winter and summer at the hot pizza ovens for up to sixteen hours at a stretch, making three or four hundred pizzas a day. They would get back home after midnight, their clothes and hair smelling of pizza, and fall into bed exhausted. But on Monday, their only day off, they could drive around in shiny American cars wearing clothes that no one had ever worn before them. My sisters rejoiced as they washed those clothes in gleaming new washing machines and cleaned their dishes in modern new dishwashers. Pizza had brought them a piece of America's prosperity.

But achieving the American dream created cracks in the unity of our vertical family compound at 369 Chandler Street. The first to move out were Olga and Dino and their four children. Dino opened his pizza parlor in 1964, using all his savings, and gave it two years to succeed. Each morning his brother picked him up and drove to work. Olga would collect the children from school at two-thirty and drive in the family car to Needham, to start work herself while the children played or read or napped on a cot in the back of the store, until they were driven home after midnight and carried on their parents' backs up the three flights of stairs to their apartment.

Olga was firmly set against moving away from Worcester and her father and sisters until one night when there was a raging blizzard and Dino, trapped with two of the children in his car, struggled for five hours to cover the twenty-five-mile drive home to Worcester. Certain they were all dead somewhere in the storm, Olga spent the night weeping and screaming. After that she capitulated to Dino's demands to find a house near his store.

My other sisters told her not to go: "You'll have no one there! Your children will become *Amerikanakia*. They'll forget their traditions, their religion and language!" But to my surprise, Father, who had opposed Dino's opening the pizza parlor, now advised Olga to move near his business. "You must follow the steps of your husband," he told her. "I don't want to make the mistake my father-in-law did. He insisted his daughter stay with her parents instead of going with her husband, and that's what killed her."

Dino and Olga had $10,000 in the bank by the time they found a small ranch house in Needham for $28,000, with a swimming pool nearly filling the small back yard. On a warm fall day in 1966 the movers came and Olga and Dino moved out. This rending of our family was so painful for Kanta and Glykeria that they stayed away from the house all day long so as not to see the moving van that was taking their sister and her family away.

My nieces and nephews had always lived together like siblings, so it was a shock to have four of the little ones suddenly leave, but Olga and Dino's offspring adjusted to the upper-middle-class community of Needham as soon as they saw the swimming pool. Although no one in the family could swim, the first thing Olga did in her new house was to have a snapshot taken of the whole family standing solemnly up to their necks in the pool, like Mao in the Yangtze — a snapshot illustrating their elevation into the bourgeoisie, which they quickly had duplicated and sent back to the wondering villagers of Lia, who had heard of swimming pools but never actually seen one.

Despite her sisters' dire predictions, however, Olga never gave up her social life in Worcester's Greek community; she drove back every Sunday to go to church and never missed a baptism, wedding, funeral, or dance. She gloried in being able to buy the expensive dresses she had always coveted, although she hid their real cost from Dino by using funds that she skimmed from her household allowance and kept in a secret stash in the freezer, wrapped in aluminum foil like packets of frozen steak.

Meanwhile, my dream job as an investigative reporter suddenly hit a major snag in the person of Joseph P. Linsey, a Boston businessman and former bootlegger who had ties to organized crime. Two of the reporters on our team were coming up with a lot of incriminating details about Linsey when the publisher of our newspaper, George Akerson, called them into his office and ordered them to drop the investigation. "Forget Linsey," he said. "There's nothing there."

This kind of statement to an investigative reporter is like catnip to a cat, so we redoubled our efforts and soon learned that Mr. Linsey numbered not only crime figures among his best friends but also our publisher, Mr. Akerson. Furthermore, Linsey was a principal stockholder in the newspaper that employed us. This was certainly bad news, for no investigative reporter with any self-respect could work for a publisher who quashed investigations of his friends. But we all had given up good jobs at great trouble and expense to come to Boston. If we quit and angered our publisher, there was no assurance that we would ever find other reporting jobs.

Just before this crisis erupted in March 1967, I was shaken by the news that my grandmother had died in the house in Lia where she had lived for the seventy-three years since her wedding day. Soon after, I learned that my grandfather was ill as well. He had been taken to the nearest hospital, in Filiates, where the doctors had told him he had terminal cancer; there was nothing to do but to go home and wait to die.

This news reached us through Glykeria's father-in-law in Filiates, who told her over the phone that my grandfather had gone back up the mountain, crawled into the bed that he had bought for my visit, and placed two gold sovereigns on the table beside him, announcing to the villagers, "I want to see my grandson Nikola or my son-in-law Christos Gatzoyiannis before I die. These sovereigns will go to the first person who tells me that one of them is coming up the mountain."

When I heard this, I felt a rush of sympathy. "One of us has to go to him," I said to my father over the phone. "He wants to tell us something. Right now I'm in the middle of some problems at work, but as soon as they're over I can go."

"I'll go," Father replied glumly. "I never wanted to go back, but if we don't show up he can't die in peace. I'll leave as soon as I can get a new passport."

On the long, tense day that our investigative reporting team agreed that we would all resign, whatever the cost to our careers, I returned to my apartment and unlocked the door to find my father sitting there in the dark.

"What're you doing here?" I asked. "Did you come into Boston for your passport?"

"No, I'm not going to Greece," he said. "Your grandfather is dead. He turned yellow and then died faster than anyone expected."

"But he was waiting for us!" I exclaimed, guiltily imagining how he must have fought to hang on to life until I came, expecting every minute to hear the sound of the taxi rattling up the road. "He died alone."

"He had Nitsa and Andreas," my father said.

"The way he felt about them, to him that was like being alone," I replied.

We sat in silence for a while, thinking of the fierce, secretive, proud old man. Then my father spoke again. "He left your mother to die alone and now he dies alone," he said. "But he thought his gold sovereigns would bring us. He always put such faith in money."

I never learned what it was my grandfather wanted so desperately to tell us, but I suspect that he craved some words of absolution before he died — forgiveness for leaving my mother to her fate. Absolution and the fate of his soul were certainly troubling him on his deathbed, I know, because the elderly village priest told me many years later that my grandfather came to him during the last days and confessed the murder he had committed some fifty years earlier.

The final irony of my grandparents' life was that after marrying in 1894, when she was thirteen and he was fourteen, enduring seventy-three years together, and fighting bitterly almost every day, my grandmother and grandfather died within a month of each other.

After my grandfather's death, I went home to Worcester to sit with my father and sisters and receive condolences from our relatives while my fellow unemployed investigative reporters from the *Herald Traveler* looked for jobs across the country. I finally went to New York, and began making the rounds of newspapers and magazines, starting with the *New York Times*. My contact on the paper, Arthur Gelb, whom I had met after the publication of his book on Eugene O'Neill, was now assistant metropolitan editor, and he arranged an interview for me with his boss, A. M. Rosenthal, who looked over my clippings and offered me advice rather than a job: "Go make a reputation somewhere, and then you won't have to ask to join our staff, we'll come after you."

To my surprise, I was eventually offered a job by the *Wall Street Journal,* even though, as I confided to a friend, I didn't know a debenture from a debutante. The managing editor of the *Journal* at that time, Ed Coney, had built his reputation on investigative reporting and encouraged it among the staff, giving reporters time away from writing daily business news to pursue an investigative story wherever it led — a policy that had won the *Journal* a number of Pulitzer prizes.

Eager to avoid covering stock splits and corporate mergers, I undertook investigations of corrupt union leaders, a phony religious foundation, and organized crime links to big business. The most talked-about pieces I did were a series on Frank Sinatra's connections to organized crime and a front-page article on prejudice within the mob, which began with the lead "The Mafia is not an equal opportunity employer."

Being back in New York meant that I could see Joan more frequently, although she was only one of several women I dated. I even helped found a social club called the Herodotus Society, made up entirely of Greek journalists, since I figured that this would be a good way to meet an attractive Greek woman who was also intelligent, educated, and interested in my field. I was making enough to pay the rent on a nice apartment on the upper West Side, and my social life became gratifyingly busy. Nevertheless, it was a shock when Joan told me, about a year after my return, that she had saved enough money to finance a long trip to Europe. She was going to travel around first, she said, then look for a job in London.

When would she be back? I asked, and she told me, with characteristic frankness, that she didn't know, but that it might be a very long time. It had been four years since we had started dating, she pointed out, and it was clear that our relationship had no future, yet her feelings for me prevented her from meeting other men. She wanted to put as many miles between us as possible.

I agreed that this was a wise decision and wished her *bon voyage*. We parted on the best of terms — she even left me her entire collection of records for safekeeping.

Joan left America on the last day of May, and within weeks the tumultuous summer of 1968 exploded all around me. There were assassinations — Martin Luther King, Bobby Kennedy. There were riots in Harlem and in Chicago at the Democratic convention. For a journalist, it was a frantic and challenging time, but I still occasionally managed to ride all the way from Wall Street to my West Side apartment on my lunch hour just to see if there happened to be a letter in my mailbox from Joan.

She wrote regularly, with lively tales of her travels. Eventually she managed to find a good job as a magazine editor in London. She also was meeting a number of English men, she wrote, including one particular young businessman whom she described as witty, intelligent, and quite successful.

For some reason these letters made me angry — so angry, in fact, that I gave all Joan's records away to my female friends in New York. That would show her! I certainly wasn't turning into a monk in her absence; I scarcely had time to wonder about what she was doing in London. The truth was, I reflected, that I was relieved Joan was meeting eligible men; after all, it wasn't as if she and I had any future together!

Perhaps not entirely by coincidence, I proposed to the *Wall Street Journal* editors an investigative series that would require me to go to London for several weeks. I had heard rumors that American organized crime figures were trying to infiltrate gambling casinos in England, and I convinced my editors to let me pose as a big-spending Greek ship owner on a Mafia-run gambling junket in which American high-rollers flew to London, stayed in hotels there, and gambled in various establishments which, I ultimately proved, the American Mafia families were secretly taking over.

It was hard work in London, maintaining my cover and gambling all night and poking around for leads all day, often taping conversations with fellow gamblers and mafiosi by means of a miniature tape recorder tucked into my sock under my pants leg. But I did find time to look up Joan, who accompanied me to the casinos and watched me gamble.

It was a memorable reunion. I realized how much I had missed her. But I also concluded it was a good thing there was an ocean between us. During my stay in London I explained my situation to her: for three thousand years, I told her, my people had married only Greeks from our own mountains. I was the first person in our entire community to get a college education. All the Greeks in Worcester looked to me as a role model for them and their children. If I were to marry a non-Greek, it would be a virtual rejection of my heritage. I would be in effect selling out my entire clan and denying my identity. I would be implying there were no Greek women good enough for me. I couldn't let my entire community down that way, I explained earnestly. It was too bad that she wasn't Greek, I said with a shrug. My father liked her. My sisters liked her . . .

Joan said that she understood perfectly. She wished me luck. She said she liked living in London so much that she never wanted to leave, anyway.

When I got back to New York, I felt like someone who had managed a narrow escape. I continued working at the *Wall Street Journal* for another six weeks, but having piled up $5,000 in my savings account by then, I decided to take a year's sabbatical and go to live in Greece. If I couldn't find the perfect Greek woman for me in America, I reasoned, then I would go directly to the source.

My sisters and father were delighted when they heard I was going back to the old country to find a bride. Father remarked, not for the first time, that he had waited far too long in marrying at thirty-three. As I was nearly thirty, he added, it was high time I settled down and provided him with a namesake.

I didn't tell my family the other reason for deciding on a year-long sabbatical. By now I felt that I had gained enough experience as an investigative reporter to begin the search for those responsible for my mother's death.

I left for Athens in December of 1968 and rented an apartment near the center of the city for the winter. In the spring I moved to an apartment in the seaside suburb of Vouliagmeni. Conscientiously, I did my best to meet eligible Greek girls. Dozens of relatives and friends introduced me to likely prospects, but it was difficult to get to know any respectable Greek women well, for in those days single dates were still frowned on in conservative circles and young people usually went out in large groups of friends.

I had many pleasant distractions, however, because a number of former girlfriends from America came to visit me in Greece. So many old flames found their way to Athens that year that I grew profoundly weary of giving guided tours of the Acropolis in the blistering heat. These visits gave me an opportunity to scrutinize my American girlfriends in the foreign atmosphere and lifestyle of my native land. Under the Greek sun, some of them seemed too flamboyant or uninhibited ever to fit into the life of my family and relatives. However, many Greek girls I met, while intelligent and well versed in Greek classical literature, had no knowledge of English literature, American theater, or the more relaxed American lifestyle I was used to. Greek girls at that time were supposed to be decorative, well dressed, and totally devoted to the domestic arts, and I began to suspect, to my dismay, that I had become too much of an American to be satisfied with a wife whose energies were completely devoted to what she wore and what she cooked.

The one girl who didn't seem out of place in either culture was Joan, who came to Greece for a visit. We had continued corresponding, and I convinced her to take a short vacation in Athens in the spring of 1969, flying on a cheap charter from London. Although her miniskirts caused a sensation in Athens, where the fashion hadn't yet become prevalent, her quiet, modest demeanor and her appreciation of Greek food and customs made a good impression on my relatives, who judged most American girls as too loose on the basis of their appearance, walk, and friendly manner.

Still without a prospective Greek bride, I was nearly as unsuccessful in my journalistic investigations. The colonels who had seized power in Greece on April 21, 1967, although strongly anti-Communist, were so reactionary that like many Greek-Americans I had been involved in anti-junta organizations in the States. As a result I was regarded with great suspicion at every government office I entered, and gaining access to military files and records about the civil war proved even more impossible under the junta than it had been under a more liberal government.

Despite my failures, the year in Greece was not wasted. I made two important discoveries. The first occurred when Glykeria and Olga joined me in the summer to go to the village for a proper memorial service for my mother. When we reached Lia I followed them up the path as far as our property, but when my sisters entered the house, I waited outside until they emerged, weeping bitterly.

The next day the whole village gathered in our neighborhood Church of St. Demetrios for the memorial service. Sun slanted through the dusty windows of the crowded church as the priest began to chant and the altar boys swung the censers, the heavy perfume mingling with the odor of decay. The schoolteacher stood up to speak. He was the only educated man in the village, and he wanted to deliver a eulogy. As soon as he said our mother's name, my sisters began to wail the keening, ululating cries that are the Greek expression of sorrow for the dead.

"This woman's death was not an ordinary one," the schoolteacher continued over the commotion. "She was executed alone, with her husband far away, because she tried to save her children. She was a victim of her fellow Greeks. This is not an ordinary memorial service for the dead; she was murdered!"

As I stood there, trying to wish myself anywhere else, the air pressed in on me, and I was aware of my mother's bones only yards away. The shrieks of my sisters stripped away the veneer of control I had built up. Even when I was a boy, on the day my mother said goodbye and again when I learned she was dead, I held my grief inside. Now it erupted. Sobs welled up from where they had been hidden for so many years and shook my body like a convulsion. The rush of emotion blurred my vision, and then my knees buckled. Two men nearby grabbed my arms, supported me out of the church, and set me on the ground, my back against the trunk of one of the towering cypress trees surrounding the graveyard.

That outburst was the first and last time I lost control and abandoned myself to my grief, but when it passed, I discovered a new strength. At last I was ready to listen to everything the villagers had to tell me about my mother's suffering and death. I knew I now would be able to follow her steps, even into the basement where she was tortured and up to the ravine where she died. I spent the rest of that summer asking questions and gathering details of my mother's last days from fellow villagers whenever I encountered them, although the Communist guerrillas' identities still escaped me.

By fall my savings were nearly gone and it was time to go back to New York and my job, but I wanted to stop in London first. After looking all over the world for a bride, like Diogenes with his lamp, I had finally realized that the woman I wanted was one I had known all the time. I had met many attractive and interesting women and I knew that I could marry and be happy with a number of them, but that would mean giving up Joan for good, and I didn't want to lose her.

In London Joan and I had some long and tumultuous conversations. Then we took a short excursion to Paris (which cost almost nothing in those days). Somewhere on the Right Bank in the rain we decided that, after six years, we should admit that we were in love and couldn't be happy without each other.

With no more formal proposal than that, without any ring or ritual, we agreed: she would quit her job and return to New York and meet me there as soon as possible, and in a year we would be married. As we rode in the bus to Orly Airport, with the rain beating on the windows, I mentioned to her that there was one more hurdle we had to cross before the wedding was firmly set. Startled, she asked me what it was. I had to get the approval of my family, I told her. Without their approval, I couldn't marry her.

Perhaps I shouldn't have been surprised that this news unnerved Joan to the point of tears. How could she give up a good job in London and move herself back to New York, where she had no job at all, she demanded, when our marriage plans might all fall through in the end?

I tried to comfort her and make her stop crying. "Don't worry about anything," I told her. "Just go ahead and pack your things and write your parents that we're going to get married. *I'll* handle my family."

Joan did as I said, and I braced myself for the task of winning over my family to my choice. This would be a very ticklish business. I recalled what a scandal it had been when my second cousin had married a Greek-American girl from Worcester. Even a hyphenated Greek woman was considered a risk as a wife: who knew what wild modern notions she might have picked up while living in America? Such suspicions sent most of my Greek cronies back to the old country, where girls were brought up strictly according to tradition, to find a bride. Announcing to my family that I wanted to marry a girl who was not only *not* a Greek, not even a Greek-American, but a Scandinavian from Minnesota — that was going to be an exercise in negotiating that would daunt Prince Metternich.

I returned to the United States, talked the editors of the *Wall Street Journal* into rehiring me as an investigative reporter, and then went to Worcester. On Sunday afternoon we all gathered at Olga's new house in Needham, resplendent with its all-new furniture and carpeting. The living room furniture was covered in velvets and shining patterned brocades, set off by a six-foot plastic orange tree with plastic oranges. Clear plastic strips covered the traffic lanes across the lush beige carpet, and more protective plastic covered the embroidered tablecloth on the imitation mahogany table, where we ate from gold-plated dishes and gold vermeil cutlery. My other sisters marveled at Olga's palace — everything so new, pristine, and modern compared to the old-fashioned shabbiness of our three-decker at 369 Chandler Street.

After dinner we gathered in the living room, and I addressed the family in my most serious voice. "We have to talk about something," I began solemnly. "You know that I've been thinking of getting married. After all, I'm thirty."

"Yes, it's time," my father said. "You don't want to wait as long as I did and be old when your children are still young."

"There are three women I've been seeing over the past three years," I went on, and named them: Joan, another American woman I had dated since my Boston University days, and a Greek girl in Athens whom they all knew. I was counting on the fact that they all liked Joan and at least one of my sisters had a strong dislike for each of the other two. "I think I can be happy with any one of these three," I went on, "but it's important to me that whichever one I marry, she doesn't upset the relationship we've always had as a family, so I want to know what you all think."

My sisters started comparing the virtues and faults of each of the three women, getting so excited as they shouted praise for the one they favored and denunciations of the ones they disliked that soon the room was in pandemonium.

"Stop!" my father shouted and rose to his feet. "Stop this shouting right now!" he ordered. My sisters all quieted down and turned to him.

"What's all this talk about these other girls?" he said crossly. "Jones is the one for Nick."

"But she's not Greek!" Glykeria exclaimed.

"So what?" he said. "You've seen those girls from Greece. They want to run everything. You think Nick can live with someone like that? As for the other one, I didn't trust her. So what's there to decide? Jones is the girl for Nick."

"But will she marry in our church? Will she respect our customs?" they asked. "You know we have to have a big wedding — you're the only son."

I assured them that Joan wouldn't object.

They finally accepted Joan as the best choice of the lot and told me to ask for her hand. I drove back to Worcester with my father, feeling pleased at how well my stratagem had worked.

As we hit the turnpike, Father said, "Tell me, what would you have done if we favored one of the other girls?"

"Well," I said, "what you all think is very important to me, and I —"

"Yeah, sure," he interrupted. "It's a good thing you have a smart father."

He chuckled for the rest of the way home, and I realized that he had been on to me from the start and had stacked the deck in favor of my choice.

Joan and I scheduled our wedding for the next year, on Labor Day weekend, when many of our friends could come to Worcester from New York. My family would need a year to prepare a wedding elaborate enough for the only son of Christos Gatzoyiannis.

Ever since Olga had moved out of Chandler Street, my other sisters had begun to feel dissatisfied with being crowded into their small quarters in the three-decker. Kanta discovered a small three-bedroom ranch house being built on Maxdale Road, one of the new residential streets carved out of the fields near Worcester Airport. She bought it and told the builder to include a finished basement, completely open, with a kitchen alcove and a bathroom. Noticing an empty lot next door, Kanta induced Glykeria to buy it for $4000, and Glykeria instructed the same builder to build an identical house to Kanta's, including the family area in the basement. My father would continue to live with Glykeria and would have his own bedroom and bath.

Eventually the finished basements would be where my sisters' families would spend all their waking hours, sitting, eating, or napping on the comfortable couches in front of the television while my sisters stood at the stove cooking or at the ironing board ironing without missing the television or any conversation that might go on. To stay in touch with the whole Greek community as well, Glykeria had Prokopi install such a long cord on the downstairs phone that she could carry on all her domestic duties without ever relinquishing the receiver tucked between her ear and her shoulder.

American visitors to Glykeria's and Kanta's houses might have been surprised at the unused kitchen, dining room, and living room on the first floor, completely furnished with stove, refrigerator, dishwasher, expensive suites of furniture, fine dishes, and crystal on display in the china closets, all of it as pristine and unused as the day it was delivered. Both Kanta and Glykeria faithfully dusted their upstairs rooms, but all the appliances, dishes, and furniture were duplicated in humbler style in the basement, where the family really lived, except for retiring at night to the bedrooms on the first floor.

The basement was where my sisters kept their family's altar, hung in the eastern corner over the TV set, with an eternal light illuminating the paper icons and a bottle full of holy water, "'case of emergency" as my father liked to say. Here they displayed the family photographs, including those of my mother, my graduation, and their own weddings. In the basement were their finest crocheted tablecloths and antimacassars, the onyx worry beads, and the huge oil painting of a village scene that Glykeria had bought for $300, which lit up when you plugged in the electric cord, all the windows of the houses and the street lamps in the scene glowing cozily.

These new houses with their spanking new furnishings, huge color TV sets, state-of-the-art audio centers, and the many electronic gadgets that delighted the hearts of Prokopi and Evangelos — tape recorders, movie cameras, and fancy phones — had all been paid for by pizza, and my family did not believe in buying on the installment plan. Even their automobiles were bought with brown paper bags full of cash.

While my family was succeeding in the pizza business, my career on the *Wall Street Journal* advanced to the point where the managing editor offered to send me to the *Journal*'s London bureau right after my wedding. This was then the paper's only European bureau, and the five openings in London were the plums sought by every *Journal* reporter, so I was pleased to get a foothold in Europe at last, with the possibility of traveling to Greece now and then to pursue my own investigations.

But the daemon who decreed that all my career windfalls would come in pairs struck again. A few days after the London bureau offer, I got a call from Arthur Gelb, by now the metropolitan editor of the *New York Times*, inviting me to lunch in the executive dining room of the *Times* offices. With his characteristic exuberance, Arthur offered me a job as the *Times* chief investigative reporter in New York, with an emphasis on organized crime, and after lunch he took me to the office of A. M. Rosenthal, the new managing editor of the paper.

"Your face looks familiar," said the legendary figure, who was transforming the venerable *Times* into a highly profitable and even more respected newspaper.

"I've come to see you before," I said.

"And what did I say to you?" asked Rosenthal.

"You said to make a reputation and the *Times* would come to me."

He smiled in satisfaction. "See, I was right!" he said. "You got our attention and now we're coming to you."

"Yes, that's true," I replied, also smiling, "but now I'm going to cost you twice as much."

Because I was torn between wanting the *Journal*'s London job and the prize assignment at the *Times*, I asked for double the $250-a-week salary I was getting at the *Journal*, and Rosenthal agreed without flinching. Then I told him I needed two weeks off in September to get married, and he agreed again. We shook hands and I realized that I had achieved my earliest career goal — I was a reporter for the *New York Times*!

While I moved from the downtown offices of the *Journal* to the huge *Times* newsroom on 43rd Street, the preparations for our wedding were proceeding apace. There was some discussion of the wording of the invitations: American tradition usually had the bride's parents inviting the guests, but this was clearly unthinkable, since the wedding was an extravaganza orchestrated by my family. I made a Solomonic decision and we ordered engraved conservative English-language invitations beginning "Mr. and Mrs. Robert Paulson request the honour of your presence . . ." and Greek-language invitations featuring a bride, groom, cupids, gold rings, flowers, wedding crowns, and entwined initials, which unfolded like an accordion to reveal gold boldface letters beginning "Mr. CHRISTOS GATZOYIANNIS and Mr. and Mrs. Robert and Martha Paulson . . ."

The reception dinner would of course be held at Putnam and Thurston, featuring the most expensive entrée available — steak. The attendants would be my nieces — Fotini's daughter, Anastasia, ten, and Olga's daughter, Eleni, eleven — two five-year-old girls who were more distantly related to me, and five of my nephews, ranging in age from six to seventeen.

Because this wedding had to reassure the Greek community that my roots and religion were still an essential part of my identity, I insisted that the ceremony be done in the most traditional way. The priest then at St. Spyridon, Father Solon Tsandikos, was a young, progressive prelate who suggested that he recite the ceremony half in Greek and half in English, but I emphatically rejected the idea. For my best man, I followed Greek custom and chose Stavros Economou, the son of Nassio and the woman who had baptized me in the village.

My sisters ordered the wedding crowns, candles, and the wedding favors — small gilded glass goblets filled with a plastic flower and Jordan almonds. Joan did the required reading and converted to the Orthodox faith. She also obtained from the priest a translation of the long Greek wedding ceremony, typed it up in pages, and had it photocopied and bound with ribbon between cardboard covers to distribute to the non-Greek guests who would come to the ceremony.

With my new wealth flowing in from the *New York Times,* I told my father to invite anyone he wanted. He ended up with over three hundred names on his list. Meanwhile, Joan invited a few New York friends and five relatives: her brother and his future wife, a cousin and his wife, and her mother (her father was too ill to make the trip). My father took care of inviting most of Worcester and supervised the plans for the reception, but I drew the line when he wanted elaborate flowers decorating the pews of the church. "The flowers we've ordered for the front are enough," I said.

"We've got to have more flowers, what will people think?" he insisted. "There was a wedding last year, the bride and groom walked through a whole archway of flowers before they got to the altar!"

"No more flowers," I snapped.

The festivities began on the Friday of Labor Day weekend, when my family went to pay a formal call on the family of the best man. Joan and I didn't get to Worcester until Saturday, however, when we arrived with the New York contingent. That night all the Greek women of Worcester brought trays of Greek foods and pastries they had cooked for a buffet dinner in a rented room at Putnam and Thurston. Our visitors from New York included reporters, editors, lawyers, former roommates, and classmates, and the enthusiasm these "foreigners" demonstrated for the ethnic food, drink, and music astonished the Greeks.

The greatest success was Joan's patrician, white-haired mother, who resembled Irene Dunne. She was resolutely charming and gracious, even though she was inwardly terrified by this exotic wedding. As the daughter of a Presbyterian minister, she had inherited a Calvinist suspicion of any form of high-church ornamentation, priests' robes, incense, and chanted liturgy. She especially dreaded the ceremony, when she would come face to face with her first Greek priest, a frightening figure to a Protestant girl from Kansas. Nevertheless, on the wedding day, Joan's mother carried on with the aplomb and dignity of Queen Victoria.

That morning the weekly Greek radio program of music dedicated by relatives for special events had to be extended an hour to accommodate all the congratulatory records in our honor. In the afternoon, Joan dressed in Glykeria's house and I got ready in Kanta's house next door. It was a perfect autumn day, and every Greek in Worcester seemed headed toward the church to witness our vows.

As at any wedding, there were a few minor slip-ups. I forgot the marriage license and had to go back to Kanta's house for it. Spiro, my oldest nephew and the head usher, lost the English translations of the vows that Joan had so laboriously prepared. And when we entered the church we found a stunning display of flowers decorating the pews; my father had decided to overrule my veto and had ordered additional flowers on his own.

As the music began and the little bridesmaids preceded her, Joan, wearing a high-necked lace dress and train from Lord & Taylor, started down the aisle, escorted by her brother. She was greeted with an audible murmur of admiration. Her mother had already made a stir arriving in an elegant street-length rose crepe dress with matching hat and white gloves. My sisters, escorted down the aisle by the ushers, had chosen long ball gowns and beehive hairdos.

The ceremony began with the priest handing me a lighted candle and making the sign of the cross. He exchanged the rings, placed the wedding crowns on our heads, and gave us wine to sip from the common cup. By the time, forty-five minutes later, he led us around the altar three times in the dance of Isaiah, our wedding crowns linked together with a white satin ribbon, even the non-Greek members of the congregation seemed caught up in the solemnity of the moment.

Then the long ceremony was over; our families and friends came forward to congratulate us, and the wedding party reassembled in Elm Park, directly across the street from the church. We were lined up and photographed in all sorts of groups and combinations. There was even a photograph of the bride and groom standing alone under the ancient trees in front of a reflecting pond and a fountain, kissing for the first time as man and wife.

The reception afterward at Putnam and Thurston outshone any event in memory. After the three hundred guests were seated, the members of the wedding party were announced as they marched in two by two, beginning with the tiniest flower girl and ring bearer. The other actors in the drama smiled as they were applauded, but my father marched in alone in his satin-lapeled black tuxedo, and when the crowd rose to its feet and the applause swelled to an ovation, he strode with a solemn, dignified mien across the floor to his place at the head table like MacArthur returning to the Philippines.

My mother-in-law, who had been terrified of falling into the clutches of a sinister, bearded Greek priest, found herself sitting next to young, urbane, clean-shaven Father Solon, who complimented her on her dress and made polite conversation until she was completely charmed and at ease. After the meal and the toasts in both Greek and English, the orchestra began to play the keening melodies of Epiros. Joan and I and our best man got up to lead the line of dancers. Even Joan's brother and her maid of honor (her brother's future wife) took their turns at the front of the ever-growing line, to the delight of the crowd. But no one received the cheers that my father did when he took the lead, this time with a glass of Coca-Cola balanced on his head, and solemnly turned and spun, spilling not a drop from the tall tumbler.

Then the New York contingent joined in and the dancing became feverish, with legs flashing beneath miniskirts, shouts and cheers, and dancers spinning on their backs on the floor or leaping like Cossacks into the air. Eventually no one was left at the head table except Joan's demure mother, and I saw her foot in a pink satin shoe tapping in time to the rhythm. A few moments later, my mother-in-law was at the head of the line, daintily essaying the sideways steps of the *kalamatiano*.

We all danced like bacchantes. I was transported by the music into more daring steps than ever before, but no one seemed as happy as my father, who was filled with a private joy that transfigured him. As I watched him dancing, I realized that he was laying down a burden that he had taken up twenty-one years before, when he found himself, at the age of fifty-six, parent to five children. Now he was seventy-seven. He had done his best by all of us, and the last of his children was finally married and settled in life. Father had found it hard to be a single parent in his old age. He had made mistakes and sometimes fumbled, but now he could take pride in what he had accomplished, saying with the Apostle Paul, "I have fought the good fight, I have finished my course, I have kept the faith."

The dancing showed no sign of diminishing as the hour grew late. Throughout the evening the Greek guests went up and handed my father envelopes containing money intended for the newlyweds but presented to him as a sign of their respect. He stuffed these gifts into a briefcase he had with him. Sometime after midnight Joan and I slipped away from the party and returned to Glykeria's house to change our clothes and leave on our honeymoon. When we were ready to carry our bags to our borrowed car, we found Father sitting at the basement table, already changed back into his casual clothes, refreshing himself with some of the Greek wedding bread dunked into his cup of coffee.

As my sisters and relatives gathered to wish us farewell, Father beckoned me over for some final advice. I might be a married man now, but that didn't make me any less in need of guidance. "Pay attention how you drive, keep the tank full," he said, lifting a pontifical finger. "And listen to your father — be nice to your wife. Put her first. Don't be like your grandfather, good to everyone outside the house but mean to your own wife and children. Home is the most important thing. If that's no good, nothing else in life is." With that he returned to his snack and we set off on a week-long honeymoon trip, which included a systematic tour of all the Greek-owned pizza parlors from one end of Cape Cod to the other.

20

John Goodman

George Cocaine

Top: Christos dancing with his granddaughter Eleni at her baptism
Bottom: Christos surrounded by his family, shortly before his death
on July 11, 1983

JOURNEY'S END

Men do what they can and suffer what they must.

— Thucydides,
History of the Peloponnesian War

SOMETHING ABOUT BEING MARRIED and starting a family of my own made me realize that my father was an old man and wouldn't live forever. He had always seemed to me as indestructible as our mountains, but the fact was that he was seventy-seven years old and I was thirty-one. Until now he had supported me as best he could — if not with money, then with encouragement and his faith in my future. He had even won over my sisters to a marriage that I knew threatened all the traditions he had taught us. Now his job was finished, and it was time for me to do something for him. I had a home and a good job, and I resolved to try to give my father three things I believed would bring him joy in the years he had left.

His greatest wish was for two grandchildren to carry on his name and my mother's. To give him that one required Joan's cooperation and a lot of luck, but the other two gifts I could manage on my own. One was a new car; he had always owned used cars, coddling them through their cranky middle age. The other was a trip back to the country he hadn't seen since 1939, the place that had formed him and still had such a strong grip on all of us.

Fortune seemed to aid me in these efforts, for Joan became pregnant almost immediately after we settled into a small apartment on Manhattan's West End Avenue and a book publisher offered me a sizable advance for a collection of my newspaper articles on the Mafia. When I went home for that first Christmas, in 1970, I told my father I had good news. "Joan is pregnant," I said, "and you're taking a trip to Greece next summer."

At first the idea of returning after thirty-two years frightened him, but

I persisted. The whole truth was, I secretly wanted him out of the country when Joan gave birth the following July. I knew how much my father longed for a grandson to carry on his name, and I was afraid that if our first-born turned out to be a girl, his disappointment would be upsetting both to Joan and to me.

"Why would I want to go back after so long?" he scoffed when he heard my offer. "All my comforts are here." But soon his enthusiasm blazed up, as he recalled his triumphant trips back to Lia in the 1930s, when he had reigned over the coffeehouse like a sultan and had gone on hunting trips for wild boar and quail on the highest peaks of the mountains.

I began to have some qualms. "The village isn't like it was in the old days, *Patera*," I warned him. "You used to have a whole family to welcome you. Now everyone's old. You're not young yourself anymore — after all, seventy-eight isn't an age for chasing wild boar!"

"Don't worry about me," he retorted. "I don't need a young *Amerikanaki* to tell me about life in the village. I remember one time playing cards in the *cafenion* for three days without sleep . . ." and he was off again on a wave of nostalgia.

When it was time to leave, on April 11, 1971, my father arrived in New York with all his luggage, including an entire suitcase of toiletries, soaps, talcum powder, and dozens of changes of underwear to help him maintain his high standards of hygiene. "I don't want to be embarrassed by having to ask someone to clean my underwear for me," he explained. "So I bought enough to change my linens every day."

He had driven his 1963 white Opel to leave with me for the duration of his trip, so that when Joan's time came, I could drive her across Manhattan to the hospital instead of having to find a taxi. As I drove him to Kennedy Airport on that warm April Sunday, he gave me advice on how to look after his car properly. When he was about to board the plane he said, "If anything happens and I should die over across, I don't want to be buried there. I want you to bring my body back to Worcester, to Hope Cemetery."

My father's return to Greece was not a success. I had warned him to do as I had and stay in a hotel when he was in Athens, because to stay with a relative could lead to arguments and hurt feelings if he selected one person's house over another or became overly indebted to one family, who might then complain that he didn't give adequate gifts when he left. He followed my advice and stayed the first night at the Grande Bretagne, but the next day he moved into the crowded home of his nephew Yianni, announcing to the family that the maids at the hotel stubbornly insisted on making the beds with sheets, a practice he considered unhealthy because sheets made him feel cold. He himself had always insisted on sleeping between two warm blankets. As a result of the sheets he had caught a terrible cold, he said, and would never stay in a hotel again. An unmentioned factor might have been that he felt less at ease in the elegant, cavernous, antique-filled Grande Bretagne than he did in a crowded, noisy family home filled with women ready to bring him his coffee, his slippers, and his glass of water (a small glass, he specified, never a large one), the way my sisters did at home.

After reacquainting himself with relatives in Athens, my father set out for the village, accompanied by Yianni. This was even more of a disaster than the Grande Bretagne. Since the death of my grandparents, Nitsa and Andreas had moved into the Haidis house, but my aunt's house-keeping had deteriorated as she grew older and her eyesight grew worse. She washed dishes and clothes carelessly, rarely swept, and allowed dust and soot to form a permanent patina on everything in the house.

As soon as he set eyes on Nitsa, Father began to berate her for slovenliness and her treachery to his wife. My aunt returned the curses and insults as forcefully as he dished them out. Despite all of Andreas' attempts to act as peacemaker, Father soon stormed out of the house, declaring he would never set foot in it again. He went to the house of his brother Foto, at the opposite end of the village and down a winding, treacherous footpath that teetered on the brink of a ravine. When my father confronted his ne'er-do-well brother, he lashed out at him too, reminding him of every misdeed throughout his misspent, lazy, selfish life and ending with the accusation that by failing to share his food during the famine, and by leaving the village and abandoning Eleni and her children as well as his own wife, Foto had been responsible for their deaths and had consigned his black soul to hell. My father evidently had been storing up these resentments and accusations for all the decades since my mother's murder, and the sight of the village and the faces of his derelict relatives caused an eruption of bitterness.

Father took a taxi back to Yannina, where he armed himself with every sort of supply: lounge chairs so he could sit under the grape arbor in the courtyard, a bottle of Petrogas to fuel the gas burner, water glasses in the small size he preferred, all sorts of food, even a wooden toilet seat to add comfort to the one-hole outhouse in Foto's courtyard. Then he returned to Lia.

Back in America I was bombarded with letters from aggrieved parties in the village. My father wrote describing his terrible treatment at the hands of Nitsa and his battles with his relatives. Nitsa wrote (dictating to Andreas, because she was illiterate) that Father had shamed her before all the village by walking out and refusing to stay in her house. Uncle Foto complained that my father was imposing on his hospitality and insulting him daily. From New York I tried to make peace between them. I sent money to my aunt, telling her to use it to hire a woman to clean her house. I wrote to my father, begging him to forget old grievances and try to make peace with the relatives he still had living in the village, but to no avail.

Father was sitting in the coffeehouse in the central square under the plane tree on July 17, 1971, when Joan gave birth by Caesarean section to a son, Christos. I immediately called my sisters, who wept with joy that I too had escaped the Gatzoyiannis curse of producing only girls. Glykeria telephoned her father-in-law in Filiates, and he relayed the news to a local taxi driver, who set out on the trip up the mountain to bring my father word of his grandson and namesake, certain that he would collect a handsome *shariki*, a reward for good news. He was not disappointed.

At the *paneyiri*, three days later, my father threw money around like confetti, treating everyone to food and drink, liberally tipping the musicians who played as he danced in joy at his good news. Within days a telegram arrived in New York from Greece: "Coming home early to see my grandson."

We scarcely had our baby son installed in the second bedroom, recently converted from an office, when it was time for me to collect my father from the airport. He came off the plane and I hugged him and then asked somewhat apprehensively how he had liked Greece.

He shook his head. "I was born there, all my children born there," he said wearily. "But my country is America. I'm glad to be home."

I could tell he was close to exhaustion from his journey. When we arrived at our apartment, he went immediately to the baby's crib, placed a $50 bill on Christos' chest, and then pinned several gold *filacta*, charms to ward off the evil eye, on the pillows around him. "That's a fine boy, my grandson," he said. "Now I need to lie down."

It was important to my father that we observe tradition, even though we lived far away from Worcester, in a skyscraper in New York. He traveled to visit us every December sixth for my name day and spent hours cooking in the pocket-sized kitchen, then we would all sit around waiting for well-wishers to come. But he was always disappointed, for Joan and I could never muster more than a few couples who either were Greek or knew the name-day traditions. I could see that it pained my father to have us living in this cold-hearted city where no one observed the feast day of St. Nicholas, while in Athens the streets were clogged with traffic as everyone visited all the Nicholases they knew.

Father visited much more often than once a year. Whenever wanderlust hit him, especially during warm weather, he would board a Greyhound bus for New York. Once settled in our second bedroom near the baby's crib, with his necessities all arranged just so on the bedside table, he would venture out into the city, traveling down to the harbor to ride the ferry to Staten Island to visit the Greeks who owned the restaurant where he had worked as a chef during the Second World War. It made him proud that he could negotiate this great city on buses and ferryboats alone. After he sailed back to Manhattan, past the huge statue of "Saint Freedom" which had welcomed him and his children to America, he would continue up to the Greek district on Eighth Avenue in the forties. But he could never stay anywhere long, and the urge to return home always struck him as soon as he had arrived. Joan and I would wake up to find him fully dressed and packed, sitting on his suitcase, wearing his hat, his hands resting on the head of his walking stick, impatiently waiting for dawn so that he could head back to the Port Authority Bus Terminal and home.

When he or my sisters weren't visiting us, we would drive to Worcester nearly every other weekend and stay in Kanta's or Glykeria's house. Submerging myself in the Greek life of my relatives, the feasts, dances, visits, and church services, gave me the strength to deal with the events that were rocking the city and my own career during the week: drug raids, corruption scandals, and a series of Mafia wars that erupted in New York in the early 1970s.

By 1974, Greece was in the throes of political turmoil. The ruling military junta tried to assassinate the ruler of Cyprus, Archbishop Makarios, and in the ensuing chaos the Turks invaded the island. The failure of the junta's colonels to stop this invasion caused the collapse of their regime and the return of democracy to Greece, events that generated daily news stories and worldwide interest in the country.

I urged my editors at the *Times* to open a bureau in Athens instead of just having the Rome correspondent cover it from afar. My ulterior motive was to get assigned there so that I could pursue my mother's story while being a foreign correspondent for the *Times*. After all, who else on the newspaper spoke Greek? But while they heeded my advice to open an Athens bureau, to my dismay they assigned another reporter to the new post. When I went to A. M. Rosenthal to complain, he told me, "I don't understand why you want to leave New York for Athens, but you'll get the post next, if it's so important to you."

The delay probably was for the best, I realized, for Joan was pregnant again and would be able to have the baby in this country. We continued our routine of visiting my family every other weekend, but because it was getting harder to crowd our growing family into Kanta's small house on these visits, I decided that we should buy our own place in the area. One day in early 1974, while visiting Worcester on my own, I saw a large, two-hundred-year-old colonial farmhouse with three acres of land in the nearby town of Grafton, located conveniently close to the turnpike and selling at a bargain price. Joan and I had been looking for an old house like this one, which had a history dating back to the original settlers in 1722. But I wanted my father's opinion before I committed myself to paying such a large sum of money. I knew my sisters would hate the place, because they had a mania for things that were brand-new. Whenever Joan and I showed them the antiques we had picked up at flea markets and auctions, they always asked, "Aren't you making enough money yet to afford something *new?*"

I drove my father over to see the house with its Greek-revival façade, wide pumpkin-pine floors, and fireplaces. His good customers in the days of his produce route had lived in such houses.

"No, I don't need to see the second floor," he said, warily eyeing the steep staircases. "It's got a nice sunny porch. All I need is a comfortable chair. Buy it!"

On weekends and vacations we struggled to make the rough-beamed rooms comfortable, and during the week I continued my reporting for the *Times,* consoling myself that I would finally get to Greece in 1977. Our visits to Massachusetts were nostalgic journeys back into Greek culture; at Christos' third birthday party, in our new/old house, someone drove his car up on the lawn to play Greek music full blast on the tape deck, while dozens of guests roasted lamb, sang, and snake-danced around the lawn, to the astonishment of our Yankee neighbors. Three months later, on October 8, Joan gave birth to a daughter, named Eleni for my mother. The baby grew to resemble her grandmother so much, with the same large blue eyes, classic features, and honey-colored hair, that when we took her to Greece, village women often burst into tears at the sight of her.

My father's joy touched everyone who saw it when he danced at Eleni's christening, on September 28, 1975. The guests all danced like dervishes, perspiring, shouting, throwing money at the musicians, and rolling on the floor as onlookers threw $20 bills at the best performers. But the stars of the show were my father and his eleven-month-old granddaughter in her lace christening gown, who held up her hands in imitation of her grandfather and danced in front of him as he led the line, glass balanced on his head, until he finally gave up to gather the tiny, solemn, dancing cherub into his arms.

Soon after the baptism, I discovered that giving my father a new car was going to be even harder than producing a boy and a girl in sequence or convincing him to go to Greece. "Why go to the expense?" he would say every time I brought it up. "My Opel is only ten years old!"

One weekend when I visited Worcester on my own, I picked up my father in a rented car and drove to Prokopi's pizza parlor. There, as my father watched, we enacted a little charade I had rehearsed with my brother-in-law. Prokopi scolded me for wasting my money on rental cars every time I came to visit, saying I should really have a car of my own. But driving a new car in New York would ruin it, I protested. Eventually, Prokopi "convinced" me to buy a new car, to leave it with my father for safekeeping, and to take his old Opel to New York, because it wouldn't matter if something happened to it.

Father was uncertain about parting with his beloved Opel, but as soon as I drove us to a car dealer on Route 9, he was drawn to a silver-gray Oldsmobile Omega like an adolescent who has glimpsed his first grand passion. "This is the one for you," he advised. "Nice lines, not too big, good space inside!"

"I don't know," I said uncertainly.

"You don't need to know!" he asserted. "You listen to your father! If there's anything I know, it's cars."

That was how my father became the possessor of the sleek silver Omega, which he cosseted and doted on for the rest of his life.

As the day approached for my departure to Greece, many fortunate omens seemed to be coming together. Joan gave birth to another girl on July 12, 1977, just two months before our scheduled departure. This child was hers to name, and she selected one that could be easily pronounced by Greeks and Americans alike — Marina — and a middle name of Zoe, the Greek word for life.

We emptied our apartment on West End Avenue, sold our furniture at an apartment sale, and arrived in Athens on September 8, taking possession of a large rented house with a walled garden in the residential suburb of Neo Psychiko. I thought I would have the resources, time, and opportunity to begin my investigation of my mother's fate at once, but as soon as we arrived, a series of international crises erupted that kept me out of the country for almost all of my first two years.

Political events in Greece had calmed down, but all over the Middle East violence raged. I found myself shuttling from Athens to Ankara to Beirut. By the spring of 1978, riots in the northern Iranian city of Tabriz were signaling the beginning of the upheavals in Iran that would end eleven months later with the fall of the shah, and I was sent at once to Teheran. There was a brief period that spring when I was allowed to return to Athens, and during that time my father decided to visit us.

He enjoyed sitting in our walled garden under the lemon, bitter orange, and fig trees like a king on a throne in his hat, suit, and bow tie, listening to his portable radio play Greek music and supervising the crowd of cats, tortoises, and children that always filled the garden. He had a whole repertoire of Greek nonsense songs that he sang while jiggling the baby on his knee, and he took a sly pleasure in popping his upper plate of dentures out of his mouth with his tongue at unexpected moments, which always evoked delighted screams from the children.

I told him that we should go up to the village now that the Judas trees were in bloom and spring had covered the mountains with wildflowers, but he was reluctant at first. Finally he relented, and I drove him and Joan up to Epiros. But my father adamantly refused to stay with anyone in Lia, insisting that I leave him with some in-laws in the neighboring village of Babouri while Joan and I went on to Aunt Nitsa's house.

The next day I collected him and drove him up a bumpy, unfinished road that was being cut up the mountain in the direction of the Church of St. Demetrios. We went together into the ossuary and lit candles over the rough box containing my mother's bones. Father studied the box in silence for a while, then he turned to me. "I want you to promise me something," he said. "When I die, I want you to bring your mother's remains to America and bury them next to me in Hope Cemetery. I've already bought the two plots and ordered the stone with both our names on it."

"I could do that now," I told him. "We could have the box sent to Worcester on the same plane with you when you go back."

He shook his head. "No, I don't want to see her buried while I'm alive," he said. "But promise me you'll do it when I die."

I promised and we walked back to the car and drove down toward the Haidis house, where Joan, Nitsa, and Andreas were waiting. But when we stopped on the road just above the courtyard my father said, "I'm too tired to go in. Just bring me a chair up here so I can sit and have a cup of coffee."

Nitsa and Andreas came up to the road and we all begged him to enter, but despite everyone's pleas he firmly refused to set foot through Nitsa's door. In the end we brought him a chair from the house and put it under a large walnut tree by the side of the road. Joan made him a cup of coffee and brought it up to him, and he sipped it in grim dignity. He was making a public display of the fact that he wouldn't enter Nitsa's house. For that matter, he wouldn't enter any house in Lia, and his behavior was the deepest kind of insult in the Greek view. I was surprised at how much anger he felt for the townspeople and how he had completely cut the village of his birth out of his affections.

Since Father clearly couldn't be convinced to spend any time in the village, we left the next day to head back to Athens, where he seemed more content. But soon his old restlessness set in and he was talking about returning to Worcester. His stomach was bothering him, he said, and he was afraid of getting sick and having to go into a hospital in Greece. He would rather be home, near his own doctors. I agreed that was probably best, since I was being sent back to Iran.

On the last day of his stay my father sat with me in the garden and said, "When you come back to America, I don't know if you'll find your father there. But before I die, I want to tell you that I'm proud of two things in life. The first is all you've done, and the second is that none of my daughters ever shamed me. For that matter, even my nieces — all the Gatzoyiannis women — they've all been virtuous and never once dishonored our family."

I was already irritated at having to return to Iran and at his behavior in the village, and now I blew up at him. "What's so important about that?" I snapped. "Why is your pride and the family honor based on the virtue of its women?"

"You don't think that honor is important?" he asked in a tone that intimidated me despite my anger.

"Yes, honor is important!" I replied. "But it should be based on what we each do as individuals, not on the sexual propriety of our women relatives. In most families some girl is going to step out of bounds. Does that mean that the entire family has to lose its good name and self-respect?"

"To me, to my friends and my enemies — yes!" he thundered. "All the men I grew up with lived in fear that one of their women would shame them. You could wake up one morning and find out that everyone you knew looked at you differently because some girl in your family did something crazy. That's why I'm proud that none of my daughters, none of the women in the whole family that bears our name, brought shame on me. I can walk with my head high before any man I know."

I decided to drop the argument. There was no way of knowing when or if my father and I would ever see each other again. But his words helped me understand both his thinking and the societies I encountered in Iran, Iraq, Pakistan, and Turkey, where women were oppressed and carefully guarded by the men but carried within themselves the knowledge that they had a weapon that could shatter their entire family in a moment.

My father returned to Worcester and I plunged back into the Iranian revolution, during which I saw one of my colleagues, Joe Alex Morris of the *Los Angeles Times,* shot dead by a stray bullet. I obtained the last interview with the shah before his flight, and watched Ayatollah Khomeini turn the country into a rigid theocracy.

As soon as I returned from Iran I was sent to war-torn Beirut, and then to Pakistan to cover the Afghan guerrillas' opposition to the Soviet invasion. By 1980 I realized that if I was ever going to devote myself to researching my mother's story, I would have to leave the *Times,* for covering Middle East hotspots kept me constantly out of the country and used up all my time and energy.

·　·　·

On October 1, 1980, I resigned from the newspaper and set out to find everyone involved in my mother's last days. The journey that followed took me all over Greece and to England, Canada, America, Poland, Hungary, and Czechoslovakia. I interviewed hundreds of people — former friends and neighbors of my mother, villagers who had witnessed her trial, false friends who had testified against her to win approval from the Communist guerrillas, and guerrilla soldiers who had carried out the policies that led to her death.

While I was traveling in Greece, tracking down witnesses and filling in gaps in my mother's story, my sisters called occasionally to tell me that my father's health had become more fragile and that his memory was going. They had a tendency to exaggerate all illnesses — their own and those of others — and when I paid a visit back to the States in February 1981, my father met me at the airport and I found him as hale and quick-witted as ever. He drove me from Boston to Worcester, and on the way, on the Massachusetts Turnpike, he pushed his little silver Omega well above the 55-mile-per-hour speed limit. Suddenly we heard sirens, and a traffic cop pulled us over. The young officer asked to see my father's license, and when he returned it he had a peculiar look on his face.

"Would you mind coming back to my car?" he asked me. When we were out of Father's earshot he said, "That license said 'Birth date 1891.' Is that right?"

"That's right," I said, proud that I had a father who could still drive at the age of ninety (or eighty-eight, if his more probable birth date of 1893 was correct).

"Would you do me a favor and drive the rest of the way?" the policeman asked, shaking his head at the thought of someone born in the 1800s tooling down Route 90.

My father was furious when I told him to move over and give me the wheel. "He told you to drive!" he exclaimed. "Why would he do that? You know I'm a better driver than you are!"

"I know it, *Patera*," I said. "But you don't want him to arrest you, do you? Let's just humor him."

"All right, this one time," he grumbled. "But I'm still a better driver than you. If they ever take my car away, that's when I'm going to lie down and die."

My father complained all the way home at this injustice, and I was reassured that neither his mind nor his reflexes had deteriorated much, despite my sisters' protestations. But after I returned to Greece he had an accident that put an end to his driving.

It was my father's habit to make the rounds every day in his little car, driving from Worcester out to Grafton to check on our empty house, letting himself in to see if everything was all right, making himself a cup of coffee, sitting on the porch in the sun for a while, then visiting a few relatives and driving on to Westboro to see how Glykeria and Prokopi were doing at their House of Pizza. One summer day, while driving along the roads in Millbury on the old route of his produce rounds, Father collided with the car of a woman exiting from a supermarket parking lot. The accident was a minor one, crumpling their bumpers, and Father exchanged names and information with the woman, but when he arrived at the Westboro House of Pizza, he told Prokopi and Glykeria in a state of agitation, "I've been in an accident and damaged my car, but I can't remember where it happened or anything about it!"

They made him drive back by his usual route, trying to jog his memory, but Father couldn't recall anything. Finally their son managed to obtain the information from the Department of Motor Vehicles, because the woman involved had filed an accident report, but Father was so demoralized by his lapse of memory that he gave in to my sisters' insistence that he quit driving alone. He had to stop his daily round of visits, looking after the property and activities of his extended family like a ruler overseeing his kingdom, but he wouldn't admit it was permanent. "Nobody touch my car," he would warn the family. "I may not take it out today, but I'm going to take it out tomorrow." But in fact his confidence was shattered and he never drove again. And when he stopped driving, he began to die.

That August, I received a long-distance call in Athens from Prokopi, who told me that my father had been hospitalized for a prostate problem and the doctors had discovered an accumulation of liquid in his lungs that could prove to be life-threatening. "I think you'd better come, Nick," Prokopi told me. "His mind is deteriorating fast, and he doesn't look good."

"That's what you and my sisters are always saying," I shouted angrily over the phone, "but when I come back, his mind is always as sharp as ever! He's eighty-eight and he's in better shape than most sixty-year-olds!"

Despite my protestations, I took the next plane for Massachusetts. When I arrived at Hahnemann Hospital in Worcester, I approached my father's room with misgivings. In preparation for traveling to Iron Curtain countries to interview exiled guerrillas and unfriendly witnesses who had testified against my mother, I had grown a beard to help hide my identity, in case any former villagers recognized me through my resemblance to my mother. Now I was worried that my father might not know who I was, that he might have become so senile he wouldn't realize this rough-looking stranger with a beard was his son.

I entered the room to see bottles suspended over the bed and tubes running down into his veins. I was shocked at how frail my father looked: small, gray, and wizened beneath the hospital sheets. With great effort, he raised his head a bit to examine me with hooded, intent eyes that reminded me of the hawks in our mountains. He frowned at what he saw, and then he raised a trembling hand to beckon weakly to a nurse who was bustling about the room.

"Come here, nurse," he croaked in a voice so faint I could hardly hear him. "Get me my jacket from the closet."

"Your jacket?" she asked.

"Yes, I need something in it."

She brought him the jacket and propped some pillows beneath his back as he fished his wallet out of a pocket, still regarding me with a look of distaste. He pulled out two dollar bills and thrust them at me.

"Here's two bucks," he said with a sly smile. "Go get a shave. I don't want a son of mine looking like a bum."

I was so relieved to find my father's teasing humor still intact that I discounted my sisters' claims that he was declining. Within twelve days, his lungs were cleared and he was released from the hospital. Convinced that he was on the mend, I headed back to Greece, to finish the research on my mother's murder.

By the end of 1981 I was done. I had interviewed more than four hundred individuals in seven countries and was ready to complete the writing of the book about my mother's life and death. On New Year's Day of 1982, I moved my family back to America, settling them in our house in Grafton. On the flight back to the States, they talked excitedly about their new home and country. Of our three children, only my ten-year-old son could remember living in America, because we had been away for four and a half years.

When we got to Boston, my sisters greeted me with disturbing news. "We didn't want to worry you, because we knew you were coming home anyway," Glykeria said. "But Father is in the hospital again. He's very ill. It's the diabetes. He bumped his foot and it won't heal. Now it's full of gangrene."

My father had had diabetes for many years, controlling it through diet and then insulin, but now he was old, his circulation was poor, and the infection wouldn't heal. I went straight to Hahnemann Hospital and was shocked to see how much weight he had lost. About thirty pounds thinner than the last time I had seen him, he now looked exactly like his older brother Foto, except that my uncle, at ninety-seven, was much more vigorous than my father, who was nine years younger but as fragile as a child. I was even more horrified when I lifted the sheets and saw the great suppurating wound on his leg. Clearly the weight of the bedclothes was aggravating the terrible sores.

I demanded to see my father's doctor and asked why nothing had been put over his infected leg to protect it from the weight of the sheets and blankets.

"We'll see if we can do something about it," said the doctor unconvincingly. "But this is normal procedure." Then he told me that they were probably going to have to amputate my father's leg.

"Amputate his leg?" I shouted. "The man is nearly ninety years old! He'd never survive!"

The doctor shrugged. If he didn't respond to medication, there was nothing else they could do, he said. Either they amputated the gangrenous leg or the infection would kill him.

Quickly I made some phone calls and learned that the best hospital in the area for the treatment of diabetes was the Joslin Clinic in Boston. I signed my father out of the hospital in Worcester and rode to Boston with him in an ambulance. In the past he had liked to tease me every time we parted, telling me, "Say goodbye to your father now, you probably won't ever see him again," always referring to himself in the third person. But now, despite his pain, he saw my fear and took the opposite tack. "Don't look so worried," he chided me. "You're not going to lose your father yet!"

He was right. The doctors at the Joslin Clinic immediately won my confidence by rigging a cagelike frame over his leg to protect it from the bedclothes. They cleaned the wound and treated him with antibiotics, and within two weeks his condition was stabilized to the point where there was no more talk of amputation. My father was much weaker than I had ever seen him, but he exulted in the outpouring of affection that filled his room with visitors who made the long trip to Boston every day to bring him dishes of Greek food and to demonstrate their respect and love for him.

Within weeks Father was well enough to be taken home to Maxdale Road, where he was installed on the sofa in Glykeria's basement so that he could lie at the center of the family's activities, surrounded by the bustle of his grandchildren, the conversations, cooking, television, and visitors, and only a few feet from the bathroom. Fastidious and proud as ever, he refused to let anyone bring him a bedpan or help him in the bathroom, but made the trip by supporting himself with a metal walker. A nurse came every day to clean the wound on his leg and monitor his condition. I dropped by daily to visit, pleased that he had been spared the pain of having his leg amputated.

Often when I came to see him, my father seemed to have slipped the bonds that anchored him to this time and place. I realized that his mind was traveling back through the decades and halfway around the world, transporting him to scenes from the past that replayed themselves within his head like pieces of a movie that had been picked up off the floor at random and spliced together with no concern for chronology.

Glykeria said she always knew when he was embarking on one of these journeys into the past because he would sit there trying to thread an invisible needle with an invisible thread. Then he would begin to sew.

"What are you doing, Father?" she would ask, and he'd reply, "Sewing on a button."

"I'll do that for you," she would say. "You don't need to mend your clothes."

"No, I want to do it myself," he would insist, and continue sewing, like Penelope, weaving the threads of his past together to complete the tapestry of his life.

Sometimes when I visited he was there in Glykeria's home with me, chiding me as usual about the scruffy beard and fishing out the same $2 so I could get a shave. But then I would come again and find he was a ten-year-old tinker's apprentice on the island of Syros, excited by the news that an English ship had sailed into the harbor and an English lord had disembarked to take refreshment in the café. "I want to see him too, where is he? I've never seen a real lord," he would say in Greek to an invisible companion. "Let's go! I want to get closer. Where is he? . . . But that's just a man! He's a man like anyone else. And such a short man! Imagine such a short lord!"

In a way I felt privileged to sit by his couch and listen to these scenes from his youth at the turn of the century. Perhaps as his journey took him closer to the bridge that separates this world from the next, the shadows waiting for him on the other side appeared clearer to his vision than the adult children sitting beside him. His mother and his dead brothers and sisters were vivid to him. "Here comes my sister!" he would cry with delight, referring to the one who died at sixteen, a victim of the evil eye. "Look how beautiful she is!" The faces of his hunting companions, when they were all *palikaria* in the flower of their strength, surrounded him and he'd shout, "Go get Nashelis! He knows how to flush out the boar. I'll stay here. They won't get past me!"

Often he spoke to my mother, and I envied him the ability to see her so close and alive while I had only my fleeting dreams. "Come sit beside me, Eleni," he would say, patting the space next to him. "Tell me the news from the T'Alonia. Leave your sweeping — someone else can attend to that. Sit down for a moment now that I'm here. But why aren't you wearing the new dress I brought you?"

By the fall I had completed the finishing touches on the book about my mother, which I called *Eleni*. Every day I visited with my father, talking with him about our friends, the grandchildren, the days when he first came to America and when his children first arrived. Other times he would be traveling in his own memories, and I would watch him as he relived conversations with lost relatives, sometimes fighting with my grandfather or Foto, trying to settle old scores, talking affectionately to his mother and the long-dead siblings who had lived with him in a land under Turkish rule, where men were required to wear the red fez and young women hid their faces in fear of catching the eye of a passing Turk and being kidnapped for the harem. His difficult first days in America passed through his personal movie show too — the bad times when he had waited in the freezing rain for the shop boss to select the day's workers from the crowd, and the better times when a newspaper or letter had arrived from Greece or a winning hand in the *cafenion* had inspired him to shout, "Ay, Costa! Treat the house!"

As the time my father spent in his private world increased, his body seemed to shrink, as if he was slowly slipping away, nearing that bridge that would finally separate us. But sometimes he was back with me, sitting on the couch regarding me with the old ironic twinkle in his eye.

"I'm writing a book, *Patera*," I said to him on one of these occasions.

"Another book? I'm afraid you'll bust your brains someday," he said, smiling. "What's this one about?"

"It's about *Mana*."

"My angel wife." He nodded. "You bring me this one as soon as it's out. I have all your other books on the shelf, right over there."

"I will," I promised.

As soon as I had a finished copy of the book, I took it to my father, but he had forgotten what I had told him about it. "I already have all your books," he said to me. "They're over there."

"This is a new one," I said, handing it to him. "It's called *Eleni*."

He looked at the front cover and then turned it over and saw the photograph on the back: a family portrait we had taken in 1946, in the brief peacetime between the end of the world war and the outbreak of civil war, by an itinerant photographer passing through our village. He had lined us up against a stone wall and set up his box camera on a tripod. Standing in the back row were my three older sisters, their hair in braids, and Aunt Nitsa. In the front row my mother was seated, wearing the heavy homespun village jacket and skirt, her hair covered by a kerchief. Fotini and I stood on either side of her as she held my right hand with her left. We were all staring solemnly at the camera.

My father studied the photograph for a while, perhaps remembering when Mother had sent it to him and he had taped it to the mirror behind the counter of the diner where he worked. "My sweet wife," he said finally, then handed the book back to me and closed his eyes, probably seeing her more clearly than he could in any photograph. I put the book on his shelf beside the others I had written, knowing he would never be able to read it.

Although my sisters knew what it was about, they also had not yet read it. But in mid-April 1983 a fact-checker arrived from the *Reader's*

Digest, which planned to run a 20,000-word condensation of *Eleni* in two issues of the magazine that summer. A slender, scholarly-looking young man with glasses named Richard Hessney, he was fanatically thorough in questioning facts. "Are you certain your grandmother's eyes were blue?" he would ask me. "Can you direct me to another person who can confirm that?"

After he and I laboriously went through the entire manuscript, with the researcher underlining and challenging every detail, he asked to interview my sisters privately, without me along, to make sure their memories of these events corroborated mine. I called Glykeria and Kanta and explained to them what he wanted and they agreed, although they were somewhat intimidated at being interviewed by a representative of a famous American magazine.

Kanta, still the most emotionally fragile of my sisters, took two tranquilizers to gird herself for the ordeal, then she went next door to Glykeria's basement, and the two women sat at the Formica table in the kitchen area as the young man from New York read the condensed manuscript aloud, paragraph by paragraph, stopping every few sentences for them to confirm that it was correct. He read to them about the arrival of the guerrillas in our village and the night that my mother and grandmother burned Olga's foot with a heated poker from the fireplace so that she would be too crippled for the guerrillas to draft as an *andartina,* and about how they took Kanta instead and finally released her in disgust because she fainted so often. He read how the guerrillas threw us out of our house and turned it into a headquarters and prison where they tortured prisoners and forced them to dig their own graves in our garden. They listened as he related how I overheard guerrillas saying they were going to take the children of the village by force, and how I ran to my mother who began to plan our escape, only to be forced to stay behind at the last moment. He went over the details of our last goodbye to her as the guerrillas led her away. His voice stumbling, he read how she was imprisoned, tried, and tortured. He described the procession of condemned prisoners being led up to the ravine past a spring, and being seen by a little girl who gave our mother water. The sight of the child made Eleni cry, "Oh, my little Fotini, where is she?" Finally he read the testimony of a village woman who was passing the ravine and heard my mother's final terrible cry — "My children!" — followed by a burst of rifle fire.

The young man had hardly started reading the manuscript to my sisters when they began to weep, but they bravely struggled on, nodding after each paragraph, telling him, "Yes, that was the way it happened." The researcher told me later with some embarrassment that before long he was also in tears as he read, moved by their pain. They spent the entire morning working their way agonizingly through the story, keeping their voices low so as not to disturb my father, who was dozing on his couch across the room. He didn't take in much of what went on around him anymore, so they didn't think he would even notice the journalist from New York. But when the ordeal was over and the last words had been read, they turned around and discovered him sitting up on the couch, his cheeks wet with tears for his lost wife.

The book was published in April, promotional tours took up most of May, and by the end of June, I was burned out and eager to take some days off. My old Greek friends Fred Malitas and Tony Deli, from the days when we stalked American girls together in the bus terminal, suggested that we all meet with our families for a nostalgic reunion in Ocean City, where I had spent the best summers of my youth. Fred by now had a whole string of pizza parlors around Philadelphia, and his young Greek wife, Aleka, had produced three sons who would someday help operate them. Tony Deli had married a Greek-American girl, who gave him two sons, and he owned a large wholesale produce business in Springfield, Massachusetts. We agreed to get together in Ocean City during the second week of July to introduce our children to each other and relive some of our youthful adventures.

On the day before we left, I stopped by Maxdale Road to see my father. I leaned over, kissed him, and said, "I'm taking Joan and the kids to Ocean City for a vacation, *Patera.* I'll be back in a week."

He nodded. "You go, enjoy your family."

"We're not leaving until morning," I told him. "Is there anything you want?"

"*Kalo telos,* a good end," he replied with a trace of the old fire in his eye.

He got his *kalo telos* two days later — the kind of death he would have wanted, surrounded by the family he loved.

On Sunday, July 10, Glykeria was celebrating the name day of her husband, Prokopi, and all the Greeks in Worcester were invited to her house for a buffet supper. The day before the party, she cooked and cleaned like a whirlwind, running up and down stairs. "Stay here," my father called to her. "Don't clean so much. Sit here so I can see you."

"You just want to chat," replied Glykeria distractedly. "I can't sit around and talk, we're having a name day tomorrow!"

"You should send me to the old age home," said Father, repeating one of his favorite themes. "I'm just a burden to you. I make you suffer too much! But when you're my age, you'll want your children to sit and talk to you too."

On Sunday the guests started coming about five in the afternoon, and soon there were over forty people crowded into Glykeria's basement.

She had put a hospital bed for my father in a small ell near the washing machines so that he could sleep more comfortably at night, but that day he insisted on sitting on the couch in the middle of the festivities so as not to miss a thing.

Everyone remembers how he laughed and joked that day, teasing all his children and grandchildren, scolding one woman because she laughed too loud and then laughing even louder himself.

Father hated the strictures of his diet and kept asking for a plate of garlicky *yigantes* beans in tomato sauce, but Glykeria reminded him that they weren't good for the diabetes. Olga came and sat by his side and fed him some rice. Then Kanta came and held a cup of tea for him to drink. "It's good, but what I really want is some of the beans," he said plaintively.

A little later he began to wheeze a bit and said to Glykeria, "Bring me some cognac or some wine to drink. There's something caught in my chest."

"*Patera,* you know that's the worst thing for your sugar!" scolded Glykeria as she brought him a glass of water. She recalled how in the old days he had enjoyed emptying his glass of *retsina* at parties after balancing it on his head and leading the dances.

By the time the guests drifted away about eleven-thirty that night, Father had lain down on the bed in the corner, but all the guests stopped by on the way out to kiss him and pay their respects. The sons of my sisters, who had all grown into young men, still went around together like a pack of brothers, and they decided to go out for some fun. First each one kissed his grandfather. Last in line was the youngest, Fotini's nineteen-year-old son Christos, an inveterate jokester like his grandfather.

Young Christos knelt beside the bed and said impishly, "May you live many years for all of us, *Papou.* Do you know who I am?"

"Who *are* you?" asked Father, squinting at him.

"Christos Bottos!" he exclaimed, laughing. "My name is Christos just like yours. I'm your grandson and I'm named for you."

"Yes, yes, my child," Father replied, patting him. "You have my blessing."

After everyone was gone, as Glykeria was picking up the dirty dishes, my father moved from the bed back to the couch in the center of the room. "I want to sleep here tonight," he said.

"But it's much more comfortable on the bed," Glykeria said.

"No, tonight I want to sleep here," he insisted.

When she was finished cleaning up, Glykeria lay down on the other couch to sleep, as she sometimes did for fear Father might call her in the night and she wouldn't hear. She thought he was asleep, but when she lay down and covered herself with a blanket, he asked, "Are you going to stay there?" When she said yes, he replied, "Good!"

Glykeria drifted off, but was awakened by my father jumping up into a sitting position, his feet slamming to the floor.

"I don't feel good," he said. "I've gotta go to the bathroom."

"Wait till I get my slippers on," said Glykeria, but he stood up by himself and then nearly fell. She caught him before he crumpled to the floor, but suddenly his mouth went crooked and she knew he was dying. She began to scream: "Help me! My father! He's dying!"

Prokopi was upstairs with all the doors closed and the television turned up high and he heard nothing, but Glykeria screamed so loudly that Kanta heard her from next door and came running over. At the same time the pack of grandsons returned and found their grandfather lying on the floor while Glykeria screamed. Her younger son, Spiro, tried to give him mouth-to-mouth resuscitation, and someone called for an ambulance.

When the ambulance arrived, Prokopi rode in the back with Father and everybody else followed behind in their cars, except for Glykeria, who was so hysterical they wouldn't let her leave the house. Father briefly returned to consciousness and indicated with gestures to Prokopi to take the wallet from his breast pocket. It contained $400 in cash — part of the small nest egg he had carefully parceled out among the children and grandchildren in his will, allocating $50 here and another $50 there.

In the emergency room, the doctors and nurses rushed him off on a gurney. A little more than an hour later, a doctor came out to tell the crowd of waiting relatives that Christos had died of heart failure. He had crossed the bridge to the other side, but not before kissing each one of his loved ones goodbye.

About three in the morning I was awakened by the telephone ringing in the apartment we had rented in Ocean City. Glykeria told me that my father had died. I hung up before she could say anything else: I needed to grieve for him alone. I didn't know him until I was nine, but God had given me thirty-four years to learn what a father I had.

We buried him on July 13, 1983, in Hope Cemetery, in the double plot he prepared so many years before. Hundreds of mourners crowded the funeral home and the church. In the church the priest chanted: "O Christ, with the saints, grant rest to the soul of your servant Christos that he may repose in a place of light where there is no pain, no grief, no sighing, but everlasting life. . . . The beauty of the countenance has withered and the strength of youth has been cut down by death. . . . Come you all who love me and greet me with a final kiss, for never shall I walk with you or talk to you again."

We all came forward to kiss his brow and his hands folded over an icon. Because Father never liked to go anywhere without money "'case of emergency," Kanta slipped his wallet into his breast pocket, with some dollar bills to pay Charon for the journey to the other side.

When we left the church, a funeral cortege several blocks long followed the black hearse to the cemetery, detouring to stop for a moment outside the house on Maxdale Road where he had celebrated and received the kisses of all his clan just three days before. At the cemetery we each went forward to throw a flower atop the casket as the priest and the mourners repeated three times: "May the memory of Christos, who is worthy of praise, remain with us forever."

Letters came from Greek senators and congressmen. Telegrams arrived from Greece. The obituary in the *Worcester Telegram and Evening Gazette* stated that "over the years Mr. Ngagoyeanes sponsored and assisted the immigration of more than 100 people from his native region to the United States." The *Hellenic Chronicle* devoted an entire editorial column to the former vegetable peddler and cook. "For 35 years after [his wife's] death Christos Ngagoyeanes was both father and mother to their children," it said. "Christos Ngagoyeanes was a leader among the *protoporoi* of the Worcester Greek community for 73 years. He worked hard and . . . achieved all the success any Greek immigrant might desire. His only regret was that his Eleni could not have been with him. . . . She was gone, but her living legacy — their five children, thirteen grandchildren, and two great-grandchildren — were there. . . . We pray God grant him much deserved rest and may He make his memory eternal among us."

. Fourteen months after my father's funeral, he and his Eleni were reunited at last when I brought her remains from Greece and buried them by his side. A new marble tombstone was ready, bearing on one side their names and birth and death dates in English, and on the other side the same facts in Greek, along with an image etched into the stone, taken from their 1926 wedding portrait: my father in his American suit, tie, and hat, my mother in her kerchief and embroidered velvet wedding costume. Engraved on it in Greek and English is a line from St. Paul's first letter to the Corinthians:

ἡ ἀγάπη οὐδέποτε ἐκπίπτει.

"Love Never Ends"